BUCKLEY

and

MAILER

BUCKLEY

and

MAILER

The Difficult Friendship That Shaped the Sixties

KEVIN M. SCHULTZ

W. W. NORTON & COMPANY

New York • London

Frontispiece: Politicards courtesy of artist Peter Green, politicards.com.

Since this page cannot legibly accomodate all the copyright notices, pages 363–65
constitute an extension of the copyright page.

For information about permission to reproduce selections from
this book, write to Permissions, W. W. Norton & Company, Inc.,
500 Fifth Avenue, New York, NY 10110.

Manufacturing by Courier Westford
Book design by Chris Welch Design
Production manager: Julia Druskin

Library of Congress Cataloging-in-Publication Data

Schultz, Kevin M.
Buckley and Mailer : the difficult friendship that shaped the Sixties / Kevin
M. Schultz. — First edition.
pages cm
Includes bibliographical references and index.
ISBN 978-0-393-08871-7 (hardcover)
1. United States—History—1961–1969. 2. United States—Social condi-
tions—1960–1980. 3. United States—Civilization—1945– 4. Nineteen sixties. 5.
Buckley, William F., Jr., 1925–2008—Friends and associates. 6. Buckley, William F.,
Jr., 1925–2008—Political and social views. 7. Mailer, Norman—Friends and associ-
ates. 8. Mailer, Norman—Political and social views. 9. Journalists—United States—
Biography. 10. Authors, American—20th century—Biography. I. Title. II. Title:
Difficult friendship that shaped the Sixties.
E841.S34 2015
973.92—dc23

W. W. Norton & Company, Inc., 500 Fifth Avenue, New York, N.Y. 10110
www.wwnorton.com

W. W. Norton & Company Ltd., Castle House, 75/76 Wells Street, London W1T 3QT

1 2 3 4 5 6 7 8 9 0

To Terra and the kids

Contents

PART III
BIRTHING PANGS (1966—68)

PART IV
THE NEW ORDER (1969—76)

It is said of the Conservative that he wishes to protect the root; of the radical that he goes to the root. One maintains, the other explores. But in the same land. There is a dialogue possible between the conservative like Mr. Buckley and the radical like myself which could prove vastly more interesting than any confrontation between liberal and conservative, or radical and liberal.

—*Norman Mailer*[1]

BUCKLEY

and

MAILER

Introduction

I t was late fall, and the old man awoke in a sour mood.

As he rolled out of bed, he saw the cold November winds outside and remembered it was only supposed to reach the mid-30s that day. He often woke up stiff anyway, earlier than he should, at hours that sometimes alarmed the help. He occasionally even showered and ordered breakfast at two o'clock in the morning. The servants obeyed, for they loved the man. But they also gently reminded him it was well before sun-up. Did he really want his eggs? Okay, sir, okay.[1]

Compounding the changing weather, he was also sick and dying, and he knew it. It might be days or weeks or months before the end came. God only hoped it wouldn't be years. So far, he had made it through emphysema, diabetes, sleep apnea, skin cancer, heart disease, near kidney failure, and various prostate afflictions. It was hard to argue that his bill of health didn't read like a medical encyclopedia cataloguing the degenerations of old age. The emphysema was progressive and incurable, too, and the heart disease could take him at any moment. He was sick and dying, and he knew it.

The most degrading part, though, wasn't confronting death per se but the measures they took to keep you alive. Most annoyingly, they had been monitoring the color of his urine, which vacillated from a deep rose color to a bright orange. There was a time when he could take for granted a normal yellow pee, when he felt at liberty to drop his trousers in the middle of New York City traffic and urinate out the door of his limousine. Some unsuspecting driver might have wondered, "Was that William F. Buckley, Jr., who just peed on us from the left-hand turn lane of Riverside Drive?" Why yes, yes it was.[2]

But not anymore. Now doctors were examining the color of his urine like a French sommelier ponders wine, judging color, density, consistency, even odor. It was awful getting old. The pain had been so bad recently, in fact, that he—a great man!—had even contemplated suicide, not once but twice. He had consulted priests on both occasions, and the spiritual ministers of his lifelong faith had helpfully advised him that his immortal soul wasn't worth the risk. The end would come soon, they said soothingly, it wouldn't be long.[3]

When he awoke this particular morning in November 2007, creaky and tired as usual, the view from his rambling waterfront home on Wallach's Point, Connecticut, an hour north of New York City, had transformed from the inviting hues of summer to the foreboding greys of winter. The vast sea gurgling its winter froth seemed to reflect his grumbly mood.

Still, Buckley, the patron saint of modern American conservatism, an icon and a living legend, raised himself up and ambled over to the garage he had converted into an office more than forty years before. He took his seat at his oversized desk, pushed aside a huge number of books and articles and a few thousand shreds of paper, and began to write.

Partly that's just what he did. You don't write forty-odd books, thousands of newspaper columns, and boxes and boxes of letters by sipping coffee too long, pondering the sports page. Someone once told him that his accumulated papers fit into so many boxes at Yale's Sterling Library that if you stacked them all on top of one another they would reach the top of the Washington Monument. To achieve that kind of productivity you get over your aches and pains, your sour moods, the greys outside, and you head to your desk to write.

In addition to habit, though, on this particular morning the old man with famously tousled reddish-grey hair also felt he had to work through something important. For that day, you see, he had just learned that yet another of his friends had passed away. This was not an uncommon occurrence for Buckley, then about to turn eighty-two. His sister Jane had died a few months earlier, and family departures were always hard, evoking memories of the family reserve. Meanwhile, his best friend of sixty years, Evan "Van" Galbraith, was in the midst of some thirty-plus radiation treatments, which would surely kill him shortly, too.

But these all paled in comparison to the passing of Patricia, his "Ducky," his wife of fifty-seven years. That was devastating. Her departure nine months earlier had created a terrible void that Buckley felt deep inside his soul, as though the rug of life had been pulled out from under him, making him now and forevermore alone. "What shall we do today?" his son, Christopher, had asked shortly after her death. "Well," replied the old man, with a sudden chill, "I guess we can do anything we want to." The realization provoked a hollowness and a dread. Too much freedom was a terrible thing.[4]

Pondering suicide had been unimaginable when Patsy was alive. But now that she was gone, well, things just seemed different.[5]

And the departures kept coming. Today, staring at him from the newspaper on this cold November morning was the face of yet another. This one was different, though, different from the rest. Sure, it sparked the usual sadness of a friend departed, but it also initiated something else. In fact, what came whirling back to Buckley as he read through the obituary pages was the excitement of an entire era gone by, when ideas seemed to matter more, when a young and vibrant William F. Buckley, Jr., and the now departed

Norman Mailer, smiling at him from the pages of the newspaper, were at the forefront of it all.

Mailer had once described theirs as a "difficult friendship," and that was certainly true.[6] There had been fights and struggles, battles and arguments. But despite their seemingly polar outlooks on America—one left, one right—the two men had been intimates during the 1960s and 1970s, when their ideas seemed to be vying for the soul of the nation. They had debated in huge venues; drunk together in intimate night spots; exchanged dozens of private letters; socialized together at the most memorable parties of the era; traded books, articles, and laughs, and, perhaps most vitally of all, had shared a deep love of America. They had dramatically different visions of what the country was and of what it could become. But they loved the promise and the dream. Their efforts to shape and improve America had made them key players in the revolution that was the 1960s.

Now his old adversary was gone. What made it worse, though, was that nobody seemed to understand Mailer's importance anymore. The obituaries were full of platitudes. Everyone seemed to have forgotten the high stakes of the 1960s. They seemed to have forgotten why that decade was so voluble, so contentious, so wide open. Was Norman Mailer nothing more than a struggling writer unable to fulfill his obnoxious promise to write The Great American Novel? Was Mailer now easily dismissible as just another "Sixties radical"? Was Mailer right when he wrote, all those long years ago, "I had tried to become a hero, and had ended as an eccentric"?[7]

The obituaries Buckley flipped through almost universally focused on Mailer's first novel, *The Naked and the Dead*, which was written way back in 1948 and was in no way the measure of the man. Yet all the papers highlighted it, the way the writers of the wispy television show *Gilmore Girls* had fallen back on that sixty-year-old World War II book in order to educate its young audience when Mailer appeared on the show in 2004.

And then there were the seemingly mandatory lists of the number of wives Mailer had had (six), the number of lovers (legion), and the number of jousts with the cream of the intellectual crop of the 1960s—friends and enemies like Gore Vidal, Truman Capote, James Baldwin, Arthur Schlesinger, Jr., John Kenneth Galbraith, Allen Ginsberg, Kate Millett, Joan Didion, Germaine Greer, and more.

But none of the obituary writers seemed to understand Mailer's larger project, his effort to remake the country, to open its possibilities, to divorce it from its lineage of Cold War liberalism and deadening technological bureaucratization in a grand scheme to create something more fulfilling, more in touch with what it means to be human. In short, they missed all the reasons Buckley loved the man, and loved to argue with him. They missed the most important part.

And so Buckley ambled over to his huge desk to write an obituary of his own. He would try to explain it all. "Norman Mailer, R.I.P." were the first words he typed.

"How to deal with Norman Mailer?" came out next, Buckley's first ponderous sentence in an obituary that would be printed in *National Review*, the journal Buckley had founded in 1955, more than five decades earlier.[8] The two men, Buckley reflected, had lived remarkably parallel lives. Born in the early 1920s, both had been largely shielded from the Great Depression. Both had earned Ivy League degrees. And both were World War II veterans, though mostly on the periphery of action. Both gained early success in the postwar era through popular books, and both, within weeks of each other in fall of 1955, helped found lasting journals that reflected their unique perspectives on American life, Buckley with *National Review* and Mailer with the *Village Voice*. Both men came into their own as public intellectuals in the early 1960s, gaining widespread attention as icons of a particular kind of politics. Both had seen their stars rise throughout the 1960s, as their faces appeared on the covers of all the big magazines and their articles received record commissions. Both had even run for mayor of New York City, Buckley in 1965 and Mailer in 1969. But by the early 1970s, both had watched the movements they had come to symbolize drift on without them; both were still famous as celebrities but no longer as vital players in the game. They continued to write best-selling books into the 1980s, 1990s, and 2000s, but their work was no longer central to the times.

Beyond the obvious parallels, though, Buckley and Mailer had been tossed together as adversaries in the early 1960s, one from the right, the other from the left. But they quickly discovered, much to their joint surprise, that not only did they like one another personally, they shared a common complaint about America. It turned out the two men's ideas actually sprung from a similar frustration, a joint disgust at the central assumptions that dominated postwar America from the 1940s to the mid-1960s. However much they differed in their recommendations about how to make Americans freer and more fulfilled, they saw the malady of postwar life in almost exactly the same way.

Even more than this, both men had acted with a seriousness that led them to become not only respected adversaries but genuine friends and, most importantly, citizen intellectuals willing to get their hands dirty in an effort to create a better tomorrow. Both had been unafraid to venture along the precipice to offer daring alternatives, and both had sought to make the individual more liberated from the stale Cold War pieties and the invidious presence of corporate capitalism. It was liberation they both wanted and, in a sense, it was liberation they got.

It would turn out, though, that their diametrically opposed prescriptions for the nation, which seemed to be duking it out in a tectonic struggle during the mid-1960s, would be only partially realized by the end of the decade. Both were blindsided by the number of visions that emerged to vie for control of the national consciousness during that turbulent decade. Both were unmoored by the precipitous rise of violence. Both were shaken by a growing lack of concern for the commonweal. When the changes each man had been pushing for finally did come, both revolutionaries were uncertain if the revolutions they helped midwife would improve the nation or end up tearing it down. Like expectant fathers, they had helped initiate all of the changes but then recoiled at the blood and violence of the birth; they were then uncertain that they even recognized the child when it breathed its first breath. Our children do not always turn out as we wish.

And in this recognition of the limits to their power, it was hard to argue that the intellectual and emotional journeys of these remarkable men hadn't echoed that of much of the nation, that their understandings of the Cold War, the civil rights movement, Vietnam, and the women's movement weren't simply microcosms of the debates that had reverberated throughout the country. The divides that polarized the nation were the same ones that separated Buckley and Mailer. And they were the divides that, arguably, destroyed the commonweal as well.

When Buckley looked back down at his typewriter, he quickly agreed with all of the other obituarists that Mailer was a great writer, that Mailer was "a towering figure in American literary life for sixty years, almost unique in his search for notoriety and absolutely unrivaled in his co-existence with it." Mailer had, Buckley wrote, "created the most beautiful metaphors in the language," sometimes more than a dozen on a single page.[9] It was a compliment Buckley had paid Mailer many times before.

Supplementing his literary talent, though, was Mailer's grand project, his attempt to project his vision onto America during the 1960s. But after Buckley introduced this vital subject into his obituary, at that key moment when he might have helped clarify Mailer's ambitions and hopes, Buckley fell back onto one of his worst traits: He hedged and grew vague and took his readers nowhere meaningful. It was a nasty tic, typically emerging when it came to defining the principles of the modern American conservative movement. "What did it all mean?" more than one person had asked. Well, er, uh. . . . Intellectually speaking, Buckley often left his readers wondering.

And it happened here again. Instead of pinpointing Norman Mailer's importance for his readers; instead of delineating the stakes of the 1960s and of Mailer and Buckley's transformative presence within it; instead of articulating how Mailer and Buckley, radical and conservative, in fact shared a common complaint about postwar America and wished to push the country in more fulfilling directions, Buckley fell back on anecdote, story, and wistful memory. He recalled their first meeting, at a Chicago debating hall in 1962. He recounted the experience of having Norman Mailer look over his shoulder as he typed a column for the next day's paper, passing ferocious judgments as the lines rolled past. He talked about being with Mailer in his heyday, of sharing a laugh, of sharing a drink.

But just as he was about to conclude his difficult friend's obituary, Buckley recognized that he had fallen short. "But Norman Mailer is a towering writer!" his essay concluded. "So why this small talk? Perhaps because it no longer seems so very small," he wrote, "wondering out loud whether the obituaries are, finally, drawing attention to the phenomenon of Norman Mailer from the appropriate perspective."[10]

To do that, to find "the appropriate perspective" in which to understand the man, one has to understand Buckley and Mailer together in the 1960s; why one went left, the other right; how their particular form of engaged public intellectualism was a bellwether of what American democracy might cntail; and to determine, finally and at long last, who ended up winning their vibrant debate over the heart and soul of the nation.

PART I

DEBATING THE FUTURE (1962–63)

1

The Nature of Man

Buckley and Mailer first met in the fall of 1962, right in the sweet spot of America's last great age of public intellectuals. President John F. Kennedy was inviting artists and academics to the White House and wining and dining New York and Hollywood, hoping to win glowing reviews from both coasts. But it was also an age when the nation seemed to be on the verge of major changes, as the America Eisenhower created came under quiet attack from both the right and the left, both of which saw American culture as profoundly hollow, with voices from the fringes too long submerged. As writer Gore Vidal put it in 1960, "in a society such as ours, where there is no moral, political or religious center, the temptation to fill the void is irresistible. There is an empty throne so . . . *seize* the crown."[1] Norman Mailer and William F. Buckley, Jr., both in their thirties, were trying to do just that.

It was an equally young and brash promoter named John Golden who brought them together. At thirty-two, Chicago-born Golden had big plans for himself. He had dropped his birth name of Robert, he said, because "I've never known a Robert who got very big." (The reporter who heard Golden say this proposed a debate on the subject between Robert Graves and Robert Frost, with Robert Kennedy moderating.)[2] Like many of his peers,

Golden detected an undercurrent of rebellion swirling through the country. The youngest baby boomers were in their teens in 1962, and the economy was so good that worries about financial security didn't really animate their frustrations. Instead, they were concerned about the seemingly authoritarian structures of family and culture that supposedly limited their possibilities. Discipline and rule-following may have made sense when the atmosphere was rife with depression and war. But by the early 1960s, that was all gone. Making it worse was the ever-present specter of the Cold War, which could end the hard-won peace and prosperity in an instant if the people in charge, the grown-ups, didn't act to stop it. As the young poet Allen Ginsberg put it in 1956, "America when will we end the human war? / Go fuck yourself with your atomic bomb."[3]

Golden knew there was a rebelliousness inside the hearts of the young, a yearning to be freed from the prevailing culture, a spiritual hunger for more. A person had only to turn the pages of the country's leading magazine, *Life*, to see a wide-ranging debate about the lack of "national purpose" in America. In 1960, that glossy Henry Luce production, which more typically showed oversized pictures of horses drinking from straws or elephants balancing on beach balls, devoted its pages to a five-part series on the problems that ailed the nation. Historian Clinton Rossiter captured the theme best when he said in his article that during depression and war, there had been a sense of mission for the country, but by 1960 America had become overweight and middle aged, had lost its vigor. "We are fat and complacent," he said bluntly. Adlai Stevenson, a distinguished diplomat and two-time loser as Democratic presidential nominee, posed the memorable question, "With the supermarket as our temple and the singing commercial as our litany, are we likely to fire the world with an irresistible vision of America's exalted purposes and inspiring way of life?"[4] He didn't bother to answer the question.

And if you missed *Life*, you only had to peruse the titles in the local bookstore to see shelves of books pronouncing some sort of crisis. Sloan Wilson was warning about the hollowness in becoming "The Man in the Gray Flannel Suit." David Riesman saw the whole country as a "Lonely Crowd" searching for affirmation from others without any inner sense of what it meant to do or be good. Erich Fromm was urging Americans to "Escape from Freedom." J. D. Salinger's *Catcher in the Rye*, Arthur Miller's *Death of a Salesman*, and James Dean's *Rebel Without a Cause* were all variations on the theme. Americans were "mass men," "conformists" in a "consumer society," bound together by hollow tradition that was summarily limited in possibility. All yearned for greater freedom.[5]

Yes, there was an itch among the young, thought Golden, a search for a new way to live beyond the liberal pieties of Eisenhower's America, or even of Kennedy's, which had once promised so much but now seemed little more than a better-looking version of the rest. Golden saw all this and felt that by 1962 the postwar generation had a choice. It could either become "beat . . . living in a pad and lamenting life," or it could take daring action, doing things that were "important and necessary" to change the country's direction.[6] He himself didn't know what those "important and necessary" actions might be, but he sensed three possible paths forward: conservative, radical, or liberal. The liberals had run things so far, and had created much of the mess. They were the ones who had forsaken a grand purpose for the nation while embracing the dreariness of the bureaucrat and the salesman. This middle road may have made America affluent, but it hadn't made it satisfied.

By 1962, though, there was action from both flanks. On the left, there were voices like those of Michael Harrington, Rachel Carson, and even Martin Luther King, Jr., each of whom criticized certain aspects of the liberal order. And from the right, there was James Burnham, Robert Welch, and Barry Goldwater, with Goldwater going so far as to write in his 1960 manifesto *The Conscience of a Conservative*, "The preponderant judgment of the American people, especially of the young people, is that the . . . Liberal . . . approach has not worked and is not working."[7]

So Golden imagined a public debate pitting a voice from either side that could illuminate possibilities for the future. He wanted the representatives young and brash and just as angry as everyone else, but also famous enough to attract attention. From a promoter's perspective, bringing together Mailer and Buckley to debate the future was ideal. As Golden put it in a letter to Buckley, "the interest in this debate would reflect the thinking of all those of our generation, whether conservative, beat, liberal, et al. And therefore we felt proud of it as our own original idea."[8]

Golden knew Mailer would be a magnetic draw. Now thirty-nine, Mailer had been famous since 1948, when he was just twenty-five. It was *The Naked and the Dead* that had propelled him to great fame. That World War II book was a powerful depiction of a single platoon in the Pacific destined to go on an aimless patrol and encounter unnecessary violence. On the one hand, the book's extensive use of the word "fug" had done wonders for promotion. People didn't use words like that in acceptable literature, but Mailer's point was that soldiers didn't talk like the characters in the popular literature of the time. Beyond "fug," though, it was the book's intense look at power relations during war and its detailed descriptions of a wide swath of prototypical Americans that made the book so popular. Critics hailed it, and Mailer's first royalty check from his publisher was so large—forty thousand dollars—and he looked so young and disheveled that the bank clerk had to ask his manager if Mailer really could deposit a check that big. The checks would come for years.[9]

But Mailer had struggled ever since. Two weak novels from the 1950s hadn't helped, and his angry, tabloid-worthy lifestyle throughout the decade, during his partying, womanizing, slumming, and soul searching, had made him the living emblem of a Rebel Without a Cause. This notion was all but confirmed when, in late 1960, he was arrested for stabbing and nearly killing his wife, Adele Morales. Their relationship had been deteriorating for some time, and late one drunken night at a party, after hours of physical and verbal abuse, she confronted him in the kitchen and called him out for lacking courage: "Aja toro, aja!" she said. "Come on, you little faggot, where's your *cojones*, [or] did your ugly whore of a mistress cut them off, you son of a bitch!" Mailer took out a three-inch penknife and stabbed her in the chest and then in the back. When someone tried to help her, he pushed the man away, kicked her, and said, "Let the bitch die."[10] The puncture had landed just centimeters from her heart and Morales barely recovered from the wounds, but she never pressed charges against Mailer, who therefore spent only two weeks in Bellevue Hospital Center's psychiatric facilities before being set free. The newspapers ate up the story of an edgy artist unable to contain his emotions. He was frustrated by his personal failures, the story went, and the only way he could relieve that frustration was through violence. While Mailer himself was primed for a social revolution, there was none forthcoming from the society around him.

Still, Mailer could write, and for many Americans his odd 1959 book, *Advertisements for Myself*, helped give voice to the frustrations of a generation. Mailer had initially imagined *Advertisements* as little more than a conventional collection of old essays, an author's clearing of the throat before the next project. But one idiosyncratic quirk turned the book into something a whole lot more. For reasons that are still unknown, Mailer decided to introduce and conclude each of his literary works with italicized commentaries that revealed his thoughts as he was writing that particular piece. The commentaries, which he called "advertisements," were so honest and socially brilliant they struck a nerve. He described his personal depressions; his bouts with alcohol and marijuana; his insecurities as a writer and human being; his views on women, on homosexuality, on social taboos, on other writers, and, above all, on himself. Historians would later see in *Advertisements* the foundational workings of what almost a decade later came to be called New Journalism, the genre that made the writer a major figure in the proceedings. When people finished reading *Advertisements*, they felt as though they knew Mailer intimately. Judge him if you'd like, the book dared, but it was clear Mailer was already ferociously judging himself.[11]

The other remarkable thing about *Advertisements* was how forthrightly Mailer critiqued Cold War America, castigating the cultural weight of the buttoned-down 1950s. "The shits are killing us," he said.[12] In page after open-hearted page, Mailer lambasted the postwar American culture, called into question its dual commitments to corporate capitalism and the Cold War, and declared he would, in words that would make the book famous, "settle for nothing less than making a revolution in the consciousness of our time."[13] He wanted to shake America from its moorings and get the country to see that its current path was unfulfilling. He wanted to open up the possibilities, make America more humane, and make his country more capable of greatness. In this way, he transformed himself from a once-successful novelist on the wane to a profound social critic of the moment. By 1962, Mailer had become a rebel *with* a cause.

From the other flank was an equally vivid attraction. Buckley, at thirty-six, was already well known as the *enfant terrible* of American politics, the darling of the right, and the founder of a journal that many Americans loved to hate (Buckley had begun the *National Review* when he was just twenty-nine). But if many Americans hated *National Review*, others saw it as a guiding light in an interminable winter of postwar liberalism. Latter-day conservatives tell story after story of receiving the magazine in its brown wrapping paper every other week, aware that friends might hold them in contempt if they knew what they were reading. The most famous person to tell a story like this was Ronald Reagan.[14] For conservatives in the 1950s and early 1960s, *National Review* expressed their frustrations about postwar America as well as their worries about the seemingly unchecked growth of the government, the country's half-hearted attitude toward the Cold War, and its general departure from America's time-tested truths.[15]

Buckley, young and smiling, articulate with an air of preciousness, seemed like a breath of fresh air for America's conservatives. Finally someone was fighting the good fight—and doing it without looking like a hate-filled kook.

Eager to advance their respective visions for the country, both Buckley and Mailer quickly accepted when they received Golden's invitation to debate each other. Golden wisely scheduled the debate two days before and in the same city as a heavyweight championship fight between hard-working, soft-spoken, church-going Floyd Patterson and brooding, angry Sonny Liston. In the midst of the emerging civil rights movement, the boxers' personalities eliminated the need for metaphor. It was good versus evil, darkness versus light, Martin Luther King, Jr., versus Malcolm X, and whom you rooted for depended on your perspective on American life. With sit-ins and Freedom Rides blaring across the headlines in 1962, with the Cold War threatening to end it all in one apocalyptic flash, with mainstream liberalism failing to provide adequate answers, the atmosphere in Chicago was electric. "Everybody was going bonkers," the fight's promoter Harold Conrad said, "they always do at a big title fight, but this was more than just a fight. It's a scene, a promoter's dream."[16]

Golden tried to capitalize on the scene by promoting his own showdown. The marquee blared "Buckley / Mailer." Posters labeled the Buckley–Mailer battle "the Debate of the Year," billing it as the "forceful philosopher of THE NEW CONSERVATISM . . . AGAINST . . . America's angry young man and Leading Radical," and teasing, "The Conservative Mind clashes with the Hip Mind for the first time, at a no holds barred discussion."[17]

By September 22, the evening of the debate, Golden had taken in ticket sales of about eight thousand dollars—a full house of more than three thousand people. He had also successfully sold publication rights to *Playboy* for several thousand dollars more. With the shadow of the fight looming, and *Playboy* now involved, it was a highly masculine environment. The sports writers put the odds at 2.5 to 1 in favor of Buckley. Several writers took the bet.

The crowd streamed in early: "College kids, the Cohn and Bolan set, and about two hundred newspaper guys."[18] The college kids were rowdy and rambunctious, eager to see if Mailer could hold his own against Buckley's intellectual acrobatics. Some were worried. "I know that Buckley might make Norman seem ridiculous," said one young librarian. "But then people will feel sorry for him and he might get their sympathy."[19]

The "Cohn and Bolan set," meanwhile, referred to a hardnosed style of youthful conservatism represented by Senator Joseph McCarthy's defense attorney, Roy Cohn, and Cohn's equally spirited law partner, Thomas A. Bolan. Both men were articulate, tidy, and unflinching in their conservative ideology. Along with Buckley, they were role models for a certain portion of the youth. The radicals on the left may have been more visible with their rock 'n' roll and their Freedom Rides, but that didn't mean they were more numerous.

Mailer was nervous. Partly that was his natural condition. The tiresome bravado he typically projected simply masked his fear of being misunderstood, his dread at being exposed as a charlatan, his worry about incurring a wound to his delicate machismo. As was his wont, he spent weeks preparing. As was equally his wont, he ended up drinking his way through those preparations. Bourbon was his drink, two, three, or four fingers high, sometimes mixed with awful combinations like cranberry juice or fruit punch. Mailer later said, "I had honed myself like a club fighter getting ready for the champion," but friends saw it differently.[20] "If boozing is the way you train for a debate," said one, "Norman wins this one hands down."[21]

Staying at the Playboy Mansion probably didn't help. To keep things safe, Hugh Hefner kept the partying to the main floor of his Lake Michigan mansion, as Rocky Marciano, Archie Moore, Joe Louis, and hundreds more showed up for the debate and the fight. But Hef kept his bunnies upstairs, hidden away from the action, and he stayed upstairs with the girls until he was hungry. Then he would come down for a peanut-butter sandwich and a visit with the guys before heading back to his den of women. "It was the most sexless hangout I've ever seen," said one of Mailer's friends. But the booze poured freely.[22] Hefner was impressed by Mailer's stamina: "It was a pleasure having you as a house guest and I hope you enjoyed yourself," Hef wrote before answering his own question. "I think you must have, for you certainly kept things hopping all week long."[23]

Still, Mailer's thirty-minute opening speech was hammered out weeks before, and he memorized several of Buckley's interviews that he could, and would, deploy at a moment's notice. Buckley, Mailer wrote to a friend, "is the leading young Conservative in the country, and in fact, the most important Conservative in the public eye after Barry Goldwater. Buckley is very able and I have my work cut out for me. I don't think it will be an easy debate."[24]

Buckley wasn't nearly as nervous. One almost imagines him whistling as he walked down Michigan Avenue, one hand in the pocket of his light-grey suit, a red checked tie effortlessly setting off the whole outfit. Having successfully portrayed himself and his budding conservative movement as underdogs to the juggernaut that was America's Liberal Establishment, Buckley knew a loss to Mailer would do little to harm his cause. Any bad publicity could be easily dismissed as the liberal media showing its bias once again.

But Buckley was also a confident debater. Indeed, the debater's persona—adversarial, humorous, derisive, quick-witted, if not necessarily intellectually honest—was his natural style. In any debate against Mailer, the photogenic Buckley would (ironically enough) play Kennedy to Mailer's sweaty, unfurled Nixon. Buckley arrived in Chicago just a few hours before the debate, his remarks just half composed.

As Mailer peeked beyond the curtain, he saw that the seats were all filled, and the architecture of Chicago's grand Medinah Temple—a lavish fin-de-siècle theater with its long balconies circling perilously close to the stage—made the energy palpable if not downright threatening to the combatants onstage. "The crowd was high partisan that night," Mailer later wrote, "and cheered separately for us with the kind of excitement one expects in a crowd at a high school football game."[25] The combatants even refused to meet before the debate, in order to keep their psychological edge.[26]

The topic under consideration was "What Is The Real Nature of the Right Wing in America?" Golden had dreamed it up as a way to get Mailer and Buckley to attack. But he also knew that the American right was in its ascendancy in the early 1960s, and it was hard to tell if it was just a collection of conspiracy-laden eccentrics or a serious threat to the established order. As agreed upon beforehand, each man was to give a thirty-minute speech, then, after a brief intermission during which some folk singers were to entertain the crowd, each man would have twenty minutes to interrogate his opponent.

They started out cautiously, "throwing out light literary jabs," as the constant boxing metaphors in the press would have it. But Buckley, who went first, quickly got personal. He didn't think he could maintain Mailer's interest in the right wing, he said, because "I am not sure we have enough sexual neuroses for him."[27] The crowd laughed with Buckley. Mailer, as everyone knew, was a staunch advocate of obliterating sexual boundaries in American life, and he had famously already gone through two wives and moved on to his third. His books were lurid, too, boasting quick scenes where a beautiful starlet might complain to the mirror that her "mouth's a little too thin," just before her nearby lover quips, "It wasn't last night."[28] It wasn't the first time Mailer had been called a libertine.

Buckley then stuck the knife in: "I do not know anyone whose

dismay I personally covet more; because it is clear from reading
the works of Mr. Mailer that only true demonstrations of human
swinishness are truly pleasing to him, truly conform to his vision of
a world gone square." Buckley playfully thought the whole debate
would be useless because Mailer would never "raise his eyes from
the world's genital glands."[29]

The crowd loved the juvenile putdowns, as "whispers of overcon-
fidence began to stir through the Buckley sections" in the crowd.[30]
But before the audience grew tired of the personal assaults, Buckley put forward his real arguments. He knew he'd have to defend
against the widespread accusation that the American right was
nothing more than a collection of crazies feeding their neuroses
by blaming all the world's evils on commies, liberals, blacks, Jews,
Mexicans, Puerto Ricans, women, the poor, or any other scape-
goat. He had to prove there was something more to the right than
a politics of emotion, all seethe and anger, signifying nothing but
greed and fear.

No, as Buckley told it in the latter half of his opening statement,
in their heart of hearts conservatives were simply fearful the country was being unmoored from the Great Western Tradition, which,
to him, was centered on a constellation of things: a less-regulated
free-market economy, standards of traditional living (including
a return to Christian ethics), and a respect for local governance.
Reaffirming and fighting to preserve those things was really what
the right wing was all about.

Buckley had spent years helping to cobble together a new American right from the ashes of the one that had died in the 1930s
during the New Deal. He had worked hard to keep together the
three main groups in the coalition—libertarians who hated the
state when it was used for anything other than self-defense, traditionalists who loved stability and order, and anti-communists who
thought communism was a bona fide menace to the American way
of life. There were irreconcilable differences between the three
groups for sure. How could you balance the libertarian's harsh

anti-government stance with the traditionalist's yearning for stability, which typically required a strong state? Buckley's answer had
been to remove from his movement the ideological purists in each
camp. Ayn Rand's brand of harsh libertarianism, for example, was
dismissed as a dangerous road toward selfish greed and a dark
path toward the decline of all social relations. Meanwhile, people
who saw communists everywhere, like Robert Welch and his John
Birch Society, were similarly excommunicated for their extremism. Even the pope had been chastised in the pages of *National
Review* for not toeing the traditionalist line far enough (with the
famous quip, "Mater si, Magistra no," a line suggesting that Catholics should respect the traditions of the Church if not its teachings
on economic justice).[31]

Buckley recognized the importance of having a handful of readily available glues to keep the coalition together. The Cold War
was a useful one, garnering respect from all three groups, and he
harped on it often. But nothing helped keep his troops together
better than abusing an internal enemy, and Buckley in the 1950s
had famously given it a name: the Liberal Establishment. As Buckley put it in the debate with Mailer, it was the Liberal Establishment
that was losing the war for the soul of humankind: "The Liberal
community accepts calmly and fatalistically the march of events
of the past years," he said, unsubtly blaming liberals for the rise of
communism in Russia and the Eastern Bloc of Europe and China,
as well as the expansion of the bureaucratic state in America with
its high taxes and probing regulations. To Buckley, the liberals had
sacrificed "an operative set of values" and were willingly departing
from "the Great Tradition" in America in order to safeguard false
idols like "fairness" and "equality." The Liberal Establishment,
he said, had "no ground wire," and "without grounding, the volt-
age fluctuates wildly, wantonly chasing after the immediate lines
of least resistance."[32] To preserve their image with the country's
Jews and secularists, for instance, liberals had sacrificed Christian
morality in the name of bland religious tolerance. Meanwhile, to

keep from appearing heartless to the poor, the nation had given up free-market capitalism for an increasingly socialized and corporatized welfare. The country was being too nice and too tolerant, and, in the process, it was giving up on its time-tested truths.

"The American Right," Buckley concluded, his arms starting to dance around in the air, "is based on the assumption that however many things there are that we *don't* know, there are some of the things we *do* know; on the assumption that some questions are closed, and that our survival as a nation depends on our acting bravely on those assumptions, without whose strength we are left sounding like Eisenhower, which is to say organically unintelligible; rhetoricizing like Kennedy, which is what comes of hiring Madison Avenue to make non-action act; or writing like Mailer, which is to write without 'beginning to know what one is, or what one wants.' "[33]

The audience laughed at the swipe at Mailer, but before they could get carried away, Buckley hammered home his point. The departure from the received truths meant that "Euclidean formulas, Christian imperatives, Mosaic homilies become, all of them, simply irrelevant; worse, when taken seriously, they get in the way of that apocalyptic orgasm which [Mailer] sees as the objective of individual experience."[34]

Buckley's point was that by swaying from the country's Grand Traditions, the Liberal Establishment had opened the way for the likes of Mailer, whose goal, Buckley unfairly claimed, was hedonistic bliss without concern for anyone else, an apocalyptic orgasm. "The true meaning of the American right wing," Buckley finally said, "is commitment, a commitment on the basis of which it becomes possible to take measurements." And "If [Mailer] wants to learn something about the true nature of the American right wing," Buckley added, "I recommend to him the works of Presidents Matthew, Mark, Luke and John."[35] These were the solid anchors to which America should hold fast if it were going to correct course and get back on a vital path toward righteousness.

Mailer was up before the applause died down. He approached the lectern like a bull. He was not the smooth operator Buckley was, nor half the performer, and the force of his ideas seemed to spew forth uncontrollably—plus, Mailer had a tin ear when it came to warming up an audience. But to everyone's surprise, he began by agreeing with one of Buckley's central tenets.

Yes, said Mailer, mainstream American liberalism was exactly as sick as Buckley made it out to be. It was shockingly unable to offer remedies to the messes it had created since the end of the Second World War. After all, it was liberalism that had ushered in a falsely premised Cold War based on a phony commitment to Christianity. And it was the liberal elite whose corporate capitalism wasn't bringing freedom to anyone, putting men in all those grey flannel suits and shipping them off to work for their pensions. The current liberal order, Mailer said, had created "a deterioration of desire, an apathy about the future, a detestation of the present, an amnesia of the past. Its forms are many, its flavor is unforgettable: It is the disease which destroys flavor." And if you didn't see it all around you, just lift up your eyes to look:

> Its symptoms appear everywhere: in architecture, medicine, in the deteriorated quality of labor, the insubstantiality of money, the ravishment of nature, the impoverishment of food, the manipulation of emotion, the emptiness of faith, the displacement of sex, the deterioration of language, the reduction of philosophy, and the alienation of man from the product of his work and the results of his acts.[36]

Mailer insisted he hated the Liberal Establishment just as much as Buckley did.

But Buckley's conservatives, Mailer said, were hardly better. In fact, he said, at least half of the so-called conservatives in Buckley's coalition were not conservative at all. They did not want to conserve any meaningful past. Instead, all they sought was the triumph of the business classes. All that red baiting about communism? All those discussions about "preserving the Grand Tradition"? Smoke-screens, Mailer said. In truth, it was laissez-faire capitalism that was the real demand.

Just look at their hero, Arizona senator Barry Goldwater, Mailer went on. How could he get away with his contradictory demand for both smaller government *and* the expanded military that would be required to win the Cold War? By pushing this contradiction, Goldwater was either a fool who didn't understand basic econom-ics or was engaging in a horrifying bait-and-switch. "[T]here are conservatives like the old lady who wished to save the trees," said Mailer, "and there are conservatives who talk of saving trees in order to get the power to cut down trees."[37] *That* was the contradic-tion at the heart of modern conservatism. Which was Mr. Buckley? Mailer asked. Did he want to conserve a real past, or did he want to use the emotional tug of that past in order to obtain the power to bring further wealth to the free-market capitalists?

Some in the crowd shouted "*Olé!*" to root him on.

Aside from the capitalists and the true conservative conserva-tionists, the only other folks Mailer could find on the right were those afraid of losing it all in a changing world, of losing status and place, and who acted angrily in order to preserve a fading past. To Mailer, these folks were more sympathetic than the capitalists. At least they were honest. Fear was a justifiable emotion. But these people promised no bright future. Yearning for the past gets you nowhere. Hadn't they read *The Great Gatsby*? Well, probably not, he surmised, but still. . . .

Mailer then began to paint a verbal picture of his own, an image of a more robust public life, where creativity was rewarded and greatness not defined by one's ability to toe a party line. Mailer's greatest fear was totalitarianism, and his understanding of it was more than just political. He believed there were aspects of business and culture and government that could grow so big and powerful they would act only to preserve themselves. Giant corporations didn't care about the lowly worker. Huge press conglomerations put limitations on the voices one might hear. People bowed to technological solutions to problems, which made scientists the new moral arbiters—even if their technology simply insulated people from what was authentic in life.

Like Buckley, Mailer sought more freedom from the Liberal Establishment. But Mailer's freedom came with different anchors than Buckley's, without foundations in a Christian heritage or walls imposed by laissez-faire capitalism. He had called himself a "libertarian socialist" in the past, a socialist when it came to providing a certain economic and educational level for everyone, but, once that base was provided, a libertarian when it came to the state trying to define and ensure "the good life." That attempt was, as Mailer saw it, the vital plague of midcentury American liberalism, an ideology premised on giving gifts that nobody had asked for.[38] "Do we accept the progressive collectivization of our lives which eternal cold war must bring," Mailer wondered in his conclusion, as the audience flanking him on either side began to understand his disdain for a society where two-thirds of every federal dollar went to the defense budget, "Or do we gamble on the chance that we have armament enough already to be secure and to be free, and do we seek therefore to discover ourselves?"[39]

Mailer then uttered the most dramatic line of the evening: In order to embrace this creative endeavor, in order to launch his vision of libertarian socialism, the United States must "end the Cold War" immediately. Coming well before Vietnam sparked widespread consciousness about the perils of the Cold War, Mailer hollered to the young crowd, "Let communism come to those countries it will come to. Let us not use up our substance trying to hold onto nations which are poor, underdeveloped, and bound to us only by the depths of their hatred for us."[40] For Mailer, the real war was not "between West and East, between capitalism and communism," but between "the conservative and the rebel, between authority and instinct, between two views of God which collide in the mind of the West." Are men born into God-ordained rungs, he asked, rich or poor, smart or foolish, without the freedom and capacity to rise above the stations of their birth? Or are men capable of "seeking to shift the wealth of our universe in such a way that the talent, creativity, and strength of the future . . . will come to take its first breath, will show us what a mighty renaissance is locked in the unconsciousness of the dumb[?]"[41]

Both men were irked at the apparent limitations of the present. But one man looked back toward reestablishing "the Great Tradition," while the other sought to "serve as God's agent" in an unknowable future freed from the tyrants of the past. One man loved commitment rooted in history while the other sought an unknown tomorrow.

After intermission, the two men squared off directly. "Are you prepared to say that it is distinctly the right wing that wants to win the Cold War?" Buckley asked Mailer.

Mailer shouted, "No, it is the right wing that wishes to blow up the earth."

"Why?" asked an incredulous Buckley.

"You think it is better to be dead than Red," Mailer responded.

"Is it not better to be alive and free?" retorted Buckley.

"Yes," said Mailer, "but the way to be alive and free is to end the cold war."[42]

For Buckley, this made no sense. He saw communism as expansive in nature and therefore an inching threat to the American way of life he was struggling to preserve. All efforts should be made to stop communism before it could make safe harbor on American shores. For Buckley, it *was* in fact better to be dead than Red.

On religion, Mailer argued that Buckley's call to return to Christianity was baloney, absent of any genuine faith. For most conservatives, Mailer argued, God's demands were almost always trumped by man's. Was this yet another smokescreen to safeguard the economy for the capitalists? Or was it an attempt to root out religious minorities who threatened "the Great Tradition"?

Buckley laughed nervously, his Catholic faith propping him up, and asked Mailer if he could name anyone on the left who was devoutly religious.

"Well, I can only speak very modestly," said Mailer, "but I think *I'm* religious."[43]

The crowd laughed at the noted radical, but Mailer was being honest. He had just recently overcome a bout of youthful atheism, coming to believe that both God and the Devil were active in the world, fighting it out for the future. The outlook he expressed derived more from his World War II experience and his readings in existentialism than his Jewish upbringing. But it was a theology (called Manichaeism) that lasted the rest of his life. And it was the Devil who was ushering in all the totalitarianism he saw around him, from plastic to cancer to bad architecture to the Cold War to the Liberal Establishment. Man needed to side with God and fight back.[44]

Buckley didn't buy it. Here was Mailer once again traversing the easiest path without concern for tradition. "Now at a certain point," Buckley replied, "the Right Wing presumably asks the question of whether or not there is a common vocabulary on the basis of which people can speak to each other purposefully."[45] Anyone can make a religion out of anything, but that was not a demonstration of anything greater than oneself, that "apocalyptic orgasm" he had been talking about earlier.

From there, the two went on to debate civil rights, states' rights, and politics. It was a profound conversation. At a deep level, they were not only talking about politics, but also about the meaning of human freedom, the definition of "the good life," and the place of God, man, and the Devil in the world. This wasn't a normal debate. It had turned into a discussion about the kind of life worth living. At one point early in the discussion, Mailer grew tired of Buckley's attempts to win rhetorical points in order to score points with the audience. Exasperated, Mailer simply threw his hands up and declared, "I'm trying to talk about the nature of man!" And that's what it was all boiling down to. Each man was after a revolution in the consciousness of their time, and all in an effort to expand human happiness.

For at least one audience member, the debate helped clarify the various ways forward. People would later come to know Abbie Hoffman as one of the most prominent antiwar protestors of the 1960s, all Jewfro and anger, arrested for attempting to incite riots and levitate the Pentagon. But in 1962 he was a twenty-five-year-old college graduate searching for ways to express his spiritual longings. He came to the Buckley–Mailer debate to see the future. Later, he said, "you felt on a gut level that William Buckley was representing everything you didn't like in your college experience. All the rah-rah baloney, the genteel and gentile power structure, the martini set and the Madison Avenue gray flannel suits. Buckley represented the empire," said Hoffman, "and Mailer was challenging the empire as a hip ethnic street fighter. That was extremely appealing to me. There was no doubt emotionally about whose side I'd be on."[46]

Of course, not everyone agreed. "When it was over, everybody (including the audience) had done a lot of shouting; nobody had changed anybody's politics; and the battle between Mr. Buckley (a clever jabber with a tiptoe stance) and the novelist, Mr. Mailer, (who hooked with his fists as he spoke) was considered to have ended in a draw." Or so thought Gay Talese in the pages of the *New York Times* the following day.[47]

Mailer was flabbergasted by Talese's assessment. He thought Buckley had been too cute. "[M]ost of the people who were there seemed to think that I had won it," he wrote a friend.[48] And he was right. According to *Newsday*, "Non-partisan judges gave the decision to Mailer by a 6-3-1 vote," adding, "Mailer accepted congratulations graciously."[49]

But the graciousness departed once Mailer read Talese's report. Mailer's ego was unsettled. Sure, both debaters had scored points, but he felt Buckley hadn't countered Mailer's central arguments that the right was simply a politics of emotion, or that the Cold War was a falsely premised battle used to prop up a near-totalitarian culture, or that the conservative response wasn't the proper one to the liberal malaise. Returning to the anchors of the past was no way forward when the world had so profoundly changed.[50]

The next day, Mailer came across Talese at a party. The room was crowded, but Mailer picked Talese out of the crowd and, drink in hand, walked straight toward him. Talese thought he looked like a bull aiming to gore the matador. He didn't want to fight, especially because Mailer's reputation was that of a man who took boxing lessons and got into head-butting competitions for fun. Somewhat absurdly, Talese also looked down at his own three-piece tan gabardine suit and didn't want to ruin it.

"*Draw?*" Mailer said to Talese ferociously. "What do you mean *draw?* There was no draw. I annihilated him. I wiped out Buckley."

Talese tried to make light of the situation, saying he wrote the *Times* piece as a spoof on the sports writing that was going to dominate the papers after the boxing match the following day. But Mailer wasn't having it. He continued his barrage, lifting his drink threateningly.

"Don't throw that drink at me," Talese said, remembering his suit.

For some reason the comment awoke Mailer from his anger, and he stood upright and replied that he had no intention of doing so.[51] Instead, Mailer offered his own assessment. "When the debate ended," he later wrote, "I had succeeded in pushing a salient into the intellectual territory of the Right which was not counterattacked by Buckley. So I claimed victory. If we ever debate again, Buckley will be hunting for mountain lion. Knowing my opponent he will doubtless use an elephant gun."[52]

For his part, Buckley also claimed victory. "Do you know who

Norman Mailer is?" Buckley wrote in his newly syndicated newspaper column the Sunday after the debate. "He complains bitterly because he supposes you do not, and the right *not* to know Norman Mailer is *not* an American right, however free is this land of the brave." Mailer, Buckley wrote, "wants to influence those who are alive at this time," and has therefore become "a teensy-weensy bit of an exhibitionist, striking garish public poses with the aim of luring people into his tent, where, where. . . ."[53]

Buckley used the time-honored tradition of beating Mailer with his odd and lurid biography, a common tactic to avoid taking Mailer's ideas seriously. But unlike others who performed this trick, Buckley refused to leave it at that. His ponderous line at the end, "where, where. . . . ," pointed to a question Buckley really wanted an answer for: *What is it you want, Mr. Mailer?*

Buckley pondered Mailer's wanderlusts through different social philosophies. "God is dead! Nietzsche announced," Buckley wrote. "[No,] God is dying! Mailer corrects him. It is of course the duty of creative men to add to our store of knowledge and accommodate new experience and contingencies. But the boys to worry about are those who want to start completely afresh—who want, in the words of the disgusted back-bencher, to 'send a man to the guillotine to do away with a case of dandruff.' "

The Mailer of the 1950s served for Buckley as a perfect symbol of what happens when someone goes searching for truths without maintaining ground wire. Buckley had called Mailer a "moral pervert" in *National Review* in the past.[54] As opposed to the "American conservative," who believes "that the cluster of truths which are loosely referred to as our 'Judeo-Christian tradition' are—well, are truths," men like Mailer, Buckley wrote in 1962, "chase about wildly through hipsterism and existentialism and humanism and Freudianism and communism and fascism and objectivism and what have you, just to say you've got the blackboard clean."

But still, Mailer's earnestness during the debate had sparked Buckley's interest. Even if "he doesn't know what it is he wants to say," Buckley concluded his column, "his desperate anxiety to say it, fired by his incandescent moral energy, makes him very much worth watching."[55]

Mailer saw something attractive in Buckley, too. When asked about his adversary a few weeks later, Mailer said, "Buckley's all right, a charming guy, a dirty fighter, and fun to debate with."[56] He knew they were both prophetic voices, standing outside the mainstream, offering critiques from a higher moral plane. They were both asking America to live up to its better angels, but both disagreed on what those angels might say.

As they left the Chicago stage, then, both had an inkling that it wouldn't be long before they saw each other again. All they'd need was an excuse.

2

Placid Seas

I n October 1962, just a few weeks after the Chicago debate, Mailer drove his motorcycle an hour north from his brownstone in Brooklyn to Buckley's rambling waterfront home in cushy Stamford, Connecticut, a mansion Buckley had owned since 1952. It was business that provoked the meeting.

For one thing, the two men had to iron out the transcript of their Chicago debate before it could be published in *Playboy*.[1] They also had to discuss a new offer from John Golden. The sparks from Chicago had been so fierce, and the ticket proceeds so plentiful, that the John Golden Productions Company wanted to keep the Mailer–Buckley ticket alive a little while longer. Golden had sent an open-ended invitation to both men, asking if they would entertain the idea of conducting a series of twelve debates, one per month, crossing the country from east to west while sparring in large theaters.[2]

Negotiations could have been handled through letters, or lawyers, or over the phone. But it seems there was a third issue that both Buckley and Mailer wanted to weigh: whether or not it might be interesting for them to form a serious and meaningful friendship. With this final motive in mind, Buckley called Mailer to invite him and his wife to Connecticut for a visit. The Mailers eagerly accepted.

As Mailer dismounted his motorcycle in Buckley's driveway, he must have looked like the embodiment of social rebelliousness. At five feet seven or eight inches tall, he was just below average height, a Napoleonic stature that filled him with angry ambition. This was reflected in his barrel chest, which always seemed to precede him into a room, announcing visceral intention. His legs were strong if thin, and his longish curly dark hair immediately identified him both as an American Jew and as an outlaw against American social norms. The tidy cropped look of the technocratic age never appealed to Mailer, and it wouldn't have looked right, either. He didn't do skinny ties like a Kennedy.

Sartorially speaking, Mailer stuck to loose khakis on casual days, rolling up the sleeves of a wrinkled dress shirt or, if his mood were particularly bad, wearing just a white undershirt, his big chest making the shirt a bit too tight against his increasing burliness. On formal occasions he donned oversized dark double-breasted suits, usually from Brooks Brothers and often adorned with thick ties.

Above all, though, what set Mailer apart were not his clothes or his build but his eyes, piercing and oceanic blue. Everyone from gossip columnist Liz Smith to literature professor Steven Marcus felt compelled to comment on them, suggesting they hinted at profound vision and deep insight, both of which Mailer possessed. His eyes could be bullish and narrow, or wide and warm. Either way, it felt as if they were examining the depths of one's soul. And they made more than a handful of women swoon.[3]

Mailer's wife at the time was Jeanne Campbell, or rather, *Lady* Jeanne Campbell. She was a large-boned Brit who wore tweed suits and bounced gaily through life. In contrast to Mailer's middle-class Brooklyn background, she was a bona fide aristocrat, the daughter of the Duke of Argyll and the granddaughter of the powerful Anglo-Canadian news magnate Lord Beaverbrook. She had pursued a career in journalism, taking a job in her grandfather's publishing empire, and during the course of her career also had

been in the employ of *Time*'s Henry Luce. The job grew into something more than that, though, and Campbell and Luce ended up
having a well-publicized affair. Considering *Time* embodied all the
stolid pieties of Liberal America that Mailer hated—the hawkish
dislike of Russia, the sanctimonious embrace of corporate capitalism, the aggressive imperialism of "the American Century"—more
than one person wondered if stealing Campbell from Luce was
Mailer's way of sticking it to *Time*. "Norman," said his friend Midge
Decter, "was not unaffected by the fact that she'd been Henry
Luce's mistress."[4]

Buckley, meanwhile, looked quintessentially WASPy, with perhaps an Irish twist. He was tall, angular, and graceful, with a
skinny frame and arms that were always on the go, as if conducting
the orchestra of his ideas. His hair was lightly colored and sometimes looked almost red, a wavy mane pushed casually to the right.
When it hadn't been cut in a while, Buckley's hair would sometimes droop uncooperatively over his eyes, forcing him to push it
back into place. But this was more a suggestion of a prep-school
past than a rejection of social norms.

Buckley's clothes would have confirmed the prep-school past,
too—a day's work done in loose khakis, a tucked-in button-down,
and an understated tie, often loosened to reveal the shirt's open
top button. For any other event, his attire was always scrupulously
proper. For tennis, there were whites. For a night out, a tux and
tails. When he traveled, his wife would pack for him to make sure
everything matched. In truth he didn't care much about what he
wore, but it was a casual indifference, the kind that comes with
having been in these situations so many times that choosing what
to wear was second nature. When Buckley undressed for the evening, he would leave things wrinkled on the floor for someone else
to pick up, just as his father had done before him.

Buckley's eyes were as powerful as Mailer's, but in a different way.
They weren't quite swoon-worthy, nor did they project insights into
the depths of one's soul. Instead, they were playful and provocative

as they bounced in the middle distance, pausing for effect here and there, searching for affirmation at other times. In some ways they were like a salesman's eyes, as though Buckley were trying to sell something he knew you didn't really want to buy.

And then there was his voice, which would become famous later after all those television appearances. It was slightly high-pitched, a bit nasal, and it could linger on a word while his whole head shot up to examine something on the ceiling before crashing back to earth to unleash a rhetorical onslaught. He spoke with a slight affectation, too. Was it British? Was it a reflection of the fact that his first and second languages had been Spanish and French, respectively? There was a bit of Upper East Side snootiness to it as well. And something of the South.

All of this was coupled with a marvelous vocabulary. As a boy, Buckley had tried to impress his father by learning a new word every day, then deploying it that night at dinner. By the time he was grown up, Buckley was famous for having even the most erudite professor searching for the dictionary.[5]

Buckley's wife was Patricia, or Pat, or, as she and Buckley called one another, "Ducky." Just as tall as her husband, bird-like and more graceful, she had been born to a Canadian industrial magnate and exuded the wealthy background from which she came. Pat was a tart conversationalist who didn't suffer fools, although she was no intellectual. Buckley couldn't remember her ever opening a work of nonfiction. When she died, it would turn out that nearly all of her closest friends were gay men more interested in fashion than ideas.[6]

As the two couples mixed drinks in Stamford, Mailer was the obvious outlier. He was the only Jew in the room, although what that meant for Mailer was poorly understood by everyone, perhaps by Mailer himself most of all. He had been a religious skeptic since his bar mitzvah, when, under the mentorship of a Marxist Hebrew teacher, he spoke gleefully about the seventeenth-century Dutch philosopher Baruch Spinoza, who had been excommunicated from his small Jewish community for redefining God, for seeing Him in everything and not just as a divinity upholding a covenant with His people. Twenty-five years later, Mailer still loved Spinoza. Here was a man willing to take on his community in order to fight for what he believed. Plus, Spinoza's notion that God was everywhere, in everything, appealed to him. "Organized religion has never meant much to me," Mailer later said. "I do believe in God, but it is a very personal faith and I find in myself . . . no detectable desire to join any church. Too many churches seem like prisons of the spirit to me."[7]

To call Mailer a cultural Jew also misses the mark, however. He didn't associate solely with other Jews, married only one (the first of his six wives), and did not belong to any temple. Instead, for Mailer, Jewishness was more of a cultural code. For him, a Jew was a law-abiding and dutiful striver, someone filled with middle-class ambition and without the guts to challenge authority. It was a condition he saw everywhere growing up in Brooklyn, all those boys asserting their masculinity not through athletics or romance but through books and earnestness. To be a man in that world was to be filled with economic and professional promise. The whole culture consisted of strivers who never bothered to ask what they were striving for, what that middle-class status would mean. Nowhere was this truer than with his mother, Fanny, a woman so filled with chutzpah she made her husband, a dapper South African Jew who was also a cad and a degenerate gambler, all but disappear. It had been her idea to give Mailer the middle name "Malech," which means "king" in Hebrew. When a cousin pointed out the pretentiousness of the name, Fanny changed it to "Kingsley" instead. But the change was only nominal.[8] At nearly forty years old, Mailer still dined with his parents almost every Friday night.

Getting beyond the sheen of middle-class Jewish respectability was Mailer's compulsion. When he came back from the Army after the Second World War, he returned not only with an even fouler mouth than before but also with an obnoxious Texas drawl he would deploy when drunk or angry. It was an odd acquisition, but it made some sense. During the war he was assigned to the hard-scrabble 112th Cavalry, initially a horse cavalry from San Antonio but which lost many of its horses and dozens of men in various battles early in the war. The 112th became the first U.S. Army unit in the Pacific to use bazookas and flamethrowers. By 1944, when Mailer joined them, the senior guys in the 112th were hardened Southerners, mainly Texans, all tobacco spit and four-letter words with bazookas to boot. Mailer had never met a Southerner before, much less a Texan.

Mailer observed them closely, watching them abuse one other but also admiring them for their strong sense of honor. He came to see them as primal savages, much closer to their wants and desires than the aspirational Jews he knew in Brooklyn. He respected their proximity to their innermost yearnings, but also feared it. Violence always seemed lurking and almost completely untamed.

In fact, the Texans reminded Mailer of what the character Charles Marlow had discovered in Joseph Conrad's *Heart of Darkness*. As Marlow takes his journey into the depths of Africa, he becomes aware of all the useless Victorian refinement that coats the Western world. But Marlow also sees something even more frightening—the carnal brutality associated with the Africans, who more freely expose the dark heart at the center of humanity: the violence, the urgency, the hatred, the despair. As Mailer well knew, *Heart of Darkness* was a critique both of Victorian sensibilities—the dulling veneer of the West—and of the heart of darkness the Victorian veneer was designed to suppress.

Mailer equated the Texans of the 112th with Conrad's Africans. But what to do? Where was the balance between frank human desire and reining in the yearning of the individual in order to build and develop a society? It was an enduring question for Mailer. Later in life, when he would deploy his over-the-top Texas drawl, everyone hated it, but they also knew exactly what it meant:

that Mailer was leaving behind his middle-class respectability in order to engage his more violent self, the heart of darkness all his own.

For Buckley, there was no such burdensome past to overcome, no wanderlust in search of more authentic happiness, no running from middle-class respectability. He was by nature not introspective, a fact he was well aware of and often bragged about. But more than this, Buckley came from wealth. His childhood home in Sharon, Connecticut, had 114 rooms and a name ("Great Elm"), and came with all the highfalutin extravagances of the rich, including private tutors, horseback riding, personal servants, and six pianos.

This wealth came with ideas, too, not the least of which was his father's deep libertarianism, an anti-government stance hardened after Buckley, Sr., lost his fortune in Mexican land and oil when the Mexican Revolution tossed and turned in a manner that would have made Robespierre proud. Governments could be dangerous, his father had learned, and the younger Buckleys, all ten of them, listened at his knee.

Plus, Buckley had Catholicism. Both of his parents had been raised with a Continental Catholicism, which was much sterner than the accommodating kind embraced by the Irish. For Buckley, Catholicism was a deeply transcendent faith that gave one direction and certainty. It created order, taught one one's place, and gave one the confidence to fight to ensure proper hierarchies of authority remained in place. Buckley prayed harder and longer than all of his siblings, came to his own understanding of the faith in one mystical moment at boarding school at the age of fourteen, and claimed to have never once wavered in his beliefs. He possessed The Truth, he knew, and The Truth gave guidance to his life. When a professor at Yale suggested Buckley broaden his perspective and take a class in metaphysics, Buckley replied, "I have God and my father. That's all I need."[9]

Buckley's struggle was not to overcome the expectations of middle-class respectability, as Mailer was doing, but to preserve the kind of life he had lived throughout his childhood, where wealth and moral righteousness went hand-in-hand. After all, a conservative ought to have something to conserve.

To do this, he'd become a salesman, not a thinker. The economist John Kenneth Galbraith liked to tell a story about Buckley that concerned their time together in college. Right after graduating from Yale in 1950, Buckley and Galbraith visited the home of their classmate, William MacLeish, son of Archibald MacLeish, the famous poet and Franklin Delano Roosevelt's Librarian of Congress. Buckley made the most of being in the presence of greatness. He asked the elder MacLeish if he should heed the advice of his parents, who thought Buckley should go to graduate school in political science.

After a thoughtful minute, MacLeish said, "That would be very good; it would be very helpful in causing you to know what you think."

Buckley surprised everyone when he replied: "No, I *know* what I think. The question is whether this will be helpful to me as a salesman. Will this credential help in getting heard?"[10]

Buckley never went to graduate school. Instead, there was *God and Man at Yale*, the 1952 book that propelled him to the forefront of American intellectual life by probing the contradictions of the liberal elite and calling for a restoration of religion and free-market economics; *McCarthy and His Enemies*, a 1954 book that attempted to defend Joseph McCarthy's cause; and, in 1955, the creation of *National Review*, the magazine that by 1962 had become the popular and powerful voice of reasonable if forceful conservatism. All were efforts to be heard, the work of a salesman pitching the outrageous idea of conservatism in a time of liberalism.

As the two men pondered business, they thought seriously about Golden's offer of twelve debates in twelve cities over the course of a year. No doubt the debates would be fun. Each man would have to refine his vision a bit more, and that would be worthwhile. This was especially pertinent because in the month since Chicago, not only had the country confronted the Cuban Missile Crisis, which brought the world to the edge of annihilation in the name of the Cold War, but also the enrollment of James Meredith at the University of Mississippi, a signal event in the burgeoning civil rights movement. Things seemed to be coming to a head.

Mailer, though, was concerned that twelve debates over the course of a year might be too much work considering his other commitments. He had books to write, journalism to attend to, revolutions to spark. Spending two weeks each month in preparation for debate would be debilitating. And there was also the issue of money. How much would it take to get a guy like Norman Mailer, a much-in-demand author, to give up a year's worth of writing in order to travel the country to debate? Mailer thought he and Buckley were "show business" people who could command "show business" prices. But Golden had already resisted one appeal to pay them more than was customary for literary intellectuals, "appealing to your ethical nature," he had said to both Mailer and Buckley. This meant, of course, that Mailer and Buckley weren't show business people after all and that they'd have to be content to earn less.[11] But, of course, they weren't.

After a while Buckley, born rich and married superrich, got bored. The yearlong debates would be fun but impractical. So they decided they'd skip it. Mailer responded to the promoter:

> As you know, a debate once a month of the sort you suggest would be the cruelest and most impracticle [sic] invasion of my time. I don't say it's impossible but I do say it's impossible unless you can guarantee me a minimum of $2000 each appearance. If I were to make that kind of money and if you could find me a lecture on the side, the day after the debate for $500 to $750 there'd be some sense to the venture. Other-

wise the only recourse is national TV, but where could we ever
get paid enough to make that worthwhile?[12]

They'd see what the promoter came up with.[13]

Business done for the time being, Buckley moved on to the
meeting's third motive, determining the possibility for friendship.
And he did what he always liked to do at times like this: he invited
Mailer sailing. It was an aristocratic gesture to be sure, putting on
display the serenity and gracefulness he had honed since childhood. Buckley also may have wanted to introduce, or even seduce,
Mailer to the fruits of conservatism. It wouldn't have been the first
time Buckley won a convert by dangling the allures of aristocratic
living in front of them.[14]

But the invitation was also a sign of how quickly the two men
were becoming friends. Buckley's typical afternoon sail took him
south from Connecticut across the Long Island Sound toward
either Eatons Neck or Oyster Bay, which sits on the northern shore
of Long Island. They would then turn east or west, drifting along
Long Island's coast before turning north and heading back toward
Connecticut. The trip would take two or three hours, depending
on the wind.

Perhaps the speed of their intimacy shouldn't have surprised
the two men. After all, they had quite a bit in common. They were
both privileged white males at a time when white male privilege
was still the norm. They were also both Ivy Leaguers who had
chafed at the indifferent students who had surrounded them.
They were both young and famous, too, and both were free spirits,
playful but possessing serious challenges to the dominant culture
around them. They were confident and cocky, comfortable speaking to, and on behalf of, the entire nation. And, perhaps most of
all, they shared a common enemy: the Liberal Establishment. In
1959, Buckley had derided the dominant culture around him as a
culture of "lotus-eaters," making reference to Book IX of Homer's
Odyssey, when Odysseus comes across a blissful island where people

sit around all day doing nothing but eating lotus leaves. The leaves contain a narcotic that makes the islanders waste away in blissful apathy. Odysseus orders his boat away, "for fear someone else might taste of the lotus and forget the way home."[15]

"During the Eisenhower years," Buckley had written in 1959:

> [T]he tendency . . . is to yield to the passion for modulation. Even in literature, one does not often find oneself concerned with kings and knaves, fair maidens and heroes, treachery and honor, right and wrong; one speaks in greys, and muted hues, of social problems, and life adjustment, and co-existence and intercredal amity. Increasingly, we are called upon to modulate our voices. Increasingly, the convention of tact brings us to modulate not only our voices, but also our dogmas. . . . Compulsive gentility has far-reaching moral consequences.[16]

His point was that, among the Liberal Establishment that then dominated American life, people were asked to temper their views, to speak in greys, to scuttle deeply held positions, to be respectful of others above all else.

Mailer couldn't agree more. The limiting sheen of respectful obedience was exactly what he was pointing to when he had said, also in 1959, "the shits are killing us."[17]

But even more than this, both men had come to identify three foundational ideas central to the Liberal Establishment. Buckley and Mailer disagreed about which of the three most needed overhauling, and to a great extent that was what separated right from left in postwar America. But that there were three common assumptions within the Liberal Establishment there was no doubt.

The first of these assumptions was a profound belief in rational thought. Problems were out there in the world, sure, but they could be detected, debated, and then coolly dispatched with technological precision. In order to fix things, what was needed was a bird's-eye gaze that could show Americans how to best react.

Buckley and Mailer, and many others, saw President Dwight Eisenhower as embodying this component of mainstream liberalism. Here was a four-star general removed from the action but monitoring it all from the oversized map on the wall at headquarters, the action done by small-thinking bureaucrats on the ground. Ike even lent his name to one of the most rationalizing aspects of the 1950s, the Eisenhower Interstate Highway System, a linear graph of mostly straight lines crisscrossing the nation with four- or six-lane highways, all done in the name of efficient, easy travel. It was unimportant to consider the fate of cities that lay a few miles off the highway because the planners had prioritized efficiency over human contact. As Eisenhower put it, "[W]e don't want to try to stop that many automobiles coming. . . . We want them. They mean progress for our country. They mean greater convenience for greater numbers of people, greater happiness, and greater standards of living. But we have got to learn to control the things that we must use ourselves."[18] Along these roads Americans zoomed, blissfully unaware of the hardships and livelihoods of the towns they passed, the mountains they climbed, and the temperature outside. The rational highway system leveled the highs and lows of the landscape, all in the name of efficiency and ease.

Robert Moses was another emblem of the Liberal Establishment's belief in the power of the rationally thought-out plan. As New York City's primary planner for the middle decades of the twentieth century, Moses would look at a map of New York City and determine how it should be organized and developed, irrespective of a borough's history or the placement of its people. When he looked at Flushing Meadows, in Queens, from the vantage point of an aerial map, he thought it would be the perfect place for New Yorkers to relax—why not put a baseball stadium there? Brooklyn Dodgers owner Walter O'Malley disagreed, saying (among other things) that his team's fans lived in Brooklyn, not Queens. That didn't matter to Moses. From his bird's-eye view, a stadium in Brooklyn no longer made sense—there was no parking, not enough access from mass transit, and therefore limited potential for growth. Queens was where the flow should go. At loggerheads, O'Malley took his team to Los Angeles. Moses would not be deterred. He eventually got his team in Flushing Meadows a few years later, when the New York Mets were created, their blue and orange colors a legacy of the Dodgers and the Giants, those teams that had refused to play ball with Moses.

Moses's liberal credo was clear: "In the physical sense there are no insoluble urban problems, once we get in the mood to be serious, honest, cooperative and unselfish about them. We can rid ourselves of slums, untangle traffic except at infrequent peak loads, provide all the modern works and services that are good for us, stimulate trade, commerce and business, welcome and encourage the arts, provide wholesome recreation and generally establish the framework for happy and productive living."[19] Moses and his rational plans won the day. Urban renewal, like the highway system, proceeded apace. Neighborhoods were torn down and reorganized on the basis of efficiency, orderliness, and structure. It was in our power to systematize and control. Why not do it? Just give the bureaucrats a map.

Technology was a key feature in this lionization of rational thought. Today's hurdles would be fixed by tomorrow's technologies. Why worry now? We had built the atomic bomb just in time to win the war; polio had been beaten; open-heart surgeries were now available. Who was going to say we couldn't get to the moon by the end of the decade; develop faster, more efficient automobiles; and be able to travel across the world in just a few hours? Someone would fix these problems eventually, and technology would be his or her handmaiden.

Progress, therefore, was inevitable. Humankind, when freed from the dogmas and mythologies of the past, could be systematized and improved. Using our powers of rationality, we could shape the economy, endorse productive traditions, eradicate nonproductive ones, and generally fulfill the American "pursuit of happiness," all by allowing the technocrats to do their thing. "Our usual method of remedying wrongs," wrote Moses, "is to create new agencies, . . . created to provide some service for which there was a popular demand or to complete the perfection of mankind."[20]

To complete the perfection of mankind. There it was, the goal stated plainly. Rationality, progress, and technology have long been features of American life, but far more than at other periods of American history, midcentury liberals eschewed the irrational and put its trust in the cool workings of the bureaucrats. It was difficult to blame them. Government agencies had fought the Depression. The military had won the war. And by the 1950s, America had become the wealthiest nation the world had ever seen. As journalist Theodore H. White put it in 1960, this "was a new generation of Americans who saw the world differently from their fathers. [They were] brought up to believe, either at home or abroad, that whatever Americans wished to make happen, would happen."[21]

Yet in a country known for self-made men inclined to go their own way, the irrational can only remain dormant for so long.

If an unswerving commitment to rational thought was the central tenet of midcentury American thought, the second article of faith was a strong belief in the moral righteousness of corporate capitalism. Its success was something of a surprise, too.

Before the 1930s, government-supported laissez-faire capitalism dominated the economic life of the nation. The government might, for example, give away huge land grants to railroad companies, then more or less back away, allowing them to do their business, build their monopolies, work their child laborers. This system incurred some challenges during the Progressive Era at the turn of the twentieth century, when some monopolies were broken up and labor laws were first passed, but it suffered its deepest setbacks during the Great Depression. Tellingly, and contrary to Karl Marx's predictions, it wasn't the working classes who took control of things when laissez-faire capitalism faltered in the

1930s. Instead, it was a collection of government bureaucracies. At first, during Franklin D. Roosevelt's New Deal, these bureaucrats worked in conjunction with local leaders, handing government largess to locally controlled political and economic machines. As the 1930s progressed, however, and especially with the onset of the Second World War, the federal government grew in both size and importance. Ivy Leaguers crowded Washington to help direct the economy, advancing certain businesses here, restraining them there, and generally tinkering with the economy to ensure things operated at a maximum.

John Maynard Keynes became the economist most associated with these new arrangements. He was a brilliant and witty Cambridge don ready to use his talents to improve the lot of the common folk. Believing that levels of investment were the key to a stable economy, Keynes argued that the role of the government should serve as something of a ballast. In good times, Keynes believed government should use its power to moderate investments, and in bad times, it should not only encourage investment but also invest money itself. He called his notion "a somewhat comprehensive socialization of investment." Keynes understood that the Great Depression ended only with the onset of World War II, once the federal government began investing heavily in the war effort and in giant corporations that made war matériel.[22] And he hoped that federal governments would continue to be the stabilizing force in the sometimes turbulent seas of free-market capitalism.

By the end of the war, nearly everyone in power considered himself a Keynesian. When Eisenhower detected a slump in the economy in 1953–54, the first measure he took was to increase military spending. The aeronautical companies who built machines for the military amped up production and hired more workers. The workers bought more goods, and an upward spiral ensued. Friendly relations between the government and corporate America thus seemed vital to the life of the nation. This is what president of General Motors and newly named Secretary of Defense Charles

Erwin Wilson was pointing to in 1953 when he said he could make a decision to the detriment of GM, but he couldn't imagine how that could happen, "because for years I thought what was good for the country was good for General Motors, and vice versa." Corporations, therefore, didn't struggle too much when asked to contribute to the commonweal. Personal income tax rates began increasing in 1932 and eventually soared as high as 94 percent of income for the very wealthiest Americans in 1942. Rates hovered in the low nineties until the mid-1960s.

By 1960, more than 50 percent of the American workforce was employed by a large corporation. Meanwhile, labor unions, the historic counterbalance to giant corporations, were growing in size but also losing their teeth. Why? Because they, too, subscribed to the vital importance of corporate capitalism. For example, when labor unions saw the potential for workers to achieve the long sought-after goal of health insurance, they realized it would come not through the federal government in a single-payer plan, as in Britain or Canada, but instead through corporations. Every-one was invested in the free-market system, and even the opposi-tional arm that could propose an alternative structure had been neutered in the process.

Alongside rational thought and corporate capitalism, the third of the common postwar assumptions was the most easily visible and therefore the most easily challenged. It was a profound belief in the moral righteousness of something that came to be called "the American way of life." This way of life could and did possess all sorts of different meanings, but it's perhaps best thought of as a series of rules that dictated the norms of society. And, as always, The Rules were simply the embodiment of a deep set of assump-tions about who controlled the country and how everyone else knew his or her place.

The Rules of postwar America are easy enough to identify. For example, proper Americans were expected to dress properly, which meant a collared shirt and tie for men and dresses for women, with sweaters or shirts whose necklines were well above the cleavage. Hemlines had to be modest, at the knee or below, and there were organizations that would help you understand that guideline more precisely if you needed some help. If a man showed up at your door in a T-shirt and jeans, he was more than likely there to fix your pipes. Women did not wear pants and always wore panty hose. Shoes were easy enough to understand, too: pumps if you were a woman, or maybe flats, and lace-up dress shoes (but not formal ones) if you were a man. If men wanted to display fashion flair, they might wear a thin tie, or perhaps even cowboy boots, but slip-on shoes were for overly stylish Italians. Hair was to be cropped short for men, above the neck and ears. Women typically wore their hair long, but could get away with short hair if they looked and dressed like Audrey Hepburn, which is to say, still feminine. Sex was to be avoided before marriage, and women were always to be treated formally and with respect. Petting could occur, but cautiously. If an unintended pregnancy resulted, it meant marriage. Divorce was mostly for the wealthy and should be rare. Birth control was hardly discussed, and it was for loose women anyway. Women could work, but were supposed to quit after they were married, which was the ultimate goal. Husbands were supposed to support their wives while they cooked and took care of the kids and house. Children were to be seen and not heard, and to realize their role as positive and playful influences in the family. At work, the boss was to be respected even if you didn't like him (almost always a him). More than that, all authority figures were to be respected and obeyed, including church or community leaders, even your school principal (almost always a him). Church was for Sundays, and even if you didn't go, you lied and said you did. Jews went to services on Fridays and were part of the Judeo-Christian tradition that undergirded American political life (democracy made sense because man was created in the image of God). But some of the odder practices of the Jews, like not eating pork or resisting Bible readings in school, were exactly that: slightly odd. Meanwhile, emotions were to be controlled and outbursts kept rare, and always apologized for later. Adults were to be addressed as Mr. or Mrs., as were all strangers, even from one adult to another. Homosexuality was, of course, anathema, and usually illegal. Foul words were to be avoided. So was pornography.

There were more, but these were some of The Rules, and they were codified in a series of organizations, through churches or the Boy Scouts, through Little League or charity organizations. There were even television shows and public service announcements that taught them. The price of deviation—a huge price—was to be deemed "abnormal," as though there were something deeply and inherently wrong with you. A well-adjusted person observed The Rules and didn't ask too many questions.

The Rules might vary slightly from place to place, but buried within them were the basic assumptions of society. Proper women were to be respected, but men were the strong caretakers. It was John Wayne and Frank Sinatra who were the masculine heroes of the era. Women were more delicate, sometimes overly emotional, and so couldn't be trusted in places of power. They honored the things that eased one's soul, such as family and church. Atop the hierarchy were Anglo-Saxon Protestants, and their rules and authority were to be unquestioned, or at least questioned with care. White Americans were situated above African Americans and other minorities, not so much because they were biologically better but because they practiced The Rules better. Rights claims often went unheeded if they violated The Rules. To speak out in the name of one's rights was to challenge what was perhaps the central tenet of the Rules: obedience.

When it came to politics, there was a huge middle in which to operate, the liberal middle. But options on the left and right were greatly circumscribed. Republicans and Democrats still fought for power, but they didn't really differ in their fundamental outlooks on the economy, the role of the state, or even foreign policy. In

1960, sociologist Daniel Bell published a seminal book called *The End of Ideology: On the Exhaustion of Political Ideas in the Fifties*, which argued that there was only one triumphant ideology then in existence among "sensible" people. It was a society premised on a powerful federal government led by wizard-like bureaucrats who nursed a New Deal–style corporate capitalism. This political sensibility had come to be labeled by everyone in postwar America as "liberalism," and there didn't seem to be much opportunity to move beyond it. "In the Western world," Bell wrote, "there is today a rough consensus among intellectuals on political issues: the acceptance of a Welfare State; the desirability of decentralized power; a system of mixed economy and of political pluralism. In that sense, . . . the ideological age has ended."[23]

We might imagine the three components—rational thought, corporate capitalism, and a rules-based society—as a triptych, an altarpiece of three paintings, each able to stand on its own but diminished in the absence of the others. In the center would be the belief in rational humanity, with the gods of progress and technology readily apparent in the picture. On the right, let's put corporate capitalism, with its large companies, friendly relations with the government, and bureaucratic authority. And on the left we can place The Rules, their hierarchies and norms, the notion that everyone has a proper place and needed to conform to it for the good of everyone else.[24]

During the two decades following the Second World War, the gilded framing that bordered each picture in the triptych and indeed helped hinge them together was the Cold War. Not only did the battle between the Soviet Union and the United States make upholding this tripartite structure seem like the most important thing in the world, but it also put any deviation in apocalyptic terms. A missile gap? Poverty? These could be solved by a rationally thought-out plan emerging from our technocrats and their technology. Any attempt to curtail the structure of corporate capitalism? Derided as socialism. Any strain against the structures of traditional living, such as homosexuality, women vying for nontraditional roles, or atheism? Dire attempts to destroy our way of life.

There was, of course, a spectrum of opinions about the Cold War, but it did not include things like complete isolationism, at one extreme, or formulating friendly relations with the Soviet Union on the other. What was debated instead was the size and nature of the resources that should be deployed in the fight. The parts of the left that sought warmer relations with the Soviet Union had died a quiet death during Henry Wallace's presidential campaign in 1948, when, running as a Progressive Party candidate, FDR's former vice president got crushed by Harry Truman, winning only 2.4 percent of the vote. (To be fair, in addition to advocating peaceful relations with the Soviet Union, Wallace supported other unpopular programs like ending racial segregation, granting full voting rights to America's black people, and creating a national health insurance plan.) On the other end of the spectrum sat hardliners from the right, including many Catholics like William F. Buckley, Jr., who viewed the Cold War as nothing less than an apocalyptic struggle between good and evil, between God and the Antichrist, between life and death. If Soviet-style communism were to triumph, they argued, humankind would lose its freedom to an all-powerful state.

These hardliners got a more receptive hearing than the pacifists on the left, and their ideas were often taken with some seriousness by the Liberal Establishment. They did, however, risk succumbing to conspiracy theories. The most famous person to fall victim was Robert Welch, the Boston candy maker (Sugar Daddies, Milk Duds, Junior Mints) turned conspiracy theorist who accused President Eisenhower of being a closet communist helping foment worldwide revolution. Welch founded the John Birch Society to circulate his views, and it was only in the mid-1960s that the Birchers were expunged from the mainstream right—by William Buckley.

In short, the Cold War helped cement into place most aspects of the liberal order. Homosexuals were at best "security threats" (because they could be blackmailed) and at worst moral perverts out to embrace communism's egalitarianism. Women worked in industrial plants in communist countries because they had to; in America, women could choose to work (for less pay than men, and less opportunity for advancement) or they could stay home and raise their God-fearing children, which was really the expectation. The specter of the Cold War curtailed options, and helped bind together, tightly, the three images in the triptych.

Dissent existed, of course, and it came from both the left and the right. On the left, critics like sociologist C. Wright Mills saw the rise of a "Power Elite," where technocrats from business, military, and government all graduated from the same schools and operated on a revolving door in and out of various ventures. There was no balance of power here, Mills argued, and the control of the bureaucrats was concentrated in so few hands that ordinary citizens had little ability to effect change. Democracy was becoming a farce. Others on the left saw the bureaucracies pushing the nation toward inauthentic goals, removing people too far from the more visceral aspects of life. This was the most common complaint of the cultural radicals of the 1950s—the Beat poets, James Dean, the underground homosexual minority—all of whom went on a personal search for "authenticity." Jane Jacobs became a symbol of this kind of yearning with her virulent protests against New York City's centralized planners, men like Robert Moses, thinking (not wrongly) that they sought to destroy organic ("authentic") neighborhoods in favor of a Disneyland version of the city. Jacobs's classic work, *The Death and Life of Great American Cities*, was published in 1961 and made her a star.

Still others on the left, like Michael Harrington, Martin Luther King, Jr., and Betty Friedan, sought to remind Americans that liberalism hadn't exactly brought everyone to the promised land yet. In his 1958 book, *The Affluent Society,* John Kenneth Galbraith made the case that Americans should use their growing personal wealth to expand the commonweal as well. Most of the protestors on the left, though, did not want to tear apart the triptych, just more justly distribute its rewards.

The right was not without its share of protestors. Many didn't care for the "managerial revolution" of the technocrats either, and in fact it was one of their own, James Burnham, who criticized the emerging management shifts in the first place. Burnham, who wound up working with Buckley at *National Review,* predicted that the new class of managers would operate solely in their own interests, forsaking the commonweal and the people they claimed to serve. One of Robert Moses's books may have been called *Working for the People,* but it wouldn't have surprised Burnham that years later Moses's biographer would label Moses "the power broker," bending the organic developments of a society to his own will.[25] Burnham went on to ungenerously compare the rise of the bureaucrats in postwar America to Soviet-style communism.

Others on the right, such as Ayn Rand, thought the current version of corporate capitalism was too coddling. Premised on the notion of fairness and equality, Rand argued that the liberal order was detrimental to individual creativity and entrepreneurial reward. Alongside Rand were business leaders who thought the bureaucrats were taking too much of the nation's wealth for themselves and redirecting it in nonproductive ways for unexceptional people. And then there were anti-communists like Robert Welch, who kept finding conspiracies everywhere.

By the early 1960s, then, there was a growing undercurrent of dissatisfaction. Critics from the left and right were complaining that mainstream liberalism was stifling individual freedom in the name of collective prosperity while at the same time shutting down creativity for the sake of order. And among the loudest of the critics were Norman Mailer and William F. Buckley, Jr.

———

As they concluded their three-hour sail across the Long Island Sound, Buckley looked over to his new friend Norman Mailer. Surely he would have laughed had he known *Playboy* was going to call Mailer "a Liberal" in its upcoming article about the Chicago debate. "The Conservative versus The Liberal" was easy fodder for a magazine editor. When the title did appear a few months later, Mailer responded with a brutal letter to the editor: "I wish you hadn't billed the debate between William Buckley and myself as a meeting between a conservative and a liberal. I don't care if people call me a radical, a rebel, a red, a revolutionary, an outsider, an outlaw, a Bolshevik, an anarchist, a nihilist or even a left conservative, but please don't ever call me a liberal."[26]

Just before they returned to shore, Buckley caught Mailer's eye and motioned to the wheel. Did Mailer want to steer them home? Mailer immediately accepted. He eased over to the wheel, feeling the energy, the wind in his hair, the excitement of power.

There is some dispute as to what happened next. According to Buckley, it was nothing worth recording. In his memories of the evening, he mentions hunding over the tiller, but little more. "He could not believe it when I turned the wheel over to him," wrote Buckley. Then came dinner.[27]

By Mailer's account, though, Buckley handed him the tiller in a narrow channel, and Mailer nearly crashed the boat before Buckley grabbed the wheel and navigated safely to shore. Mailer said he learned that day that Buckley "will never attack you in public, and never let you touch his sailboat in private."[28]

Regardless of what really happened, the two men disembarked as newfound friends and near-allies in the battle to overturn the Liberal Establishment in America. But they were heading into uncharted waters, and it was still wildly unclear which of their visions would carry the day.

3

American Golem

n the year after the sail, Buckley and Mailer's friendship blossomed. Almost immediately after they returned to shore, a flurry of letters went back and forth. "Might we meet somewhere in between your place and mine?" Buckley wrote in one.[1] Jeanne phoned Pat several times to chat and set up dinners. While on their annual ski vacation in Switzerland, Pat wrote chatty letters to Mailer: "I spend my time in Rome or Paris but Bill can always be found at his typewriter (thinking up new nasties about you) or hurling down the horrid slopes." She added, "If you come over [to Europe] we would love to have you come and visit."[2]

In his letters back, Mailer continued to call Pat by the nickname he had given her during their first night together in Connecticut: "Slugger." And Pat continued to call Mailer "Chooky Bah Lamb," a Scottish expression she had learned from her nanny, used to refer to someone you find deeply endearing. Her letters sometimes began, "Dear Chookie B.L."[3] Buckley, meanwhile, was equally chatty: "Will return toward the end of March," he finished one letter. "Hope to see you."[4]

When Lady Jeanne left Mailer in early 1963, resulting in Mailer's third divorce, Pat expressed her condolences: "I really am sorry about you and Jeannie—love to you both."[5] But Mailer seemed okay with things. He and Jeannie were an odd match anyway, he noted, and he hoped his new single status (always temporary) would not jeopardize their budding friendship. When the Buckleys returned from Switzerland, Mailer wrote Buckley: "Glad to have you back. The scene has been quiet in your absence. I'm going to be out of town for a week or so but when I get back perhaps we could spend an evening—you, me, Slugger, and I'll bring a girl—and at a certain point we [the two men] might retire to a side room and have a private debate with no audience. . . . We do have a lot to talk about, but I have come by now to suspect that we won't be able to do it in public, since each of us has invested too much interest in past positions, and all that."[6]

The offer put on display Mailer's willingness to shift views if he could be convinced that his understanding of human nature was wrong. As Buckley well knew, Mailer was not inclined to score easy points, but sought a deeper understanding of the human condition. It is unlikely Buckley would have willingly shown that kind of ambivalence. It wasn't his style.

The two men were, however, far too busy to develop a sustained social life together. Their calendars were remarkably full. Mailer was being asked to travel the country to give dozens of speeches; he was under contract to write another book; and he paid the bills (and alimony and child support payments) by writing the journalistic pieces that were growing increasingly popular.

Buckley, meanwhile, was constantly on the lecture circuit, editing *National Review*, working on multiple books, and writing his weekly newspaper column, which was about to go from once a week to three times a week. "I am terribly sorry," Buckley wrote to Mailer at one point, "but I just plain don't have any time at all [to get together], except late Monday afternoon. Advise."[7] On another occasion, when Buckley wrote to ask Mailer's forgiveness in declining an invitation: "We are both most anxious to see you but we cannot profane our Saturdays and Sundays by going to New York."[8] Mailer wrote back: "We are all such blessedly busy people, bless us."[9]

But Mailer never swayed far from Buckley's thoughts, at least intellectually. When Buckley was on the road in 1963, he typically began his lectures by referring to the debate he had had with Mailer in Chicago, using the points raised there to help illuminate the merits of his conservatism versus Mailer's radicalism. Even if Mailer was correct to lambast the Liberal Establishment, Buckley said, Mailer's alternative was dangerous, leading the nation's young people to float around without any fixed points of reference.

On one instance in December 1962, students at the University of North Carolina had invited Buckley to speak, and, as he typically did during those months, he simply recited the lecture he had given during his debate with Mailer. The Cuban Missile Crisis hadn't given him the slightest pause in his staunch defense of the Cold War. Nor had the budding civil rights movement altered his defense of tradition, premised as it was on the superiority of white people.

The lecture went well enough, Buckley thought. A thousand people showed up; a group of organizers invited him to get beers afterward (Buckley paid); and one even approached Buckley to sign the copy of *Playboy* that had just arrived in his mailbox, which was the first time Buckley saw the Chicago debate in print.

Playboy, Buckley noticed, had offered full coverage to the debate. His and Mailer's names appeared on the cover, next to a bunny drinking a martini. There was a two-page photo spread featuring each man glaring away from each other (Buckley to the right, Mailer to the left). The January issue in his hands featured their opening statements in full, while February's was to feature the exchange that followed (their names would appear on the cover then, too).

But of course magazines appear on newsstands well before the publication dates that appear on their covers. Not being aware of just how early *Playboy* printed, Buckley had felt comfortable giving his Chicago speech in mid-December, thinking January's *Playboy* wouldn't come out until later in the month.

Sure enough, the following week, several UNC students wrote to the school newspaper, *The Tar Heel*, to complain. Buckley, they wrote, hadn't come to Chapel Hill prepared. His ideas were empty and baseless. And worst of all, he had "soaked" UNC by charging four hundred and fifty dollars to simply rehash a speech readily available that same day in *Playboy*.

The editors of *The Tar Heel* read the angry letters and sent them to Buckley, asking if he wanted to respond. Ever the opportunist, Buckley took up the cudgel. He was shocked, *shocked!*, to be scolded so. He talked about how professional speakers do their business, by constructing a handful of adaptable speeches, "working out a formulation, and updating it from time to time, until events have anachronized it, at which point he tosses it away; or, as in my case, donates it to the Library of Congress." As for the four hundred and fifty dollars, "I'd like to talk less, and earn more. But I don't regularly aspire to the $800 that Martin Luther King charges, or Norman Cousins' $750—I am not envious, understand. I am a conservative: I know my place."

And on reproducing the Chicago speech, "There had been no effort whatever to dissimulate. I told the audience my talk had crystallized at a debate with Mailer, and told my hosts it had been bought by Playboy. . . . And anyway, would you refuse to invite the January Playmate to Chapel Hill because she had already revealed her charms?"

On a more serious matter, several of *The Tar Heel* letters complained that Buckley had used unnecessary sexual imagery during his talk in an effort to be hip. Buckley called the students prudes, referring to a fictional "Old Lace Society" that supposedly served as the morality police in Chapel Hill: "What a difficult time the Old Lace people must be having," he wrote, and one could almost picture Buckley fanning himself to cool down. But then he reminded the students that sex was a key subject of Norman Mailer's quest to challenge The Rules. Sex, Mailer had argued, was one of the key topics being confined and covered over by the liberal elite; it needed to be confronted, discussed. To Buckley, this meant that one had to engage with it in order to engage with Norman Mailer and the emerging left that Mailer seemed to represent. "My friends," Buckley wrote, "you must read Norman Mailer and try to understand the role that sex plays in his social philosophy." Mailer was "taking a serious social-philosophical position—which one must speak about seriously, on the assumption that one is addressing grown-ups, and need not strew over one's language with fig leaves. Kant defined marriage (quite seriously) as the 'mutual monopolization of the genitalia.' Now how're you going to discuss Kant without, well, without arguing with Kant? I guess you argue outside Chapel Hill, where they can take it."[10]

It wouldn't be the last time Buckley would come to Mailer's defense, trying to educate the lotus-eaters about the national treasure that was Norman Mailer. Buckley would, however, retire the 1962 Chicago speech, though not before reproducing it in collections of his writings not once, but twice.[11]

Mailer too was hounded by the debate. A few months after Buckley spoke at UNC, Mailer gave a speech to students at the University of Chicago. Sure enough, during the question-and-answer period he was asked his opinion of Buckley. Buckley's method of debate, Mailer said, was to hurl "unspeakably churlish invective." But as a man he was "the best fellow you ever met off stage."[12]

At the same time, both Buckley and Mailer were encouraged by what they had heard from Hugh Hefner. It turned out that the issue of *Playboy* that featured their debate had become the magazine's all-time bestseller. As Hefner wrote to Mailer, "You will be pleased to learn, I think, that the January issue, including the opening statements for your debate with Buckley, is not only the greatest seller PLAYBOY has ever had, but at one dollar an issue it has sold more copies in thirty days at that kind of premium price than any other publication (magazine, book or newspaper) in history—a total of over 1,550,000 copies."[13]

For both men the allure of celebrity was magnetic, and despite their reservations about what happened to public intellectuals when they become too public, Mailer and Buckley both sought another magical night of debate. At one point in 1963, Buckley even hatched a plan to see if a new group called the Young Presidents' Club might be interested in having Mailer and Buckley appear at one of their conventions. "Only remember," Mailer said to Buckley, "that they must pay us very well indeed." The debate didn't happen.[14]

Nevertheless, throughout 1963 their respective stars were on the rise, and each man was being presented with unique opportunities on his own. As befit their parallel status, though, they were often presented with the same opportunities.

Mailer, for instance, had been impressed with the outrageous comedy of Lenny Bruce, who throughout the 1950s went on stage to provoke the establishment and break The Rules. Bruce's topics always verged on the crass—defecation, urination, variations on bad words—and his talent was to make his audience squirm at the shattering of taboos. Bruce was in fact provoking the exact kinds of reactions Mailer was seeking, thumbing his nose at the rules-based society and causing his audience to think hard about the water in which it swam. Mailer saw at least two Lenny Bruce shows at the Village Vanguard in the late 1950s, and both times Bruce ended up being hassled by the police for breaking obscenity laws.

Mailer wanted to do much the same. So when a promoter asked him if he'd like to present "An Evening with Norman Mailer" at Carnegie Hall, Mailer jumped at the chance. He was nervous about performing, and knew he would have a hard time maintaining the line between being humorous and being offensive (a skill he never mastered), but he agreed to do the show anyway. "Best of luck," the Buckleys telegrammed Mailer on the evening of the show.[15]

The night was a disaster. For one thing, the promoter scheduled the event the day after Memorial Day, and the theater was half empty. Mailer looked out at the audience and said, "Now I know what Robert Frost meant when he said, 'Hell must be a half-empty auditorium.'" By the end of the night, the hall was finally filled to a respectable level, although writer Richard Kluger "had the feeling vans were prowling the Village . . . rounding up stray hipsters and rushing them uptown."[16]

The crowd wasn't the worst of it. Mailer had lousy comedic timing, and when nervous he didn't fall back on humor but on mean-spirited satire. In person he just wasn't funny; he was too aggressive.

The show fell flat. The libertine who was supposed to shock instead came on stage as a slightly paunchy, angry New Yorker in a wrinkled blue suit talking about the horrors of cancer. Who could laugh at that? When an audience member tried to bring some energy to the floor by asking Mailer's views on homosexuality, Mailer took the audience on a long journey describing how homosexuality was a mistakenly chosen vice that defeated human virility. Feeling as though he were losing his audience with his long-winded response, he suddenly closed his show by reading the part of his Carnegie Hall contract where he agreed not to swear, then he proceeded to read aloud an obscene poem.

With a deadening thud, he walked off stage.

Some in the audience were embarrassed. There had been no humor and little provocation. What was the point? A more sympathetic reading suggests that many in the audience understood what he was trying to do, just that he didn't do it well. Mailer naturally agreed with the more sympathetic assessment. "Carnegie Hall was a great relief," he wrote to Buckley. "It turned out not to be a disaster, which, if you remember, was precisely what I was fearing. But on the other hand, it was nothing extraordinary either and of course everything went wrong."[17]

Buckley wanted details, all the details, because he too had been asked to do something later in the year: "An Evening with William F. Buckley, Jr." Buckley, a tad fearful of holding the audience by himself, wrote fretfully to Mailer, saying in Latin, "*Non licet bovi, quod licet Iovi,*" which roughly translates into "Cattle may not do what Gods can do."[18]

Mailer's response was typically funny:

> I would tell you to have nothing to do with Fulton [the promoter], except that I ended to my surprise liking him personally. He did everything wrong for me and made a number of stupid and brutal mistakes, so of course I can hardly recommend him, but on the other hand, he was learning his trade with me. While I remain a fool, he has perhaps graduated. At any rate, he's a funny, funny man. You might find it interesting to talk to him although I warn you he's not in the least your type: he has a hug like a bear.[19]

Buckley never did the performance.

It was right at that time that David Susskind called. Over the previous two decades, Susskind had parlayed his position as World War II communications officer in the Navy into a variety of jobs in the entertainment industry, becoming not only a manager of talent like Dinah Shore and Jerry Lewis but also a producer, talent scout, and press agent. But it was as a television personality that most Americans came to know him. His talk show debuted in New York in 1958 and was called *Open End* because it would last until Susskind called it quits—which could be after an hour, but sometimes after two or three or four. The show came about in an effort to compete with the only other hard-hitting talk show then on air: Mike Wallace's *Night-Beat.* By 1961 *Open End* had gone into national syndication, though in the process the network capped it at two hours. But the show nonetheless earned cachet as a prominent place for intellectuals because Susskind, as a powerful television producer, could get top-class talent to appear. It helped that he lived next door to Truman Capote in the United Nations Plaza apartment complex along the East River and could invite Capote or any of his neighbors (including Robert Kennedy, Johnny Carson, Walter Cronkite, and Arthur Goldberg) at almost a moment's notice. Susskind was interested in figures from the worlds of politics, literature, movies—anyone he thought might be interesting. By 1963 *Open End* had featured not only Vice President Richard Nixon (in a show that lasted three hours and forty-five minutes) and Martin Luther King, Jr. (prompting Malcolm X to complain in a call to Susskind that he hadn't asked about King's marital infidelities), but also Soviet Premier Nikita Khrushchev, the only American television show to get the Soviet leader to sit down for an interview. President John F. Kennedy was even said to be a viewer.[20]

American public life in 1963 teemed with public figures of intellectual or cultural renown, but not all of them were right for Susskind's show. There were writers like James Jones (*From Here to Eternity*), William Styron (*Lie Down in Darkness*), Jack Kerouac (*On the Road*), and Saul Bellow (*The Adventures of Augie March* and *Henderson the Rain King*). But these men were mostly storytellers who tended not to speak beyond the world of books. And then there were politicos like Arthur Schlesinger, Jr., John Kenneth Galbraith, Daniel Bell, Walter Lippmann, and James Wechsler. But most of them were committed left-liberals likely to toe a party line. There was also a collection of New York intellectuals, mostly Jewish, many of them former communists, such as Irving Howe, Norman Podhoretz, Lionel Trilling, Clement Greenberg, Irving Kristol, Alfred Kazin, Philip Rahv, Leslie Fiedler, and Sidney Hook. They were almost always both politically and culturally engaged, but often were too academic, too highbrow for a popular television audience.

When Susskind surveyed the terrain, there were only a handful of candidates he deemed proper for primetime. James Baldwin was one, a powerful and articulate voice for civil rights. Gore Vidal was another, a writer whose temperament and fierce left-wing politics made him constantly entertaining. Truman Capote had emerged as a spirited personality with a unique view on American life, too.

There was also Mary McCarthy, Carson McCullers, Diana Trilling, Hannah Arendt, and Jane Jacobs—but women were a striking minority in this realm. Susskind himself was aware of this, though scarcely to women's advantage. A noted philanderer, he often hired women because he saw them as overlooked talent he could hire for cheap. When Susskind moderated a show about the "American Sexual Revolution" in 1963, for instance, the discussion was not about women's liberation but about increases in premarital sex and the license men felt to sway beyond the traditional bounds of marriage. Hugh Hefner was the featured guest.[21]

Alongside the likes of Baldwin, Capote, and Vidal were Mailer and Buckley. Susskind, like Golden before him, knew that while they came from seemingly opposite ends of the political spectrum, the two were almost always a draw in articulating the conflicting movements then on the rise. In 1963 Susskind knew Mailer and Buckley were looking for a venue to debate each other again, so he invited them on *Open End*, hoping sparks would fly once more.[22]

President Kennedy had just been assassinated, too, and the country was seemingly adrift, risking, perhaps, a reinforcement of liberal pieties rather than displaying a willingness to try something new. Buckley had been no friend of Kennedy's, seeing him as little more than a smug emblem of the Liberal Establishment. Just before the assassination, Buckley had written, "Our President emerges as the ultimate man in the gray flannel suit: the great accommodator, the weather vane on the perfect ball bearings soul free, immune from any frictions of reality."[23] But after the assassination, Buckley was moved by the violence and put a blockade on any negative lines about the dead president in *National Review*.

Mailer had been equally moved by the assassination. It was the third moment he could recall when the entire nation was completely connected, alongside Pearl Harbor and the death of President Roosevelt. But Mailer also took the assassination hard because Kennedy's presidency had coincided with Mailer's own transition into a political writer. Mailer saw his function in the Kennedy years go "from some sort of mysterious half-notorious leader of the Beat Generation . . . to something quite other, a respected if somewhat feared leader of the literary Establishment."[24] He saw himself, rightly or wrongly, as an emerging minister of culture. When Kennedy was killed, it marked for Mailer the departure of "an intangible good." Under Kennedy, the right and the left had been able to make their critiques within the culture, but it was unclear if that would continue now that Kennedy was gone.[25]

Susskind wondered the same thing, especially amid speculation that it might have been either a communist or a deranged right-winger who had done the deed. There was no better way to find out than to invite a prominent member of the left and the right on his show.

Both men eagerly accepted, with Buckley writing Mailer a few days before the taping with "a suggestion. Let's meet for lunch and have champagne before the *Open End* taping. I think it will loosen us up a little. And we'll send the bill to Susskind."[26]

Despite the addition of champagne, the topics were more or less the same as in Chicago—the Cold War, the inadequacies of the Liberal Establishment—but the violence of Kennedy's assassination seemed to temper both Mailer and Buckley, and Susskind, too. Mostly they got bogged down in a discussion about how celebrity status was altering American political and intellectual life. At one point, Mailer brought up Buckley's idea that all intellectuals must alter their personality when they become public figures, when they enter what Buckley had called "the freak show."

Buckley then kindly smiled at his friend and said, "I think you are a freak."

It elicited some laughs. But not from Mailer. Looking hurt, Mailer said somewhat tartly, "Why then do you get on television with a freak?"

Buckley retorted with flair: "You are a magnetic field in this country," he said. But he quickly added, a bit contritely, "A lot of people get on television with me who think I am a freak. Freaks are not necessarily to be boycotted."

Despite the tension JFK's assassination created, the second debate turned out to be less fulfilling for everyone. A *New York Times* writer described the show as "two hours of friendly chitchat, not so friendly argument and miscellaneous conversation." The title of his article said it all: "Mailer and Buckley Talk on 'Open End.'" Gone were the fireworks.[27]

When one viewer wrote in to complain to Buckley that the show was too lightweight, too much point-counterpoint, Buckley fired back:

> You are quite incorrect about why Mr. Mailer and I met before the television cameras. We were not there to learn—any learning was pure serendipity—but to express views on the basis of previous, and I might say diligent, efforts to learn something about each other's positions. I have read all of Mr. Mailer's books and columns, and he has read my books and many issues of National Review, and the engagement therefore was projected as a confrontation, not as a seminar.

It was a statement indicative of Buckley's intellectual intransigence. While Mailer repeatedly offered to learn from Buckley's insights, it seems that, at least publicly, Buckley showed no such willingness to return the favor. When the viewer complained about what she deemed Buckley's "annoying phoniness of manner," Buckley responded:

> I honestly don't know what to do about it, or even, exactly, what it is. I do not cultivate any manner at all, and am resigned to my own, not because it pleases me, but because I would not know how to change it. I say resigned, because I have annoyed some people for years and years, ever since I was in fact a boy. I am sorry to hear from you that it grows worse. In one

respect, then, I can say that I am harnessed to the entropy of
the universe.[28]

Buckley sent a copy of his rebuttal to Mailer. Mailer wrote back
quickly: "Your answer is a masterpiece. I'm tempted to frame it."[29]

But Mailer privately seethed after *Open End*. "Mr. Mailer," the *Times*
had reported, "who is more articulate on paper than he is on television, could not match Mr. Buckley's quiet style and at-home com-
posure."[30] It was clear to everyone, including Mailer, that Buckley
had won this one. He wrote to his long-serving Japanese translator and friend, Eiichi Yamanishi, that he was furious at himself for
not taking the time to prepare properly and that because of it he
had been on the defensive. "A lot of people," he added, "were kind
enough afterward to tell me that I won. The newspapers were all
on Buckley's side. And between us two, I think I must confess that
the best I obtained in the second debate was a draw."[31]

That he hadn't prepared, however, is a joke. Mailer's archives
reveal dozens of notecards and quotations about Buckley and his
recent work. One sheet catalogues twenty-six articles from *National
Review* that Mailer read in preparation. Not all of the articles were
written by Buckley either, meaning Mailer had probed the entire
landscape of American conservatism, learning its inner quibbles
and the soil on which Buckley trod. Buckley was right, or nearly
so, when he said Mailer had read everything Buckley had ever
written.[32]

The notes also reveal Mailer's long-standing critiques of Buckley's major points. On Buckley's desire to return to "the laws of
God and for the wisdom of our ancestors," Mailer asked bluntly:
"[W]hat are they?" Which aspects of the past were worth conserv-
ing and which deserved to be tossed aside? A blanket endorsement
of "the wisdom of our ancestors" was downright stupid. It was hard
to make a case, say, for slavery.

Mailer called Buckley's complaint that knowledge and education don't always lead to wisdom "Buckley's fundamental authoritarianism." Here he was thinking of the conservative's awareness
that the creative mind will inevitably challenge tradition when he
or she sees it as limiting creativity. Copernicus may have been abra-
sively challenging tradition, but this didn't mean he was wrong.

Mailer also delved into their persistent dispute about the seriousness with which they should take the Cold War. To Mailer, of
course, it was not a holy fight between God and the Antichrist, as
Buckley saw it. Instead, Mailer saw this interpretation as a bastard-
ization of faith, once again placing man's needs over God's: "The
hole in faith is here," Mailer wrote. No, to understand the Cold
War one needed to be a bit more cynical about humanity, more
aware of the forces that drive people to action, aware of greed and
intolerance and the inertia of routine. *Cui bono?*—who benefits?—
shouldn't only be the mantra of lawyers, but of intellectuals as well.

As he filed these things away (he was a voracious filer), it's likely
Mailer came across an unpublished clipping he had written after
their first debate (in an undated folder simply labeled "Buckley").
The clipping is a long, drawn-out metaphor about America and
about his and Buckley's place in it. In the clipping, Mailer compared America to a giant man, acknowledging that the country
had a virtuous, well-meaning "American" heart. But this heart was
struggling against all the muck that lived inside him. Mailer gave
each of the two lungs names: Republicans and Democrats. They
breathed life into the body, but Mailer worried that "Too much
bad air had gone into those lungs." They were being corroded by
money and power, and now everything they emitted simply made
the heart sicker. As the capillaries closed from corruption, the
lungs needed more air, "Which is to say more taxes, more government, more billions for armament, more load for the hull." The
roads, the schools, the support for the arts, all the good things a
government does to keep the heart happy, were being crowded out

to accommodate the government's less savory endeavors, its corruption and corrosion.

While the lungs were being corroded, the rest of the body was faring just as badly. The ribcage supporting the lungs was "the labor unions of the Left and the FBI on the Right." They kept the parties in line. And the body "had the government and the corporations for its torso, which is to say its belly was composed mostly of Republicans, Democrats, and that part of the economy which went to national defense, that huge part of the economy." The structure of corporate capitalism that was vital to midcentury liberalism was overburdening the good American heart.

The head of this American golem was the mass media, "which permitted nothing too Left or too Right to disturb the sleep of the citizens." Rules were to be enforced. Its legs, meanwhile, were branches of the American military, and "its toes," Mailer suspected, "were the Mob, the Syndicate, the Mafia, that part of the Center which was always attacked, but lightly, by the mass-media of the center."

"What a giant. What a dead and deadening giant," Mailer concluded.

Both Buckley and Mailer wanted to topple this corrosive golem, but both wanted to do so while preserving that virtuous American heart. "Buckley and I had been attacking this Center from our opposite flanks," Mailer wrote. Buckley's project was to sever the wedge connecting the honest heart to the bilious lungs—by cutting taxes and choking the beast. "That was the real meaning of the Right Wing in America as far as I was concerned," he wrote. "They were a force which drew upon themselves the powers of rectitude." Buckley "led the intellectual wedge of the *National Review* . . . against the plastic tube which connected the honest heart . . . to the sludge-deadened lungs of that administrative machine in the center."

Mailer understood the impulse to kill the giant. But he worried about what would be lost in the effort: "I did not see how it would be improved if Buckley's wedge fretted a hole into the tube. What was left of the heart might drain through that hole."

On the other hand, "What I had wished to do was simple enough," wrote Mailer. "It was murky, it was often blind, but it was real to me. I wished to keep a certain voice alive, a certain kind of voice. To be shameless about it, let me say it was the natural American voice, to wit, it was the vanishing voice of any man who was a natural democrat." Like Buckley, Mailer wanted to clean the place up, but he wanted to do it by reminding the country of its own brilliant heart, letting the heart beat more freely, absent the corrosiveness of liberal politics and corporate capitalism. The question was how could he do this, and would he be able to do it before Buckley had succeeded in starving the beast to death?[33]

Little did he know it then, but that battle would represent much of the story of the remainder of the 1960s.

PART II

IMPREGNATING THE HOST

(1964–65)

4

The Fires

The 1964 Republican National Convention surprised nearly everyone with its energy. It surprised everyone even more with the way it redefined the Republican Party. Defeated were the moderates, those who had brokered deals with Keynes, the bureaucrats, and the Liberal Establishment. Victorious were the ideologues, the Buckleyites looking to vent their rage at being ignored for so long. San Francisco, where the convention was held, had turned overnight into ground zero for what Mailer called "the fires of the right."[1]

There were many who could take credit for the rise of the ideologues in 1964, not the least of which were behind-the-scenes engineer F. Clifton White, who helped organize the primaries in dozens of small states, and Clarence Manion, the former dean of Notre Dame Law School who had become a radio personality and chief recruiter in a grassroots campaign to create a conservative electorate.[2] There were also politicians like Barry Goldwater and Ronald Reagan who spoke the language of conservatism and provided a political outlet for its expression.

But it was fair to say that William F. Buckley, Jr., was the most celebrated of the bunch. It was he who had harnessed the energy in the mid-1950s with *National Review* and then stoked it into life

during the early 1960s. It was he who had articulated the talking
points and given the cause an elegant voice. With Buckley's support, and more importantly with that of his followers, it was clear
Goldwater was destined to win the party's nomination in 1964.
A gun-toting Arizona senator, Goldwater had shot to prominence
with his 1960 book, *The Conscience of a Conservative*, which articulated, point by point, the dominant features of Buckley's brand
of conservatism—its tempered libertarianism, its hallowed respect
for tradition, its unbending stance on the Cold War. Indeed, the
book had been ghostwritten by Buckley's right-hand man, his old
Yale debating partner and now his brother-in-law, Brent Bozell. At
the Cow Palace convention center in San Francisco, those ideas
were featured front and center, destined to be the central planks
of a new Republican agenda for the country.

When Mailer landed in San Francisco on Sunday, July 12, 1964,
the day before the convention convened, he was impressed and
even a little bit frightened by what he saw. Commissioned by *Esquire*
to write about the convention, Mailer assumed Goldwater would
win the nomination. What amazed Mailer, however, was not Goldwater's likely victory but the energy of his supporters. It provoked
in him a "sense of barbarians about a campfire and the ecstasy
of going to war."[3] This newfound right wing in America, bound
together by its staunch opposition to the Liberal Establishment,
looked formidable.

The police were estimating that more than 40,000 people were
going to try to cram into a convention hall that seated 14,500,
and the estimates were probably low. The streets throughout San
Francisco were jammed with partisans waving signs and singing
songs. All hail Barry! Down with the liberal Republican contender,
Pennsylvania governor William Scranton. Taxis and trolleys sometimes had to wait half an hour for a path to be cleared through
the thousands of conservatives screaming, "We are the Goldwater
armyyyyyyy of liberation!" Liberation was their call, liberation from
the Liberal Establishment, from the threat of encroaching com-

munism, from the demands of the civil rights movement, from the impulse toward moderation and appeasement that conservatives saw everywhere coming from the culture of the lotus-eaters.

But there was more to it than just calls for freedom, Mailer saw. There was also fear. Sensing the bubbling-up of deep frustrations from the American heartland—that bureaucracies were taking over the country, that the calls to support the commonweal had become too demanding and too far-removed from traditions they understood—Mailer could see that Goldwater was the man for the moment, a cowboy hat–wearing Westerner ready to ride into Dodge to save the day. As Mailer looked at the convention floor, he saw the conventioneers "loaded with one hatred: the Eastern Establishment was not going to win again, this time Main Street was going to take Wall Street. So Barry had his brothers, three or four hundred of the hardest delegates in the land, and they were ready to become the lifelong enemy of any delegate who might waver to Scranton."

"That," Mailer wrote ominously, "was the mood."[4]

Liberal Republicans made an effort though, first and foremost by recruiting a popular politician like Scranton to run against Goldwater. Scranton was as plain as they came, solid if uninspiring. With Scranton's mellowness in the forefront, someone from his team released a below-the-belt letter saying, "Goldwaterism has come to stand for a whole crazy-quilt collection of absurd and dangerous positions that would be soundly repudiated by the American people in November." The liberal Republican strategy was to throw Goldwater off-kilter, to get him to speak openly and, as often happened, frighteningly. At the convention, liberal Republicans like George Romney pushed back against the blind free-market rhetoric of the Goldwaterites, saying, "Markets don't just *happen*." There must be *some* role for government.[5] Henry Cabot Lodge similarly declared, "No one in his right mind would today argue that there is no place for the federal government in the reawakening of America. Indeed, we need another Republican-sponsored

Marshall Plan for our cities and schools."[6] Ideological purity didn't make sense when you actually had to govern.

It was all for naught. In 1964, the "barbarians" were having their moment. They wanted libertarian economics and traditional morality, all tied with a bow of hard-line anti-communism. At a lavish Republican Party fundraiser that Mailer labeled "an Establishment gala," there was no energy, and it was clear to everyone that this "was in degree a wake. . . . The dance floor," he said, "was not to be crowded this night."[7] President Eisenhower was there, the Luces were there, as were Henry Cabot Lodge and Governor Scranton. But Goldwater didn't bother to attend.

Meanwhile, there was, Mailer said, "excitement watching Barry go to work with a group, an intensity in the air, a religious devotion, as if one of the most urbane priests of America was talking at a Communion breakfast, or as if the Principal-of-the-Year was having a heart-to-heart with honor students."[8] Mailer was awestruck when an incredibly good-looking woman stopped her car in the middle of San Francisco traffic as Goldwater walked by. "You go, Barry, you go, go," she yelled. It was then that Mailer heard the "anger and elation in her voice, as if she were declaring, 'We're going to get the country back.'"[9] Pulling the lens back a bit, as Mailer looked at the masses in and around the Cow Palace, he saw "a convention murderous in mood. The mood . . . spoke of a new kind of society. Chimeras of fascism hung like fogbank."[10]

For his part, Buckley was elated by everything. It seemed to be reflection of all his successes. He saw fresh-faced kids by the boatload, whistling, singing songs, gaily stuffing envelopes, knocking on doors, cavorting around, and having a good time. These young conservatives knew what Buckley had done for their movement. When he stepped off the airplane in San Francisco, hundreds of young conservatives, whom he knew were coming to be called "Buckleyites," gathered to greet him. They shot off confetti bombs and sang "Won't You Come Home, Bill Buckley?"[11] Looking around the airport, he must have thought he had. This was Marilyn

Monroe landing in England. Hell, many of the young Republicans had even started to dress like Buckley and talk like him. When an observer had previously referred to "a flock of little Buckleys" milling around the conservative movement, Buckley hadn't known how correct he was until now. William Buckley was who all these young conservatives wanted to be. There was a "glamour," said one young conservative, "of being amidst the likes of Bill Buckley."[12]

More than that, though, there was a huge number of volunteers working on the Goldwater campaign. They seemed to be everywhere and to have come from nowhere. The postmortem after the election would reveal that Goldwater had a record 3.9 million volunteers, twice as many as President Lyndon Johnson, who could pull from a pool twice as large. Around the country, Johnson's own men would later report that Goldwater bumper stickers outnumbered those backing the president by a ratio of ten to one.[13]

It was not just a momentary blip associated with Goldwater's candidacy, but a reflection of a new mood around the country. The syndicated column Buckley had signed up for in 1962 had expanded into new markets, now reaching close to one hundred and fifty newspapers across the country. Called "On the Right," it had set the talking points for the conservative movement, effectively teaching his followers how to talk back to their liberal friends. *National Review*, meanwhile, had been so successful that it no longer required his full-time attention. Subscriptions had increased sharply during the first years of the decade, from fifty-four thousand in 1961 to ninety thousand in 1964, exceeding even Buckley's optimistic hopes.[14] He had hired able businessmen to handle the money, and his sister Priscilla was so competent at day-to-day management that Buckley could be gone for long stretches of time without anyone really noticing.

Buckley never handled boredom well, so he increased his speaking engagements to nearly a hundred per year. Aligning perfectly with his stated goal in life, he had become a traveling salesman for his cause. He was a headliner, too—when he went to college cam-

puses or Rotary Clubs, he was usually booked in the largest audi-
toriums, and on Friday or Saturday nights. The money he earned
helped support *National Review,* and the speeches helped salt the
earth with young conservatives.

In San Francisco all that work seemed to be paying off. He
looked at the crowd at the airport and knew immediately that most
of them were members of an organization called Young Americans
for Freedom (YAF), a group launched four years earlier at Buckley's father's home, Great Elm, in Sharon, Connecticut. Buckley
himself had been instrumental in the group's creation. In Chicago
in 1960 he was standing beside a conservative organizer named
Marvin Liebman when they witnessed the energy of a small group
called Youth for Goldwater, a collection of conservative students
eager to get Goldwater nominated for president in 1960. Nixon
would win the nomination in 1960, of course, but Buckley was
impressed by these young right-wingers. He and Liebman invited
them to host a meeting at Buckley's parents' home to codify the
energy. Winning the kids would be key to victory, Buckley thought.

"What is so striking in the students who met at Sharon is their
appetite for power," Buckley wrote in *National Review* after the
meeting at Great Elm. "Ten years ago," he wrote, thinking of his
own time as a recent college graduate, "the struggle seemed so
long, so endless, even, that we did not dream of victory." These
YAFers, though, seemed to have no doubts about winning. "It is
quixotic to say that they or their elders have seized the reins of history," wrote Buckley. "But the difference in psychological attitude
is tremendous."[15]

In 1960, Buckley reviewed the group's mission statement, known
thereafter as the Sharon Statement, and it more or less toed the
National Review line of balancing traditionalism, libertarianism, and
anti-communism—all in an effort to beat down the Liberal Establishment. "In this time of moral and political crisis," the statement
began, "it is the responsibility of the youth of America to affirm
certain eternal truths." Echoing Buckley's argument from the Chi-

cago debate with Mailer, it went on to mention "God-given free will," "that political freedom cannot long exist without economic freedom," and "that the [only] purposes of government are to protect these freedoms through the preservation of internal order, the provision of national defense, and the administration of justice." According to Lee Edwards, one of the young conservatives who met at Sharon, "[Buckley's] presence, having it at his family home, lent a flavor of glamor to the event. I was particularly under his spell."[16] Edwards was not alone. The year after the founding of the YAF, subscriptions to *National Review* went up by twenty thousand.[17]

Now, at the Cow Palace four years later, the fruit had ripened. From having just ninety members at its founding convention in 1960, a year later the YAF reported 24,000 members at 115 schools.[18] In 1962, Ronald Reagan joined YAF's advisory board and would remain involved in the group through his presidency. The YAF was out in force in 1964 San Francisco, throwing streamers at their hero, Bill Buckley and singing songs about soon-to-be–presidential candidate Goldwater.

They weren't alone in the budding conservative movement. In addition to YAF, local businessmen had started the Philadelphia Society and the Conservative Party of New York State in the early 1960s, joining older groups like the Intercollegiate Society of Individualists and the Foundation for Economic Education. Buckley was at the center of things here, too. In the founding of New York's Conservative Party, Kieran O'Doherty and J. Daniel Mahoney were the real catalysts, but they took their cues from Buckley. While still a student at Columbia University in 1955, Mahoney had recruited Buckley to speak on campus and had remained in correspondence with him ever since. O'Doherty had met Buckley earlier, too, when he had gotten him to speak at a local Catholic Action meeting in New York. Together, O'Doherty and Mahoney teamed up to create a third party in New York, not necessarily to win elections, but to destroy the state's Republican Party, which, to them, was overly stocked with liberals. As they put it in their founding statement, they sought to "bring down the liberal Republican *apparat* in New York State."[19] Buckley urged them on, advised them, and then sent out the party's prospectus to wealthy contacts. He lent his star appeal, helping, as he called it, "midwife an intellectual revolution."[20]

But now, standing before him, was Barry Goldwater, and Buckley thought his movement's success might have happened too quickly. Was his youthful rebellion really ready to take control of a major national party? When *Time* asked Buckley how a cowboy hat–wearing Arizonan could possibly appeal to Buckley, who was more comfortable in a sailor cap on a yawl, Buckley replied, "Barry Goldwater is a man of tremendously decent instincts, and with a basic banal but important understanding of the Constitution and what it means in American life."

Wait a minute. Had Buckley really said "decent" and "banal" about the conservative standard-bearer?

Time followed up: "But what would happen if he were elected President of the United States?"

"That," said Buckley, a smile seeming to sneak out the corner of his mouth, "might be a serious problem."[21]

Throughout 1964, Buckley had made difficult compromises with the Goldwater campaign, effectively accepting Goldwater's decision to push him into the background lest Goldwater lose whatever chance he had to win the political middle. There was little for Goldwater to gain in standing side-by-side with the nation's most identifiable conservative. And Goldwater's method for pushing Buckley away—by having subordinates leak a story to the *New York Times* suggesting Buckley had tried to hijack the campaign, but been solidly rebuffed—was hurtful.[22]

Plus, Buckley had his own doubts about Goldwater. He didn't think Goldwater was all that smart. Neither he nor Brent Bozell thought Goldwater had read *Conscience of a Conservative* before it was published under his name in 1960.[23] More importantly, though, Buckley didn't think the time was right for an out-and-out conservative to rise to the national stage. He feared that a huge loss for Goldwater might bring down the entire movement he had worked so hard to build and which seemed just on the verge of becoming a lasting presence in American life. The energy around him notwithstanding, he didn't think the nation was ready for a conservative revolution.

Indeed, after Goldwater won the Republican nomination (on the first ballot), Buckley found himself shocked to "labor under the visitation of a freedom-minded candidate for the presidency of the United States" and relieved that "A great rainfall has deluged a thirsty earth."[24] But still, he was worried. He just didn't think Goldwater could win. Not only that, Buckley also felt the conservative movement was not prepared to sustain the critiques that would come not only from radicals like Norman Mailer but from the entire Liberal Establishment, whose ideas may have run their course but whose place in power had yet to be dislodged. The rainfall had "deluged a thirsty earth," Buckley said, but it had come "before we had time properly to prepare the ground."[25]

Buckley gave a speech to a group of YAFers a few weeks after the convention, one he knew wouldn't be popular. "The beginning of wisdom is the fear of the Lord," he told them. "The next and most urgent counsel is to take stock of reality." Buckley then added: "I speak, of course, about the impending defeat of Barry Goldwater."

The crowd of young barbarians, knuckles callused from knocking on all those doors, taste buds dead from licking all those envelopes, became stonily quiet. Here was Buckley, their hero, crushing their dreams.

They shouldn't be discouraged, though, Buckley said, rushing to his point. Conservatives were "an army on the march." Morale was high. But for Goldwater to win in 1964:

> would presuppose a sea change in American public opinion; presuppose that the fiery little body of dissenters of which you are a shining meteor suddenly spun off nothing less than

a majority of the American people, who suddenly overcame a generation's entrenched lassitude and, prisoners all those years, succeeded in passing blithely through the walls of Alcatraz and tripping lightly over the shark-infested waters and treacherous currents, to safety on the shore.

"The Goldwater movement," he said, "is in the nature of an attempted prison break."[26]

But it would not succeed, not this year. "The glorious development of this year," Buckley concluded, "was the nomination of a man whose views have given the waiting community a choice" between liberalism and conservatism. But it was too soon for it to succeed. They were the avant-garde of a major transformation, and they had to be satisfied that they had infused "the conservative spirit in enough people to entitle us to look about, on November 4 [the day after the election], not at the ashes of defeat but at the well-planted seeds of hope, which will flower on a great November day in the future."[27]

When he finished, there was no applause. The YAFers were stunned. All this for nothing? A few among them must have recognized that Goldwater had arrived before his time. The ground wasn't ready yet; the fortresses of liberalism were still too strong. Still, it was a difficult admission to make after all the blood, sweat, and tears that had been shed.

Buckley would turn out to be right. Despite the energy of the volunteers, President Johnson soundly defeated Barry Goldwater on November 3, successfully doing what Scranton and the liberal Republicans couldn't: making Goldwater and his movement seem dangerously extreme. All Johnson's team had to do was point to the one sentence most people remembered Goldwater saying at the convention: "Extremism in the defense of liberty is no vice! And . . . moderation in the pursuit of justice is no virtue!"[28] But Buckley had been smart. His speech to the YAF had served its purpose by inoculating his movement from Goldwater's defeat, making the spirit of the movement last longer than just one election cycle. He may have lost friends that night, but he had done much to preserve his movement.

Not quite everything was coming up roses for Buckley in the early 1960s. For a long time he had been contemplating writing what he called a "Big Book" on modern American conservatism. His long-time publisher, Henry Regnary, was harping on him to do it. Students asked if he was planning to explain the key tenets of modern conservatism. His father wanted him to do it, and so did his friends at *National Review*. He wanted to do it, too. He always thought writing a big book that challenged an era's primary assumptions was the highest calling for an intellectual. In 1961, he signed a contract with Putnam's for "an untitled book on conservatism."[29] It was to be his magnum opus.

The thing was: he couldn't pull it off. It wasn't his style. He didn't enjoy pondering a single topic for too long. He could craft an eight-hundred-word column in just thirty minutes. But the sustained thinking required to write a big book was something altogether different. Buckley tried. He drafted an outline. He even adopted a title, *The Revolt Against the Masses*, a play on José Ortega y Gasset's *The Revolt of the Masses*, a popular book from the 1930s arguing that democracy granted too much power to average people whose tastes were not worth ennobling. Buckley's spin on it was to show how the Liberal Establishment had successfully plotted a revolt *against* the people, its torpid way of life sucking the marrow out of the otherwise good people of America, the bureaucratic yoke too heavy on the noble heart. In 1960, Buckley had written that he would "sooner live in a society governed by the first two thousand people in the Boston telephone directory than in a society governed by the two thousand faculty members of Harvard University."[30] His big book would explain what that meant.

Buckley intended to write the book in Switzerland in 1963, during his usual winter holiday. But he couldn't concentrate. Distractions seemed to be everywhere. As a thinker, he just couldn't perform the difficult work of smoothing out the contradictions within modern conservatism. Indeed, the first contradiction he confronted—whether or not average working- or middle-class people really were worthy of being in power—proved an insurmountable stumbling block. He knew the liberal elite was not up to the task, at least in his mind, and he was coming to see that his own movement was tapping directly into the anger of lower- and middle-class Americans who hated the liberal snobs. But his own elite background prevented him from enjoying the same kinds of things commoners enjoyed. Did he really want to be led by "the first two thousand people in the Boston telephone directory"? If so, he probably shouldn't have earlier proposed that the illiterate and uneducated be denied access to the ballot, which, to him, put democracy in the hands of dolts. In thinking about where to draw the line between the desires of the elite and those of the masses, the contradictions were too difficult for him to overcome. "I hope you're well and writing up a storm," Buckley wrote Mailer from Switzerland. "My own book is not forthcoming. I have temporarily put it aside."[31]

But who could blame him for putting aside such a hefty intellectual project? Looking at the excitement among conservatives at the Cow Palace in 1964, Buckley had spent his energy well enough. To succeed, conservatism didn't seem to need a big book by Bill Buckley at all. His work as a salesman had been quite successful.

Mailer understood. His own big book, the promised "great American novel," wasn't forthcoming either. But nevertheless, just like Buckley, it seemed his ideas were beginning to take hold in the early 1960s, too.

San Francisco was a perfect example. Alongside all those spiffy, Buckley-wannabe conservatives, a counterrevolution on the left was also coming into view. Just north of the convention, in fact, at the intersection of Haight and Ashbury Streets, a collection of radicals had embraced the kind of existential politics Mailer had been talking about for years. While Barry Goldwater was sucking up the plaudits at the Cow Palace, the intersection up the way was the target of a bus of "Merry Pranksters," headed by writer Ken Kesey. Later to be remembered as the country's first hippies, the Pranksters put a mocking poster on the side of their bus that read: "A VOTE FOR BARRY IS A VOTE FOR FUN!" They did drugs, stopped at psychedelic drug explorer Timothy Leary's commune, did more drugs, and eventually made it to the intersection of Haight and Ashbury. Corporate capitalism? Rational thought? The Rules? All were ridiculed by the Merry Pranksters.

Mailer's general sense of the early hippy movement was that their complaints had merit, but their avoidance of democratic politics was dangerous. Besides, there was more serious activity coming from the left. During the convention, for instance, church and labor activists had sponsored a forty-thousand-strong civil rights march through the middle of San Francisco, displaying provocative signs like "GOLDWATER FOR FÜHRER" and "GOLDWATER '64, BREAD AND WATER '65, HOT WATER '66." A casket labeled "FREEDOM IS DEAD" rose above the crowd.[32] These were the kinds of creative protests Mailer had been hoping to see.

Even beyond San Francisco, by 1964 there were plenty of signs of vitality on the left, of people challenging The Rules, questioning corporate capitalism, and rejecting the technocrats. A little more than a year before the Republican National Convention, for example, a journalist and housewife named Betty Friedan had stoked the flames of the women's movement with a barn burner of a book called *The Feminine Mystique*. The book distinctly challenged The Rules, which Friedan blamed for a widespread depression among smart middle- and upper-class women in America. In examining the post-collegiate lives of her peers from Smith College, Friedan discovered that, fifteen years on, most of her classmates were suffering from a psychological malaise she labeled "the Feminine Mystique." According to The Rules, she wrote, "truly feminine

women do not want careers, higher education, political rights. . . .
All they had to do was devote their lives from earliest girlhood
to finding a husband and bearing children."[33] The Rules, Friedan
argued, had to change.

At roughly the same time Friedan's book came out, the African American freedom movement arrived in Washington, D.C.,
to March on Washington for Jobs and Freedom. The men wore
ties and the women proper dresses, but the marchers were quick
to point out that their rights were being infringed and that the
hierarchies inherent in The Rules were contradictory. If The Rules
didn't change, what choice did African Americans have but to
demand their rights? This was not radical lawlessness, but it was
an interracial challenge, more people willing to see The Rules as
hollow and dangerous and self-serving for a particular subset of
the population. Threats from the left were mounting.

Meanwhile, college students were voicing complaints, too. The
Free Speech Movement in Berkeley, which kicked off radical student activism for the decade, began a month after Goldwater left
town. But the action in Berkeley was in many ways just the politicization of a broader movement that had begun four years earlier,
in 1960, the same year that Buckley's YAF was founded. It was then
that a small group called the Students for a Democratic Society
(SDS) formed in Ann Arbor, Michigan. SDS was almost always
much smaller than YAF, in part because there was no equivalent to
William F. Buckley, Jr., to help it along. At its opening convention,
for instance, there were just twenty-nine participants (as opposed
to YAF's ninety). By late 1961, SDS counted 575 members in 20
chapters (compared to YAF's 24,000 members in 115 schools).[34]
But it was the start of the youthful rumblings of the left.

SDS's mission statement, the Port Huron Statement, perhaps
unwittingly invited comparisons to the Sharon Statement, too,
although there were some notable differences. While YAF had
gathered at Buckley's father's home, the student leaders of SDS
met at a United Auto Workers educational camp in Port Huron,

Michigan. While the Sharon Statement was a two-page brief, the Port Huron Statement was long and ponderous. Crafted in 1962, largely by Tom Hayden, its opening line set the tone: "We are people of this generation, bred in at least modest comfort, housed now in universities, looking uncomfortably to the world we inherit." It would be wordy and theoretical throughout; indeed, it totaled sixty-three pages when it was complete. The general sense of the Port Huron Statement, though, was that the Liberal Establishment had betrayed its goal of increasing human happiness in the world. Instead, liberalism had created a "remote control economy" with an "authoritarian and oligopolistic structure of economic-decision-making." There were huge bureaucracies that destroyed connections between people. There was a badly fought Cold War that limited dissent. "Men," it read, "have unrealized potential for self-cultivation, self-direction, self-understanding, and creativity." Claiming "the life of the nation is spiritually empty," the call of SDS was for a spiritual rebirth. "The goal of man and society," it read, "should be human independence."[35]

By 1964, the group had 2,500 members in forty-one chapters. That number would explode in 1965 and 1966.[36]

As these kinds of radical protest gained sway, a lot of people on the left began to recognize that Mailer had been making similar complaints for years. In 1963, for example, Mailer received a letter from his old friend Diana Trilling, who told Mailer about an evening she had just enjoyed with one of the de facto deans of American letters, Jacques Barzun, the commanding literature professor at Columbia University. Trilling had cultivated Barzun to be her first reader. "I always send him everything I write," she told Mailer. She clearly respected Barzun, and he her. Otherwise, he wouldn't have read her stuff.

At the dinner, Barzun remarked that there was no real voice of protest in modern literature, no voice of serious dissent. All the current writers, he said, seemed interested in complaining about the current shape of American culture rather than analyzing it and plotting creative ways out.

Trilling quickly corrected him, suggesting that while this was generally true, there was one primary exception: Norman Mailer. Barzun was surprised, knowing Mailer mostly for his gossip-page exploits and his poorly received novels of the 1950s. He asked Trilling what it was about Mailer's work that made her of this opinion. She suggested Barzun read *Advertisements* "right thru from cover to cover," and leaped up to retrieve her copy, which she lent to him on the spot.

"So last night," Trilling reported to Mailer:

> [Barzun] phoned me. He owed me an apology, he said, for having voiced a judgment on insufficient knowledge of your work. Now he totally concurred in my good opinion of you; my praise was now his praise. You were infinitely more serious than he had realized and more on the ball. And you were the only person of your generation with a satiric view of your time instead of a self-pitying, self-indulging impulse; you were way out in front in thoughtfulness. So far, indeed, did he have to go as to acknowledge that you were saying many of the same things he is now trying to say in his new book!

For Trilling, it was proof that her positive assessments of Mailer had been correct, making her "feel the same kind of pleasure you have when the racket and the ball meet the way they should in tennis . . . with just the right ping."[37] For Mailer, it was a sign of his acceptance as part of the outlaw literary establishment, as a celebrity intellectual baptized by greats.

Mailer had other successes as well. His piece on John F. Kennedy entitled "Superman Comes to the Supermarket," which appeared in *Esquire* in 1960, was widely recognized as being transformative to the entire genre of journalistic inquiry. In its blend of Mailer's personal experiences with the future president and First Lady, vivid descriptions of the people surrounding him, and penetrating descriptions of the supermarket culture that Superman was coming to save, its style was revelatory. "As we sat down for the first time," wrote Mailer:

> Kennedy smiled nicely and said that he had read my books. One muttered one's pleasure. 'Yes,' he said, 'I've read . . .' and then there was a short pause which did not last long enough to be embarrassing in which it was yet obvious no title came instantly to his mind . . . but the hesitation lasted no longer than three seconds or four, and then he said, 'I've read *The Deer Park* and . . . the others,' which startled me for it was the first time in a hundred similar situations, talking to someone whose knowledge of my work was casual, that the sentence did not come out, 'I've read *The Naked and the Dead . . .* and the others.' If one is to take the worst and assume that Kennedy was briefed for this interview (which is most doubtful), it still speaks well for the striking instincts of his advisers.

Mailer concluded the piece championing Kennedy, urging voters to go to the polls in what would inevitably be a close election, saying, "Counting by the full spectrum of complete Right to absolute Left, the political differences [between Kennedy and Nixon] would be minor, but what would be not at all minor was the power of each man to radiate his appeal into some fundamental depths of the American character. One would have an inkling at last if the desire of America was for drama or stability, for adventure or monotony."[38]

Mailer had begun taking the personal revelations of *Advertisements* and bringing his powers of observation to politics—and it worked. "I was already working at the *Post* in '60," said the writer Pete Hamill, "and I remember that suddenly most of the younger guys were talking about this amazing piece. . . . It showed us that there was a way to do journalism that was not as rigid as we had thought it was. It was as if Mailer had taken the form and expanded, shoved it around, and said, 'Okay, here's what you can do with this fuckin' thing.' "[39] There were other journalists doing experimental work too, but "Mailer had come along and put himself at the center of the action," Hamill said.[40]

The editors at *Esquire* noticed, and in late 1962 they offered Mailer a monthly column. His first columns were about Marilyn Monroe and Ernest Hemingway, headline grabbers that might ensure readership. But his articles used those hooks to make profound critiques of American life, of the idiocy of The Rules and the deficiencies of the liberal assumptions about the world. After a few columns, he eventually began addressing the president directly, giving JFK thoughtful but sometimes absurd advice on how the nation should be run.

The columns caught on. People began buying *Esquire* just to see what Norman Mailer might say. As *Esquire* editor Carol Polsgrove recalled, "He had the audacity to address the President of the United States directly from our pages, thus we acquired the audacity. He spoke out boldly on politics, sex, architecture, literature, civil rights, cancer, anything that challenged his imagination. Most of the time, when he shouted people listened."[41]

A few months before the San Francisco convention, Mailer collected his *Esquire* pieces and nearly everything else he had written since 1959 and put them in a collection called *The Presidential Papers*. It was *Advertisements* gone political. Mailer fashioned the book as "written *to* the President, *for* him." It turned out to be a remarkably prescient statement of the politics of the left then coming into existence. He began by bemoaning the bureaucratic rationality inherent to liberalism. "The President suffers from one intellectual malady," Mailer wrote: "intellectual malnutrition." The rational bureaucrats had taken over, and the president's "information is predigested—his mind is allowed as much stimulation as the second stomach of a cow." Thus, "there's no feeling of a new political atmosphere in the country" despite Kennedy's flashy promise. Instead, "The liberals pump up their balloons, the conservatives flush out their bile and bilge, but a real issue is never found." America, in turn, was becoming "more economically prosperous and more psychically impoverished. . . . The President has commissions and commissars and bureaus and agents and computer machines to calculate the amount of schooling needed to keep America healthy, safe, vigorous." But the President simply didn't know how to use them. In *Presidential Papers*, Mailer gave JFK 40 percent for passion, 50 percent for rhetoric, 98 percent for arithmetic, and zero for imagination.[42]

Mailer was there to help. The rest of the book was filled with crazy, creative solutions designed to reawaken the country. For example, Mailer proposed the abolition of capital punishment except in those states that opted to retain it, with the lone condition being that executions had to be performed as public spectacles by trained executioners allowed to use only their bare hands.[43] He suggested giving huge subsidies to cancer researchers, who would be "put under sentence of mortal combat (with a professional executioner) if they have failed to make progress in their part of the program after two years." This would help in the search for a cure, "since one may suspect that only a brave man living in the illumination of approaching death could brood sufficiently over the nature of disease to come up with a cure which was not worse than the illness." Mailer also sought to legalize drugs and send the country's best advertising agents to Russia ("If our hucksters have been able in fifteen years to leech from us the best blood of the American spirit, they should be able to debilitate the Russians equally in an equivalent period"). And of course he advocated abolishing all forms of censorship, saying, "pornography is debilitating to sex—the majority of people would stay away from it once they discovered how wan it left them." On this, though, he did reserve the right to be wrong: "It is possible I am indulging a shallow liberal optimism, and America would become a cesspool of all-night pornographic drive-in movies, the majority of the population becoming night people who meet for cocktails at one in the morning."[44]

He called the book an introduction "to existential styles of political thought," and it was a creative onslaught.[45] But it had the bad timing of being released just two weeks before Kennedy's assassination. Sales were poor. The nation was not in the mood for existential experiments when the times seemed to demand certainty and assurance.

Nonetheless, several reviewers understood what Mailer was doing and knew that his ideas, wacky as they were, were striking a nerve in American society. "What Norman Mailer is doing," Richard Kluger wrote, "and doing more prolifically and more provocatively and occasionally more preposterously than any other literary figure we have, is to tell what life is like now in America."[46] Mailer was grateful for Kluger's review, cutting it out of *Book Week* and saving it for posterity.

The problem with the book, however, was the thing that most separated him from Buckley. Buckley was willing to sacrifice some of his ideological commitments in order to work in the dirty trough of politics. He was a salesman working to close a deal, even if it meant tamping down the enthusiasm he saw within his own camp. Mailer, on the other hand, was as always more of a philosopher. If he had been willing to leave aside implausible ideas— medieval jousts in Central Park for juvenile delinquents, such as he proposed in *Presidential Papers*—he might have been better able to capture the emerging anger from the left and harness it into a coherent movement, the way Buckley had done for the right. But that wasn't Mailer's strength. It would turn out that no one on the left was really up to the task.

The country's mainstream liberals knew Mailer's lurid biography was a vulnerability, and in 1963 they casually dismissed him as an eccentric. John Kenneth Galbraith wrote bitingly of *Presidential Papers* that, "This book is a definite forward step in the development of Norman Mailer's fiction, for it has a plot." He went on to criticize its personal tone and its preposterous proposals.[47] The picture that accompanied Galbraith's dismissal was an unflattering portrait of a drunken Norman Mailer sitting in a near-miniature rocking chair, looking bewildered and, well, off his rocker.

National Review assigned Garry Wills to review the book. Wills was Buckley's favorite reviewer and probably the best writer on its staff, Buckley included. But Wills missed the humor in *Presidential Papers* and perhaps the point as well. He saw the book as a way for Mailer "[t]o distract himself and others from the fact that he has no books to write." Wills tapped cruelly into Mailer's personal frustrations as an author, arguing that the book derived from the fact that "President Kennedy . . . failed in his major task—the construction of A Society In Which Mailer Could Write Another Novel," adding: "Mailer, who thinks he got Kennedy elected with a single article on Mailer-and-Kennedy, expected to become something of a Cultural Minister, who would redo the White House in Early Neanderthal and set up a Department for Improving the Orgasm." That hadn't happened, and so, wrote Wills, Mailer made these absurd suggestions. Mailer "deserves the title for all-around ability to take absurdities seriously," Wills asserted. "Look how seriously he takes himself."[18]

Nevertheless, if his books weren't quite good enough to harness the power of the underground tumult that was barely underground anymore, Mailer was gradually realizing his limitations as an author—he found it hard to come up with stories. But if the story was provided by the country itself, if the story *was* the country itself, well, was there any better way to deploy his remarkable powers of observation? Mailer's story on the 1964 Republican National Convention would help solidify his role as reporter to the soul of the nation.

Mailer was both electrified by the strength of the resurgent right and horrified by it. The barbarians of the right were at the gates, taking charge of a major national institution before those on the left could get organized. The battle between the two flanks seemed to be turning in the wrong direction. For a short while, Mailer even considered voting for Goldwater in order to derail mainstream liberalism and help stoke the fires of the left. At least then there would be some balance.

But he couldn't bring himself to do it. He recoiled too strongly at the rage that lay beneath the energy at the convention. When the nominations began, a million tiny pieces of gold foil dropped from the ceiling, meeting the spotlights in the room. "There was an unmistakable air of beauty," Mailer wrote, "as if a rainbow had come to a field of war, or Goths around a fire saw visions in a cave. The heart of the beast had loosed a primitive call. Civilization was worn thin in center and to the Left the black man raised his primitive cry; now to the far Right were the maniacal blue eyes of the other primitive. The jungles and the forests were readying for war. For a moment, beauty was there—it is always there as tribes meet and clans gather for war."[49]

But war was not what he wanted. Like many in the nation, Mailer was struggling to find the balance between the sheen of civilization and the loosening of individual freedoms. The Liberal Establishment had not found it, leaving the country "fearful, half mad, inauthentic. It needed a purge," he wrote. But, he feared, if the purge came solely from the right, the country might fall back upon the center, where, as Mailer put it, "a mighty Caesar had arisen, Lyndon Johnson was his name, all hail, Caesar."[50]

As Mailer left the convention hall, he saw the protestors from the left marching against Goldwater and knew he was with them. But he also had a premonition about what was to come. In their midst was a beautiful, quintessential WASP woman: "Yes, kill us, says the expression on the face of the nunlike girl with no lipstick, you will kill us but you will never digest us: I despise you all." And Mailer understood this image above all others would provoke fear within the Buckleyites inside the convention center, "for the girl is one of theirs, no fat plain Jewess with a poor nose is this one, she is part of the West, and so their sense of crisis opens and they know like me that America has come to a point from which she will never return. The wars are coming and the deep revolutions of the soul."[51]

Buckley and Mailer would both turn out to be prescient in their assessments of the election of 1964. Goldwater and the conservatives took control of the Republican Party in August and then got crushed in November, just as Buckley predicted. Goldwater won only six states: his home state of Arizona, plus five states in the Deep South, which voted for Goldwater largely because Johnson had embraced the civil rights movement. Those states would have voted for the Four Horsemen of the Apocalypse before they voted for Lyndon Baines Johnson. And just as Mailer predicted, not only had the rise of Goldwater led Americans to rush to the center and vote for Johnson, but Johnson also saw his electoral triumph as a mandate for midcentury liberalism. In the weeks following the election, Johnson took his platform to Congress and got almost everything he wanted, his own Great Society. In 1965, LBJ passed both Medicare and a school-aid bill costing $1.3 billion. Immigration reform came shortly thereafter, and then another civil rights bill, this one concerning voting rights. Urban redevelopment proceeded apace as well. The juggernaut that was the federal government continued its dramatic growth. The percent of government spending as part of the nation's gross domestic product had risen from 17.1 percent in 1948 to 27.7 percent in 1964, and showed no sign of slowing.[52] While most liberals interpreted this as the United States simply catching up to the rest of the Western world when it came to the expansion of social welfare policies, it was undeniable that the central liberal proposition—that all problems could be rationalized and solved and that government, especially the federal government, was the proper organization to do it— seemed destined to continue. "I wanted the power to give things to people," Johnson told one of his biographers, Doris Kearns Goodwin. But it never occurred to him that his control over those gifts might breed resentment, for they might be the wrong gifts. It was demeaning to have no say in the kind of society in which one lived. Over the course of their relationship, Kearns Goodwin recalls receiving twelve electric toothbrushes from President Johnson, a repetition of which he never seemed aware. The gift-giver wanted kudos for giving the present, unaware at how ignorant the gifts were. By 1965, that ignorance would help stoke the fires of the left. It was the gift-giving without care for the desires of the recipients that Mailer, and lots of others, began to resent.[53]

After the election, Buckley wrote to Mailer to ask if he'd comment on a piece that was about to appear in *National Review.* "I would be interested in your comments," said Buckley, "whether for publication or otherwise."[54] The piece wasn't about the election or the liberal malaise or the rise of modern conservatism. Instead, it was about another issue then challenging the heart and soul of the nation: race. Mailer declined. "I'm not likely to be writing on this subject for a long time," he wrote to Buckley.[55]

As it turned out, he lied. Ever since those college students in Greensboro, North Carolina, had started the sit-in movement at their local Woolworth's in 1960; ever since the Freedom Riders had gone south to integrate public facilities and faced the violence of the Klan in 1961; and ever since Martin Luther King, Jr., had told the nation in 1963 that he had a dream, race had propelled itself into the nation's consciousness in a new way. A 1963 Gallup Poll found that, for the first time, a majority of Americans thought civil rights was the most serious problem confronting the nation.[56] And so, with the civil rights movement sparking into life and the vibrancy of Mailer's broader critiques of America's potentially totalitarian culture beginning to catch on, in the back of Mailer's mind was a novel that would capture the tensions of the time. The question was: after a decade away from novel writing, did he still have the gift?

5

American Dreams

Mailer had been fascinated by race for a long time, and not just out of an effort to understand a system designed to make a significant portion of the population servile. Instead, he was interested in the psychodrama of segregation, of the anger and insecurity required to abuse a person just because of the way he or she looked, and, from the other perspective, the courage required to live in a world where the vast majority of your fellow citizens wouldn't be bothered by your death. The turmoil challenging this drama that came to be called the civil rights movement had fascinated Mailer from its beginnings in 1954, with the Montgomery Bus Boycott, when African Americans began to demand recognition as equal members of the human race. But as with most white people, Mailer just didn't know too many black people, and his relations with them were always fraught with misunderstanding.

His relationship with James Baldwin was especially complex. Mailer first met Baldwin in the Paris apartment of French writer Jean Malaquais in the mid-1950s. Baldwin was not yet well known, and he respected Mailer for not putting down a struggling writer: "He didn't pull rank on me," Baldwin recalled. "He was famous and I wasn't, he had money and I hadn't, [and] he was white with all its advantages."

"But then," Baldwin added slyly, "I didn't pull rank on him either, though being black I knew far more about that kind of extreme outlaw experience he was pursuing than he would ever know."[1]

The two men respected each other, with Mailer even offering to review Baldwin's work in big magazines and newspapers.[2] But their relationship was also filled with fights, misunderstandings, and jealousies. "[W]e had a lot in common," said Baldwin, "even a bad habit of suspecting that others are trying to put us down and therefore striking first at *them*. The time came, of course, when we faced each other the same way—suspiciously—and struck."[3]

By 1965, Baldwin was indisputably famous. His novels from the late 1950s had received attention, most especially his first novel, *Go Tell It on the Mountain*. But it was the civil rights movement that propelled him to great fame. In the early 1960s, a hesitant Baldwin went south at the behest of an editor just as the civil rights movement was gaining momentum. Baldwin's essays on the experience appeared in *Harper's* and *Partisan Review*. Their success led to invitations from *Mademoiselle*, *New York Times Magazine*, and *The New Yorker*, whose editors found his 1962 essay, "Down at the Cross," so exceptional they decided to devote two entire issues to publishing it. They even added pages to the magazine in order to fit the whole thing. That essay later became the signature piece in Baldwin's 1963 book *The Fire Next Time*, which made Baldwin a household name. When his face appeared on the cover of *Time* in May 1963, the editors announced: "There is not another writer who expresses with such poignancy and abrasiveness the dark realities of the racial ferment in North and South."[4] To many, Baldwin possessed the hope of Martin Luther King, Jr., but the threat of Malcolm X.

Baldwin had tried to teach Mailer about black people throughout the late 1950s and 1960s, especially in direct response to Mailer's celebrated 1957 essay, "The White Negro," in which Mailer attempted to explain the increasing appropriation of black mannerisms by white kids. Black Americans, Mailer argued, had been living outside the confines of the Liberal Establishment for two centuries and therefore seemed to live authentically, "in the enormous present," living for "Saturday night kicks, relinquishing the pleasures of the mind for the more obligatory pleasures of the body." Not knowing if they'd be alive tomorrow, Mailer claimed, the black person lived today, giving "voice to the character and quality of his existence, to his rage and the infinite variations of joy, lust, languor, growl, cramp, pinch, scream and despair of his orgasm."[5] White people's search for authenticity had led to the appropriation of black culture and mannerisms in the 1950s, including the rise of a species Mailer labeled "the hipster," young white existentialists appropriating what Mailer saw as the black way of living.

There was plenty of racism in Mailer's article, and any number of gross generalizations. There was also a profound ignorance of the growing black middle class that followed The Rules scrupulously. Instead, from the great distance of his white Jewish background, Mailer glamorized African Americans, and sexualized them, yearning to be like them without an awareness that his assessment could be limiting.

Baldwin hated that piece, deeming it a white fantasy of black life. When Baldwin read "The White Negro," he countered with a long article in *Esquire* called "A Black Boy Looks at a White Boy," which he called a "love letter" to his friend Norman Mailer. Baldwin expressed disbelief that, with people like Mailer, "It is still true, alas, that to be an American Negro male is also to be a kind of walking phallic symbol: which means that one pays, in one's own personality, for the sexual insecurity of others."[6] But Baldwin didn't want to single Mailer out, just expose him as having a typical white, middle-class misunderstanding about black people, one Mailer and others seemed resistant to give up. If someone as brilliant as Mailer perpetuated the extreme sexualization of black men, how on earth could Baldwin expect lesser lights to learn? All white folks, it seemed, simply "wanted their romance."[7]

In 1963 and 1964 Mailer decided to take another crack at it. He knew the fires of the left were coming together and he wanted to capture them, and he knew that the frustrations of black Americans were beginning to boil over. He also knew that with three ex-wives and several children to support, he was having financial trouble and needed to make some money in a hurry.

So Mailer hatched an idea. Thinking through the possibilities to make some quick cash while exploring the tumults then shaking society, Mailer believed he could turn himself into a modern-day Charles Dickens, serializing a novel about contemporary times over the course of eight months in the pages of *Esquire*. One chapter a month with no possibility of rewriting, set to begin . . . well, now. As Mailer wrote to one of his old Army buddies in late 1963: "I decided the only way out of my financial hole was to take a jump, and so I contracted with *Esquire* to write a novel in eight parts, each installment (ten thousand words) will appear in a successive month, and since I didn't have anything behind me when I started, it comes down to writing a book in eight months."[8]

Esquire loved the idea, although the editors knew the risks. Was Mailer up to it? He hadn't written a novel in a decade and was famous for taking his time in rewrites. But still, it was a compelling prospect, one they decided worth the risk.

In addition to being paid by *Esquire*, Mailer also contracted with Dial and its paperback subsidiary Dell to publish the eight chapters as a book, to be released shortly after the serialization was complete. For that, Mailer would be paid a then-astronomical $125,000 advance.[9] The price, Mailer said, "was so large it's crazy."[10]

He started the installments with a horrific bang. The protagonist, a Mailer doppelgänger (Harvard educated, World War II experience, self-proclaimed "existential psychologist") named Stephen Rojack, kills his wife in the first installment, strangling her in the middle of a violent fight. "She strained in balance," Mailer wrote in the death scene, "and then her strength began to pass, it passed over to me, and I felt my arm tightening about her neck. . . . She gave one malevolent look which said: 'There are dimensions to evil which reach beyond the light,' and then she smiled like a milkmaid and floated away and was gone."[11] The shocking murder ends the first installment. In the second, Rojack throws the body out a skyscraper's window, calls the police, and claims his wife has killed herself. He then ominously hangs up the phone, concluding the second installment. Would he get away with it? As Mailer wrote to a friend, "I've finished the first installment which is sheer cliff-hanger, and the second installment, which is sheer cliff-hanger. Can I keep it up?"[12]

It turned out Mailer could. He didn't enjoy it, though: "It's like giving a hot fuck to your beloved," he wrote a friend, "and having to pull your cock out eight times for her to inspect it."[13] But this nevertheless turned out to be yet another of his literary talents. Writing under pressure had its benefits: "It makes me work," Mailer wrote:

> Since it's been eight years since I've set out to write a novel and finish it, I think I would have taken forever to get somewhere if it weren't for the fact that I have to make my decisions in great haste and stick by them. It's a little like playing ten-second chess. You have to take the bold choice each time, because you know you can depend on getting something out of the bold effects—the subtler choices may prove too subtle and fail to come to life in the speed with which you have to write.[14]

After lying to the police and getting away with the murder (for the moment), the remaining installments tell of Rojack's two-day quest through New York City to evade arrest and search for the source of the thing inside himself that allowed him to kill his wife and feel no remorse. Rojack goes to Harlem, meets a beautiful blonde nightclub singer named Cherry and a Miles Davis–like jazz musician named Shago Martin, and has numerous fights and love affairs. He ends up in Park Avenue's Waldorf Towers, where he confronts his now-deceased wife's father, one of the richest men in America and the book's personification of evil. After staring down his father-in-law, Rojack begins to feel that everything important in the world is part of a fight between God and the Devil. It's thus hard to understand anyone's true intentions. Who is winning the existential battle that propels our actions, binds us to others, and allows us to be free?[15] The book ends on a sour note, with Rojack's image of purity, the promiscuous nightclub singer Cherry (Mailer wanted Cybill Shepherd to play Cherry in the movie)[16] dying an odd death and Rojack heading to Mexico, a place that might be rougher and tougher than New York City, but which was also some-how more honest. When the book came out, Mailer called it *An American Dream*.

It was a notable story coming from a man who had in fact nearly killed his wife then gone on a two-day bender. In addition to the biographical similarities, Rojack also shares many of Mailer's ideas. He believes in the anti-rational world of magic and in some-thing akin to voodoo, where looks and curses possess meaning. He professes to hate contraception, seeing it as yet another "plastic" device that divorces humanity from itself. And he believes in sex as an analogy to power, to get beyond the sheen of civilized mid-century life.

In one of the most infamous and memorable scenes in *An American Dream*, right after Rojack kills his wife but before he decides to make it look like a suicide, he stumbles across their German maid, Ruta, masturbating in her bedroom. She had heard the fight, thought it was rough sex, and gotten excited. Rojack makes eye contact but utters no words as he slowly undresses himself before having sex with her. Rather than fade to black and allow the reader's imagination to do the work, Mailer gives a graphic description of the act. "She was hungry," he wrote, "like a lean rat she was hungry, and it could have spoiled my pleasure except that there was something intoxicating in the sheer narrow pitch of the smell, so strong, so stubborn, so private. . . ." The scene ends with Rojack alternating between anal and vaginal sex, debating with himself about where he should climax: "So that was how I finally made love to her, a minute for one, a minute for the other, a raid on the Devil and a trip back to the Lord." In the end, the Devil wins, and the maid is ecstatic: "I do not know why you have trouble with your wife," she says. "You are absolutely a genius, Mr. Rojack."[17]

When Mailer turned this section in to *Esquire*, the editor in chief, Arnold Gingrich, wanted the whole serial called off. He had never been a fan of Mailer's, and this scene confirmed why. The other editors thought better of it, though, and convinced both Mailer and Gingrich that if the scene could be made more metaphorical, more consciously a debate about which path Rojack should follow—God or the Devil?—it would work. Surprisingly, both parties agreed. Mailer revised it, and the scrics continued.[18]

Another memorable scene occurs when Rojack debates the murder with his father-in-law. To exonerate Rojack for the crime, his father-in-law forces him to walk a long parapet along the roof of a tall New York skyscraper. With the winds howling a hundred stories up, Rojack can overcome his wrongdoing only by summoning all of his courage. A cliffhanger in a near-literal sense, the scene is electric, and readers arc not sure if they want Rojack to fall to his death or make it across.

As Mailer was writing, he was thinking of the book in terms of a movie—not so he could sell the rights to Hollywood (although that was always in the back of his mind), but instead because he thought only movies were capable of penetrating the American psyche anymore. Technology had sped things up so much that deep, considerate thinking was becoming increasingly rare, and visual images had taken hold of American creativity. Mailer was beginning to feel that the literary age was fading away. He himself had been deeply affected by Stanley Kubrick's *Dr. Strangelove, Or: How I Learned to Stop Worrying and Love the Bomb*, the farcical anti–Cold War film that echoed many of Mailer's own critiques about Cold War America. "It's the only great movie I know which is great not because it's great as a movie but because it's sociologically great that thing was made," he wrote to a friend.[19]

Now Mailer sought to critique the assumptions of American life through a novel that resembled film. "So far as I know," he wrote:

> this is the first I know that an author has tried to make a serious novel out of a story which derives in its style of plot from the movies. The serious reason for this is that by now the only myths and legends we have in America are those unconscious ones in our minds by the American movie. And so I thought it would be more interesting to try to write a novel which embodied one of these modern myths or legends rather than, let us say, trying to bring Oedipus Rex up to date.[20]

Does Mailer ever "deal with" the act of murder? No. Does he think Rojack has made a mistake in killing his wife? No. Does Rojack get away with it? Yes. Was the book seen as a giant, nightmarish dreamscape coming out at what was otherwise the high point of the Liberal Establishment in America, when LBJ's Great Society was in full bloom?

Well, that was exactly the point. Amid the backslapping and self-congratulation within liberal America, Mailer was revealing a darker side of the story, the tensions in the room. There was still poverty, racism, corruption, and a general lack of courage within the population. Mailer consciously called the book *An American Dream*, not "The" *American Dream* to demonstrate the blindness within the American Liberal Establishment. It was also a play on one of the darker novels Mailer read early in his life, Theodore Dreiser's *An American Tragedy*, a book about a young man full of promise who can't contain his libido and eventually kills the pregnant working-class girl who stands in the way of his upward mobility.

Mailer was nervous about the book's reception. A few days before it was published, Jason Epstein, a friend and editor at Random House (though not the book's editor, who was E. L. Doctorow, before his own career as a writer), exchanged a number of letters with Mailer about the manuscript and its meaning. Mailer asked Epstein what he thought of the book. Epstein wrote back to say he wished Mailer had made the idea of a dreamscape more explicit, so readers wouldn't have to decide if Rojack was mad or if the reader was supposed to find her or himself rooting for him. This was too much work, thought Epstein, and Rojack was simply too unlikeable. Conflicted feelings in the reader would come to be normal in the later 1960s and into the 1970s, when books like Mario Puzo's *The Godfather* would provide much the same effect. But Mailer was ahead of the curve.

Epstein held on to his critical letter for a few days before sending it, and then read it again. Before sending it, he added a postscript: "I've let this sit for a while, and now it seems to me harsh and ungenerous. I know you will understand that I would not write this way to a writer whom I do not greatly admire, whose talents and courage are in a different category entirely from those of his contemporaries."[21]

Mailer, ego appropriately stroked, pointed out to Epstein that "Rojack is neither mad nor sane, but in that extreme state of fatigue and emotional exhaustion where the senses are crystal clear and paranoia substitutes its vertical salience for the horizontal measure of daily reason, and everything takes place somewhere between a fever and a dream. . . . It is, after all, not insanity but an existential state, but I may have been wrong in assuming that people would recognize it as equivalent to some kind of crisis in their own lives."[22]

This explanation made something click for Epstein. He finally understood Rojack as a metaphor for America. Epstein wrote back: "The point, I suppose, is that the whole culture is in a state of emotional exhaustion, and . . . we seem to be behaving in a way that Rojack would probably understand very well. It's a commonplace now, though still to me a most peculiar development, that the culture as a whole lives beyond good and evil, or as you say in the case of Rojack, in a state of paranoia which has replaced reason."[23]

This was exactly the point Mailer had been trying to make for nearly a decade. The country had accepted intrusions on its individual freedoms from organizations like the CIA, all out of a paranoid feeling that everything had to be controlled. The nation's soul was strung out from the attempt to rationalize everything, but no one seemed able to push beyond. "[I]f the novel has large merit," Mailer wrote, "it is because the attempt is made to write about the dramatic history of a man's soul over thirty-two hours rather than about his character, his life, or his fortune. And while I'm not so grandiose as to compare myself to Dostoevsky directly, it is necessary to say that no one has tried to write this way before or since Dostoevsky."[24] And just as Dostoevsky is noted for capturing certain large aspects of whatever is meant by "the Russian soul," Mailer sought to be the American equivalent.

Unsurprisingly, reviews of the book were split. As Mailer wrote to his daughter, "It got the craziest reviews of any of my novels. It got the very best and the very worst."[25] Both the *New York Times* and the *New York Review of Books* were tough on it, not really engaging with the book's ideas, not seeing it as a metaphor for the times, but merely as an attempt to fictionalize Mailer's recent past without confronting the anger his acts had provoked. "It is a sad parody of itself," Eliot Fremont-Smith wrote in the *New York Times*, "because Mailer shows no more awareness [of the book's lack of believability] than . . . of the hopeless vacancies of his ideas."[26]

Of course, not everyone was critical, and support came from some unsuspecting sources. In *National Review*, Buckley tapped Joan Didion to write the review of *An American Dream*. Didion, just thirty-one years old, had been writing for *National Review* for several years and had already developed a unique and powerful voice.

Like Mailer, she would come to be seen as one of the most perceptive observers of the 1960s. Her 1968 book, *Slouching Towards Bethlehem*, is still widely considered a classic firsthand account of the
era. Buckley recognized her literary talents and championed her
even if she wasn't an avowed Buckleyite conservative.

Didion loved *An American Dream*. Calling it an almost "perfect novel," she saw Mailer as the era's F. Scott Fitzgerald. They
both, she said, "share that instinct for the essence of things, that
great social eye." Didion felt that Mailer and Fitzgerald both had
"some fascination with the heart of the structure, some deep feeling for the mysteries of power. For both Mailer and Fitzgerald,
as for the tellers of fairy tales, there remains something sexual
about money, some sense in which the princess and the gold are
inextricably one." It was a most American fascination. In addition, both Fitzgerald and Mailer had "immense technical skill,
the passion for realizing the gift. The deep romanticism. And
perhaps above all the unfashionableness, the final refusal to sail
with the prevailing winds. Fitzgerald was 'frivolous,' and Mailer
is 'superstitious.'" Both would be pilloried for these traits, but
both were great because of them. "If it has always been easy to
laugh at Mailer," Didion wrote, "it was never easier than when
he announced, clearly in trouble, running scared, that he had
dared himself to write a novel in installments for *Esquire*. ('Only
a second-rater would take a stupid dare like that,' as Lulu says in
The Deer Park.) Nonetheless, that novel, *An American Dream*, is one
more instance in which Mailer is going to laugh last, for it is a
remarkable book."[27]

Mailer was delighted with the review. He immediately wrote
to Buckley, "What a marvelous girl Joan Didion must be. I think
that's one conservative I would like to meet," adding: "And who
would ever have thought that the nicest piece I am to read about
myself four weeks after publication should come in the *National
Review*. Well, this is the year of literary wonders. What do you think
the odds would have been for a parlay of good reviews in *National*

Review, Life, the *New York Times Sunday Book Review,* Paul Pickrel at *Harper's,* and the *Chicago Tribune.* One hundred fifty million to one, or would we have picked it by light years?"[28]

One other person who was perhaps inexplicably charmed by the book was Pat Buckley. Even though she wasn't exactly a prude, she was unlikely to have enjoyed the blunt sex scenes or the murderous chain of events. But Mailer had played her right. He always liked her nickname for him, "Chooky-bah lamb," so he used it in *An American Dream* during a literary flourish, a playful discussion between Rojack and an otherwise expendable character. Mailer had asked Pat how to correctly use the phrase. She told him. He used it, and then sent her a copy of the book. Pat wrote back: "Norman luv—The book is great—Really. Chooky Bah Lamb is spelt thusly—I sent the book to my old Nanny in darkest Scotland—She is beside herself with delight that her old Pa's expression has been immortalized. Lots of love—long to see you. P."[29]

But that paled in comparison to Buckley's own gusher of a review, "*Life* Goes to Norman Mailer."[30] Buckley had allowed the Didion review to stand as *National Review*'s official position, but by September 1965, the book was getting so much attention that Buckley felt compelled to weigh in. He took as his cue a long article on Mailer in *Life* that was supposed to be *Life's* cover story until some of the first images of earth from outer space came through. Buckley had been interviewed for the piece, and when *Life* arrived in his mail that month he immediately scanned it for any mentions of his name. He was not disappointed. He was used early on to set up the theme of the piece, which was why Mailer insisted on a "reckless quest" for confrontation, "always, incorrigibly, contending, whether in vinous debate with rightwing publisher William F. Buckley, Jr. about what Norman calls 'Red dread,'" or any other number of Mailer's pet projects. For seemingly no good reason, *Life* argued, Mailer insisted on pushing people's buttons, enjoying the confrontation without concern for what fruit it might bear.

Buckley took his pen and underlined his own name when he came across it. As he scanned further, Buckley saw that *Life* concluded with a long quote from him, too: "I like him," Buckley had said of Mailer, "but I disapprove of him. He's a terribly good measure of the current disturbances in the air. A sort of lightning rod. Yet he does have a strange formality about him, doesn't he? Despite the fact that he's supposedly the god of spontaneity. A very sweet streak in him."[31] *Life* took this to mean, not incorrectly, that Mailer's constant efforts to understand more, to know more, despite his personal frailties, endeared Mailer to millions of Americans. He was, if nothing else, authentic.[32]

The quotation was right on, and Buckley had liked *An American Dream*, in a way. But it was frustrating to Buckley that so many people, now including *Life*, still didn't understand what Mailer was trying to do with his critique of the country and its culture, still thought Mailer was "reckless." Twelve pages in *Life* magazine, thought Buckley, certainly meant Mailer was "big on the literary scene, and more, that he is big on the American scene, for reasons that most critics do not know how to explain but, by their friendly activity in trying, go so far as to acknowledge that the Quest to Explain Norman Mailer is itself worthwhile."[33]

"And indeed it is," Buckley added.

Now, in his syndicated column, he'd tell them why.

"Mailer is interesting in two respects," Buckley explained.[34] "The first—and here is why I love him as an artist—is that he makes the most beautiful metaphors in the business, as many as a dozen of them on a single page worth anthologizing." This was a fair point, but also a common refrain about Mailer. "The second reason why he is interesting," continued Buckley, "is that to many who read him hungrily (and perhaps too seriously) he represents present-day America. He expresses their feelings that America today is shivering in desolation and hopelessness, is looking for her identity after a period of self-alienation marked by a couple of world wars, a depression and a cyclonic advance through technology and automation." The shits are killing us, Buckley was saying, and Mailer was not only telling us why, but trying to articulate a way out, even if it sometimes sounded crazy.

But Buckley didn't think Mailer was quite there yet. He was still a work in progress, too eager to reject things without concern for what it truly takes to build something new. "As a citizen, he is wild," Buckley wrote, "defying not only those starched conventions that are there primarily to stick out your tongue at, but the other conventions, the real McCoys: those that are there to increase the small chance we have, whether as children or as adults, for a little domestic tranquility." Mailer was out to break The Rules, but it was all too wantonly.

"On the domestic scene, he is a so-so socialist," Buckley asserted, "because even though he finds he can float only in the cool waters of the left, he is transparently unhappy, really, as a socialist." On international relations, Mailer was "an utter and hopeless mess," with Buckley adding: "If there is an intellectual in the United States who talks more predictable nonsense on the subject of foreign policy, I will pay a week's wages not to have to hear him."

But still, somewhere deeper in Mailer's quest, Buckley found merit. "As a philosopher, however, Mailer is—dare I say it?—in his own fashion, a conservative," Buckley wrote. "Wrestling in the 20th century with the hegemonies of government and ideology, the conservative tends to side with the individualist." And so did Mailer. Buckley could relate to that.

"In his most recent novel, *An American Dream,*" Buckley continued, "a hero as screwy as Mr. Mailer lurches from Gomorrah to hell and back, but always depends on himself to get out of the jam." Buckley went on to confess that "Mr. Mailer's tours through the nightspots of hell are not my ideas of recreation, even with pad and pencil in hand to jot down what one has Learned About Things. I do not enjoy spelunking in human depravity, nor do I wish my machine around to tape-record the emunctory noises of psychic or physical human excesses. Even so, there is hope in Norman Mailer's turbulent motions."[35]

It was, in many ways, a moving tribute, respectful of his friend's quest to understand human nature, to find authenticity in an increasingly inauthentic world, to find freedom when the waters of totalitarianism seemed to be rising all around. Buckley of course rejected Mailer's findings, but declared the quest to be in no way reckless.

When Mailer read the affectionate but challenging piece (which Buckley sent him prior to syndication), he immediately wrote back: "What the hell does emunctory mean?"[36]

"Anyway," Mailer continued, "you're just an old fraud. You offered to pay a week's wages not to have to hear anyone who talks more predictable nonsense on the subject of foreign policy than myself. Sailor Bill, I come close to loving you here. When the hell did you ever earn a week's wages, you bleeding plutocrat. Of course if you were really indicating you were ready to give up one-fifty-second of your yearly income, then I will go look for such an intellectual and split the swag with him. Maybe Mario Savio would like to cut up a five-thousand-dollar pie with me."[37]

Buckley laughed at the barb, and responded in full satire.

"What the hell does emunctory mean?" he wrote. "NL emunctorium, fr. L emunctus (past part of emungere to blow or wipe the nose, fr. emungere, akin to mucus) . . . archaic (note: not reactionary—WB) an organ or part of the body (as the kidneys or skin) that serves to carry off body wastes. . . ."[38]

Buckley delighted in giving Mailer a vocabulary lesson. His larger point of course was that he, unlike Mailer, did not like to dwell in the more savage, more visceral, aspects of human depravity. That didn't lead to enlightenment. No need to investigate the smell of a lay, the chunks in the blood, or the joy of a fart. Searching for deep meaning there, thought Buckley, was purely prurient. There were other ways to attack the liberal monster that Mailer had elsewhere so marvelously excoriated.

What is perhaps surprising about all the reviews of *An American Dream* is that none of them, positive or negative, commented much on Mailer's treatment of race, a fact that angered James Baldwin even if it didn't surprise him. When Baldwin first read *An American Dream*, he realized that his old friend Mailer hadn't learned anything from their friendship, at least nothing about black people. In fact, despite the novel's grappling with the inner horrors of postwar American life, the knife-edged anxiety of trying to find a code to live by when the horrors of nuclear annihilation compressed the boundaries of individual experience, Mailer's representation of black people perfectly embodied almost every liberal assumption Baldwin had been trying to overturn. When Baldwin was asked about *An American Dream*, he simply said Mailer "must have been joking." Baldwin refused to take the book seriously.[39]

With good reason, too. In *An American Dream*, Harlem is portrayed as a dangerous, exciting destination, where taxi cabs refuse to go but where Rojack seeks primal purity. The one black character of any substance is the musician Shago Martin, the epitome of cool, "skin dark as midnight," with a reputation for being impossibly attractive and perhaps the world's greatest lover. Rojack is constantly trying to measure up to Shago when he meets Cherry, who happens to be Shago's ex-wife. When Shago says things like, "Listen, Sambo, you look like a coonass blackass nigger jackaboo to me cause you been put-putting with blondie here, my wife, you see, dig? digaree? Evil! Evil? Why the white girl's evil, you see," Rojack scores points by not being intimidated by all that hipness and overt sexuality.[40]

When Baldwin read that, he just threw his hands in the air. Mailer had supported the civil rights movement. In 1962, he had sent a telegram to Attorney General Robert F. Kennedy advising him on how to handle James Meredith's integration into the University of Mississippi. He had even volunteered to serve as a presidential ambassador to the South. (Kennedy passed.) And the one and only time Mailer ever congratulated Lyndon Johnson was for passing the Civil Rights Act of 1964. But Mailer, like a lot of post-war liberals, had developed a mythology about the twenty million black people in America. It was a common refrain. In Norman Podhoretz's 1963 essay in the then-left-wing *Commentary*, "My Negro Problem—and Ours," he demonstrated a nearly identical sensibility: black people were, to him, "free, independent, reckless, brave, masculine, erotic," while his Jewish brethren were "sissies."[41] Baldwin's perpetual point was that interpretations like these were premised on a false notion of black people, that the mythology of the hyper-sexualized black man had more to do with white insecurities than black realities. Still, as late as 2007, Mailer answered a question about what, if anything, he would want to be reincarnated as with: "a black athlete. I don't care where you put me, I'll take my chances, but yes, that's what I want to be, a black athlete."[42] Mailer's sought-after radical freedom seemed to possess limitations Mailer himself didn't understand.

In the end, *An American Dream* sold well. It wasn't a runaway best-seller like *The Naked and the Dead*, but it didn't fare badly, either. "The publisher estimates fifty thousand copies in hard cover will be sold before its sale is done," Mailer wrote three months after the book's release, "and so far we've done better than two-thirds of this figure."[43]

"I think actually," Mailer added, in his typically perceptive way, "what is going on is that two counter-waves are meeting, and I am being bounced like a cork at the confluence. So everything you will read about me for the next year is likely to be choppy, very good, very bad, both at once."[44] The right and the left were emerging to challenge the liberals in the middle, and Mailer saw himself, rightly or wrongly, as a touchstone for all involved.

6

The Most Hated Man in America

With the challenges of the civil rights movement sparking worldwide discussion about the importance of individual rights and the limitations of tradition, the students of the Cambridge Union Society dreamed up a humdinger of an event to celebrate their one hundred and fiftieth anniversary in February 1965. Coming in the throes of the civil rights movement, when the hopefulness of the early movement had yet to give way to the more violent reactions of the latter half, the students thought a debate between James Baldwin, the most articulate voice emerging from black America, and William F. Buckley, Jr., the most persuasive conservative, would draw a significant amount of attention. They were right. More than seven hundred students showed up, filling every seat. An overflow room set up to pipe in the debate also filled quickly. The only black face in the audience was that of Baldwin's friend, Sidney Poitier. The rest were white students from Cambridge, sitting alongside numerous reporters, including one from the *New York Times*, which would print the debate almost in its entirety a few weeks later.[1] The proposition under consideration was "The American Dream is at the expense of the American Negro."

For Buckley, who had long opposed the civil rights movement, it seemed to be a perfect venue for him to explain his position. It was a formal affair at tux-and-tails Cambridge, away from the hot emotions in America, and he knew well the rules of collegiate debate: wear formal attire instead of a business suit (as Baldwin wore); answer only the questions from the audience you want to answer and skip over the rest (Baldwin seemed ruffled at being interrupted); and address the president of the Union instead of the entire audience (a deficiency that actually may have helped Baldwin).

But knowing the rules gets you only so far. Sometimes you simply can't win an argument if your ideas are worse than your opponent's. And with the help of some tactical nudging from Baldwin, it didn't take long for Buckley's shoddy ideas about race to come unmasked.

National Review had come of age alongside the civil rights movement, having published its first issue a year after the *Brown v. Board of Education* decision that outlawed segregation in public schools and two weeks before the arrest of Rosa Parks. From the beginning, *National Review* could have endorsed the traditionalist notion that changes should come slowly within a society but should happen nonetheless, and that the rule of law need be respected above all else. Or it could have taken a libertarian stance that the state shouldn't be in the business of segregating people at all.

But it didn't take either of these paths. Instead, it fomented a direct assault against civil rights, embracing nearly all of the most offensive and discredited arguments against the movement, including the idea that black people were inherently inferior to white people. It routinely dressed up the racist resistance to civil rights with respectable-sounding arguments about states' rights and constitutional law. As a signal crafter of conservative talking points in the midcentury years, throughout the 1950s and 1960s *National Review* developed arguments to oppose every motion in favor of civil rights, indiscriminately using sometimes contradic-

tory ideas in order to pursue a single goal: the continued subjuga-
tion of America's black people.

Buckley himself had developed two arguments against civil
rights, both of which were little more than disguised racism, both
of which led the line at *National Review*. The first emerged early in
his career. Since the 1950s, Buckley had argued that civil rights
should be opposed not because black people were biologically
inferior to white people, but because they were not yet "civilized"
enough to take part in democratic government. Or, as Buckley put
it in 1959, "There are no scientific grounds for assuming congeni-
tal Negro disabilities. The problem is not biological, but cultural
and educational."[2]

This "lack of civilization" argument has a long pedigree dating
back to the country's earliest thinkers on the subject, including
Thomas Jefferson. Even some black leaders, like Booker T. Washington, expounded on the idea, if with different motives. In the
1950s and 1960s, the argument pushed Buckley in surprising
directions. After repeated questioning, he was sometimes forced to
admit that, in his view, all uneducated people, black, white, brown,
red, or yellow, should not be allowed to vote if they didn't pass
some sort of competency test. This was an undemocratic stance
to say the least, but at least it was consistent with his idea that only
"civilized" people should rule.

As he pushed this line of thought in the pages of *National Review*,
Buckley argued that no one knew what levels of education should
be mandatory to participate in a democracy better than local
arbiters. Thus, for Buckley, the federal government had no business declaring equal access when it couldn't differentiate between
uneducated black people in Alabama and black graduates of
Harvard. The federal government should butt out; states should
decide. If Massachusetts wanted to limit the franchise based on an
IQ test, that should be its prerogative.

Of course, no one in Massachusetts was advocating restrictions
on voting rights for uneducated white people, and thus Buckley's

argument displayed a willful ignorance about the abuses that had taken place throughout the South during the previous one hundred years, when literacy tests, poll taxes, and grandfather clauses kept the vast majority of black people from voting. Nevertheless, Buckley relied on this states' rights argument for much the rest of his life. Buckley's reaction to *Brown*, for example, was that it was "one of the most brazen acts of judicial usurpation in our history, patently counter to the intent of the Constitution, shoddy and illegal in analysis, and invalid in sociology."[3] He later added, "Support for the Southern position rests not at all on the question of whether Negro and White children should, in fact, study geography side by side, but on whether a central or a local authority should make that decision."[4]

He didn't stop there. In 1957, Buckley wrote *National Review*'s most infamous editorial, entitled "Why the South Must Prevail." Is the white community in the South, he asked, "entitled to take such measures as are necessary to prevail, politically and culturally, in areas in which it does not predominate numerically?" His answer was crystal clear: "The sobering answer is *Yes*—the White community is so entitled because for the time being, it is the advanced race." Buckley cited unfounded statistics demonstrating the superiority of white over black, and concluded that, "it is more important for any community, anywhere in the world, to affirm and live by civilized standards, than to bow to the demands of the numerical majority." He added definitively: "the claims of civilization supersede those of universal suffrage."[5]

And what method should be used to enforce the maintenance of "civilized standards"? According to Buckley, it should be a no-holds-barred defense, even including violence. "Sometimes," he wrote, "it becomes impossible to assert the will of a minority, in which case it must give way, and the society will regress; sometimes the numerical [white] minority cannot prevail except by violence: then it must determine whether the prevalence of its will is worth the terrible price of violence."[6]

In other words, it was up to the white community to decide when violence was appropriate. Through its White Citizens' Councils, the resurgence of the Klan, and the general refusal to prosecute crimes committed against black Southerners, by the 1960s the white South had made its decision. And rather than condemn it, Buckley stayed the course. In 1958, *National Review* printed a cutting article on the black politician Adam Clayton Powell, Jr., entitled, "The Jig Is Up." Buckley professed not to know the racial connotations of the word "jig." In his 1959 book, *Up From Liberalism*, Buckley responded to an African nationalist, saying, "Your people, sir, are not ready to rule themselves. Democracy, to be successful, must be practiced by politically mature people among whom there is a consensus on the meaning of life within their society."[7] In his next breath, Buckley turned to American civil rights leaders, saying, "In the South, the white community is entitled to put forward a claim to prevail politically because, for the time being anyway, the leaders of American civilization are white—as one would certainly expect given their preternatural advantages, of tradition, training, and economic status."[8]

In a 1961 article in the nationally prominent *Saturday Review*, Buckley answered the titular question of "Desegregation: Will It Work?" with his first, all-capitalized word: "NO." His rationale? For it to do so would require the dramatic intervention of the federal government, and conservatives should always oppose such an occurrence. Meanwhile, things weren't so bad in the South, he said. Martin Luther King, Jr., was simply "more sensitive, and so more bitter, than the average Southern Negro, and hence unqualified as a litmus of the Southern Negro's discontent."[9] Meanwhile, Buckley allowed two open racists, sociologist Ernest van den Haag and editor James J. Kilpatrick, to write long pieces on civil rights for *National Review* (it was a piece by van den Haag called "Negroes, Intelligence & Prejudice" on which Buckley had asked Mailer to comment in 1964). Both van den Haag and Kilpatrick became the magazine's authorities on the matter.

"My position on the moral aspect of segregation," Buckley wrote to a sixteen-year-old correspondent in 1964, is that "[s]egregation is morally wrong if it expresses or implies any invidious view of a race, not so if it intends or implies no such thing," and in the South in 1964, despite all the images of dogs attacking black children, of violence against black citizens seeking to vote, of hatred bubbling up against black students enrolling in schools, Buckley didn't think there was much racism in the South. He saw such images as simply an effort to preserve civilization. "It is for each man's conscience to decide in the specific case whether segregation is being practiced morally or immorally," he said.[10] It was, once more, an example of Buckley using sophisticated language to endorse the brutalities of segregation.

If Buckley's first argument against civil rights sounded good to white Southerners worried about the erosion of their long-standing privilege in the South, his second argument, which he developed only in 1964 and 1965, helped lure Northern whites to his cause. This second argument might be called the bootstraps argument. Its premise was that generation after generation of white immigrants had come to the United States and pulled themselves up by their bootstraps, working hard to give their children a good education, pushing the next generation into jobs and careers that ensured success. Why were African Americans the exception? Might there be something within the black community that prevented it from rising up, too?

As with his "not yet civilized" argument, there was more than a little willful ignorance here. The argument ignored the enormous structural inhibitions to black achievement, including the deliberate underfunding of schools in black neighborhoods (North and South), the devaluing of homes in black sections of towns (especially in the North), and the denial of benefits and promotions that had long been a primary way white immigrants had risen to middle-class status (especially in Northern-based unions and via the GI Bill).[11] It was exactly these things that President Johnson was referring to in his 1965 speech promoting affirmative action when he said, "You do not take a person who, for years, has been hobbled by chains and liberate him, bring him up to the starting line of a race and then say, 'you are free to compete with all the others,' and still justly believe that you have been completely fair."[12]

Despite Johnson's counterargument, Buckley knew working-class white people in the North were concerned about the decay of their cities and sensed that black people were recipients of special benefits solely because of their color. For them, the bootstraps argument had appeal. If their families had worked hard to succeed, why hadn't the same things happened for black people? The structural inhibitions to achievement were often hard to see.

It's unclear why Buckley took the anti–civil rights stance he did, especially because there were good conservative arguments in support of civil rights. Traditionalists, of course, privileged the right of law, which, after the *Brown* decision in 1954 and the Civil Rights Act of 1964, clearly outlawed segregation. Libertarians, meanwhile, argued that the government should not be creating or upholding laws that tell people whom they can or cannot sit next to—in fact, quite the opposite. Indeed, in 1956, three short pieces arguing as much appeared in *National Review*. If black people in Alabama wanted to create their own all-black bus system in order to oppose the discriminatory public bus system, the pieces argued in good libertarian prose, they should be allowed to do so.[13]

But Buckley scoffed at these arguments, defending "the right of the few to preserve, against the wishes of the many, a social order superior to that which the many, given their way, might promulgate." Siding with what was "civilized" made it "responsible" for white folks "to refuse to enfranchise the marginal Negro."[14] No other articles sympathetic to the civil rights movement appeared in *National Review*.

One plausible explanation for why Buckley acted the way he did is that he was simply refracting the racism he had inherited from his mother, an affluent Louisianan who reflected the worldview of her upbringing. Another plausible reason for Buckley's opposition to civil rights is that he knew how deeply ingrained racism was in America, and he was a political pragmatist. He had seen Southern politicians outdo one another in their allegiance to "massive resistance" to civil rights. He saw middle-of-the-road politicians voted out of office in favor of staunch segregationists. If he wanted to perpetuate his burgeoning conservative movement, he'd have to find a balance between opposing civil rights while not looking like an out-and-out racist. He'd have to clean up the arguments and make them safe for public consumption.

That's what he had done in *National Review*, and that's what he'd try to do in his debate against Baldwin.

Two Cambridge students spoke first, welcoming Baldwin and Buckley before spending five minutes advocating either side of the proposition. The student alongside Baldwin gave a fine speech, using statistics to prove that the American Dream had in fact come at the expense of the American Negro, whose plight and comparatively lower chances for success were indisputable.

The student on Buckley's side then gave a sterling talk, showing a keen awareness of the dynamics of the room. He said, over and over again, that the success of the American Dream has occurred "in spite of the suffering of the American Negro, but not because of it." He was careful to acknowledge that black suffering did in fact exist in America, and he repeated again and again that he was not arguing that civil rights should not come for black Americans ("that would be a very easy vote"), just that the American Dream was something that black people could now, at long last, access. In a revealing display, he discussed the income and educational achievements of African Americans, arguing that while they were significantly lower than those of white Americans, they were nonetheless higher per capita than the average Briton. This was not a failure of a people, but the story of a long-denied promise finally being fulfilled.

Buckley would have done well to listen to his co-combatant. Instead, he looked over his notes, appeared distracted, and smiled wistfully. His mind seemed elsewhere.

When Baldwin rose to go next, he first laid a trap for Buckley. Anticipating that Buckley would rely on his two main arguments against civil rights, Baldwin dismissed them in advance, saying, "The white South African or Mississippi sharecropper or Alabama sheriff has at bottom a system of reality which compels them really to believe when they face the Negro, that this woman, this man, this child must be insane to attack the system to which he owes his entire identity." Buckley, Baldwin was saying, was identical to the Alabama sheriff who just couldn't understand why someone would attack a culture that had allowed him to prosper. Buckley may or may not have been an outright racist, but that was beside the point. He simply couldn't understand the plight of the downtrodden because he himself had been so successful. If someone failed to succeed, Baldwin imagined Buckley thinking, this wasn't a social problem, it was their own. If Buckley tried to counter that argument, he would inevitably end up sounding like the Southern racists he was trying to justify.

But Baldwin had a lot more to offer than a trap. He talked movingly about what it was like to be a black child in America and to realize at age five, six, or seven that you were black, and therefore must confront an entire mountain of resistance to your very success as a human being. "It comes as a great shock," Baldwin said, "to discover that the flag to which you have pledged allegiance, along with everybody else, has not pledged allegiance to you. It comes as a great shock to see Gary Cooper killing off the Indians, and . . . that the Indians are you."[15]

Addressing the exact motion under consideration, Baldwin then argued that the harbors, ports, roads, and railroads of the country "could not conceivably be what they are if it had not been for cheap labor," and so, in a very real way, the American Dream had in fact come at the expense of the American Negro.

Then, in the most moving moment of the night, Baldwin said slowly: "I am speaking very seriously, and this is not an overstatement: *I* picked the cotton. *I* carried it to the market. *I* built the railroads under someone else's whip, for nothing, for *nothing*." He emphasized the *I* in every telling, the pronoun reverberating through the hall, and then echoing back through the loudspeakers in the overflow room. The echo made Baldwin's voice akin to the voice of God. "The Southern oligarchy which has still today so very much power in Washington, and therefore some power in the world was created by *my* labor and *my* sweat and the violation of *my* women and the murder of *my* children," Baldwin said. "This, in the land of the free, the home of the brave. None can challenge this statement. It is a matter of historical record."

Coming back to his trap, Baldwin talked with faux-generosity about how four hundred years of wrongdoing had actually been worse for Southern white folk than for black Southerners. "What happens to the poor white man's, the poor white woman's, mind?" he asked. How can a human do such despicable things to another human being? "Their moral lives have been destroyed by the plague called color." If only, he said, they would accept their history, accept the fact that black people have been contributing to the good of American society for four hundred years, accept the fact that "our ancestors are both black and white, that on that continent we are trying to forge a new identity, that we need each other, that I am not a ward of America, I am not an object of missionary charity, I am one of the people who built the country. Until this moment comes there is scarcely any hope for the American dream."

The television announcer sitting in a balcony above the proceedings had called Baldwin "the star of the evening," and he had lived up to expectations. As "the voice of actual experience," the announcer said when Baldwin concluded, he had delivered an incredibly moving account, not only revealing what it meant to be black in America, but arguing the point at hand. When Baldwin was done, the crowd rose as one, sustaining an applause that lasted several minutes. The announcer, who had been covering Cambridge Union debates for decades, had never seen a standing ovation before and wondered out loud if it was the first such ovation in the Union's 150-year history.

Baldwin took his seat before the applause died down and looked a bit stunned at the extended ovation. Eventually he rose again, waved his hand to the audience, and smiled. Buckley had his work cut out for him. Buckley would "need all his skill" to win the argument, the television announcer said. But sure enough, when Buckley stood up to speak, rather than listen to Baldwin's arguments and push back, he stepped directly into the role of the Alabama sheriff who just couldn't understand what Baldwin was saying. In a flash, Buckley morphed into Bull Connor.

"You cannot go to a university in the United States where Mr. Baldwin is not the toast of the town," Buckley said, making the point that the United States could not be nearly as bad as Baldwin was arguing because Baldwin himself had been so successful. He then added a churlish personal attack, suggesting that Baldwin had even affected a fake British accent in order to win over this particular crowd (the crowd booed Buckley for the first time here). And then, somewhat remarkably, Buckley said that, in order to argue the point at hand, he'd have to consider Baldwin the equal of a white man: "It is quite impossible in my judgment to deal with the indictments of Mr. Baldwin unless one is prepared to deal with him as a white man, unless one is prepared to say to him that the fact that your skin is black is utterly irrelevant to the arguments you raise."

At this moment, the camera cut to Baldwin, whose eyebrows rose up high, accentuating his already slightly protruding eyes to create the appearance of utter shock. *Did you just say what I think you said?* the look suggested. *Was whiteness so normative in America that you would equate being color-blind with being white?*

He had and it was. It was Buckley's inelegant way of suggesting

Baldwin might receive special treatment because of the color of his skin. All of a sudden, Buckley started to look like the Alabama sheriff Baldwin had warned everyone against.

Quickly realizing his normal mode of derisive attacks was not going to work (the boos increased as he proceeded), Buckley moved to his arguments. He began with the bootstraps claim. White people in America *do* care about black people, he said, but the structural problems that perpetuate racism are complex. And so, while white people are working out the politics of desegregation, black people had a duty to continue on their course of uplift. They had to rectify the "failure of the Negro community itself to make certain exertions which were made by other minority groups of the American experience." Irish, Italian, and German immigrants had all pulled themselves up by their bootstraps; it was time for African Americans to do the same. Citing Nathan Glazer and Daniel Patrick Moynihan's *Beyond the Melting Pot,* a recently published book about New York immigrant groups, Buckley pointed out that in 1900 there were 3,500 Negro doctors in America. In 1960, there were 3,900, an increase of just 400. Why so few? It wasn't because of discrimination in medical schools (a partial if not complete lie), but instead, "It is because the Negro's particular energy is not directed toward that goal." Instead of demanding laws from the federal government, Buckley thought Baldwin "should be addressing his own people and urging them to take advantage of those opportunities which do exist. And urging us [white Americans] to make those opportunities wider."

But if African Americans promised to bring "The Fire Next Time," as Baldwin's bestseller threatened, "our determination," Buckley said, "will be to wage war not only for the whites, but also for the Negroes," because white folks would act in the best interest of civilized people everywhere.

This was a subtle nod to Buckley's idea that black people in America weren't fit to rule, an argument that received jeers from the crowd. Didn't James Baldwin look civilized? One student even shouted, "One thing you might do, Mr. Buckley, is let them vote in Mississippi." To which Buckley responded: "What is wrong in Mississippi, sir, is not that not enough Negroes are voting but that too many white people are." The crowd laughed, thinking Buckley was joking. He put his arms on his hips and looked around the room, not quite understanding that they didn't know he was serious.

By the end, the students were not impressed by either of Buckley's main arguments, and they distanced themselves from his derisive attacks, which seemed little more than coded racism. They gave Buckley a polite applause, but no more.

When it came time to vote, Baldwin easily carried the day, 544 to 164.

It was a tremendous defeat, but Buckley didn't see it that way. In a conversation with Garry Wills shortly after the debate, Buckley told Wills, "I didn't give them one gaw-damn *inch*! They were infuriated [that he hadn't granted Baldwin's critique of America]. . . . But I walked out of there tall, so far as self-respect goes."[16] He felt his arguments were solid, and that the only reason he had lost was because Baldwin was a bigger celebrity.

On April 4, 1965, a little over a month after the debate in Cambridge, Buckley was invited to give a speech at the New York City Police Department's Holy Name Society's annual communion breakfast. The fact that the vast majority of New York City's cops were Catholic meant that the breakfast was the police department's largest social event of the year. Like most cops in America, New York's had been under siege in the mid-1960s. Not only had crime rates gone up in New York despite the addition of nearly seven thousand officers during the previous few years, but the increasingly violent resistance to civil rights in the South had made even police officers look generally suspect. The Rules' emphasis on authority was now under attack, even when it came to cops. Buckley was invited to the breakfast to prop up the cops. He did just that, but perhaps too emphatically, exposing once again his lack of empathy for those demanding civil rights. It would be the second time in a period of a few weeks that the issue of race would plague William F. Buckley, Jr.

As he began his speech to the police officers, he used as his opening gambit a riff on the recent civil rights marches in Selma, Alabama. A cadre of civil rights activists and mainstream religious leaders, black and white, had marched to protest the lack of black people registered to vote in Selma. Half the population there was black, while 99 percent of registered voters were white. The fifty-four-mile march from Selma to the capital city of Montgomery was intended to help local citizens register and put on display the injustices of segregation in the South. When the police and a collection of Klansmen joined together and ordered the marchers to halt on a narrow bridge halfway through the march, the protestors knelt down in prayer. They might not make it to the capital that day, but they would face their rebuke with God on their side. After a two-minute interval, the police and the Klansmen, some on horseback, started to clear the bridge. The effort swiftly became violent as cops and Klan members beat up the civil rights and religious leaders—with the media taking pictures the whole time.[17]

The violence spurred a second march a few days later. It was equally unsuccessful, although there was no violence. A judge refused to issue a permit for the march, and the law-abiding Martin Luther King, Jr., made an agreement with the local police. He would march to the bridge, kneel in prayer once again, then turn back to Selma. Some civil rights leaders thought King had lost his edge, but people all over the country admired his nonviolent determination. Some watched the events on TV, got in their cars, and drove to Alabama to help.

In response to the two unsuccessful marches, President Johnson himself took to the floor of Congress and delivered what many deem to be his best speech. In pushing Congress to pass a voting rights bill that would validate Selma's cause, Johnson said, "At times, history and fate meet at a single time in a single place to shape a turning point in man's unending search for freedom. So it was at Lexington and Concord [during the Revolution]. So it was at Appomattox [during the Civil War]. So it was last week in Selma, Alabama." Johnson began the speech referring to the civil rights protestors as "they," but by the end he had shifted to "we," making the cause for civil rights a cause for all Americans. "Their cause must be our cause too," he said. "Because it is not just Negroes, but really it is all of us, who must overcome the crippling legacy of bigotry and injustice. . . . And we shall overcome."[18]

In Congress, "There was an instant of silence," recalled Richard Goodwin, LBJ's speech writer, and then seventy-year-old congressman Emmanuel Celler jumped to his feet in applause. Soon all of Congress was standing. Senator Richard Russell, from staunchly segregated Georgia, called Johnson that night to say that even though he couldn't vote with him on the Voting Rights Act, it was the best speech he had ever heard a president give.[19] In Alabama, Martin Luther King. Jr., watched the speech on television and wept.

With the might of the federal government now behind them, a third, much larger, protest took place a week later. The permit for the march from Selma to Montgomery only allowed three hundred people to be walking at any one time, but more than eight thousand showed up to make the trek. They constantly had to alternate to ensure that only three hundred marchers were on the street at a time. When they reached Montgomery, the marchers were joined by thousands of others, as up to twenty-five thousand people took the final steps to the state capitol building. Several thousand military police, U.S. marshals, and federalized Alabama National Guardsmen lined the streets to ensure the march's success. The marchers had made it to Montgomery.

The Klan had its revenge, though. Immediately after the march, Klan members hunted down and murdered a white Catholic housewife from Detroit named Viola Gregg Liuzzo, who had been spurred to Selma after watching the violence of the first march on television. Civil rights "was everybody's fight," she told her husband as she packed her car and headed to Selma. She was murdered on an Alabama back road while driving young black activists home. The Klan targeted her specifically in an attempt to ward off Northern assistance for the movement. An undercover informer ratted out the murderers and justice was eventually served, but it came far too late.

The Selma March, with its highly religious atmosphere, its national exposure, its violence, and its somber success, was the emotional peak of the civil rights movement, a moment, if there was one, that justified all the work that had been done—and put on display the work that remained. It was, in short, a poor event for Buckley to use to prop up the New York City police.

But Buckley didn't see it coming. He began his Holy Name speech more or less justifying Liuzzo's murder: "So the lady drove down a stretch of lonely road in the dead of night," said Buckley, a bit too casually, "sharing the front seat with a young Negro identified with the protesting movement, and got killed." Who should be surprised at that?[20] "Why, one wonders, was this a story that occupied the front pages from one end of the country to another, if newspapers are concerned with the unusual, the unexpected?" Sure, "the lady" didn't deserve to get killed, but by going to Montgomery, Buckley seemed to be saying, she had brought it on herself.

Buckley then segued from the murder to the civil rights movement in general. When the newspapers told the story of what happened on the bridge, Buckley said, they failed to account for the restraint the police had initially shown. They had, after all, waited several minutes after ordering the marchers to disband before they cleared the bridge. And anyway, the protestors were the ones deliberately disobeying orders. Perhaps the police were a tad overzealous, Buckley said, but that didn't make them outlaws. They were the ones protecting tradition in the face of lawless calls for individual rights. "You must know that you will be hated for doing your duty," he told the police at the Holy Name breakfast, "and be reviled by those who misrepresent you. But bear this in mind, that there are the two worlds I speak of, and that though the voices of the one [the liberals] seem sometimes so very much noisier than the voices of the other [Buckley's movement on the right], that other world, the world of sensible men and women, looks on you with pride and gratitude."[21]

It was unclear how much those in attendance applauded his words about Selma, but the cops did appreciate his respect for their work. At the end of the speech, he received a sustained ovation. Many in the audience thought he had spoken the truth.

The assessment in the press was much harsher. They were aghast that Buckley would try to defend the actions of the police in Selma. That was little more than Klan-orchestrated, police-assisted violence against people who were simply demanding the right to vote. The *New York Times* headline read: "Buckley Praises Police of Selma." A *New York Post* editorial read: "Large disquieting issues are stirred by the ovation some 6,000 New York policemen accorded a defense of the Selma police force . . . delivered by William Buckley, Jr., the noted thunderer of right-wing extremism. . . . The ordeals of police service in these times in no way justify the salvos of applause that greeted the impassioned apologia for the Selma possemen recited by Buckley [in his] spirited whitewash of Southern police terrorism."[22] Every paper drew blood.

Buckley was surprised, thinking the liberal press had done it again, misquoting and misinterpreting him. In his recollection, the cops may have cheered his speech, but no one applauded Liuzzo's death. He vowed to prove the papers wrong.

Buckley soon discovered the speech had been recorded by one of the fathers of the Holy Name Society. Buckley immediately called a press conference while a *National Review* staffer collected the tape (which no one had yet heard). The harried staffer arrived to find a completely full press conference. Everyone leaned in as the tape began. But then, right at the crucial moment when Buckley began to discuss Selma, the player jammed. Everyone leaned in further. They waited. And waited. It took more than ten minutes to repair the player (an act performed by one of the cameramen from the press), and when it was finally fixed a vital thirty seconds were missing. It all looked a bit suspicious. Nonetheless, Buckley thought the portions of the tape that remained exonerated him. The press, he felt, needed to retract their hateful stories about cops cheering on murder.

The press did no such thing. The stories that came out the following day were just as bad as the previous ones. There were a few corrections to bits and pieces, fixing the work of a journalist working on the fly and misquoting a rapidly spoken voice. But there was not a single apology.

Searching for a lifeline, Buckley sent the transcript to Roy Wilkins, executive director of the NAACP, suggesting that Wilkins' earlier comments condemning Buckley were out of line and that the transcripts proved it. Wilkins was unmoved, saying the full text of the speech provoked "even more cause for alarm."[23]

Buckley was at a loss. He didn't know what he had done wrong. He felt his argument was sound. He thought he was being deliberately misunderstood. More than that, though, Buckley's own sense of righteousness, which had given him the confidence to do all the work he had done to prune and bind together the various strands of American conservatism, didn't allow him to recognize the error of his ways. His profound sense of confidence, grounded in his childhood, his faith, and his talent, didn't allow him to think he could be wrong, or that his actions might be hurtful to those who didn't deserve it. If welfare recipients only worked, he thought, if black people only pulled themselves up, they wouldn't be in the positions they were. It was inconceivable to him that his arguments might be wrong. He didn't recognize that supporting the Klan-backed police could be in any way problematic when it was done on behalf of something he could so easily justify.

In a moment of true friendship, Mailer was there to help. "Dear Bill," wrote Mailer. "I write you this letter in great envy. I think you are going finally to displace me as the most hated man in American life. And of course that position is bearable only if one is number one. To be the second most hated man in the picture will probably prove to be a little like working behind a mule for years."

Buckley recognized his friend's humor, and insight.

But Mailer quickly got to the point: ". . . which brings me to your address before the police department's Holy Name Society." Mailer had been in Alaska doing research for a book he was planning to write about how technology and corporate capitalism were wasting the lives of American youth when the story about Buckley thumbing his nose at the civil rights movement hit the press. When Mailer came back to New York, he got his "first inkling in the *New York Post* that some sort of bomb had gone off."[24]

"I was not surprised," continued Mailer, "when I read your speech today to find that it was literate, moderate in relation to your own position, and felicitously phrased. And of course I don't agree with your fundamental premise. On that I think you're all wrong." Giving his own take, Mailer described the "extraordinary tortured psyche" of the police, who actually make on-the-spot judgments about right and wrong, about when to press an issue and when to back off, knowing violence is always lurking. Dealing with police was a grey area, and Buckley had missed all that, falling into the same trap as the liberals of seeing everything in black and white, and then righteously defending his position without admitting possibilities for growth. "There's no doubt in my mind," Mailer continued, "that the newspapers misquoted you shamefully, and the net result of that is to deepen one's sense of an oncoming disaster; for I think humanly it could only drive you further into some of your own most charming surrealisms." He hoped Buckley wouldn't retreat back to his core of supporters, back to being a big man in a small pond.

Buckley, for once, needed to learn: "[L]isten," Mailer wrote, "I think our public debating days are probably over—for a time at least. As wrestlers we are now both villains, and that excites no proper passions. Still, it may open something interesting—which is that the two of us have a long careful private discussion one night, because I think in all modesty there's much in your thought which is innocent of its own implications and there's much surplus in mine which could profitably be sliced away by the powers of your logic." He knew (and hoped) Buckley's politics weren't intended to be mean-spirited or evil. The conservative movement had a lot of good ideas in it, Mailer thought, but these ideas risked being clouded by the "innocent implications" of its premises, most especially its unnecessary lack of compassion for the downtrodden. Mailer was trying to tell Buckley that his hatred of the Liberal Monster had led him to support the Klan. And that, Mailer said, was a shame.

After writing the letter, Mailer felt compelled to protect himself from what he knew would be Buckley's anger about the Holy Name incident. He hastily added to the bottom of his letter: "And you, esteemed scallawag [sic]—I can't imagine why you would ever wish to quote from this letter, but if the impulse should take you, please clear it with me first. I say this with pain, because I hate to get in the way of your only vice. . . . Incorrigibly yours, Norman."[25]

Mailer knew that Buckley would try to write his way toward justification, and that having a juicy quotation from a noted lefty like Mailer would lend support to Buckley's claim that he had been misquoted. Mailer was also aware of the lack of nuance in the press, and that if he were quoted as being sympathetic to Buckley, he might be seen as opposing civil rights completely.

It turned out Mailer was wise to make the request. A few days later Buckley wrote back: "Thanks for your warm and amusing letter. I have a lot more to teach you than merely how to reason." Buckley then added, "Can I quote that part of the letter that refers to the 'shameful destinations' of the press? Corrigibly, Bill."[26]

Mailer never answered, which Buckley understood to mean no.

Sure enough, when Buckley wrote his take on the Holy Name incident a few months later, he included his entire speech, and

offered a heavy dose of justification (alas, he *still* didn't get it). But
to ensure that Mailer knew he hadn't been quoted, Buckley sent
Mailer a copy of the book in which the essay appeared, having
first inscribed in the index, next to Mailer's name (where he knew
Mailer would look first), "Hi!"

The index revealed that Mailer had been quoted a few times,
but not concerning the Holy Name Society.[27]

It would take Buckley nearly all his life to figure out that his position against civil rights was little more than dressed-up racism.
Only in 2004 did he come to regret his position, answering a
Time magazine question about whether there were any previous
positions he had come to regret: "Yes," he said. "I once believed
we could evolve our way up from Jim Crow. I was wrong: federal
intervention was necessary."[28] But if Buckley really did believe
America could "evolve [its] way up from Jim Crow," he certainly
didn't preach it in the 1950s or '60s. Instead, he championed segregation under the guise of "states' rights" and even endorsed
the use of violence in order to maintain white rule. He had done
little more than dress up the language of racism so it could be
used at dinner parties and in the press without offending modern
sensibilities.

In a surprising twist, although Buckley's opposition to civil
rights worked to the detriment of the nation in general, it nonetheless helped him locate a surprising new base of support for his
conservative movement—the white working classes in the North.
In 1964, 60 percent of white men voted Democratic. Four years
later, after all those civil rights laws, all those challenges to The
Rules, all those challenges to the understanding of what it meant
to be an American, that percentage plummeted to forty-one. And,
said Kevin Phillips, one of the prime observers of this growing
conservative constituency, "the principal force which broke up
the Democratic (New Deal) Coalition . . . was the Negro socio-
economic revolution."[29] Buckley's dressed-up racism may have

cost the nation some of its integrity, but it also helped sustain the Republican coalition he was trying to build and maintain. This became altogether clear when Buckley, preposterously and against all odds, decided to do something unthinkable for the most hated man in America: run for mayor of New York City.

1

Catching All the Falling Bodies

I n the wake of Goldwater's huge loss in 1964, conservatives seemed to be getting crushed everywhere: socially, economically, and in the voting booth. LBJ's landslide victory over Goldwater had been followed by the passage of several banner laws, ushering in the high point of American liberalism. The Buckleyite moment seemed to have passed and failed. Indeed, in Congress, conservatives ran scared as both parties seemed to have largely accepted liberal principles and appeared eager to do the president's bidding. The fires on the right and the left might be burning, but in 1965 the liberal center still held firm.

But Buckley wasn't worried. He knew that part of his quest in the 1960s was to orchestrate a takeover of the Republican Party, pulling it away from moderate conservatives who were willing to kowtow to the liberal line and placing it in the hands of firmer conservatives, those who embraced the ideas Buckley prioritized in *National Review*. The Goldwater campaign had been one brick in the wall. Shortly after Goldwater's defeat, Buckley imagined himself placing another.

It was hard to know if the foundation was ready yet. Throughout 1965 the economy continued its stellar postwar boom, as GDP climbed for the sixteenth straight year to its highest point in his-

tory. The country needed to be reminded by Michael Harrington
in 1962 that poverty still existed in the United States. When LBJ
lit the National Christmas Tree in December 1964, he said, "These
are the most hopeful times in all the years since Christ was born in
Bethlehem. . . . Today, as never before, man has in his possession
the capacities to end war and preserve peace, to eradicate poverty
and share abundance, to overcome the diseases that have afflicted
the human race and permit all mankind to enjoy their promise in
life on this earth."[1]

This optimism masked a tremendous crisis that lay just beneath
the surface—one Buckley hoped to take advantage of. America's
cities had taken a series of hits in the 1950s and early 1960s. The
famous suburbanization of postwar America, with all those Levit-
towns idealized and laughed about on Leave It to Beaver, helped
begin the hollowing out of cities. Industries had begun to take
advantage of new transportation and communication innovations
in order to depart the union-heavy cities along the Northeastern
seaboard for the South and the West. The middle class began to
leave, too, as cities became balkanized between rich and poor.

New York City was the poster child for this dark side of liberalism. More than a million middle-class residents, almost all of
them white, left the city between 1955 and 1965, mostly for the
green suburban ring encircling the metropolis. The city's economy began to look like an hourglass, with a wealthy elite living a
fortressed existence in a few select neighborhoods while the rest
of the city became increasingly slum-like. Tax revenues departed
with middle-class whites, too, and many schools closed or suffered
deep declines. Real estate taxes shot up by 75 percent to pay for
programs already in place, but that led businesses to move out.
When they left, they took their tax payments with them. The city's
deficits spiraled from $92 million in 1964 to $256 million in 1965.
New York had the highest rate of unemployment of any metropolis in the nation. Violent crime doubled; property crimes nearly
tripled. Adding salt to the wound was a severe water shortage that

eventually resulted in New York City being declared a Federal Disaster Area. Signs from the Water Department appeared: "Don't Flush for Everything." The city was in trouble.

The dark undertone of the crisis was racism. Fear that black people might integrate white neighborhoods led many of the million middle-class whites to leave in the first place. In 1965, New York City elementary schools would report that, for the first time in their history, a majority of their students were black or Puerto Rican. The previous summer, the killing of a fifteen-year-old black teenager by a New York City police officer had touched off a week-long riot in Harlem that left one dead and as many as five hundred injured. The riots eventually spread all the way to Philadelphia and Chicago. After the 1964 Harlem Riot, any police action that occurred in New York's black neighborhoods seemed to threaten more violence.

A long January 1965 series in the *New York Herald Tribune* summed it up. Entitled, "New York, Greatest City in the World—and Everything Is Wrong with It," the article concluded: "For the poor, the aged, the Negro, the Puerto Rican, and the blue-collar worker who is unemployed because of automation and the exodus of business, New York today is a nightmare. . . . For the young and the middle-class white and Negro, New York has become a terrible place to live because of unsafe streets, poor schools, and inadequate housing. . . . And even for the wealthy—those who can afford the best—the air pollution, the traffic-clogged streets, and the violence have come to outweigh the delights afforded by New York's stores, restaurants, and cultural events."[2]

No politician could handle this perfect storm, and the only solution on offer was the Liberal Establishment's refrain about creating new programs, raising taxes, and spending more money. Let the bureaucrats take over, they suggested, using their rational gaze to reapportion the city's wealth and manipulate a solution to the crises from on high. Let them keep giving gifts that seemed to be satisfying no one.

John Lindsay's plan embodied all these liberal assumptions. Tall and good-looking with a toothy smile, Lindsay was an ambitious Republican congressman who sought the mayoralty in 1965, largely, it seemed, in order to raise his own public profile. The mayoralty was to be a stepping stone. "The District's Pride—The Nation's Hope" was the slogan in his campaign literature, which seemed to paper the entire city in the spring of 1965. When Lindsay announced his candidacy for mayor, his face appeared on the covers of *Time*, *Newsweek*, and *Look*. All were puff pieces. As *Life* put it, "With youthful verve and the long-legged grace of a heron, John Vliet Lindsay . . . strode into the race for Mayor of New York and Republicans all over the country broke into ear-to-ear smiles."[3]

New York had been run for more than a decade by Robert F. Wagner, a Democrat whose three terms were noted for bringing the Mets to New York, developing new housing projects and Lincoln Center, and breaking the stranglehold that the Tammany Hall political machine had had on New York's Democratic Party for the previous hundred years. When Wagner opted against a fourth term in 1965, the race was suddenly wide open. The Democrat who won his party's candidacy was Abe Beame, an accountant who had served as city budget director and city comptroller for the previous decade. But Beame was no politician. He had risen through the ranks of the Brooklyn wing of the Democratic Party machine, but had worked more as a behind-the-scenes numbers guy than as someone destined to be the standard-bearer. Still, when Wagner declined to run again, Beame was next in line. His speeches were uninspiring and pedantic. It became a real possibility that New York would elect a Republican mayor for the first time since Fiorello La Guardia left office twenty years earlier, in 1945.

Lindsay hoped to be that man. He was a liberal Republican and technocrat. He would eventually establish no less than twenty-five task forces to propose solutions to the city's problems, hire management consultants to parse City Hall operations, and bank analysts to study the budget—the experts would take over.[4] He had

special ire for Buckleyite conservatives, thinking they were little
more than reactionary Cold Warriors all too eager to court the
hand of racists. He disliked Barry Goldwater and everything the
gun-slinging Arizonan represented. Goldwater was on the wrong
side of history, Lindsay argued. The divide within the Republican
Party, he felt, was best solved by excising Buckley's wing and letting
the liberals retain control.

Buckley therefore held Lindsay in violation of all the Republican Party should stand for. Of course, Buckley was an equal-
opportunity hater of all liberal Republicans, but because Lindsay
was a national figure seeking to be mayor of what he considered
his city, Buckley carried special animus for Lindsay. "[P]olitically
he belongs in the Democratic Party," Buckley wrote of Lindsay.[5]
Lindsay responded by calling Buckley "the assassin from the
ultraright."[6]

In May 1965, immediately after Lindsay announced his candidacy, Buckley wrote a playful column entitled, "Mayor, Anyone?"
The column lambasted Lindsay for having no plan to save New
York City and no vision for the future. Task forces were fine, but
what did they accomplish? In fact, the only qualification Buckley
could find for Lindsay was "the brilliance of his teeth," adding par-
enthetically, "(Yes, that was a qualification solemnly remarked by
one major newspaper.)" Lindsay did have a gorgeous smile, was
forty-three, good-looking, six-foot-four, personable, and athletic.
But Buckley thought these were not significant qualifications for
office. Did Lindsay even recognize that "New York—and other
major cites—[have] become, increasingly, unpleasant places to
live in"? Someone had to clean up the mess, and, thought Buckley,
Lindsay was not up to the task.

In his column, Buckley outlined a ten-point plan for any future
candidate. The program included creative solutions to important
problems like crime (make parents legally responsible for juvenile
delinquents and allow neighborhoods that developed self-financed
patrols to receive tax breaks); drugs (legalize them for adults, but

require users to see a doctor before using); race (give minority-owned businesses tax breaks if they remain in depressed neighborhoods); traffic (no commercial vehicle loading or unloading between the hours of 8 a.m. and 4 p.m.); gambling ("Legalize it. Anybody who wants to bet anything with anybody may do so . . . and did you notice the workout yesterday of Lucky Sadler who is running in the 5th at Roosevelt on Election Day?"); and welfare (work programs for welfare recipients, with mothers of children under fourteen and invalids excepted). The eleventh point in his ten-point plan was: "Any election returns suggesting that the mayoralty candidate running on this program has been defeated will be challenged at the courts."[7]

Just as Mailer had done for JFK in 1962 and 1963, now it was Buckley's turn to offer a concrete platform to help solve the country's problems. It was a reflection of how deeply both men thought about the life of the nation—and how highly they thought of their ability to speak to it. *National Review*, which often reprinted Buckley's columns, reprinted this one, too. It even put a teaser on the magazine's cover that read: "Buckley for Mayor." According to Buckley, it was his sister, Priscilla, who had suggested the teaser. Buckley only allowed it because "no reader in his right mind would be likely to infer from the streamer that Buckley was actually announcing that he would run for Mayor and that this was his trial balloon."[8] Others were less certain, thinking this was Buckley showing a little ankle, seeing if anyone was interested. If so, it worked.

Barking at the moon in New York City at the time were the two founders of the Conservative Party of New York State, Kieran O'Doherty and J. Daniel Mahoney. They were the men who three years earlier had rekindled New York's Conservative Party with Buckley's help. They had so far run no-name candidates whose campaigns were ignored. But this was okay, because the point was not yet to win elections but to advance the conservative arguments Buckley had been making for years.

In 1965 they were as usual having a hard time filling their slate, with O'Doherty himself having already run for New York Senate, which, Buckley argued, had killed O'Doherty's chances of becoming a partner at his law firm. Finding candidates was always tough because, as Buckley put it, "the mission ahead [was] didactic and disciplinary, the personal inconvenience enormous, and the retaliatory animus high."[9]

When O'Doherty and Mahoney saw the "Buckley for Mayor" teaser on the cover of *National Review,* they took notice. Thinking strategically, they asked Buckley to help locate a conservative candidate to run for office. They suggested *National Review* publisher William Rusher, who was becoming a television personality. Rusher immediately said no. Buckley may have hoped Rusher would reply that way (at least that's how Rusher interpreted the whole thing), because shortly afterward, Buckley himself decided to run. He called it his "jury duty" for the movement. But this was mostly faux reluctance. Buckley was eager to play the role of candidate: "What the hell," he told his biographer later, "this is kind of interesting."[10]

Buckley of course loved the spotlight. But he also felt he could articulate conservative ideas better than anyone else. If the idea was not to win but to air ideas, who better than himself? In addition, there was the opportunity to take potshots at Lindsay. It was plausible to think that maybe Buckley could steal enough Republican votes to prevent Lindsay from winning, thus ensuring that liberalism would remain the credo of the Democrats while making the Republicans the voice of conservatism.[11]

Buckley sought Pat's approval. She gave it reluctantly. Then he went to O'Doherty and Mahoney. They were delighted. They were less delighted when Buckley said he would not be a full-time candidate. He had *National Review* to edit, and three newspaper columns to write each week, and lectures to help finance the juggernaut. Plus, in a week there was a sailing race to Nova Scotia. After that, he'd work nights and weekends as a candidate. He'd release position papers when he could, hold a press conference or two, and debate other candidates when he was available. But he wouldn't stump. The point was to publicize alternative ideas, not run a serious campaign. Frustrated, O'Doherty and Mahoney nonetheless accepted Buckley's conditions, and so, in that haphazard way, William Buckley became a bona fide candidate for mayor of New York City.

True to his promise, Buckley drafted a nine-page statement announcing his intention to run. Fifty reporters showed up at the Overseas Press Club and listened as Buckley, still just thirty-nine, clad in a light grey suit, playfully plunged his hands into his pockets and presented his candidacy: "I am a Republican," he said, but "because the Republican designation is not, in New York, available nowadays to anyone in the mainstream of Republican opinion . . . I have declared my availability to the Conservative Party."

While he made his hatred for Lindsay clear, he also reflected on the larger problems within the country. The "major candidates," Buckley said, "while agreeing that New York City is in crisis, are resolutely opposed to discussing the reasons why it is in crisis. Their failure to do so . . . is symptomatic of a political disease that rages in New York, and threatens to contaminate democratic government everywhere in the United States." Their solutions? "The passion of the last generation has been to refer our problems to extra-local government agencies, most particularly the Federal Government," Buckley said, adding, "increasingly the government of New York becomes the vassal of the government at Washington" and New Yorkers were stuck "approaching Washington as supplicants, begging it to return to the City some of the income it has taken from it." Against this situation, "someone, somewhere, ought to speak out. I propose to do so."[12]

After his speech, which went on to echo the sentiments of his ten-point plan, the *New York Post* asked Buckley—who everyone knew lived in Connecticut and only owned an apartment in New York City (a triplex no less!)—how long he had lived in New York.

Buckley had clearly prepared for such questions, as he answered: "I have lived in New York longer than Bobby Kennedy did when he decided to run [for Senate]." When he was asked if he really wanted to be mayor, he paused, flashed his famous smile, pulled out a cigar, lit a match, and, a perfect instant before lighting it, said, "I have never considered it." When asked how many votes he expected to get, he replied, "Conservatively speaking, one." And who would that be? "My secretary."

The humor continued. At his second press conference, Buckley was asked what he would do if he won, and he replied, "Demand a recount." He later refined his answer, saying he would also rush over to the sidewalk below the *New York Times* to catch all the falling bodies.[13]

A few months later, in October 1965, Mailer accepted an assignment to cover the mayoral campaign for the *Village Voice*, and one suspects it was so he could write paragraphs like this about his friend Bill Buckley:

> . . . no one I suspect is more majestically unsuited for here becoming Mayor since it is possible Old Bill has never been in a subway in his life. . . . Buckley's personality is the highest Camp we are ever going to find in a Mayoralty. No other actor on earth can project simultaneous hints that he is in the act of playing Commodore of the Yacht Club, Joseph Goebbels, Robert Mitchum, Maverick, Savonarola, the nice prep-school kid next door, and the snows of yesteryear. If he didn't talk about politics—if he was just the most Camp gun ever to walk into Gunsmoke, I'd give up Saturday nights to watch him. But he does talk about politics time to time, and his program for New York is to drop an atom bomb posthaste on the atom bomb of the Chinese.

"A man like that," Mailer concluded, "cannot be kept from getting an enormous minority vote."[14]

It was a great line. Buckley himself loved it so much he codified it into the historical record by adding it to the book he eventually wrote about his campaign, *The Unmaking of a Mayor*.[15] There were of course profound insights into William F. Buckley there, too. Buckley *was* most of those things, a constellation of conservative ideals, able to keep it all together by the power of his personality. Just like Bret Maverick on TV's Western show *Maverick*, Buckley was something of a libertarian cowboy, constantly suspicious of the federal government. But he was also a traditionalist—"the snows of yesteryear"—who sought to retain what was great about a bygone era. He recalled the blissful simplicity of his childhood, and he thought the country could learn a lot by looking back. Buckley was also a grand propagandist for his ideas; okay, likening him to Joseph Goebbels was a bit extreme, but the point was clear: Buckley was the salesman par excellence for modern conservatism.

Buckley was also a devout Catholic calling for Christian renewal, just like Girolamo Savonarola, a fifteenth-century Dominican friar who got the Medicis tossed out of Florence and (temporarily) created what he hoped would be a New Jerusalem, rich and mighty, morally stringent, the center of the Christian world. Paralleling Savonarola, Buckley's hardheaded advocacy for the Cold War was nothing if not a religious crusade against a perceived Antichrist. Of course, Buckley probably hoped that he, unlike Savonarola, would not be burned at the stake for his efforts.

Buckley was also silky smooth ("the nice prep-school kid next door") with a huge vocabulary and a casually ruffled elegance that appealed to legions of admirers. But he possessed a dark undertone that championed the continuation of certain unsavory aspects of American life, like its racism and its poverty. Robert Mitchum had just appeared as a Southern rapist antihero in *Cape Fear*, and there was that sailing reference—"Commodore of the Yacht Club"—an inside joke. But the reference also suggested an elite America, a world of white male privilege where aristocracies of wealth concocted a life unknowable to most.

Buckley loved the irreverence of Mailer's *Village Voice* quotation. In a personal letter to Mailer, he only complained about the word "Camp": "Either you don't know what 'camp' means, or I don't know what it means. Needless to say, the former is more likely."[16]

When New York City's newspapers went on strike in the middle of the campaign, election coverage moved from newspapers (which often thoughtfully disagreed with much of Buckley's platform) to television, which played perfectly to Buckley's demeanor and wit. Buckley became the star of the four televised mayoral debates, succeeding in every instance at making both of the mainstream candidates, John Lindsay and Abe Beame, look inept. In one instance, Buckley listened to each of the other two candidates claim that he was the properly qualified candidate and the *other* was a mess. Buckley jumped in: "Now, if in fact long public service entitles you to make accurate judgments about each other, it would seem to me a fair inference that both of you should disappear from the public scene."[17] Buckley didn't appear as an angry conservative in the mold of the reactionary Birchers or the unfeeling Ayn Rand or the frightening Barry Goldwater; he came across as funny, sensible, and likeable.

The press loved Buckley's humorous side. "He is more fun to listen to than most professional comedians," said one. "Love him or hate him," wrote another, "TV fans found it difficult to turn off a master political showman. His rolling eyes, deft handling of the English language and razor-sharp debating techniques were exciting to watch. Even tall, handsome and personable Lindsay found himself being upstaged time and time again." Murray Kempton, a veteran newsman who Buckley later named as one of his best friends but who nonetheless supported Lindsay for mayor, compared Buckley to a work of art: "To attempt to convey the tone of his press conferences by quotation would be to pretend to play a Mozart glass harp concerto by printing the notes."

But Kempton also recognized that Buckley and Lindsay were playing different games—Lindsay a short-term game to win an election, Buckley a long-term quest to change American life: "Mr. Buckley has said," wrote Kempton, ". . . how surprised he is that John Lindsay has no sense of humor. But he is thinking about the aesthetics of a different game. A debate between him and say, Norman Mailer, is really a contest to see who can save the other's soul. But the great candidates [like Lindsay] do not think about souls; to them, the other man is simply an object."[18]

With favorable if not-quite-serious coverage in the press and his playful disparagement of the powers that be, Buckley started to do well in the polls, receiving as high as 20 percent of prospective votes. To his surprise, however, much of his support was coming from an unexpected, and perhaps unwanted, source—the white working class.

When he decided to run, Buckley had thought he was going to appeal to anti-tax professionals tired of the bureaucratic nonsense imposed by the Great Society, or maybe educated people frustrated by the increasingly cavalier breaking of The Rules. Instead, Buckley was attracting construction workers disdainful of politics in general and white workers threatened by the inroads of the civil rights movement. Nixon would later call these hard hats his "Silent Majority." In 1965, they were called Buckleyites.

Neal Freeman, Buckley's twenty-five-year-old aide-de-camp, later said, "I suppose that I was expecting our supporters to be *National Review* types—car dealers, academic moles, literate dentists, dissenting students, whatever. As soon as we hired halls, though, we learned that [Buckley] was speaking for the people who made the city go—corner-store owners, cops, schoolteachers, first-home owners, firemen, coping parents."[19] These people were angry and worried. They were watching jobs slip away and were being pinched by the transformations of the time. They didn't necessarily have a principled beef with the Liberal Establishment; they were simply looking for a lifeboat to carry them to safety as the times they were a-changin'. Was the decline of industry a dangerous prospect for them? Sure it was. Was it easier to blame black workers and the new affirmative-action guidelines than the larger structures of corporate finance? Of course. And who lambasted the current order with humor and style? Who seemed to be one of those guys but was instead speaking for them? Why, William F. Buckley, Jr. The white working class did not sound like reactionaries when Buckley was their mouthpiece. They sounded like Yale-educated political philosophers.

Their actions sometimes belied their aspirational yearnings. When Lindsay went to New York's working-class outer boroughs, his car was almost always mobbed by Buckley supporters who aggressively called Lindsay a "fake," a "traitor," or a "communist." These protestors were often more prevalent than Lindsay's supporters. Lindsay eventually even hired a team of bodyguards—called "Lindsay's Raiders"—to protect him from the Buckleyites. At one stop in Coney Island, a heckler ripped Lindsay's shirt with his Buckley placard. When the Lindsay campaign sought police protection, they discovered the police were wearing BUCKLEY FOR MAYOR buttons.[20]

If the press loved Buckley's wit and humor, it hated the Buckley campaign's embrace of this working-class anger, about which the candidate himself seemed blissfully unaware. Walter Lippmann, one of the most imperious of American editorialists (and a Lindsay supporter), worried that Buckley was "determined to wreck the [Republican] party in order to rule the wreckage." Buckley, thought Lippmann, was taking the politics of rage too far. Meanwhile, columnist Joseph Alsop wrote, "[Buckley] is one of the people who have been trying for years to impose a new and thoroughly nasty pattern on American politics. . . . By all sorts of hints, and very shrewdly, Buckley has appealed to these people's prejudices. . . . A big Buckley vote, therefore, such as the wiseacres now expect, could set back the cause of sanity and decency."[21]

But, still, Buckley continued to gain support. It never occurred to him that the working-class whites he was attracting had been classic New Deal Democrats who were increasingly disaffected by the workings of the state. If Buckley stole too many of these Democratic voters from Abe Beame, he could, ironically enough, ensure a victory for Lindsay. Unaware of the source of his growing support, however, Buckley never contemplated this outcome.

Over the course of the campaign, Buckley spelled out what he would do as mayor. He proposed cutting down traffic by building a huge aerial bike lane, twenty feet above the ground and twenty feet wide, above Second Avenue from First Street all the way to One Hundred Twenty-Fifth. All this biking would cut down traffic and get New Yorkers healthy.

He also proposed higher prices for toll roads, and charging out-of-state cars (whose owners didn't pay local taxes) more than local vehicles. He proposed universal water metering; fees for using most government services; and simplified business taxes using a single, European-style value-added tax (VAT), which would take a business's gross revenues minus the cost of all previously taxed goods and services, and then tax that. Small businesses wouldn't need an accountant to manage a VAT. It would be easy.

Buckley made other individualistic free-market proposals, including having Walt Disney convert the Flushing Meadows fairgrounds that was then being used for the 1964–65 World's Fair into what Buckley called "Disneyland East." It would create jobs and tax revenue. Drug addicts, meanwhile, were to be quarantined from the rest of the population, while "chronic welfare cases" would be relocated outside city limits.

How feasible were these solutions? Not very. What city would willingly take New York's chronic welfare cases? None. Unless Buckley meant to establish city-owned camps where poor people would be forced to live, the proposal was a nonstarter. While some of his ideas were just risible—everyone laughed at bike lanes and "Disneyland East"—others proved toxic. Buckley's opponents quickly labeled his plan to relocate welfare cases "concentration camps." They played on the image of hard-hearted conservatism. As with his stance on race, Buckley was once again unaware of the consequences of some of his ideas.

Nevertheless, in the end, what came through from the Buckley campaign was not only a wild collection of creative if unfeasible ideas to complicated problems, but also the notion that New Yorkers needed to start taking responsibility for their city to clean up the mess. Buckley wanted to crush government bureaucracies and cut the city's debts. He did not want the government responsible for defining the good life or for telling people how to live. Governments, he was saying, should only deal with collective problems that were too big for individuals to handle.

When it came to air and water pollution, for instance, Buckley wrote: "Here is a legitimate concern of government—a classic example of the kind of thing that government should do, according to [Abraham] Lincoln's test, because the people cannot do it themselves." At other times, he made similar statements: "Obviously the power of government is needed, for instance, to control the traffic problems in New York. . . . Obviously the power of government is needed to decide such questions as what to do when the water reservoirs begin to empty. The question is whether the necessity to increase the powers of government—yesterday there was no traffic problem, no water scarcity—for specific purposes, has resulted in unnecessary increases in state power for general purposes."[22]

Above all, Buckley argued that government should be used to preserve the things that made a city livable. Throughout the campaign, he described New York City's beauty as one of "its principal assets" and "a public trust." To protect that beauty, he wanted to eliminate "the schematic designs upon [the city] of the social abstractionists who do not look up from their drawing boards for long enough to recognize what it is that makes for human attachments—to little buildings and shops, to areas of repose and excitement: to all those abstractions that so greatly inconvenience the big-think social planners. The obsession with urban renewal must, in due course, be tranquilized, before the City loses its hold on human sentiment."[23]

Jane Jacobs couldn't have put it better. Or Norman Mailer.

Watching the election from the wings, Mailer loved Buckley's campaign. Buckley was performing exactly the kind of existential politics Mailer had been hoping for. Most of his proposals were farcical, intended to make you think about larger problems within society. And even if Buckley's solutions sounded harsh and unfeeling, at least they prompted you to think. Disneyland East? As absurd as it sounded, it was indisputably an original idea. Preserving the beauty of the city by building a giant bike lane over Second Avenue? Mailer loved it.

Of course, when Buckley proposed some routine political thinking, Mailer called him out. "Running for Mayor has made you mellow," Mailer chided at one point, when Buckley showed signs of looking like a real candidate.[24] But most of the time, Mailer was pleased with the spectacle. Mailer even threatened to vote for him, which Buckley laughed off. "Yes, by all means we must meet in the fall," Buckley wrote Mailer at one point, "and well enough in advance of election day so that I can persuade you not to come out for me for Mayor, which would be quite disastrous."[25]

"Dear Bill," Mailer responded, "Don't worry, even for a smile from my beloved Patsy I could not come out for you."[26]

At a certain point, Buckley offered to give Mailer "the final word on the subject" of the election.[27] Mailer jumped at the chance. "Does that mean I could write a few hundred words for your column?"[28] But Buckley was joking. Mailer never ghostwrote a column for Buckley.

Right before election night, Buckley made a bet with his brother and his campaign manager about how many votes he would get. Buckley guessed 340,000, his campaign manager 280,000, and his brother 400,000.[29] Buckley turned out to be remarkably close.

Despite polling as high as 20 percent, Buckley ended up winning 13.4 percent, or 341,226 votes.

That was a lot of votes, and Buckley was pleased. But the success was tempered by the fact that he hadn't stolen enough votes from Lindsay to prevent him from winning. Lindsay got 43.3 percent of the vote to Abe Beame's 39.5 percent. Buckley finished third.

For Buckley though, the revelation that his ideas were attracting a certain portion of the electorate was both troubling and delightful—and instructive for those who came later. In the end, Buckley had earned a large number of votes from the white working-class, mostly German and Irish Catholics, but also broader swaths of workers generally. Since Franklin Roosevelt's New Deal, these voters had been reliably Democratic, listening to their guts, to their union bosses, and to the party machines that supported the Democratic Party when it came time to vote. But when Buckley ran for mayor, these voters abandoned the Democratic Party and voted Conservative or Republican, many for the first time. If the Republicans ever produced a truly conservative candidate, these working-class voters would be Republicans. It was an instructive lesson for the future. In the meantime, however, and as no one expected, it was Buckley who had stolen these votes from Beame, thereby handing the election to Lindsay.[30]

Despite Buckley's reticence about serving as the voice of the angry white working class, he still took great joy when the *New York Times* invited him to its offices for an interview just a few days before the election. Buckley knew it would turn into an ambush (it did), but as he walked from the sidewalk up to "the august quarters" of the *Times*, he had "to pause every step or two to shake gratefully the outstretched hands of porters, clerks, secretaries, elevator men, who, spotting me, wanted to wish me well, several of them whispering to me their subversive resolve to vote for me the following Tuesday." Buckley had promised to clean up the place, and they thought that was exactly what was needed.[31] In them, Buckley saw the future of the Republican Party. As he interpreted it, the hunger for a candidate like him "was fueled in part by the long diet of blandness that had produced a body lacking in tone and coordination; but also by telling critiques of the liberal ideology." He called this new conservative concoction "the Goldwater effect," which, he concluded, "was not, in the experienced judgment of Mr. Theodore White [in *The Making of the President, 1964*], a freak geological tremor, unlikely to recur in another thousand years."

"Something," Buckley said, "was stirring."[32]

Mailer, unlike nearly everyone else, had predicted this exact outcome. When he wrote about the Goldwater campaign of 1964, Mailer wondered, "Would the best of the young in every hick town, washed by the brainwater of the high school and the [American] Legion, come to join this conservative crusade because Goldwater made an appeal to freedom, to courage, to change?" Mailer shuddered at the thought. "What a swindle was in the making," he wrote, "what an extinction of the best in Conservative thought."[33] The politics of emotion seemed to be taking over.

Buckley was now confirming that fear. By tapping into the frustrations of the people, Buckley could not "be kept from getting an enormous minority vote," Mailer had written.[34] And so he did. As Mailer elaborated, "Of course, Buckley's votes will not come from people who even know the word 'Camp,' no, his sort of votes come from the kind of girls who want to work at Bell Telephone," the working-class, hourly wage-earners.[35] Even more than this, the feeling of resentment about liberalism's unfulfilled promises "has been cutting into the righteous wrath of all us Wagner-aged citizens—we are finally apathetic about the great dump in which we live, we laugh at Buckley, we laugh with him, we say let the city burn, let it burn, and Lindsay goes wrong, a little solemn, a little empty, too earnest much."[36] The anger and the fear of a changing America was no longer merely the possession of the downtrodden. It was spreading.

As 1965 went on, Buckley and Mailer had discussed getting together for a meal for months. "We owe you dinner, I'd like to make it a good one, so Beverly will be calling Patsy soon," Mailer wrote at one point, referring to his latest wife, Beverly Bentley. "Would you like to meet Norman Podhoretz, and Stephen Marcus of *Partisan Review*, at that time? To balance things out, perhaps we ought to invite some friends of yours at the same time, Brent Bozell, or anyone you'd care to name—you are, after all, much too much of a tiger if everyone's against you at once."[37]

Buckley replied: "Delighted. Yes I'd very much like to meet Mr. Podhoretz. Brent is never in town. Why not Jim Burnham, or Irving Kristol?"[38]

The dinner never happened; they were still too busy. Buckley was away for two weeks when the Mailers called, then the Mailers were out of town, then the Buckleys headed to the Caribbean, then the Mailers went skiing in Vermont, then the Buckleys left for Switzerland. Mailer joked to Buckley, "it's a relief if we're both becoming so popular. Now one day sometime in the future we'll even be able to go on television and have a calm if crazy conversation in which neither of us need feel that a political catastrophe will occur if the other scores even one small point."[39]

In time, however, the invitations slowed. It turned out that in 1965 and 1966 they'd finally come up against one subject that irreparably divided them. Unlike their collective excoriation of the Liberal Establishment, or their differing views on civil rights, or their growing awareness of the anger coming from the white working classes, or the ongoing battles between the fires on the right and the fires on the left, something else would finally push the limits of their difficult friendship. As Mailer bluntly wrote to Buckley in 1965, "I think this is the wrong time for us to have dinner, because instead of having a nice calm quiet and lively conversation about the future of conservatism, my left conservatism and your right conservatism, there'd be too much pressure to have a screaming match about Vietnam."[40]

PART III

BIRTHING PANGS
(1966–68)

8

Fly in the Ointment

In the summer of 1966, Frank Sinatra and his young wife, Mia Farrow, joined George Plimpton, Truman Capote, and a handful of other well-known cultural figures for lunch at Bennett Cerf's country estate in Westchester County, New York. The estate was called "The Columns" because Cerf's various newspaper columns had paid for the thing. A founder of Random House, a television personality since the 1950s, and the author of several books of jokes, Cerf nonetheless knew what his bread and butter was.

After lunch, the group moved to the pool to sit in the sun. With her famous short hair and transfixing eyes, Farrow was one of the most alluring sex symbols to arrive on the scene recently. She reclined on a chaise longue by the pool in a plummeting black bathing suit. While the men chatted, Farrow lay still, eyes closed, basking in the warmth of the sun. She remained so still, in fact, that out of the blue a swallowtail butterfly felt compelled to land softly on the exposed part of her breast, the untanned décolletage that had animated the imagination of more than one viewer of *Peyton Place*. The scene entranced Plimpton. Removing himself from conversation, he simply stared at Farrow and the butterfly. "Absolutely beautiful," he recalled, ". . . because [the butterfly] had picked Mia to land on, faunlike, childlike." The other men noticed too, and all conversation stopped. The butterfly kept its wings straight up, then would fan them up and down quickly, then hold them straight up again. Farrow's eyes remained closed.

And then completely shattering the moment, an oblivious Truman Capote blurted out in his shrill, nasally voice, "What about the Goetzes? Should I invite them, or consign them?" The butterfly flew away. Everyone exhaled and turned to Capote in disappointment.[1]

Capote was at the time obsessively planning his Black and White Ball, a party ostensibly designed to honor *Washington Post* president Katharine Graham, but which was really intended to honor the success of Capote himself. His recent book, *In Cold Blood*, was then topping the bestseller list, and Capote wanted to celebrate. He had rented out the giant ballroom of the Plaza Hotel and compiled a guest list of A-list personalities from Hollywood, New York, Washington, and Europe. Later he would claim to have invited five hundred friends but made fifteen thousand enemies.[2]

To many, there seemed to be much more going on with the party than Capote's tony celebration of himself, but no one could really put it into words. Rich men offered bribes for the coveted invitation. One woman threatened suicide if she wasn't invited. The press covered it as though it were an important event in the life of the nation. It was almost as if there was an urgency to be a part of a moment that seemed to be slipping away.

And in fact, there was. It was right at that moment that the war in Vietnam would help push all the bubbling protests from the right and the left beyond the tipping point, when the liberal center could no longer hold, when the unity and goodness of the nation could no longer be taken for granted. It would be the war that would prompt the fires of the right and fires of the left to tear into each other, and into themselves. When the violence finally slowed, what emerged was a dramatically reformed set of assumptions guiding American life. Capote's party happened to be timed right at that transitional moment.

Until the mid-1960s, the goings-on in Vietnam hadn't really concerned most Americans. The Cold War had been a part of daily life, but it typically focused on debates about the Soviet Union, the spread of communism in Cuba or China, or civil defense at home. Even as late as December 1964, "The simmering conflict in Vietnam," writes historian James Patterson, "did not preoccupy the American public . . . in spite of the subtly escalating U.S. presence in the country."[3]

It was no surprise, really. Vietnam had been of marginal concern even to the American government until the early part of the decade. It had been a French colony for more than a hundred years through the 1950s, and its war for independence had emerged in force only during the Second World War. The French had superior technology, but the Vietnamese were fighting for independence, a fact that proved decisive. And as what was called the First Indochina War dragged on, the French persuaded the United States to help based on the fact that the leader of the Vietnamese revolution, Ho Chi Minh, was a communist. The United States, fearing the establishment of another communist country in Asia (after China had "fallen" in 1949) offered funds. By the end of Truman's second term in 1952, the U.S. was subsidizing 40 percent of the French costs to run the war. By 1954, the total was up to 75 percent.[4]

Despite American assistance, in 1954 the Vietnamese inflicted a final, brutal defeat on the French, leading the two countries to engage in peace talks in Geneva. The peace talks temporarily divided Vietnam into two sections, north and south, as the French regrouped in preparation to leave. The peace convention promised that in 1956, after two years, an election would be held to reunify the country.

But the United States wasn't going to let that happen. President Eisenhower later said in his memoirs that he knew that if free elections were held in Vietnam, Minh would receive something close to 80 percent of the vote, thus ensuring the establishment of Vietnam as a communist country. Eisenhower's response was to allow Minh to continue controlling the northern section of the country while creating a counterweight nation out of the southern part, something eventually called the Republic of Vietnam.[5] Eisenhower helped install a staunch anti-communist prime minister, Ngo Dinh Diem, to lead the Republic. Diem was not only an anti-communist, he was also a Catholic (the religious remnant of French colonialism). And even more than that, he had close connections to American Catholic leaders, including the powerful Cardinal of the Archdiocese of New York, Francis Spellman, who introduced Diem to then-senator John F. Kennedy, among others. Senator Kennedy went on to join a pro-Diem lobby called the American Friends of Vietnam when it first formed in 1955.

But Diem had his problems. He was a micromanager who slowed governance to a crawl. He unfairly favored his fellow Catholics over the country's overwhelmingly Buddhist population. And he reinstalled many of the bureaucrats who had supported the French colonial regime. To many Vietnamese, the United States had simply replaced the French as their colonial overlords. Despite the rhetoric of American freedom versus Soviet totalitarianism, there was little love for the USA in much of Vietnam.

As Diem became increasingly repressive, guerrilla warfare began. Diem tried to curtail the insurgency by forcing his mostly rural citizens into easily monitored villages. But moving people from their farms or paddies into "strategic hamlets" led to deep resentment against Diem and his American protectors, especially when their former homes in the countryside were destroyed by American fighter-bombers.

To ensure the Diem government stayed in power, President Kennedy sent 2,067 American "military advisors" to Vietnam in 1961, many of whom were pilots and technicians. By 1963, Kennedy realized that Diem was growing increasingly unpopular. He informed leaders in the South Vietnam military that the U.S. would not intervene should a coup materialize. In November 1963, the military took control of South Vietnam. Diem was killed shortly thereafter.

From the perspective of the American government, the trouble in Vietnam was that every leader who was not Ho Chi Minh had to be propped up by the United States, and, after a hundred years of colonial rule by the French (and a thousand years of fighting to keep the Chinese at bay), any leader backed by an outside force would inevitably be unpopular. To the vast majority of the Vietnamese, this was not a battle between communism and capitalism; it was about becoming a free nation.

Still, no American president wanted to "lose" Vietnam to communism, another fallen domino in the Cold War. By the end of 1963, the United States had 16,300 "advisors" in Vietnam and had spent $500 million there in that year alone. In 1964, under the guise of a responding to a questionable attack on an American ship patrolling the Vietnamese Gulf of Tonkin (the "attack" was later found to be a result of faulty radar in bad weather), President Johnson increased the American military presence to 23,000 "advisors" and expenditures to about two million dollars a day. An overwhelming majority of Americans supported the effort, seeing it as little more than a small brush fire in a larger battle over the world's future. When the Senate passed the August 1964 Gulf of Tonkin Resolution, which authorized Johnson to send troops to Vietnam, the vote was unanimous. In the House, there were only two dissenters.

By 1965, the guerrilla warfare that emerged to fight Diem was now targeting American installations, an occurrence that led President Johnson to increase his commitment to war. In the spring, Johnson began sending large numbers of U.S. Marines to Vietnam, initially to protect American air bases, but then to patrol local villages. He also began large-scale bombing campaigns against guerrilla bases. In April 1965, hating the war but uncertain how he could end it while still claiming victory, Johnson gave a speech at

Johns Hopkins University where he offered "Peace Without Conquest" to the North Vietnamese. Ho Chi Minh rejected it. The north seemed to be winning. Why would he settle for a divided nation now? Angry, Johnson sent combat troops. This was no longer a battle among "advisors"; American troops began receiving combat pay to go to Vietnam.

The escalation of the war in 1964 and 1965 ignited an opposition already in the mood to protest. Young people, right and left, had already been chafing at the seemingly restrictive culture that both Mailer and Buckley had excoriated during the previous decade. They had witnessed or been a part of the protests over civil rights, a regional dispute over segregation that had quickly turned into a nationwide debate about liberty and equality. And when Johnson came up empty with "Peace Without Conquest" and increased his commitment to war, Vietnam became the central force that brought out almost all of the disparate voices of discontent. Ten days after "Peace Without Conquest" fifteen thousand students protested in the streets of Washington, D.C., marking the first large-scale protest against the war.

As might be expected for men of their stature, Buckley and Mailer were in the forefront of the debate over the war. For his part, Mailer became an early celebrity opponent of escalation. As he had said in his 1962 debate with Buckley, "Let communism come to those countries it will come to. Let us not use up our substance trying to hold onto nations which are poor, underdeveloped, and bound to us only by the depths of their hatred for us." That sentiment perfectly embodied his position on Vietnam.

In November 1965, Mailer was asked to speak against the war at a huge, two-day antiwar rally at the University of California, Berkeley, one of the largest protests in the nation at that point. Mailer "speaks to the unconscious of this country," said one of the organizers, a twenty-three-year-old Jerry Rubin, adding that, "Like a rock star, he interested a larger audience than the people who were just against the war."[6] Rubin had called Mailer and urged him to speak to the crowd at Berkeley. Mailer was no student, and his presence would lend credibility to the protest and perhaps allow it to be heard beyond college campuses.

It would turn out to be one of the best speeches he ever gave. Mailer looked over the soccer field filled with ten thousand protesters, some of whom had been there for more than thirty hours, sleeping bags in tow, some hanging off rooftops to listen, and he poked fun at Johnson's overall liberal vision, in which "the colleges would look like factories, the housing projects would keep looking like prisons, the corporation office buildings would be indistinguishable from the colleges, and not even an airline hostess would know where the airport ended and the motel bedroom began."[7] The war in Vietnam, he said, was the result of an illness affecting all of American life, and thus these protests should be recognized as more than just complaints about the war. The students were exactly right to be protesting so vociferously.

Then Mailer went on to explain how the war was connected to the anemia of the nation's larger liberal vision. He told the students that LBJ was smart enough to detect the surges coming from below, from the right and the left, out to challenge the entire social order. And to distract the population from liberalism's shortcomings, "it came to the President," Mailer said: "Hot damn, Vietnam."

Over the course of the next hour, Mailer argued that the only sensible explanation for the war was located in the psyche of the president, a supreme narcissist who sought to be a leader endeared to all, loved for his gifts without ever asking what one wanted. "Caesar gave promise to unify the land," Mailer said of LBJ. "But at what cost? For if the ideology were liberal, the methodology was total."[8] Johnson wanted Vietnam to be the U.S.'s victory, its feel-good moment, where its citizenry could adulate the president and thank him for his strength and for showing it theirs. In the face of mounting criticisms against liberalism, Vietnam would show Americans it was all worth it.

To Mailer, this was a sham. So what if Vietnam came under the leadership of communists? How much succor could we take by defeating a banana republic on the other side of the globe that posed no credible threat to America? As Mailer built to his crescendo, he invoked the image of JFK, how he had promised to bring America to a New Frontier, and how Kennedy's victory in the Cuban Missile Crisis of 1962, "the biggest poker game we ever played," had given Americans a sense of triumph. But with JFK's death, the wound of anemia reopened. We returned to "going mad" under the liberal malaise. Now Johnson wanted to return the sense of triumph, and Vietnam was his platform.

"Hot damn, Vietnam!" Mailer repeated.[9]

As he amped up the audience in preparation for his conclusion, he said:

> Only, listen, Lyndon Johnson, you have gone too far this time. You are a bully with an Air Force, and since you will not call off your Air Force, there are young people who will persecute you back. It is a little thing, but it will hound you into nightmares and endless corridors of nights without sleep, it will hound you. For listen—this is only one of the thousand things they will do. They will print up little pictures of you . . . the size of post cards, the size of stamps, and some will glue these pictures to walls and posters and telephone booths. . . . These pictures will be everywhere. These pictures will be pasted up everywhere, UPSIDE DOWN.

The point was "that not all Americans are unaware of your monstrous vanity, overweening piety, and doubtful motive." He demanded the students declare "that we trust our President so little, and think so little of him, that we see his picture everywhere upside down. . . . Everywhere, upside down. Everywhere, everywhere."[10]

"[W]hen he finished," the emcee recalled, "the response began to build rhythmically, getting louder and louder. The cheering was so powerful I just waited. I couldn't go on while he was still out there, I didn't want to interfere with that moment."[11]

To the crowd at Berkeley, Mailer had made sense of what the war was about and offered a crazy way to resist. He had also tied their protest against the war to the larger malaise confronting the nation. He demanded a rejection of The Rules in the name of a higher morality; he sanctified their existential politics of protest. "It was the first time anybody had made fun of the President," Rubin recalled, "and here he was telling the country to take LBJ's photo and turn it upside down. He qualitatively changed the event. What he was really doing was giving us permission to insult a father figure, indicating it's okay to ridicule the president."[12] Obedience, perhaps the signal feature of The Rules, was now under assault. For several minutes the crowd roared its approval.

As the crowd roared, those who could find pictures of the president raised them above their heads, upside down. Abbie Hoffman said the speech led the counterculture "into the guerrilla theater" they widely adopted later. Mailer's speech, Hoffman said, "showed how you can focus protest sentiment effectively by aiming not at the decision but at the gut of those who make them."[13]

The speech was such a success that comedian and antiwar activist Dick Gregory, who was slated to speak next, refused to go on. He turned to a friend and said, "I ain't gonna follow that shit."[14]

A few weeks later the radical magazine *The Realist* reprinted the speech and put on its cover a picture of Lyndon Johnson, upside down. Printed in New York during the water shortage, *The Realist* captioned the image "Don't Flush for Everything." When Mailer reprinted the speech a year later in a collection of essays called *Cannibals and Christians*, he dedicated the book to Lyndon B. Johnson, "whose name inspired young men to cheer for me in public."[15]

"[I]t was certainly the largest audience I ever spoke to in my life," Mailer wrote to a friend, "and they were a marvelous audience . . . and were kind enough to give me, when I finished my hour's speech, a standing ovation which went on for many minutes. The first time in my [life] that had happened, too."[16]

Buckley had a position on the war just as prominent as Mailer's. He had been arguing for years, with Mailer and others, that the Cold War was fundamentally a battle between good and evil, between individual freedom and collectivized un-freedom. Worse, thought Buckley, was that communist leaders, prioritizing the morality of their cause over basic human decency, would do anything to win. They didn't care about the welfare of the individual, or about getting elected. All they wanted to do was win in the name of their ideology. War might be necessary to do so, but that was okay, because communism promised bountiful earthly rewards. As promised in their manifesto, heaven could happen here and now, so why not fight till the death for the good of the cause? And why not fight dirty?

When viewed like this—as a moral cause being fought to the death by an enemy willing to die to win—how could anyone who loved individual freedom *not* be a hardline Cold Warrior seeking to halt the coming rule of communism? Because of the stakes, Buckley thought the United States should broker no compromise.

The *National Review* was brutal in its assessments of Russia, China, and Vietnam. In 1959, Buckley had even protested the visit of Soviet Premier Nikita Khrushchev to the United States. "Khrushchev is *not* aware," Buckley said, "that the gates of hell shall not prevail against us. Even out of the depths of despair, we take heart in the knowledge that it cannot matter how deep we fall, for there is always hope. In the end, we will bury him."[17] In 1962, Buckley endorsed preemptive strikes against China's nuclear facilities, which he thought would "probably have the effect of damping down the trend toward general war" by showing that the United States was serious about stopping communism.[18]

Buckley even endorsed a plan that was much bolder than the

government's official policy of "containment," which sought to contain communism where it was and not let it spread further. Following the lead of Buckley's friend and *National Review* correspondent James Burnham, the *National Review* advocated a policy called "rollback," which argued that, out of consideration for the people behind the Iron Curtain or in China, the United States should not simply contain communism but should try to roll it back to where it came from. In the late 1950s, *National Review* asserted that the U.S. should militarily intervene in order to roll back communism in Hungary and the Middle East. After the Cuban Revolution of 1959, it was clear to Buckley what the United States should do: attack. After the Cuban Missile Crisis of 1962, which most Americans viewed as a victory, the *National Review* argued, "Even today, the most critical threat of a Communist Cuba is not from any missiles that may be there, but from the political and subversive warfare against which navies alone can do nothing." The U.S. shouldn't stop fighting until Castro and the communists were removed.[19]

With rollback in mind, Buckley endorsed Diem in Vietnam until the bitter end. When Diem was overthrown and killed in 1963, Buckley looked for alternatives, eventually landing on the idea that no matter who took control in Vietnam, it couldn't be the communists, and the United States should not rest until ensuring this outcome. He even went so far as to endorse the tactical use of nuclear weapons in Vietnam in order to end the war decisively in favor of the South Vietnamese.[20]

By the mid-1960s, Buckley and Mailer's positions on the war had become so well known that the question of another major debate between the two was raised. In August 1966, a young conservative named Donald Lambro proposed that Mailer and Buckley face off. "The debate will center about [sic] the topic of Vietnam," Lambro wrote in the invitation. He promised civility: "It will be conducted at the best possible level of taste and decorum. A promi-

nent member of the Washington press corps will serve as moderator." But Lambro knew it was a contentious topic. To Mailer he
wrote, "We feel very strongly that you are one of the few people in
the literary field who could make a very moving presentation for
your point of view. We believe that such a discussion can serve a
worthwhile purpose . . . to broaden an understanding of two very
divergent opinions on the war."[21]

Mailer told Lambro the invitation was "directly appealing" but
said there were obstacles, the most formidable of which was, as
usual, money. "One doesn't just debate William Buckley," he wrote,
"one gets ready for it, which means I must spend a couple of weeks
preparing, which in turn means I lose a lot of time from working
on a novel, plus momentum, plus, plus, plus." He asked for at least
nine thousand dollars, twice what he made in 1962. "I leave you
with that financial hand grenade," he wrote.[22]

There was another reason to pause before the two could conduct any public debate: Mailer didn't think he and Buckley could
remain civil on the matter for much longer. The war was egregious,
people were dying, and neither he nor Buckley seemed willing to
back down. For Mailer, the war symbolized everything that was
wrong with postwar America, the conjoining of all the corrosive
elements snuffing out the honest American heart—and the price
was being paid in human flesh. For Buckley, the war was a struggle
worth dying for because it was designed to stop an insipid enemy,
an enemy out to rob all that was good in the American Way of Life.
The stakes on both sides were thus incredibly high and, unlike on
almost any other topic, compromise seemed impossible.

Just a few months earlier, in February 1966, Buckley had drafted
his typical fund-raising letter for *National Review* and sent it to subscribers and previous donors. Mailer was a subscriber, so he got
the letter too.[23] "Your letter was the best letter I ever read by an
editor asking for funds," Mailer wrote to Buckley. He didn't think
National Review was all that great, suggesting, "it's not so good as
it ought to be, and often it's tiresome, especially when one knows

in advance what your trusted old line contributors are going to say." But Mailer sent a check anyway. Why? "As a personal mark of respect for you," he wrote.

"Besides," Mailer added, "I have the hope that some day our minds will meet somewhere between your real and essential conservatism (as opposed to your outrageous—in my opinion—right-wingerism, which I still see as the last of your sophomoric salts). [Y]es, I still see some future rapprochement between your love of fine trees and mine, for that, old buddy, is where some existential notions (like mine) touch the conservative base."

The check, however, was "in lieu of dinner," Mailer wrote. Because, as he explained once again, "For as much as I miss you and a certain wife of yours for the pleasure of a fine evening, I'm not so certain we can have it now, with Viet Nam to pass the wine. But then I've said this before. . . . That's the trouble with bad wars. They spoil the continued existence of difficult friendships."[24]

The breaking up of difficult friendships, the sense that the nation was on the verge of a potentially irrepressible conflict, was the sentiment in the air at Truman Capote's Black and White Ball. The night might be the final moment before the rupture. Capote was a compelling figure to host a celebrity ball, too. He was of course a famous writer, one of the best of his generation, even if his pieces often went down like truffles, delightful but unfulfilling. Several of his books were well received, none more than *Breakfast at Tiffany's*, a short novella about a young woman named Holly Golightly who overcomes her Southern hick past in order to become what Capote called "an American Geisha" in New York City, constantly searching for some idealized version of happiness as the mistress of the wealthy. Even that book was lightweight, a perfect confection offering a quick taste of something, but in the end, saying nothing important about America.

Despite his appreciation of *Breakfast at Tiffany's*, Mailer had grown frustrated by Capote's inability to use his talents to probe depths that needed probing. Mailer felt he knew about Capote's courage, living as an unrepentant and flamboyant gay man in the homophobic 1950s. Mailer often told the story of when they first met, in about 1958, when the two men dropped into the first bar they came across in order to talk shop over drinks. It happened to be an Irish bar, "at which," Mailer recalled, "were lined up fifty reasonably disgruntled Irishmen drinking at three-thirty in the afternoon. We walked in. Truman was wearing a little gabardine cape. He strolled in looking like a beautiful little faggot prince. It suddenly came over me: My God, what have I done? I've walked into this drunken den of sour male virtue with Truman!" But not to worry: "Truman just floated through. As he did, the eyes—it was a movie shot—every eye turned automatically to look at him with a big Irish, 'I've seen everything now.'. . . He walked right through to a table in the back, sat down and drank. . . . Afterward, I thought, 'My God, if I were that man, I couldn't live, I'd die of adrenaline overflow.' I was very impressed with what it cost him to live," Mailer said. "That quality—that he had a special life and was going to live it in a special way—is enormously exhausting."[25]

While Mailer appreciated Capote's brass balls in the way he lived, he didn't think Capote had the guts to use his talents to say something transformative about the country in his writing. As Mailer had written of Capote in *Advertisements*, "he has less to say than any good writer I know. I would suspect he hesitates between the attractions of Society . . . and the novel he could write of the gossip column's real life, a major work, but it would banish him forever from his favorite world."[26]

These lines were prescient. Capote did love High Society, with its parties, elegance, and gossip. He loved it all, especially the company of a stable of wealthy ladies he called "his swans." Beautiful, rich, and thin, they brought him like a lapdog on their Mediterranean cruises, trips to the Alps and the French Riviera, basking in his gossip and tales. Capote would never risk the access he had in order to tell the story of what he saw, and of what it said about

American extravagances. Indeed, when Capote finally did delve into that material for a book called *Answered Prayers*, his swans cut him off immediately. The pain, he discovered, wasn't worth the reward. He never completed the book.

In 1959, Capote had become captivated by the murder of the Clutters, a farming family in Kansas, which seemed to be nothing more than a random crime in rural America. With the help of his childhood friend Harper Lee—who had just sent a draft of *To Kill a Mockingbird* to her editor and was awaiting feedback—Capote went to investigate the Kansas crime on assignment from *The New Yorker*. He grew obsessed with the details he gleaned from the small-town folk in Kansas. And when they arrested the killers in Las Vegas a few months later, at least one of them turned out to be articulate and interesting. Capote knew he could turn the story into much more than an article for a magazine; it merited a book. The intensity of the case helped bring out the best in his writing, too. What finally emerged, after a five-year stay of execution (which was finally revoked, giving Capote the awful, deadly conclusion to his book), was the book called *In Cold Blood*.

In the fall of 1965 *The New Yorker* began to serialize the book over four issues. By the third installment, readers were waiting outside newsstands to buy the magazine. Reviewers were already beginning to pronounce the book "a masterpiece" and it hadn't even been published yet. When it finally came out in January 1966, the serialization, along with the remarkable self-promotion of Capote himself ("a boy has to hustle his book," he told *Newsweek*), made it seem as if there were little else going on in the literary world. Twenty-four major newspapers reviewed the book on the very same Sunday, and all the big weeklies chimed in as well. Many put Capote's face on the cover. The all-important *New York Times Book Review* called it "a modern masterpiece."[27]

By the summer of 1966, with production companies offering to buy the movie rights and book sales skyrocketing, Capote found himself with lots of money, lots of fame, and no imminent project.

He decided to celebrate, turning his energies into throwing him-self a world-class party. He scheduled it for November 28, 1966.

Capote made a few decisions that would make the party stand out. First, it was to be highly formal, black-and-white attire only, elegant enough for Fred Astaire and chic enough for Audrey Hep-burn. He would also make it a bal masqué, where the most famous people in America would be asked to mask their faces only to reveal themselves at midnight. He also consulted with his friend Evie Backer, a sharp-tongued woman with an eye for décor whom Capote called "Tiny Malice," and asked her to help decorate the ballroom. She decided that what the party needed was nothing. She skipped huge floral centerpieces and dramatic table decora-tions in favor of simple golden candelabra wrapped in subtle green vines. At Capote's party, "all the other beautiful people would be the flowers," said one commentator.[28]

In contrast to this decorative simplicity, Capote wanted two bands so there would be no downtime in the dancing. He wanted his favorite food, the Plaza's famous Chicken Hash, as well as whim-sical spaghetti and meatballs, along with the usual finger foods. He would have four hundred and fifty bottles of Taittinger cham-pagne at the ready, dispensed from four separate bars strategically situated throughout the ballroom.

One of the most important details was Capote's selection of the evening's Cinderella. He could easily have chosen one of his New York swans, someone like Babe Paley (the elegant wife of Wil-liam S. Paley, head of Columbia Broadcasting) or Gloria Guinness (the graceful wife of millionaire Thomas Loel Guinness). But that would have limited the reach of the party, making it little more than a New York affair. Instead, Capote chose Katharine "Kay" Graham, the Washington, D.C., matriarch who had become the powerful publisher of the *Washington Post* after her husband's sui-cide. "Honey, I just decided you're depressed and need cheering up," he said to Graham on a visit to Saratoga Springs in 1966, "so I'm going to give you a party."[29]

Graham was in fact in the final stages of mourning her husband, emerging as a powerful woman who didn't need sympathy from anyone. "I don't need cheering up and what are you talking about?" she responded.

"Yes, yes, I've always had this idea for a black-and-white ball."

He went on to explain that he'd always loved the black-and-white scene at the racetrack in *My Fair Lady* and that the Plaza was among the places where he was happiest. There would be no stopping Capote. "I felt a little bit that Truman was going to give the ball anyway and that I was part of the props," Graham said. "Perhaps a 'prop' is unfair, but I felt that he needed a guest of honor and with a lot of imagination he figured out me."[30]

It was a bold choice, but also an important one. In France, Paris is both the cultural and political capital of the nation. Britain has London. Germany has Berlin. But in the United States, the worlds of politics, culture, high finance, and society were relatively isolated, divided among New York, Washington, D.C., and Hollywood. This began to change in the 1950s and especially the early 1960s, as the power elite swam in increasingly small ponds among the liberal order. Capote, consciously or not, recognized that. "I think Truman had a very shrewd sense of this kind of process and was himself very much in the center of it," said Norman Podhoretz, who was at the party.[31] In the end, many of America's best-known people made the cut. It represented a new who's who of the mid-1960s, not just the greying folks from the Social Register. Frank Sinatra would rub shoulders with Henry Ford II. Andy Warhol would talk with Arthur Schlesinger, Jr. Tennessee Williams would chat with the Kennedys (three of whom were there). Capote spent months refining the guest list, and he carried a little black-and-white composition notebook to make adjustments. He taunted his friends, threatening to kick them off the list if they didn't behave. "Well, maybe you'll be invited and maybe you won't," he'd say to a friend who asked what he was doing with that childish notebook.[32] That's what he was doing when, at Bennett

Cerf's country estate, he had been so oblivious to the butterfly on Mia Farrow's chest.

No matter how you saw things, there was an amiability and play-fulness about the ball that suggested few were worried about the health of the nation, that despite the civil rights movement and all the other activity from the right and the left, all were still pushing for the common good and that all *was* good in America. As the *Washington Post* put it, Capote's name, "coupled with a guest list that reads like Who's Who of the World, has escalated the party to a social 'happening' of history-making proportions."[33]

It rained the day of the party. Nevertheless, the press and several hundred onlookers gathered early outside the Plaza. One woman even decorated her umbrella in black and white in order to cel-ebrate the party. The Plaza has a dramatic entryway to its Grand Ballroom, where photographers could line up to photograph partygoers—Capote knew this as well.

A consummate host, Capote showed up first, dressed perfectly proper save for his mask, a kid's mask, which he had bought for thirty-seven cents at FAO Schwarz. With Graham and a handful of other socialites by his side, he worked the receiving line, welcom-ing guests as they were announced, one by one, a midcentury hall of fame.

At the party, Sinatra and Farrow chatted with actress Candice Bergen and writer Lillian Hellman. Arthur Sulzberger, the influ-ential publisher of the *New York Times*, wore a mask crafted from old newspaper. There were Johnsons (as in Lynda, daughter of the president, who was accompanied by a dozen Secret Service agents all in black masks and tuxedos), Kennedys, Trumans, and more. The Washington matriarch Alice Roosevelt Longworth, Teddy Roosevelt's octogenarian daughter, wore a domino mask attached to her face with Band-Aids. She called the party "the most exqui-site of spectator sports," although she returned home later that eve-ning to find her house burgled, the burglars having known she'd be at the party.[34] During one moment, Arthur Schlesinger, Jr., saw his friend Lauren Bacall dancing. He began to cut in before he was stopped by a fierce look from Bacall. "Don't you see whom I'm dancing with?" she said. It turned out to be Jerome Robbins, the famous choreographer. They were jitterbugging, and she wasn't going to give up that experience in order to dance with a historian. "So I retired crestfallen," Schlesinger said.[35]

One beautiful actress, whom Capote later refused to name, spent the evening dancing with a tall, dark, and handsome stranger, wondering if he came from the world of business or politics. She surely would have known him if he was from Hollywood. It turned out to be Capote's elevator man from the United Nations Plaza apartment complex. Capote never revealed the man's identity to the smitten actress.[36]

In one of Capote's favorite comments from the evening, Gloria Guinness complained that the entwined diamond and ruby necklaces she was wearing were so heavy that she'd have to spend the entire next day in bed. Capote simply laughed out loud.[37] "Aren't we having the most wonderful time?" he asked everyone as he bounced from table to table. "I love this party."[38]

Neither Mailer nor Buckley really cared for *In Cold Blood*. Buckley recognized talent in the writing, but thought the book lacked politics. "I was on the Johnny Carson show one night," said Buckley, "and the subject of capital punishment came up. I said, 'Well, we've only had a certain number of executions in the last few years . . . and two of them were for the personal convenience of Truman Capote.' "

Capote was furious at the joke. When a mutual friend, Lee Radziwill (Jackie Kennedy's sister), informed Buckley that Capote was angry, he said, "Oh, for Pete's sake. . . . I was just making a wisecrack."[39]

Mailer was even more uncharitable about *In Cold Blood*. "It's a hell of a damned good book, beautifully written, but I do think it's limited," he said, because, by the end, "You didn't know enough about those killers finally. . . . I think Truman decided too quickly this is all heredity, that in their genes his killers were doomed and directed to act in this fashion; there was no other outcome possible. All that I thought was too quickly solved by him. Those are the kinds of questions that should keep you up at night—and they were not in that book."[40] To Mailer, of course, the culture surrounding these killers had a role to play, but Capote had refused to engage. This accords with Mailer's larger assessment of Capote, one that remained unchanged in the thirty years he knew him: "He had a lovely poetic ear. He did not have a good mind. I don't know if there was ever a large idea that bothered him for one minute."[41]

Mailer arrived at the Black and White Ball on time, mostly sober but not entirely, wearing a formal tuxedo with a slick silk bow tie. To ensure the prompt arrival of his guests, Capote had many of the most important partygoers invited to pre-party dinners held at the homes of his closest friends, who were then responsible for making sure everyone showed up on time. The Mailers dined at Sidney and Piedy Lumet's. Mailer drank a little as he sat next to Patricia Lawford, JFK's sister. She insulted Mailer playfully: "I don't know why I'm sitting next to you. I've heard you're awful." He returned in kind: "Well, that just shows how dumb the people are that you know."

"We got along like a house afire," Mailer said later, "because we did nothing but insult each other all night. It was wonderful. . . . We've gotten along ever since."[42]

As orchestrated by the Lumets, the Mailers showed up at the Plaza right on time. When Mailer arrived, though, his hair was tousled by the November winds, curls flying everywhere, and he was buried in a heavy old black raincoat. A photographer snapped a picture before he could deposit the coat in the coat check, and he went on to receive the dubious award of worst-dressed man at the ball from *Women's Wear Daily*, the fashion bible of the times, which didn't appreciate his "dirty gabardine raincoat with black tie."[43]

Nevertheless, Mailer arrived mask in hand, and with Beverly on his arm. A former actress and all-American beauty, she wrapped herself in white fur over her black bugle-beaded sleeveless dress. The whole thing was adorned by long white gloves and a dramatic white mask with a solid black border that swept up dramatically on both sides of her eyes. If Mailer was among the worst dressed, Beverly most certainly was not.

The Buckleys arrived at about the same time. Buckley was dapper as always, and generally comfortable in this milieu. He knew the cues of high society and wore a crisp tuxedo with a large, rectangular oversized mask. Pat of course had been operating at this level her whole life, and she seemed immediately at ease. At nearly six feet tall, she sparkled in a sequined spaghetti-strap dress. Her gigantic mask was bordered along the top with big strips of fur that made her appear even more feline than usual. A large Japanese fan matched her mask. Buckley smiled along, a drink in one hand, the other around Pat's waist.

In the receiving line, the Buckleys saw the Schlesingers and the John Kenneth Galbraiths. It occurred to Pat that Galbraith had made a snide comment about *National Review* a few years earlier, when he criticized another economist for deigning to write for right-wing trash like *National Review*. She turned to Galbraith and stunned him with an out-of-nowhere rebuke: "I'm going to choke you before the evening is over for what you said about Bill."

Galbraith, taken aback, apologized for whatever it was that he had said—he couldn't remember. "It was rather extraordinary," recalled Buckley, who seemed oblivious to the whole incident, "that he took the occasion to apologize for an indiscretion he felt badly about." Galbraith rushed to the top of the stairs to avoid any further wrath from Pat, and ran headlong into Capote. Pat, meanwhile, sought to steer her beau away from the intellectuals and toward the socialites for the rest of the evening. She would only be partially successful.[44]

As they entered the party, guests encountered a cadre of photographers snapping their pictures. But alongside them were a hand-

ful of journalists there to ruffle feathers. How could they attend a
lavish party like this, the journalists asked, when there was a dis-
gusting war going on? Candice Bergen recalled the scene. She was
just nineteen at the time, with little consciousness of the war. She
wore a white rabbit mask that resembled the look made famous by
Hugh Hefner. When she was accosted by the journalists, she said,
"Oh, honestly!"

Another partygoer came to her defense, saying, "The question's
inappropriate."

The reporter hollered back, "The war's inappropriate."

Bergen scurried into the party.

Mailer tried to avoid the contrarian voices and have a good time,
and he mostly succeeded. He and Beverly were socializing and
drinking, bumping shoulders with old friends and new ones, and
Mailer appreciated the event for what it was. Mailer later said, in
a remark that was not exactly charitable to his host, "It was one of
the best parties I ever went to. So much action . . . so many people
of a sort you'd never met before. For example, there was Tallulah
Bankhead! . . . It's probably hyperbole to say that everything there
felt anointed that night. Truman had certainly brought it off. It certainly was his greatest coup. For some, and I might be one of them,
that party was even greater than any particular one of his books."[45]

On the dance floor, Beverly and Norman invented a dance that
resembled one of their favorite pastimes, walking on a tightrope
with your arms out wide as though you were about to lose your
balance (Mailer had a tightrope installed in their Brooklyn home,
even forcing guests like Senator Jacob Javits to walk across it[46]). The
dance was funny enough, or copied enough, or took up enough
space on the dance floor, that a handful of other people noticed;
it made the papers the following day.

At some point later in the evening, with a few drinks under his
belt, Mailer came upon a circle of people talking about Vietnam.
His old friend Norman Podhoretz was there, as was President
Johnson's former special assistant for national security, McGeorge

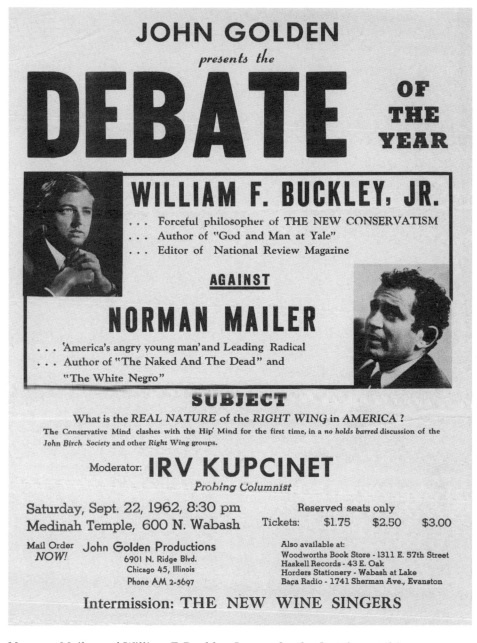

Norman Mailer and William F. Buckley, Jr., met for the first time at this 1962 debate in Chicago, which was timed to occur two days before the Floyd Patterson–Sonny Liston heavyweight title fight (and promoted in kind).

Founded in 1955 by Norman Mailer (pictured here in the early 1960s), Ed Fancher, and Dan Wolf, the *Village Voice* would come to represent the literary left's critique of the Liberal Establishment.

Buckley (pictured here in 1966) started the conservative journal *National Review* just weeks after the founding of the *Village Voice*.

Buckley ran for mayor of New York City in 1965 under the banner of the Conservative Party.

Four years later, in 1969, Mailer ran for mayor of New York City on a platform that included the secession of the city from New York State.

In November 1966, Truman Capote's Black and White Ball at New York City's Plaza Hotel brought together leading lights of Hollywood, politics, finance, literature, and New York society.

Mailer at the ball with his fourth wife, Beverly Bentley. *Women's Wear Daily* named Mailer the worst-dressed man at the ball.

Buckley with his wife, Pat, at the ball.

Both Mailer and Buckley had complex, often adversarial relationships with many leading thinkers of the 1960s.

James Baldwin

Truman Capote

Gloria Steinem

Gore Vidal

Buckley behind his desk at *National Review*. He served as the magazine's day-to-day editor for thirty-five years.

Mailer built a gigantic "City of the Future" with tens of thousands of Legos in his Brooklyn Heights living room.

Mailer (center) took part in the 1967 march on the Pentagon with Dr. Benjamin Spock (far right, with glasses and lapel pin), literary critic Dwight Macdonald (right of center, with glasses and cigarette), and poet Robert Lowell (center, with light-colored jacket).

By the late '60s, Buckley had made peace with Republicans like Richard Nixon, who had never fit comfortably with his conservative ideals.

After a 1971 debate with leading feminists including Germaine Greer, Mailer was criticized for seeking to maintain traditional gender relations.

Buckley hosted *Firing Line* from 1966 to 1999. In this episode from 1968, Buckley and Mailer discuss, inevitably, the state of the nation—a conversation they carried on for four decades.

Bundy, one of the architects of the war. As much as anyone, Bundy had been one of the chief advocates for escalating the conflict in Vietnam. And now here he was, holding forth.

Fueled by liquid courage, Mailer barged his way into the conversation and challenged Bundy on the war. After a heated exchange where Bundy held firm, Mailer said, "I paid you too much respect." It was a somewhat obscure comment but probably referred to the fact that Mailer had hoped President Johnson would surround himself with thoughtful men who would tamp down his enthusiasm for battle, but instead he had gotten the likes of Bundy.

Bundy knew about Mailer, knew he was both a staunch antiwar advocate who had sparked the crowd in Berkeley and also a man with substantial ego. Bundy patronizingly put his hand on Mailer's shoulder and said, "Well, of course, you don't really know much about it."

It was cocky and dismissive, and it immediately pushed Mailer's anger into overdrive. He became furious, inviting Bundy outside to settle the dispute in a manner that would have gratified Aaron Burr: "Let's go downstairs," Mailer growled.

"I was very brave," Mailer later recalled, "because he was obviously in better condition than I was. I was dissolute and full of drink. But I'd have killed him that night, I was so angry." Mailer added, "[O]ne night every three years you can win if you're gonna have [a fight]. That was one of those nights."[47]

Lillian Hellman, an old friend of Mailer's, was walking past when she overheard the argument. She couldn't believe what Mailer was doing. Before anything could happen, Hellman stepped between the two men and told Mailer to get out of there. Mailer told her that she didn't understand how men settled their differences, but Hellman didn't let him have enough air to make his case, telling him he was out of line and needed to control himself.

"How *dare* you, Norman!" she said.

To all who heard the commotion, it ended up sounding "like an older sister and her kid brother," Mailer remembered. "She was always such a celebrity fucker," Mailer added, the anger still not gone thirty years later. "It must be said of Lillian that when the chips were down she'd always go for the guy who had the most clout. And there was no doubt in her mind that McGeorge Bundy had a good deal more than I did. So she turned on me right in front of him." Hellman and Mailer didn't talk for two years.[48]

Mailer stormed off, likely to the bar, his pride hurt by Hellman's dressing-down in front of Bundy and the others. One drink led to the next, and Mailer turned to the crowd, looking for people he might go after in order to restore a bit of pride.

In the distance, he saw Buckley. Mailer walked straight up to him and said, "Put up your dukes."

Buckley saw booze in his friend's eyes. He detected the anger, but realized it was not directed at him. Buckley demurred. When Mailer persisted, Buckley demurred again, trying to laugh it away. But Mailer wouldn't let it go. Giving it one last try, Mailer raised his own fists to test Buckley's resolve.

Buckley knew Mailer didn't really want to fight but was instead out to save face. He saw that Mailer had approached him in "the semi-affectionate way in which we have always contended," adding, "there was nothing serious about it."[49] The threat fizzled.

Mailer never found anyone to fight that night, but the incident was more than just an unruly act. Beneath the hurt ego was a seething resentment, a fear of what was to come as the war kept drumming along, giving neither side much peace. Indeed, more than one guest recalled going to the ball and feeling a little like they were about to hear the tumbrels rolling outside, those carts during the French Revolution that carried the aristocrats to the guillotine. In the analogy, the artists, intellectuals, politicians, and social matrons at Truman Capote's Black and White Ball were the ones eating cake.

The guests left by four o'clock in the morning, and the party's enthusiasm was only punctured a bit by the 2:45 a.m. departure of

Frank Sinatra, who left to go to Jilly's, the dive bar that was one of his favorite hangouts. Seeking to minimize the stir of an early exit, Sinatra engaged the assistance of one of the waiters, who showed him a back exit. Sinatra gave him a hundred-dollar bill, which the waiter vowed to save to commemorate the night.[50]

All the major newspapers wrote detailed stories about the party, with Capote himself quietly allowing the *New York Times* society writer to see a copy of the guest list.

A year later, *Esquire* paid Buckley to write about the party. It was now 1967 and the political atmosphere was amped up even more because of the war in Vietnam, so *Esquire* proposed that Buckley write something about the politics of the ball. Buckley, who famously said he only discussed politics when someone was paying him to do it, reasoned that someone *was* in fact paying him to do it, so he drafted a long piece about the politics of it all.

Buckley's deduction: there was no politics to the party. It was simply for fun. Sure, it codified Capote's status as gatekeeper to the nation's social elite. And there were some funny jokes that bashed the lotus-eaters, as when Buckley pointed out to Capote a few months after the ball that there had been members of every modern presidential family there *except* Eisenhower.

"I don't happen to know any Eisenhower," said Capote icily, adding: "Do *you?*"

Buckley said the tone was, "as if to say: 'if you do, really, I wonder that *you* were invited.'"[51]

But on the whole, the party had been for fun.

Despite this ambition, the stench of Vietnam couldn't be avoided. Buckley sidestepped his run-in with Mailer, choosing instead to discuss journalist Pete Hamill's essay on the party. Hamill's piece had been a thudding critique, alternating between episodes from the party (". . . she looked just gorgeous in a white Balmain gown . . . Truman is a fat fellow, you know, and he was so nice and round and sweet and polite that, God, you just wanted to *hug* him. . . .") and overly dramatic events in Vietnam (*"You could*

hear the phwup-phwup of a mortar and the snapping of small arms fire
and then when it was quiet again, you realized that the young man next to
you was dead. His right eye was torn from his skull.").[52]

Buckley hated Hamill's piece. Not only was the writing bad, but
it also missed the point. "After all, one of the reasons why there is
fighting in Vietnam," wrote Buckley, "is so that people can have
fun together back home. And besides, if Society accepted the
dictum that so long as some people are suffering others may not
party together, there would never be any partying at all, especially
not on the evening of Mr. Capote's ball when the agony experienced by some of the uninvited almost certainly exceeded that of
the calm and resolute young men in Vietnam."[53]

Of all the invitees, Buckley said, only Secretary of Defense
Robert McNamara declined to attend because he felt he had to
focus on the war. Other government personnel had been present,
citing exactly the rationale Buckley offered. And anyway, more
than half the partygoers, "if called upon, could have conducted a
very long spontaneous teach-in against Vietnam. My God," Buckley reflected, "Norman Mailer alone would have been good until
five a.m. the day after the day after. And to back him up there was
Arthur Schlesinger, the redoubtable Galbraith, Walter Lippmann,
Drew Pearson, Norman Podhoretz—only Susan Sontag was
missing."[54]

That wasn't what the party was about. "It was all, after all, very
reassuring," Buckley wrote, quoting from *Vanity Fair*'s write-up:
"Jerome Robbins wondered if we weren't the list of those to be
shot first by the Red Guard; Kenneth Galbraith said no, not as
long as *he* was on it. . . . Clifton Daniel, for instance, jitterbugged
with an expertise that increased one's respect for The New York
Times. Arthur Schlesinger Jr. smiled beatifically as he performed a
spirited fox-trot."

"And," Buckley continued, "George Plimpton used a candelabra
to instruct his guest . . . in the mechanics of the Statue of Liberty
play [in football]. It was all very loose-jointed, psychedelic, very

apolitical, very anti-arbiter elegantarium; all the guests sensed, sort of, that they were *Hoffähig* [German for 'worthy of being accepted at court']; but it didn't matter much, and if there were politics in the situation, they were not explicit, nor even implicit, nor contrivable even by the most schematic imaginations."[55]

For others, the dissociation was too much. A soldier responded to *Time*'s coverage of the party with a letter saying he couldn't "bear to think of my country's future at the hands of this fat, lethargic, useless intelligentsia." Another editorialist wrote, "If this is what it takes to be 'in' in 1966 America, let us pray."[56]

Mailer shared their concern. As far back as 1964 he had written:

> The country was taking a turn, the colors were deepening, the knives of the afternoon were out, something of the best in American life might now be going forever. . . . One did not know any longer, you simply did not know any longer, but something was certain: the country was now part of the daily concern. One worried about it for the first time, the way you worried about family or work, a good friend or the future, and that was the most exceptional of emotions.[57]

By 1966, this worry had become even more pressing. Battles over the righteousness of the war had exacerbated the divide embodied by Buckley and Mailer. They had provoked deeper questions about the Liberal Establishment and made it all the more important that the fires from the right and left keep burning; after all, the cost of maintaining the Liberal Establishment was, in Vietnam at least, being paid in blood. By the mid-1960s, "The incredible war in Vietnam," said Paul Potter, president of SDS, "has provided the razor, the terrifying sharp cutting edge that has finally severed the last vestiges of illusion that morality and democracy are the guiding principles of American foreign policy." But it was more than just foreign policy that became suspect: "What kind of system is it that justifies the United States or any country seizing the destinies of

the Vietnamese people and using them callously for its own purpose?" asked Potter.

> What kind of system is it that disenfranchises people in the
> South, leaves millions upon millions of people throughout
> the country impoverished and excluded from the main-
> stream and promise of American society, that creates faceless
> and terrible bureaucracies and makes those the place where
> people spend their lives and do their work, that consistently
> puts material values before human values—and still persists
> in calling itself free and still persists in finding itself fit to
> police the world?[58]

As historian David Farber put it, "the Vietnam War had become
a prism on American society, refracting that society into bands of
linked but separate realities. Americans were not simply divided
politically over the war. The war had become much more: a way
for Americans to vent their feelings about the values, morals, and
'self-evident' truths that guided their everyday lives."[59]

The knives, in other words, were beginning to appear. Mailer
was worried, but also eager to contain the carnage. In developing the techniques of New Journalism, he had found his muse. In
deciding to write explicitly about the country, he had found his
subject. And in evaluating the war, he finally found his narrative.
But how much power did an aging radical really have?

9

A Searing Love of Country

I n early September 1967, Mailer received a phone call from Mitch Goodman, a fellow writer but also a leader of an emerging movement that would come to be called the Yippies. The Yippies were a derivation of the hippies, but unlike hippies, who mostly wanted to remove themselves from the culture of the lotus-eaters, the Yippies sought an answer in radical politics. They wanted to do what Mailer had been trying to do for at least a decade by combining the antiwar movement with the growing rebellion against social norms. Founded by Jerry Rubin and Abbie Hoffman, two longtime Mailer admirers, "Yippie" stood for Youth International Party. In 1967 it began to experiment with the kinds of guerrilla theater Mailer had initiated with his call to turn President Johnson's picture upside down. In the early part of the year, the Yippies had done things like burn money and draft cards. Now they were going to try something more dramatic.

Goodman asked Mailer if he would march with a large group of activists from the Lincoln Memorial to the Pentagon, where they would then protest America's military involvement in Vietnam and, they hoped, "invade the corridors of the Pentagon during office hours and close down some of their operation."[1] Some organizers had proposed marching to the Capitol building instead, but they

decided that would simply descend into sign-carrying and pontifi-
cating, not acting against the true enemy: America's war machine.
Would Mailer join them?

The idea was interesting to Mailer. There was some risk involved,
which he liked. Goodman also told him he would be accompanied by other left-wing literary figures, including Robert Lowell,
perhaps the most famous poet in America (whose face had just
appeared on the cover of *Time*); Paul Goodman, the cultural
critic and analyst of the youthful revolt against liberal pieties; and
Dwight Macdonald, the renowned literary critic who was also an
old friend. The Yippie leaders hoped the writers would make a
brief appearance a few days before the march at a fundraiser (held
in expectation of the legal fees they would incur), then trek to the
Pentagon with the protestors two days later and get arrested for
the cause.

While all that sounded fine, Mailer was beginning to feel a bit
disconnected from the youthful protests rising up around him in
1966 and 1967. He had once thought they would follow his plan
for social revolution against society's norms, that they would allow
him to lead. But he was increasingly coming to believe that their
actions were undisciplined and bordered on aimlessness, especially as the total removal from society practiced by the hippies
caught on. Unlike his deep complaints about the lotus-eaters, this
younger generation seemed to be anti-everything without seeking
to understand underlying motivations or struggling to propose
constructive alternatives. He wasn't sure he wanted to serve as a
symbolic leader for such a disparate group, a group who thought
total removal from society was a plausible solution.

More than this, though, he was slowly beginning to realize that
this younger generation didn't share the set of assumptions that
had grounded his complaints throughout the 1950s and 1960s.
Certain aspects of the liberal triptych he hated: the lionization
of rational thought, corporate capitalism, most of The Rules. But
others he couldn't leave behind. This younger generation seemed

eager to forego them all completely—rational thought for mystical thinking, capitalism for communism, The Rules for "do your own thing." Mailer was, after all, forty-four years old in 1967, old enough to be father to many of the protestors. When he spoke to an anti-war rally that year at Fillmore East in New York City, he opened with one of his standard, crude jokes, about a forty-year-old man who sees his ex-wife sitting with a young stud across the way. When the man belligerently asks the stud how he likes "sticking it up her worn-out old pussy?" the woman interjects: "He likes it just fine, once he gets past the worn-out part." Instead of eliciting laughs for breaking a social taboo, as had happened with older audiences in the past, the young crowd at Fillmore East grew hostile. They booed him for the lack of respect he showed and called him a fascist intent on preserving traditional power relations. Mailer hurried on with his speech, but he was aware of a growing disconnect.[2]

Still, as he weighed Goodman's offer to march to the Pentagon, he couldn't resist the opportunity to lead, especially in a protest against the war machine he had been complaining about for three decades. And unlike the other banal marches he'd seen, this one had some teeth. The warmth of the Berkeley crowd two years earlier still made him glow.

"Mitch," said Mailer, "I'll be there . . . but I can't pretend I'm happy about it."[3]

More than one hundred thousand protestors showed up at the Lincoln Memorial, a strong number, if not the quarter-million who had showed up to hear Martin Luther King, Jr.'s "I Have a Dream" speech in 1963 or the three hundred thousand who had showed up to the antiwar rally in New York City in March 1967. But this protest entailed risk. Indeed, fewer than half the protestors who showed up at the Lincoln Memorial made it all the way to the Pentagon.

Two days before the protest, at the fundraiser for anticipated legal fees, Mailer and the other celebrity protestors gave drunken speeches about the importance of what they were about to do. Mailer's speech was the most noteworthy—he affected his annoying Texas drawl and pretended to be LBJ, sentencing them all to die. Like LBJ, Mailer laced his talk with obscenities. Then he quickly shifted to an Irish accent, pretending to be an everyday working-class American who supported the war, one of those folks who voted for Buckley in 1965. This was agitprop theater. At one point, Mailer asked the members of the press to raise their hands and told them that before he'd come out to speak he had used the restroom, but the lights were out and he missed the bowl. He didn't want them reporting that the demonstrators had been unruly and debauched. He claimed that for himself.

It was an odd performance, but it had its brilliance. At a metaphorical level, by recounting the story of urinating in the dark, he was drawing parallels to what the United States was doing in Vietnam: operating blindly and missing the bowl. As he had done onstage, the United States should claim its error: "Some damn mistake had been made," Mailer had said of the toilet incident. But now he submitted himself to embarrassment and was going to "seize defeat, convert it to triumph."[4] The United States should follow his lead.

Even if they missed the metaphor, the performance worked: scads of reporters covered the event to report on Mailer's diatribe, and in that way Mailer used his celebrity and lurid imagery to promote the protest.

At the march itself, Mailer showed up wearing a dark grey pin-striped suit, a buttoned-up vest, and a maroon and blue regimental tie. This being the first time the counterculture joined the anti-war movement, he clearly did not resemble the rest of the hippy/Yippie protestors. To Mailer, they looked "like the legions of Sgt. Pepper's Band . . . assembled from all the intersections between history and the comic books, between legend and television, the Biblical archetypes and the movies."[5] He still positioned himself with them, but as older and more responsible. He made his way with Lowell and Macdonald and all the thousands of others from the symbolic center of American freedom (the Lincoln Memorial) to the symbolic center of American warmongering (the Pentagon). It wasn't a subtle message.

When the marchers got to the Pentagon, they were directed into huge cordoned-off, chain-link pens, where stages had been set up for music, speeches, and other performances. Rejecting the rational side of midcentury liberalism, an exorcism was planned to rid the country of the Pentagon. An Indian triangle, whatever that was, was forming at one end. Someone called for a "grope in." "Out, demons, out!" became a ritual chant. Mailer was sympathetic but incredulous. What was all this? It was not violent, but it also wasn't quite logical.

"You know I like this," Mailer said to Lowell, seemingly trying to convince himself as much as anyone else.[6]

Lowell was troubled by it all and shook his head. He hated chanting. He hated the war, sure, but this complete rejection was too far afield for him to comprehend. Was this how kids did things these days?

Macdonald was hopeful something brilliant might happen, but worried that things would devolve into violence. That seemed to be a growing trend these days, one he wasn't terribly fond of.

Of the thirty-five thousand protestors who made it to the Pentagon, a group of roughly one thousand were intent on provoking a violent response from the Deputy U.S. Marshals and the military police. The other thirty-four thousand were content to maintain the form of nonviolent protest inherited from Martin Luther King, Jr. When some of the violent one thousand unveiled the flag of the North Vietnamese Army and charged at the point in the pen closest to the Pentagon, Mailer, Lowell, and Macdonald shuffled away. Supporting the North Vietnamese was different from opposing American involvement in the Cold War. These protestors didn't seem to understand that. They were carried away with fervor. This was thoughtless.

"Listen," Mailer said, uncertain how the day would play out, "let's get arrested now."

"Look Norman," Lowell said, "if we're going to, shall we get away from here? I don't see any good accomplished if we're all picked up right next to a Vietcong flag."

That was not to be contested. Just imagine what the likes of William F. Buckley might say if they were arrested under the banner of the communists.

So they walked fifty yards from the flag, found an opening in the fence, walked through it toward the Pentagon, and encountered a low rope behind which two rows of military police were guarding the Pentagon.

A little too quickly, Mailer said, "Let's go," and before his compatriots had time to react, he hopped the rope and approached an MP, telling him he was headed to the Pentagon unless the MP arrested him.[7]

The MP was young and inexperienced. Unlike MPs a few years later, this one had no idea how to handle deliberate protestors to the civilized order. Mailer saw the fear in the young man's face. He was just doing his job. This MP wasn't the enemy, was he? The throes of protest had made it hard to tell.

And so the MP just stood there, too petrified to move. Mailer walked right past him to the second row of police, who, remarkably, also let him pass. Now he was starting to pick up his pace. He felt like a tailback running an end-around. He was incredulous. Would he wind up in the end zone? And what in the hell would he do if he actually made it to the Pentagon?

Finally, a collection of Deputy U.S. Marshals behind the lines of military police ordered him to return to the rope line or be arrested. Mailer repeated his line about heading to the Pentagon unless they took him in. The marshals jumped him, yanked him about a bit too harshly, and arrested him for transgressing a police line.

Lowell and Macdonald, who jumped the line a minute after

Mailer, were turned back, responsive to the marshals' demands that they leave. They would seek to get arrested several times later that day, all for naught. Lowell went home to write a poem about the event; the next time Mailer saw him he had written eight hundred lines.[8]

It was the beginning of a long afternoon of arrests made by the marshals. A total of 682 people were taken in that day, with increasing amounts of violence as the marshals' patience ran thin. When the permit for the march expired at midnight, a few hundred protestors remained in the parking lot of the Pentagon, mostly smoking pot. A disproportionate number of those who remained were women. The exhausted marshals sought to clear the lot with one brutal push, which came to be called "The Battle of the Wedge." Drained from a day of arrests and wearing their anger on their sleeves, the authorities seemed to single out the women. As Margie Stamberg of the *Washington Free Press* put it, "Slowly the wedge began to move in on people. With bayonets and rifle butts, they moved first on the girls in the front line, kicking them, jabbing at them again and again with the guns, busting their heads and arms to break the chain of locked arms. The crowd appealed to the paratroopers to back off, to join them, to just act human. They sang the 'Star-Spangled Banner' and other songs: but the troops at this point were non-men, the appeals were futile."[9] It was the first time the iron hand of reaction was shown to be so brutal when it came to the protests against Vietnam.

Mailer later speculated on why they had singled out the women: "to the Marshals and the soldiers, the enemy was finally there before them, all that Jew female legalistic stew of corruptions which would dirty the name of the nation and revile the grave of soldiers like themselves back in Vietnam, yes, the beatings went on, one by one generally of women, more women than men."[10] Mailer added: "they beat the women for another reason. To humiliate the demonstrators . . . ; they ground it into their faces that they sat there while their women were being taken off and no one of them or group of them dared to charge. . . . [T]he working class had plucked all stolen balls back."[11] The violence, Mailer surmised, was about restoring tradition.

Mailer himself missed most of this. He had already entered the world of bureaucratic mechanics. He was placed in a holding cell before being shuttled via Volkswagen to a larger courthouse that served as a temporary prison. Processing him and all the other arrested protestors took a day and a half. He missed a party in New York City that night, and, in the end, was given a sterner sentence than the rest of the protestors: five days in jail compared to one, with the judge using him as an example. His lawyers fought the heightened sentence and eventually won.

When he got arrested, Mailer (writing of himself in third-person) "felt as if he were being confirmed. (After twenty years of radical opinions, he was finally under arrest for a real cause.)"[12] Protesting the war had given him a dose of authenticity, a feeling of renewal, a sense that he was finally rejecting obedience for something righteous, a serious effort to remake America.

Others recognized the moral authority of the march, too. Robert McNamara, the Secretary of Defense, watched from the roof of the Pentagon. He was beginning to doubt the efficacy of the war himself, and he thought, perhaps wistfully, "that had the protestors been more disciplined—Gandhi-like—they would have achieved their objective of shutting us down."[13] Alas, it was the violence, not the protest, that made headlines the following day.

Feeling Gandhi-like himself, Mailer didn't want to plead "No contest" when he was arrested but "Guilty," standing up for what he had done. He also wanted to get out of jail. "I wanted to get out in one day because I had the feeling there was a book in me," he said, "and five days in jail could take the edge off that book."[14] Even at the height of an experience, he thought not only of enjoying the feeling he was always after—that of having done something courageous—but also of writing about it. After what he had seen and heard, he thought, "What a good short story I've got."[15]

His agent contacted *Harper's*, which gave him ten thousand dollars for twenty thousand words. His deadline was in a month. When Mailer ran into Willie Morris, *Harper's* new, thirty-two-year-old editor, shortly after negotiations had concluded, Mailer crouched like a boxer and said, "I will have a great twenty thousand words in one month from today."[16]

Three weeks later, Morris visited Mailer to check on his progress. Mailer had an amazing ninety thousand words.

"He had gone up there and hadn't had anything to drink for a month, leading a Spartan life with Beverly, and he had turned out this incredible ninety thousand words," Morris said.[17]

Then Morris started reading it. As he did, he realized the material was something special, much more than a simple account of the march. What Mailer had written, in fact, was a revealing portrait of the times that were undergoing dramatic changes, the birthing pangs of a new order, pangs that were dividing the nation and bringing about violence. "When I finished reading it," Morris said, "I embraced him."[18]

Morris called his boss to tell him what he had just read. His boss asked how the ninety thousand words should be broken up.

"I think we should run all of it at once," was Morris's amazing answer.[19]

Just like that, Norman Mailer's article, "The Steps of the Pentagon," appeared in *Harper's* in March 1968 and became the longest essay ever published in American magazine history. It took up every page in *Harper's*, and they still had to reduce the font size. It was published in book form shortly thereafter as *The Armies of the Night*.

Most people loved it. It not only made them laugh at Mailer and his personal wildness, but it also made them understand what the radical left was protesting—and what it was up against. The book's genius was Mailer's: the ability to locate and describe profound truths in American life through the actions of the everyday, a talent amplified by the fact that "the everyday" in this instance wasn't any normal day, but a major protest not only against Vietnam but against everything the country had become since the Second World War.

The participants themselves were shocked by Mailer's ability to remember so many tiny details, and to find big truths in those details. He was drunk the night of the fundraiser, everyone knew, but they all independently attested to his remarkable accuracy in recounting even the smallest gestures. As Robert Lowell wrote to Mailer, "everything I saw and remembered seems true as one could ask. I'm sure the rest I never saw or forgot is true too. A staggering immensity."[20]

Macdonald was equally impressed. Although Mailer took no notes, "he reproduces, with few errors or omissions I detected, the scenes and the dialogues of the weekend." After reading it, Lowell wrote to Macdonald, "when you're with [another novelist], you think he's so sensitive and alert, and then you find later he wasn't taking in anything, while Norman seems not to pay much attention, but now it seems he didn't miss a trick—what a memory!"[21]

Lowell added, in a letter to Mailer, "everywhere I go students hold up *Harpers* [*sic*] and ask if I've read it, this one question."[22] Mailer had struck a nerve.

Some of Mailer's insights are stunning. In searching for a metaphor for the Pentagon, Mailer decided it was like the tip of a giant can of deodorant. As he explained (writing again of himself in the third person), "For years he had been writing about the nature of totalitarianism, its need to render populations apathetic, its instrument—the destruction of mood. Mood . . . was a scent which rose from the acts and calms of nature, and totalitarianism was a deodorant to nature. Yes, and by the logic of this metaphor, the Pentagon looked like the five-sided tip on the spout of a spray can to be used under the arm, yes, the Pentagon was spraying the deodorant of its presence all over the fields of Virginia."[23]

Before the march began, some protestors were passing around a bag of bread and some peanut butter, schoolyard sustenance. An

African American named Harris looked at the bag of white bread and laughed. The bread, Mailer wrote, "was the comic embodiment now of a dozen little ideas, of corporation-land which took the taste and crust out of bread and wrapped the remains in wax paper." It was "television, the fun of situation comedy shows with commercials" and "the infiltrated enemy who had a grip on them everywhere, forced them to collaborate if only by imbibing the bread (and substance) of that enemy." But most significantly it was "*white* bread, not black bread—a way to remind them all that [Harris] was one of the very few Negroes here. . . . Here he was . . . with White bread—White money, White methods, even White illegalities. It was exorbitant, Mailer decided glumly, to watch such virtuosity with a hangover."[24]

At one point, Mailer stopped to consider the origins of the Cold War. He surmised that at some point near the end of the Second World War, a "consensus of the most powerful middle-aged and elderly Wasps in America—statesmen, corporation executives, generals, admirals, newspaper editors, and legislators had pledged an intellectual troth: they had sworn with a faith worthy of medieval knights that Communism was the deadly foe of Christian culture. If it were not resisted in the postwar world, Christianity itself would perish. So had begun a Cold War with intervals of overt war, mixed with period of modest collaboration."[25]

For those seeking to understand the mindset of the youth in America, these explanations helped. And for the youth who were seeking to understand why they felt the way they did, Mailer cast an illuminating light.

Along the way he even had time for a crack about his old friend, Bill Buckley. "This condition of innocence," he said about being arrested for a cause he believed in, "was not, however, particularly disagreeable since it forced him to watch everything with the attention, let us say, of a man like William Buckley spending his first hour in a Harlem bar—no, come! things are far safer for Mailer at the Pentagon."[26]

The book was a culmination of a lot of things Mailer had been saying since 1959. The reportage and third-person narrative harkened back to *Advertisements for Myself* and lots since. But *Armies* was better. The frustrations he described with America the "Technology Land" were similar to those that had appeared in previous books, only now they were crisper. The hope for a more open future? That was there too, only more chastened, realistic, and articulate.

The book got better reviews than anything Mailer had ever published, including *The Naked and the Dead*. In a gusher in the *New York Times Book Review*, Alfred Kazin compared Mailer to Walt Whitman. Commenting on how Whitman "staked his work on finding the personal connection between salvation as an artist and the salvation of his country," Kazin concluded, "I believe that *Armies of the Night* is just as brilliant a personal testimony as Whitman's diary of the Civil War, *Specimen Days*, and Whitman's great essay on the crisis of the Republic during the Gilded Age, 'Democratic Vistas.' I believe that it is a work of personal and political reportage that brings to the inner and developing crises of the United States at this moment admirable sensibilities, candid intelligence, the most moving concern for America itself. Mailer's intuition in the book is that the times demand a new form. He has found it."[27]

Richard Gilman in *The New Republic* admired Mailer's desire "to do for our present situation and by implication all our communal pasts and futures, what our traditional instrumentalities of knowledge and transcription haven't been able to do—place our public acts and lives in a human context." For this, "Mailer has put us all in his debt."[28] Even *The New York Times* came around, with Eliot Fremont-Smith saying, "Here, in this extraordinary book . . . all the facets of Norman Mailer, man and artist, settle momentarily into place; and we sense, as he senses, perhaps for the first time . . . Mailer whole and in place."[29]

Lowell's response was equally revealing. At a party before the march, Lowell had said to Mailer, "Norman, I really think you are the best journalist in America," to which Mailer snapped back, "Well, Cal, there are days when I think of myself as being the best *writer* in America."[30] Now, having read *Armies*, Lowell wrote to Mailer, "I don't want to call you a journalist again; this is non-fiction, comedy, history. . . . Let me bow to your memory, mind and stamina. May we remain as good friends in life as in story."[31]

When *Commentary* agreed to print up a short, more standard reporter's piece by Mailer on the march (which appeared as Part II of the book), Dwight Macdonald wrote, "[I] have to admit, grudgingly, it's good, solid, and imaginative—also, worse, in a quite different mode than the *Harpers* [sic] piece, so you are versatile, too, for God's sake. There must be something wrong, give me a little time, I'll find it, you watch. . . ."[32]

The reviews have stood the test of time. Decades later, one radical from the era called it "probably the best book out of the whole period," while another referred to it as "the bible of the Movement."[33]

Buckley commented on *The Armies of the Night* as well, multiple times. He wrote a column proclaiming, "Norman Mailer is the proper bard for such an age as this," adding: "He is the man to write a hundred million words on why we should all be indignant against Lyndon Johnson, and reverential toward the Communists," unfairly dismissing Mailer's radical critiques of the country as little more than the complaints of the old and familiar enemy. If *Armies* was about the left, Buckley hoped Mailer might be commissioned to write about what was going on in the entirety of the nation: "It will take just about that many words to explain what's going on," he wrote. "Perhaps the *New York Times* would devote its entire Sunday edition to it?"[34]

Buckley beat the *Times* to it, inviting Mailer to be a guest on his new weekly television show *Firing Line*.

Firing Line, which began in 1966, capped off an extraordinary run for Buckley. His syndicated column, "On The Right," had just

been expanded to run three times a week, and now a remarkable 205 newspapers across the country featured it. He had just
won an award for Best Column of the Year from a collection of
newspaper editors. Meanwhile, *National Review* had hit yet another
peak, achieving a readership of ninety-four thousand. This was
as much as any opinion journal in the nation. *National Review*
mostly preached to the converted, but the number of converted
was growing.

Capitalizing on these successes, *Firing Line* was supposed to have
started in 1965, but Buckley's mayoral campaign—yet another high
point—had gotten in the way. The weekly show began in earnest
in 1966, hosting a wide swath of intellectuals from the left who
were yearning to go toe-to-toe with Buckley. Although it varied a
bit during the first few years, the format was simple. There was a
small stage with two chairs and a table in front of a studio audience.
Buckley, holding an ever-present clipboard, would introduce his
guest that week, often with a dash of humor and casual putdown or
two. He would then start with a provocative question that inevitably
led the two into fierce debate. The debates sometimes got vicious,
which was the point: the show was modeled after the prizefights
that had inspired the Mailer–Buckley debate in 1962. "I was thinking that *Firing Line* ought to be a challenge to the liberal establishment to see if their champions could go three rounds with the boy
wonder," said Neal Freeman. "It was the fight of the week."[35]

Buckley pulled no punches. When Staughton Lynd, a radical
Yale historian who had recently visited Hanoi in North Vietnam
with former SDS president Tom Hayden, came on the show, Buckley asked: "Were you in a position where you could actually exercise your scholarly apparatus or did they simply treat you in Hanoi
the way the average observer would have expected that they would
treat you in Hanoi: simply that, here is an American idiot, whom
we are in a position to manipulate?"

When socialist and former presidential nominee Norman
Thomas spoke out against Vietnam, Buckley asked him to explain

how he could have supported the war in Korea while opposing Vietnam: "Now, is [your change of position] a function of age?"[36] When the press asked Buckley why Robert Kennedy refused to appear on *Firing Line*, he answered coolly, "Why does baloney reject the grinder?"[37]

If certain members of the liberal left began to avoid the show, viewers did not. KQED in San Francisco skipped *Firing Line* one week because the tape got stuck in transit, and more than 180 calls flooded the station within the first hour.[38] Even his antagonists hailed the show's appeal. As one of his frequent on-air battlers put it, Buckley "is an exceedingly witty, attractive and rather insidious spokesman for a point of view for which I have few sympathies. But if we don't want to die of sheer boredom, the Buckleys [of the world] should be encouraged."[39] Within three years, *Firing Line* would win an Emmy.

By 1967, Buckley's fame as a public intellectual was reaching its peak. In January, he appeared in a profile on page one of the *Wall Street Journal*. In March, *Harper's* profiled him extensively in a story called, "God, Man, and William F. Buckley." And in November, *Time* featured him in a cover story, thus solidifying his status among American intellectuals. The David Levine drawing on the *Time*'s cover—a penciled portrait drawn to accentuate Buckley's eggheaded angles—was not flattering, but the story revolved around the notion that Buckley was teaching America that "Conservatism can be fun." After describing display after witty display of Buckley's humor, *Time* quoted Buckley saying, "I feel I qualify spiritually and philosophically as a conservative, but temperamentally I am not of the breed." He had too much fun. In naming some of his best friends, Buckley named a bunch of eccentric lefties, including Murray Kempton, Steve Allen, and, of course, Norman Mailer.[40]

Buckley enjoyed *Time*'s summary of his status: "Buckley is in vogue as never before," *Time* wrote. "He is asked to write non-ideological articles for nonconservative publications. He has just finished a piece for *Esquire* on Truman Capote's masked ball, to which he was invited as a matter of course. He and Pat appeared on the cover of a recent issue of *Town & Country*. His letters are printed wherever he chooses to write them." Buckley, *Time* added, "stands in grave danger, in fact, of being adopted by the liberal establishment he deplores," citing as evidence an episode of *Firing Line* in which Democratic speechwriter Richard Goodwin tells Buckley, "Any society, and particularly the Great Society, needs a responsible force on the right. I think that all of us are very glad that you are that force. It might have been somebody who is mean and sharp and nasty and unwilling to debate the issues. As long as you're there, it protects the civilities of discourse in a free society." To which Buckley replied, "I'm going to dissolve at this rate. I'm not used to being treated so kindly."[41]

Indeed, as he sat back in his chair on the set of *Firing Line*, pen in mouth, arms behind his head, legs crossed, late 1967 and early 1968 must have seemed like a good time to be William F. Buckley, Jr. The right wing was awakening, and everyone wanted Buckley to explain it to them. He did the best he could, even if he scrupulously avoided discussing the rage he sensed lying beneath it all. Occasionally he shuddered at the disconnect between the kind of people he wanted American conservatives to be and the kind of people who crossed the street to shake his hand—the angry working classes. He worried a bit that the left's awakening in response to the Vietnam War might raise a viable alternative to his rightward pulls. But mostly he was feeling good about the status of the right in American life, and that big things were about to happen.

And now, in early 1968, sitting across from him on the *Firing Line* stage was his old friend. Their conversation would not only be crucial in helping Mailer and Buckley understand the dynamic transformations of the late 1960s, but it would also lay bare for the nation the challenges that lay ahead and the fundamental questions being asked of the traditional order.

Buckley introduced Mailer by quoting a reviewer who had said, "we are assured that our hero fought one of his brawls after getting two hammer blows to the head, that he put Kennedy in office, and could put Floyd Patterson back on his throne, that he out-debated Buckley, that he out-writes everybody since Hemingway, and out-loves everybody since Casanova. In short, that he can lick anybody in the house."

Everyone in the studio laughed, except Mailer. "I never claimed I was the greatest lover in the world," he said with dead seriousness.

"Only since Casanova that is," Buckley corrected him.

"I don't even claim that," said Mailer. Otherwise, he would accept the rest of the accolades.

Buckley then gave Mailer a hard time about one of his earlier books, a novel from 1966 called *Why Are We in Vietnam?* The book didn't have anything to do with Vietnam, at least on the surface. Instead, it told the story of an eighteen-year-old Texas kid who goes hunting in Alaska with his best friend and dad. His dad is a corporate bigwig, but the liberal premise of postwar America that made him wealthy has also hollowed him out spiritually. He needs to catch a grizzly to demonstrate his manliness. Eventually, with the help of a loud helicopter, the three find a grizzly and kill it. But the dad claims the bear for himself even though his son actually did the deed. Dejected, the son and his friend go on a long hike, stripping down naked to experience nature at its most pristine. They see a world unadorned by technology and civilization, and find it beautiful. They go home, newly aware of blood and beauty. It is technology and corporate capitalism that robs us of our humanity, the book suggested. The day after the hike, the two boys return home to Texas and are soon "off to see the wizard in Vietnam." The book's last lines are "This is D.J., Disc Jockey to America turning off. Vietnam, hot damn."[42]

Mailer knew he was challenging people with the book. The metaphor was obscure and the language, a ragtag hip-hop kind meant to resemble how young people were beginning to speak, was sometimes hard to follow. "Hip hole and hupmobile, Braunschweiger," the book began, "you didn't invite Geiger and his counter for nothing, here is D.J. the friendLee voice at your service—hold tight young America—introductions come. Let go of my dong Shakespeare, I have gone too long."[43] The rest is more of the same.

"There is a tendency among the kids in America now to talk more for the pleasure of the sound than for the literal meaning," Mailer wrote to the translator who had the unenviable job of translating the book into Japanese, "and this book is an attempt, among other things, to capture the mood of rebellion among the young people in America."[44]

It didn't work. Most readers missed Mailer's argument about Vietnam—that it was being pursued by the United States not on geopolitical grounds, or even ideological ones, but instead as a way to satisfy a spiritual hunger. Granville Hicks said in the *Saturday Review* that the book struck him "not as a hoax but as a lark, a book that Mailer, in his perhaps perverse way, got a kick out of writing." *Life* rhetorically asked, "Is it worth reading? Only because the 16-year-old behind it is a 44-year-old named Norman Mailer committing atrocity on his talent."[45]

Buckley didn't care for *Why Are We in Vietnam?* either. In an article defending the right of the wealthy to enjoy their wealth (while differentiating between "the deserving rich," who worked for it, and "the undeserving rich," who didn't), Buckley admired the artistry of, say, someone who corners the soybean market, because "My guess is that the last man to corner the soybean market, whoever he was, put at least as much time and creative energy into the cornering of it as, say, Norman Mailer put into his latest novel, and produced something far more bearable."[46]

The book was nonetheless one of five shortlisted for a National Book Award, alongside Joyce Carol Oates's *A Garden of Earthly Delights*, Chaim Potok's *The Chosen*, William Styron's *Confessions of Nat Turner*, and Thornton Wilder's *The Eighth Day*. It didn't win.

On *Firing Line*, Buckley didn't want to talk about *Why Are We in Vietnam?* He went straight to *Armies*. "I think everyone should read

[it]," Buckley said, "because I think it's an extremely interesting and enjoyable book."

Mailer interrupted, "Well, I wish someone on the Rightwing would write a book that would be as good, because it would be a great help to us on the Left."

Buckley laughed. "You wouldn't notice it if it were written."

"No," said Mailer, "I would notice it. You know, I'm a lover of literature." Mailer added that he thought Evelyn Waugh, a noted conservative, was a "marvelous" writer. "Unfortunately," said Mailer, "he's not an American."

"Yeah, umm. Unfortunately, he's dead," Buckley said of the writer, who had died in 1966.

"That too," Mailer said.[47]

But neither Mailer nor Buckley wanted to remain too playful. They wanted to discuss the morality of the surging protest movements in America, as well as talk about how one can live in a country undergoing dramatic changes, and how intellectuals can manage and control vibrant social changes without allowing them to derail the entire nation. Change is always scary, especially when it threatens to bring about a whole new set of assumptions about life.

Buckley asked about the style of the book, wondering about Mailer's "ruthless self-criticism." What was the point of the sort of mock introspection Mailer used throughout the book? Mailer didn't see the book as a "tremendous confession." Instead, he was trying to use his observations to put on display the insanity of "the social mechanisms of the country."

"Oddly enough," Mailer reminded Buckley, "we'd agree on half the social mechanisms [that] are insane and part company on the others." Using himself as a character in the book was a way to access the insanity that both Buckley and Mailer acknowledged.

Buckley then asked Mailer about a line he used in explaining why he was arrested: "I transgressed a police line," Mailer had written in *Armies*. Buckley joked: "I never thought I'd hear you utter a word with that many syllables."

Mailer laughed. "It's because of our close and continuing correspondence."

Finally, Buckley refocused the discussion, getting to the heart of the matter and asking about the book's moral, "because the book does have a moral, doesn't it?"

Mailer said he was trying to enter the psychology of the left, to shake it from its liberal pretensions, to give it a sense of style and demonstrate that some things were worth risking, even though the starched society in which they lived didn't like radicals to think that way. Blind obedience to The Rules needed to be given up; authority needed to be questioned. "People on the Left are more law-abiding than anybody else," he said. "That's why they are on the Left." He was trying to show them how to protect the wider culture without giving up on the entire commonweal.

Buckley, thinking of the hippies and Yippies, couldn't let Mailer get away with saying that those on the left were more law-abiding than those on the right. He said, to much laughter, "Explain that, would you?"

Mailer tried. "Just as the disease of the Right is greed, big-otry, insensitivity, and general stupidity—yourself excluded, sir, I assure you of that—so the disease on the Left has always been excessive propriety in family life, excessive obedience to all the small laws of daily life, such as only crossing at the corners. You'll find that many more Communists and Trotskyites and people like that will cross at corners. You see, the Minute Men or FBI men, you know, won't."

Mailer could have pointed out that the leaders of the march to the Pentagon had requested and received a permit to conduct their protest. Instead, he used as evidence the men who had crossed in the middle of the street in 1965 to ask why he didn't support Buckley for mayor. "Mailer," they said, "what have you got against Buckley?"

"I said if I didn't have an idea in my head, I'd be for him myself," Mailer said.

"You always find the right word," replied Buckley, smiling.

Mailer's point was that he was so strenuously against the war and everything it stood for that he was ready to go to jail to protest it, ready to put some skin in the game. Would he have risked life imprisonment? Buckley asked. "I'm too much of a pleasure-lover to even dream of enjoying jail," Mailer said. If that had been the threat, Mailer would have had to go underground or leave the country, or even "turn into an enemy of the country."

And that got them to the point Buckley had been after: "[A]ren't you, in one sense, an enemy of the country?" Buckley wondered if the protests of the left could be conceived as anti-American. It was a vital question, because so many on the hippy- and Yippie-left seemed willing to give up on their country, unaware of the baby in the bathwater.

"No, sir, not yet," Mailer answered.

"What do you mean, 'not yet'?"

"Well," said Mailer, "I mean I still believe that this country is a marvelous country and that one fights within this country. If one's completely wiped off the board, in other words, if you have no way to fight for your ideas any longer in this country, then you have to decide one of two things, which is either, one, your ideas [are] wrong, or two, the country is wrong." He clearly thought the latter, and he was still willing to fight to preserve the virtuous American heart.

Mailer was trying to convey the sort of renewed patriotism he had felt during the march. It had hit him while crossing the Potomac en route to the Pentagon: "the sense of America divided on this day," he wrote in *Armies*, "now liberated some undiscovered patriotism in Mailer so that he felt a sharp searing love for his country in this moment and on this day . . . , a love so lacerated he felt as if a marriage were being torn and children lost—never does one love so much as then, obviously then."[48] No, he was no enemy of the country.

But of course what Mailer saw as an irreparable divorce was

really a battle over the terms of the social order. Possessing the assumptions of an older age, he recognized his distance and his fear of "children lost." He may have confronted authority and been arrested, but he still hoped his country wouldn't slip too far from its promise. He was growing concerned that all could be lost if the youth pushed their challenges too far.

As if unable to get beyond his Cold War framework, Buckley asked Mailer if he was still sympathetic to communism. "I detest Communism," Mailer said, "I detest it much more than you do, because I know much more about it." Buckley, laughing, asked if those on the other side of the Iron Curtain "would be much less frightened by a Mailer Administration than say a Buckley Administration?"

Mailer laughed back. "I love the way we're treating each other as world leaders. You see," he said, "I'm not the only narcissist in the house."

The entire exchange was illuminating. "Seeing Buckley and Mailer on the tube yesterday, I can't get over it," wrote Mel Lyman, a musician in the process of creating the underground newspaper *Avatar*. "The greatest representation of the two extremes I've seen in a long time. Conservative meets liberal, right meets left, before meets after. Buckley didn't know what the fuck Mailer was talking about, it just jammed his computer, he even had to resort to child-ish insults to try and keep up his end."

Lyman was a man of the left, but he respected Buckley. For Lyman, though, Buckley was too much of a traditionalist to under-stand the morality of the left's protests. Buckley, like many others, was more comfortable dismissing them as either simple enemies of the country or communists. He didn't want to risk the concessions he might have to make if he took them seriously. "I love Buck-ley," Lyman wrote, "but he makes me very sad, he's completely mastered the art of living in prison but Mailer's mastered the art of what you do after you get out, and Buckley doesn't even know there is an out."[49]

At the National Book Awards that year, *Armies* took first prize in the Arts and Letters category, beating out Hannah Arendt's *Men in Dark Times*, Peter Gay's *Weimar Culture*, Gertrude Himmelfarb's *Victorian Minds*, and Gordon S. Haight's *George Eliot*. It went on to win a Pulitzer Prize and more.

There were rumors Mailer wouldn't show up to accept the National Book Award as a form of protest against the war. The rumors proved false. "[S]tanding on this podium," he said in his acceptance speech, "your speaker is here to state that he likes prizes, honors, and awards and will accept them."[50] He referenced Jean-Paul Sartre, who in 1964 had refused the Nobel Prize in Literature as a form of protest against the bourgeoisie that was using awards to coopt society's true rebels. Sartre had wanted to be known as simply "Jean-Paul Sartre" not "Jean-Paul Sartre, Nobel Prize Winner." But Mailer disagreed. "The most bourgeois elements in French society had been speaking of him for years as Jean-Paul Sartre, perverted existentialist," Mailer said. "How much better for the final subtleties of their brain if they had been obliged instead to think of him as Jean-Paul Sartre, perverted existentialist *and* Nobel Prize Winner."

Mailer went on to warn the gathered guests about what he saw coming, about the demise of the liberal center and the violent birthing pangs of a new order. "We are a savagely mechanical society poised upon the lip, no, the main of a spiritual revolution which will wash the psychic roots of every national institution out to sea," he said. "We are on the brink of dreams and disasters. We are entering a world in which the value systems of the stoutest ego will spin like a turning table, the assertions of the inner voice go caroming through vales of electronic rock."[51]

The speech exposed a lurking fear inside of Mailer, a frustration that the future was spiraling in a million different directions that neither he nor anyone else could control. He knew something was coming, but he wasn't sure what it was. And he wasn't sure he was going to like it. As he had put it in the last pages of *Armies*, at his lyrical best:

> She is America, once a beauty of magnificence unparalleled, now a beauty with a leprous skin. She is heavy with child— no one knows if legitimate—and languishes in a dungeon whose walls are never seen. Now the first contractions of her fearsome labor begin—it will go on: no doctor exists to tell the hour. It is only known that false labor is not likely on her now, no, she will probably give birth, and to what?—the most fearsome totalitarianism the world has ever known? or can she, poor giant, tormented lovely girl, deliver a babe of a new world brave and tender, artful and wild? Rush to the locks. God writhes in his bonds. Rush to the locks. Deliver us from our curse. For we must end on the road to that mystery where courage, death, and the dream of love give promise of sleep.[52]

But there would be no sleep, for the portentous signs he saw coming were just around the corner.

10

The Assassination of Politics

By mid-1968, Mailer was becoming increasingly unnerved by the times. The violence he feared seemed to have arrived. "[S]o much has happened here," he wrote his Japanese translator in June, speaking of just the first half of the year, ". . . that politics reminds me now of nothing so much as the movie serials we used to see when we were children. . . . [W]hat will this week's climax be?" He then added: "Every sign indicates that we will have revolutions, counter-revolutions or both."[1]

Mailer was referring to the seemingly perpetual cycle of social challenges being dispatched with violence in 1968, which then led to the violent radicalization of protestors who had to be put down with still more violence. In the process, the last shreds of the commonweal seemed to be evaporating.

It had been an awful year so far. In January 1968, the communist opposition in Vietnam surprised the American-supported south with a powerful assault that left several southern cities in tatters, and even the American embassy in threat. What was called the Tet Offensive (because it occurred on the Vietnamese holiday of Tet) shattered the notion that the U.S. government had been talking honestly about the war for years. This wasn't an easy battle against a pre-modern opponent. The enemy wasn't standing, as

General William Westmoreland had told the *New York Times* just two months earlier, at the "beginning of a great defeat."[2] Instead, after Tet, even those who supported the war lost confidence in the people running it. Either they were lying or they were incompetent. Neither option was terribly reassuring. It was Tet that prompted the iconic newscaster Walter Cronkite, "the most trusted man in America," to turn against the war, saying on national television it was "more certain than ever that the bloody experience of Vietnam is to end in stalemate" and that the only rational way out is "to negotiate, not as victors, but as an honorable people who lived up to their pledge to defend democracy, and did the best they could."[3]

Cronkite expected to be deluged by critical responses. Instead, he received silence, even from the president. "[I]n the past Lyndon Johnson had been quick to telephone me," Cronkite recalled. But now, nothing. "The explanation came many months later, when we learned that the President was actually stunned by the broadcast." Bill Moyers, then an assistant to the president's press secretary, watched the broadcast with the president and later told Cronkite, "The President flipped off the set and said, 'If I've lost Cronkite, I've lost middle America.' "[4]

Six weeks later, Eugene McCarthy decided to run against President Johnson in the Democratic primary, an almost unheard-of intraparty rebuke to a sitting president. McCarthy waged his entire campaign *against* the president's hawkish policy on Vietnam, using Tet to gain support. "Only a few months ago," he said, "we were told that 65 per cent of the [South Vietnamese] population was secure. Now we know that even the American embassy is not secure."[5] He was running, he said, to "alleviate the sense of political helplessness" and a "growing sense of alienation from politics" coming from the younger generation.[6] On March 12, McCarthy captured 42 percent of the vote in the New Hampshire primary. LBJ won more votes—49 percent, mostly from write-ins (he still hadn't formally declared his intention to run for reelection)—but he'd been made to look vulnerable.

Sensing the soft spot, four days later Robert Kennedy, the savvy heir to his brother's legacy, maybe smarter and more ruthless if not as good-looking, entered a suddenly congested Democratic primary. As with McCarthy, Kennedy's appeal was that he might harness the growing revolt, exorcise the demons of liberalism's mistakes, and lead the nation through a smooth birthing process. He asked the nation to empathize with the Vietnamese, a new tone coming from someone in power. He asked the country to understand the animus coming from black America. When he spoke on college campuses, he was greeted like a rock star. As Buckley put it, Kennedy "knows how to give the impression of fluidity, of that magic motion one hankers after when one is convinced that, as a society, we are stranded in the middle of the road, with great world forces careening by us in every direction."[7]

With McCarthy and Kennedy destroying any idea that LBJ was loved, the sitting president, the epitome of postwar American liberalism and its dual loyalties to the Cold War and the New Deal, became frighteningly aware he couldn't even count on the support of his own party. It was in the midst of its own civil war. He queried his staff. He looked at the polls. He was told he would probably still win in November. But he hated the possibility of getting tossed out so unceremoniously. And then he thought of the fact that his father and grandfather had both died at sixty-four, an age Johnson would reach in the final year of a second term (indeed, he did end up dying at sixty-four). He thought of his life in politics and of how he had missed watching his children grow up, and how now it was turning out to be the same with his grandchildren. He thought of how he might be hampered in fighting the Vietnam War if he had to play politics during an election year. And then he thought of losing again. So he made his decision. On March 31, the president announced he would not seek reelection. "There is division in the American house now," he said on national television, echoing Abraham Lincoln. "There is divisiveness among us all tonight. And holding the trust that is mine, as President of all the people, I cannot disregard the peril to the progress of the American people and the hope and the prospect of peace for all peoples."[8]

Buckley had a less charitable interpretation of LBJ's decision: "[P]eople built like Lyndon Johnson do not voluntarily give up their power," wrote Buckley. "They are pushed out. Lyndon Johnson was pushed out."[9] By whom? By the American people. "It seemed, for a moment," wrote David Wyatt, a young college protestor at the time, "as if the peace movement had won."[10]

But then things quickly turned dark. Shortly before LBJ's announcement, one of Martin Luther King, Jr.'s marches had become violent, and King couldn't stop it. In his hotel room that night, King had pulled the sheets over his head and said, "Maybe we just have to admit that the day of violence is here."[11] For King, that day arrived very soon indeed: just four days after LBJ's announcement, the apostle of peace was killed while standing on the balcony of a Memphis motel.

"For those of you who are black and are tempted to . . . be filled with hatred and mistrust of the injustice of such an act, against all white people," said Robert Kennedy, in a black neighborhood in Indianapolis, trying to head off rioting in the aftermath of King's assassination, "I would only say that I can also feel in my own heart the same kind of feeling. I had a member of my family killed, but he was killed by a white man."[12]

RFK's pleas didn't work. Weeks of violence ravaged cities across the country. White House secretaries reported to the president that white people in the capital's business district had surrendered the sidewalks. General Westmoreland was in Washington briefing the president on Vietnam at the time, and the two men took a helicopter ride over the capital. "It looked considerably more distressing than Saigon during the Tet Offensive," Westmoreland said.[13] Billions of dollars' worth of damage was done, as looting and arson seemed the only way to be heard. Sociologist Harry Edwards later said, "It became absolutely clear: you don't want Dr. King, you assassinated non-violent direct action, you've tried to kill the dream. OK. Here's a taste of the nightmare."[14]

King's death also provoked fierce infighting over the direction of the civil rights movement. If the apostle of peace had been shot dead by a white man, was there anything left to do but endorse those who vowed to fight back? But where would that lead? No one knew. Chicago mayor Richard Daley thought he had an answer when he ordered his city's policemen to shoot to kill any arsonists and to maim looters. The extremes were taking over.

Two and a half weeks later, students stormed the administration buildings at Columbia University, just blocks from Mailer and Buckley's apartments. As Yale University chaplain William Sloane Coffin put it, "the universities, starting as bases for protest, ended up as targets for it."[15] At issue was the construction of a university gymnasium in Morningside Park, a finger of the overwhelmingly white Columbia University reaching into a black part of town. That small spark ignited the smoldering flames of discontent among the students. They ended up occupying five buildings, initiating a weeklong strike protesting the war, the university, the entire Liberal Establishment, everything. Eventually police stormed the buildings, used axes to enter locked offices and conference rooms, and carried the student-occupiers, nearly 1,200 of them, down several flights of stairs. Many came down bloody.

"Our young people," said Columbia president Grayson Kirk, "in disturbing numbers, appear to reject all forms of authority, from whatever source derived, and they have taken refuge in a turbulent and inchoate nihilism whose sole objectives are destructive. I know of no time in our history when the gap between the generations has been wider or more potentially dangerous."[16]

Demonstrating the gap between the generations, Mark Rudd, president of Columbia University's SDS, replied, "While you call for order and respect for authority, we call for justice and freedom." When the bridge between those two couldn't be met, Rudd added, "There is only one thing left to say. It may sound nihilistic

to you, since it is the opening shot in a war of liberation [but] . . .
Up against the wall, motherfucker."[17]

Rather than a battle between respect for authority and justice
and freedom, some saw it differently: "At some point between 1945
and 1967," wrote Joan Didion in her 1968 collection of essays,
Slouching Towards Bethlehem, "we had somehow neglected to tell
these children the rules of the game we happened to be playing."
The Rules, which had for so long upheld the traditional structures
of American society, were completely under attack. Their spiritual hollowness had grown apparent. Didion, who counted herself among the failed older generation, wondered, "Maybe we have
stopped believing in the rules ourselves, maybe we were having a
failure of nerve about the game."[18]

In June, four weeks after Columbia's occupation, Robert Kennedy, one possible source of hope, was assassinated in the kitchen
of the Ambassador Hotel in Los Angeles. It was two minutes to
midnight and he was shaking hands with a young hotel employee
named Juan Romero when the gun went off. As Pete Hamill put it
in his eyewitness account:

> The shots went pap-pap-pap-pap-pap, small sharp noises like a
> distant firefight or the sound of firecrackers in the backyard.
> Rosey Grier of the Los Angeles Rams came from nowhere and
> slammed his great bulk into the gunman, crunching him against
> a serving table. George Plimpton grabbed the guy's arm, and
> Rafer Johnson moved to him . . . and still the bullets came.[19]

The photo in the papers the next day showed a wounded, soon-
to-die Kennedy being propped up by a terrified-looking seventeen-
year-old Latino. "Where other politicians found their nourishment
in the hog's trough of American mediocrity," wrote Mailer hours
later at a reporter's request, "Robert F. Kennedy seemed to drink
from the tap root of American life, from those primal waters which
might ask, 'Is our democracy epic or finally tragic?' "[20]

That was a key question for Mailer in 1968, and for America more generally. It was a question he had pondered in his debate with Buckley in 1962 and in the pages of *Armies* in 1967. It was one he mused over when he accepted the Kennedys' invitation to serve as a member of the honor guard during RFK's memorial service a few days later. Was the United States destined to achieve epic things in the name of human accomplishment, or was it finally tragic, unable to resolve the tensions that were part of the battle to preserve the virtuous heart? By 1968, the giddy optimism of the revolutionaries of an earlier era, of people like William F. Buckley, Jr., and Norman Mailer, now seemed necessarily tempered by the apparent inevitability of a sniper's bullet, where "hope doesn't last very long among us." The birthing pains of a new order seemed too violent. Voices long dismissed as too radical, too cranky, too angry were now getting a fair shake.

It was hard to admit they didn't deserve it. What had shouting them down done but suppress a latent strain of violence now being sprung from its jack-in-the-box? As President Kennedy had said, "Those who make peaceful revolution impossible will make violent revolution inevitable."[21] He might not have been talking about America then, but the idea didn't discriminate. The country was unmoored and lurching toward easy, emotionally charged outlets.

In 1968, Mailer saw all this and shuddered for the life of the nation. But he also felt compelled to capture it in his art.

To articulate the uncertainty of the times, Mailer dreamed up a movie about the 1968 presidential election. During the previous few years, he had been experimenting with filmmaking, creating some pretty bad movies about his favorite themes: law and order and the wild undercurrents of the American psyche. When he wrote *An American Dream*, he had written it in a cinematic style because, in his mind, movies were the only medium capable of penetrating the country's soul in the 1960s. Modern minds needed modern media.

His films were almost entirely unscripted, and Mailer wasn't a convincing director, nor was he a very good editor. He was a pretty bad actor, too. But he thought if he let the cameras roll long enough, if he made the audience and the actors squirm just enough, something brilliant might happen. The unconscious would be revealed; the liberal sheen of civilization would be exposed as unfulfilling; the heart of darkness would come clear.

Mailer's filmmaking flops were widespread New York fodder. His previous movies, two self-financed films called *Wild 90* and *Beyond the Law*, were made to challenge the movie industry's increasing corporatization, which he felt left little room for creativity: "commercial film-making has a natural tendency to liquidate the collective human entity of the film, and so it is a living miracle, nothing less than a miracle, when a good big-budget movie is made."[22] By making films that unleashed individual creativity and pushed beyond the "liberal, condescending, and over-programmatic" movies, Mailer believed his fiercely independent films contributed "to no less than the general weal."[23] Most everyone else thought they were pretty bad.

In July 1968, Mailer dreamed up a movie that would revel in the uncertainty of the times. It would feature as protagonist a film director named Norman T. Kingsley, who is contemplating running for president but fears assassination. The movie, as Mailer put it in his first meeting with the cast in July 1968, "takes place a year from now and we're assuming that all the present candidates— Rockefeller, Nixon, Humphrey—have been knocked off, a possibility which isn't so unlikely as it may seem. The men up for consideration in their place—about fifty—are people like Sinatra, Baldwin, Buckley, and Brando, which is also in the realm of the possible."[24]

A new federal agency has been created to prevent assassinations (which in truth was the Secret Service's new charge after RFK's killing), and its agents have been sent to watch over Kingsley as he decides whether or not he's going to run. Some in the new security team want Kingsley to win the election, but others are corrupt and intent on assassinating him for vague reasons of their own. The movie plays out all these tensions. The film would be called *Maidstone*, named after the mansion where Kingsley has gone in order to think through his options.

"By the way," Mailer said, in the most predictable line of the night, "Kingsley will be played by me."[25]

When Mailer imagined the thing, he thought Buckley might like to play himself. The two could banter their irrepressible banter, debating the future once again, although the context around them had changed so much. So he called Buckley to ask.

Mailer had already shown Buckley one of his earlier movies to try to entice him to join the effort, although it probably had the opposite effect. "I must confess," wrote Buckley, who had to leave halfway through the film, "that by the time I left it had begun to depress me. But then maybe that was what you intended."[26]

At any rate, would Buckley still show up to play himself?

Buckley hemmed and hawed over the decision. He, too, had been moved by the upheavals of the present day. Despite his unwavering political conservatism, Buckley had in fact been enlivened in recent times. He loved the constant rebukes to the status quo perpetuated by the counterculture. He could understand their anger and frustration and he, most at home as a provocateur, had never been one to toe a party line. He loved to be irreverent. Throughout the mid-1960s, he grew his already wavy hair even longer and could be seen darting around New York City on a Honda motorcycle, often with a passenger in tow. He had no problem publishing articles in *Playboy* and proved consistently curious about the most popular fads in youth culture. Buckley's first take on the Beatles was that they were "not merely awful, I would consider it sacrilegious to say anything less than that they are God-awful. They are so unbelievably horrible, so appallingly unmusical, so dogmatically insensitive to the magic of the art, that they qualify as the crowned heads of anti-music." But as the Beatles' popularity soared, Buckley felt he had missed something. By 1968, he gave in, finally finding something to love about the Beatles: "I mean how can one prevail against them? The answer is: One cannot. And even if they are hard to listen to, there is an exuberance there that is quite unmatched anywhere in the world."[27]

Even when it came to his beloved Catholicism, Buckley embraced some of the changes to its social doctrine. He never wavered in his faith, nor did he support the papal encyclicals that challenged laissez-faire capitalism, and he certainly didn't approve of Catholics who protested the Vietnam War under the banner of faith. But Buckley did take positions on social matters that were far more progressive than those of his Church. He urged the Church to allow married priests, for example, and he never followed the hierarchy in opposing birth control or divorce. He even chided the Church for politicizing its opposition to abortion, arguing that the doctrine of religious liberty that the Church had recently endorsed during the Second Vatican Council mandated that Catholics not impose their position on others.

But the violence of 1968 shook him, too. As someone who gleefully shirked the establishment, he nonetheless couldn't help but understand the turn to violence as a direct result of an increasing spirit of lawlessness. "The scholars tell us that political assassination prospers when there is a loosening of the repressive traditional regime," he wrote in October 1968 in a piece for *Esquire* that he entitled, "The Politics of Assassination." The challenges that brought about the student revolt, the antiwar protest, and the shirking of The Rules, he concluded, had led directly to the assassinations of Martin Luther King, Jr., and Robert Kennedy. "Political assassinations such as that against Robert Kennedy are 'unimaginable,' we keep reassuring ourselves," he wrote. "But so also, in another frame of reference, is the occupation of the office of the President of Columbia University unimaginable, not to mention defecating in his wastebasket, scribbling obscenities over his family pictures, or destroying ten years' research material in an adjacent scholar's office."[28] The Rules were not only being broken, they were being broken with such glee that the traditional boundaries of social decorum were disintegrating. That was not something Buckley could get behind.

When it came to performing in Mailer's movie, then, Buckley decided to pass. "I have thought and thought about it," he wrote, "and decided against it." He thought to portray himself in a fictional movie would be to parody himself, to make his ideas seem beyond the realm of reality, not serious but fanciful. That would defeat much of what he had accomplished during the previous decade. Indeed, it was for this very reason Mailer opted against using his own name and instead named his character "Norman Kingsley" (premised on Mailer's middle name). "When you told me that you were using Norman Kingsley instead of Norman Mailer," wrote Buckley, "and gave the reasons why, I was encouraged to believe that you will understand that for reasons akin to those that prompted you toward this self-effacement, I am moved to prudence."

You can tell from the letter, though, that Buckley had thought about it deeply, not because he thought Mailer was a great filmmaker but because he thought the times were in need of new expressions. A consummate salesman, might this have been yet another arena for Buckley to hawk his wares? He finished his letter wistfully, referring to the times as "a chimera." Then he trailed off ambiguously, saying, "But I don't know, I don't know."[29]

It was an uncharacteristic pause for Buckley, who was more at ease deploying a pun or a barb than a wistful note about the uncertainty of the times. It was a rare moment of longing, one reserved for good friends you can trust. How could a conservative of Buckley's mold respond to all the bloodshed? The explanations of yesteryear—a hard line on the Cold War, a staunch upholding of The Rules— seemed to carry little weight in this new era when efforts to enforce them ended in violence. He often fell back on simple patriotism, an easy way out that he himself hated: America "needs us all as her devoted bodyguards, even as Messrs. Kennedy and King needed more bodyguards than they had, at the crucial moment in *their* histories," Buckley said two weeks after King was killed. "She needs us, however quarrelsome we are; however disparate our views; however pronounced our separations." But Buckley knew that selling simple patriotism was hard going in 1968—and he didn't think he could blame anyone for their reticence. He disliked himself for falling back on it.[30]

"I can understand your cautions to be prudent," Mailer wrote back two weeks later, immediately after filming had been completed, "and perhaps it's just as well. We worked at such incredible speed that any scenes we might have played together could have come out farcical."[31]

The film would turn out to be farcical as a whole, another of Mailer's movie-making disasters, although by far the most accomplished of the bunch. He ended up with forty-five hours of film, during which nothing much happened. "Loss was everywhere in the forty-five hours," Mailer recalled, before describing the process of cutting the film down to two watchable hours as "not unequal to separating uranium from pitchblende." That said, latter-day movie-watchers should be relieved that Mailer ignored the advice of Jean-Luc Godard, who advised Mailer to let the forty-five hours stand as it was.[32]

Morale among the actors suffered not only because of the lack of coordination and plot, but also because of the booze that had been freely provided, and most especially because of the fact that the mansion where Kingsley was supposedly considering his run for the presidency also happened to serve (for unclear reasons) as a male house of prostitution called the Cash Box. What had started as a political thriller devolved into late-1960s drunken pornography. It was generally awful, although there were some beautiful scenes of unshorn lovemaking.

The film was saved, such as it was, by an unscripted moment

that occurred once the five days of filming had officially ended. Mailer decided to use some of the leftover film to make family movies, with Beverly and his younger kids running around the Eden-like estate on Long Island. As the camera captured scenes of Mailer and his children, one of the frustrated actors, Rip Torn, realizing the film had no resolution, ominously stalked Kingsley/Mailer with a hammer. Out of nowhere, with the family completely unaware, Torn emerges from the trees and attacks Mailer, hitting him on the head with the hammer three times, drawing blood.

Mailer had no idea Torn was coming. He panicked, uncertain of the boundary between fiction and reality. The two men wrestled to the ground, screaming obscenities at each other. Beverly and the children came upon them, terrified. A baby starts to scream in the background. Beverly screams and shouts herself. It was a pure, unscripted moment.

As the men wrestled on the ground, Torn yells, "You're supposed to die, Mr. Kingsley. *You* must die, *not* Mailer."

Torn, drunk as he was, knew what he was doing. He had turned the hammer sideways to ensure he hit Mailer with the blunt side. Mailer was uncertain, though, straining with all his might to stop the attack. The cameraman thought to himself, "*What am I doing?*" passively filming a scene as Mailer was turning blue in Torn's bear hug before eventually biting off a piece of Torn's ear to get himself free.[33]

The two men separated, staring at each other in an ambiguous standoff. Mailer, blood rolling down his cheek, was angry. He didn't know what had happened, and he hated Torn for his insolence. Torn, blood coming from his partially torn ear, kept saying that Mailer knew Torn would have to do something: "The picture doesn't make sense without this, you know that," Torn said.

"I can't forgive you for doing this in front of my kids, that's what I can't forgive," Mailer said.

"When, when, when is assassination predicted?" asked Torn, hitting the exact tenor of the times.

"I'm taking that scene out of the movie," yelled Mailer. "Just wait, I owe you one. Just wait, 'cause I'll pull it. . . ."

But the scene ended up saving the film. Mailer did as promised and left the whole episode out of the first cut, until those who knew better told him it was the only vital thing in the movie, which was, after all, supposed to be about assassination and instability. As Mailer came to realize, Torn was "a superb actor at a pitch of intensity [who] was there finally to reveal the premise on which a film had been built, even of the essence of a method which might yet become the future of film."[34]

As he had so many other times, in *Maidstone* Mailer had predicted and even helped bring about violence. But when it came he hadn't wanted it. In his heart, he wanted to use the movie to bring together a large collection of friends from disparate backgrounds. He wanted to explore the tensions between them, to study the chemistry, to allow the stench of humanity to appear. But he didn't want violence. Only later did he recognize that violence is a necessary part of the process. Still, he didn't have to like it.

For his part, Buckley heard about the hammer blows and the fight, which was covered in the newspapers, and was relieved not to have been there. Who knows, perhaps he, too, might have lost part of his ear? "Tell me," he wrote Mailer, "was the party discussed in the *New York Times* a part of the movie script?"[35]

Mailer spent $150,000 editing the film, and it ended up earning him nothing. He was broke, as usual, and had to write for money, as always.

No matter: the 1968 presidential conventions were just around the corner, and *Harper's* was sending him to cover them. Buckley was heading to the conventions, too. He had been hired to comment on them for ABC. Perhaps something there might restore his sense of confidence about the world, his hope for the country, his notion that in politics might lie an answer beyond violence. But he couldn't be sure.

"See you in Miami," Mailer wrote to Buckley.[36]

11

Halfway to Burke

I t was hot in Miami that August, and it seemed foreign to those who flew in from New York and Washington and Seattle and Omaha for the Republican National Convention, too tropical, almost un-American. "Wealthy, superoptimistic, pushy, sparkling Miami Beach," wrote the *New York Times* in an eleven-page profile, "has in less than one lifetime grown from a dense mangrove swamp inhabited by snakes and rats into one of the great resort and convention centers of the world."[1]

Mailer and Buckley both hated it. As Mailer put it, the heat and humidity "was not unlike being obliged to make love to a 300-pound woman who has decided to get on top. Got it? You could not dominate a thing. That uprooted jungle had to be screaming beneath."[2] It was yet another instance where the heart of darkness was straining to get out, and, like elsewhere, it was unclear how long the liberal sheen could remain in control.

Mailer also pointed to the irony that "in a year when the Republic hovered on the edge of revolution, . . . the party of conservatism and principle, of corporate wealth and personal frugality, the party of cleanliness, hygiene, and balanced budget, should have set itself down on a sultan's strip."[3] By holding the convention in Miami—the first time a Republican convention was held south of the Mason-Dixon line in a hundred years—the Republicans not only wanted to shore up Florida for its candidate Richard Nixon, but also make it look like a vacation from the violence taking place back in the real world. If anyone could tamp down the dangers below, it was the Republicans. They appreciated the fact that Miami Police Chief Walter E. Headley, Jr., was famous for using the newly legal "stop-and-frisk" policy in black areas, which allowed cops to stop and search anyone with or without probable cause. "They must have been smoking marijuana the night before, to make that decision," said Chief Headley of the U.S. Supreme Court's *Terry v. Ohio* decision. "It's the first time they've ruled in favor of the public for years."[4]

Despite things looking good for the Republicans that year, Buckley was not terribly excited to be there. After all, he was supposed to spar with his old nemesis Gore Vidal, the thought of which nearly made him sick. Buckley had contracted with ABC to provide commentary on the convention, and to do so with someone from the left who would counter Buckley's surefire conservatism. An executive at ABC had asked Buckley whom he might like to debate, and Buckley gave eight names, including his two favorites, John Kenneth Galbraith and Norman Mailer. The executive also asked if there was anyone Buckley *didn't* want to debate. He put down just one name: Gore Vidal. Buckley and Vidal had had a famous spat on *The Jack Paar Tonight Show* a few years earlier. They had sued each other over it and remained bitter enemies. Politics had become personal between Vidal and Buckley, and Buckley didn't think the nation would be best served by the raw emotion that might surface if the two of them appeared side by side.

But by 1968 Buckley had already made his deal with the devil. He was no longer just a public intellectual, he was also a paid pundit. He was a bona fide celebrity, and he was expected not only to espouse his ideas, but to entertain. No one knew this more than he did; he had, in fact, sought the role his entire life, to be a salesman for his ideas.

Now he was feeling chastened by the bargain. No one benefited when politics devolved into pure entertainment—except the networks, of course, which made money on the whole thing. And so, unsurprisingly, ABC picked Gore Vidal to be Buckley's sparring partner in 1968. In the end, ABC got its money's worth.

As the two men settled into their seats high above the convention floor and made their opening statements to viewers at home, Vidal deliberately ruffled Buckley's feathers by saying the Republicans were nothing more than a "party based almost entirely upon human greed."

Buckley countered by saying of Vidal, who was bisexual and whose recent novel, *Myra Breckinridge*, featured a transsexual hero, "Now the author of *Myra Breckinridge* is well acquainted with the imperatives of human greed. . . ."[5] It was a homophobic line premised on the notion that gay people are ravenous lovers eager to please only themselves.

Quicker than quick, Vidal shot back: "If I may say so, Bill, before you go any further, that if there were a contest for *Mr.* Myra Breckinridge, you would unquestionably win it. I based the entire style polemically upon you—passionate and irrelevant."

And so they began. It would be more of the same the entire four days. Buckley's wife, Pat, hated the whole thing, especially Vidal's innuendo that Buckley was the role model for his fictional transsexual hero. She said angrily, "Two hundred million Americans think William F. Buckley is a screaming homosexual."[6] As they left Miami, Buckley even called the producer at ABC to ask if he could get out of the deal. The producer said no. From the producer's financial perspective, this was a smashing success.[7]

Buckley found a bit of succor when he gave a speech to the Young Americans for Freedom, the shock troops who had provided all that energy to Goldwater's campaign in 1964. But in 1968, with the unpredictable, not-definitively-conservative Nixon as frontrunner, they lacked the same spark. As Mailer put it, "Nothing this night could begin to recall that sense of barbarians about a campfire and the ecstasy of going to war which Barry Goldwater had aroused in '64."[8]

In 1968, Buckley embodied that lack of energy. Something had changed in America. The hope was tempered; *his* hope was tempered. The anger of 1964 was now, in 1968, not out to demand a brighter future premised on conservative values, but instead was yearning for security and revenge. Law and order were in the air. Nixon epitomized that feeling, and played on it. "I think it is time the doctrine of civil disobedience was analyzed and rejected as not only wrong but potentially disastrous," Nixon said. "[F]rom my own trips across the nation, I can affirm that private conversations and public concern are increasingly focusing upon the issues of disrespect for law and race turmoil."[9] In early 1968, a report was released on the presidentially appointed Kerner Commission, which analyzed the structural racism that had led to the 1967 race riots and which possessed the standout line, "Our nation is moving toward two societies, one black, one white—separate and unequal." Nixon coolly said that the report "blames everybody for the riots except the perpetrators of the riots."[10]

Not thrilled by Nixon's ascension, Buckley arrived at the YAF meeting tired from jousting with Vidal and injured from a recent boating accident (he had broken his collarbone while sailing). He had to entertain his troops, but his performance was dreary, a reflection of his cooled enthusiasm. "If anyone in the room is planning to shoot me, this is an excellent time to do it," he said.[11] No one knew whether to laugh or cry.

Although Nixon would go on to win the nomination on the first ballot, the star of the convention was John Wayne. Wayne was a longtime Republican backer who had supported Nixon in 1960 and Goldwater in 1964. He appreciated President Johnson's stern handling of the Vietnam War and had friendly relations with the president, but he hated both the counterculture and the critics of the Cold War. When those two forces came together in 1966 and 1967, Wayne thought they imperiled the nation.

As he got up to speak on the first day of the convention, sleepy journalists roused and hurried to cover the story. Here was Hollywood's most macho star out to hurl red meat to the lackluster conventioneers. TV networks began rolling their cameras. Wayne recounted a conversation he'd had with Dean Martin, who asked him about his hopes for his daughter. "I told him," said the Duke, "I wanted her to be as grateful as I am. Grateful for every day of my life that I wake up in the United States of America." He was planning to teach her the Lord's Prayer and the Psalms, and "I don't care if she memorizes the Gettysburg Address, but I hope she understands it." As the *New York Times* put it, Wayne "got the biggest applause for his patriotic remarks and rugged demeanor."[12]

Buckley was appalled that it took a Green Beret–wearing movie star to rouse the crowd, but he thought he understood the appeal. The politicians had been unable to harness hope, to spark energy. People were almost ready to walk away from it all. Then the Duke appeared. "He is not merely a patriot," Buckley wrote with a snicker in his pen, angry at the Republicans for abandoning their true principles in favor of law and order, angry at America for the violent birthing processes:

> but an explicit patriot. Having committed *The Green Berets*, he is very much out in the Kulchur world. He takes the mike, says 'I know this sounds corny but . . .' and proceeds to say the corniest imaginable things but, *mirabile dictu*, the delegates suddenly stop talking, and start applauding, . . . They make you feel that the applause is not because there is a spontaneous enthusiasm for patriotic sentiment; but because the delegates are somehow afraid that the folks back home will be sore if they *don't* respond to the Duke paying tribute to our boys in Vietnam.

Buckley explained this reverence for celebrity as a sign of the new era. Candor was now everywhere, and everything was image.

There was no substance anymore. "Everybody is supposed to tell everybody about everything," he wrote of the spectacle, "especially his sexual habits; especially if they are abnormal (abnormal, what's that? Typical Republican). And putting on the dawg is tempting even to network broadcasters. What is strange is how easily many of them are wowed." Poor, dumb voters, Buckley thought; poor, dumb America. "If only they knew enough to turn off the set."[13]

Instead they were responding to machismo and unsophisticated patriotism. Law and order were destined to win the day, and that was not Buckley's kind of conservatism.

When Nixon won the nomination, Buckley was lukewarm about it. He had history with the man. They were of the same generation and had similar experiences. Both had used anti-communism to stoke their respective ascensions, Nixon by showing his enemies forever pink, Buckley by keeping together the factions of American conservatism through his prioritizing a common hatred of communism.

But Buckley also saw Nixon as unprincipled, a politician to the bitter end, perhaps with no core at all, no fixed principles. He understood the need for politicians to be that way, but he hadn't enjoyed playing Nixon's pawn, of being loved or hated by Nixon depending on the prevailing winds. Was Nixon for Buckley's movement or against it? Buckley didn't know. What was more troubling was that he didn't know if Nixon knew either. The man was too unpredictable.

In 1968, Buckley supported Nixon but always kept him at arm's length. Of '68, Buckley famously said he'd back Nixon because there was "No sense running Mona Lisa in a beauty contest. I'd be for the most right, viable candidate who could win."[14]

Now, that candidate was, unenthusiastically, Nixon.

Oddly enough, at that very moment, Mailer began, shockingly, to gain some respect for the grizzled would-be president. This surprised Mailer as much as anyone. He had long seen Nixon as the epitome of the plastic culture he so despised, an obedient soldier for his own cause, someone willing to answer the demands of the party that would give him the mantle. To Mailer, Nixon was alternately a bulldog for anti-communism or a cuddler of corporate capitalism or a liberal demanding an activist state, an amoebic figure who would manipulate the country's schizophrenia if they let him lead once and for all. Mailer had hated the man, calling him someone "who would press any button to manipulate the masses," and whose "presence on television had inspired emotions close to nausea."[15]

But now here Nixon was, chastened by history, by losing Ike's love and having to grovel to win it back in 1952, by getting knocked from what was rightfully his in 1960 by someone richer and prettier, by getting his knees chopped from under him on the very first step of the comeback trail in California in 1962. By 1968 Nixon's face showed the deep wrinkles of experience, the grizzled exhaustion of someone who knew a thing or two, who, as Mailer put it, "had finally acquired some of the dignity of the old athlete or the old con—he had taken punishment."[16]

In 1964 Nixon had been smart enough to pull his wife back down to her seat when she spontaneously rose to applaud Barry Goldwater's famous "extremism in the defense of liberty" line. Nixon supported Goldwater, but not with enthusiasm meriting a standing ovation. It was clear, he saw, that the hardcore conservatives dancing around the fires in 1964 would be necessary to win the Republican nomination, but that you couldn't become president just yet if you were one of them. Mailer respected the discipline that showed. And like Mailer, Nixon also seemed aware that he was nothing more than an actor in the biggest show of them all, America, and that 1968 might be his starring moment. As Nixon said in his first press conference in Miami, "this is the time I think when the man and the moment in history come together."[17] He would, of course, be right.

Mailer used his typical incisiveness to detect the changing winds within the Republican Party. It had always portrayed itself as the party to clean up the mess, and had been better suited for that role than one as visionary empire-builder, where its hubris had taken it to extreme and dangerous places. Goldwater's failure was an example. But when it came to cleaning up the place, well, they were the party for that.

And there was a lot to clean up. Nixon could talk that talk. As Mailer looked around the convention hall, he noticed "many of the women seemed victims of the higher hygiene. Even a large part of the young seemed to have faces whose cheeks had been injected with Novocain."[18] This was a tied-down crowd, ready to retake their country. More tellingly, as they entered the convention hall to pick their man, Mailer realized something about himself, too, that he "did not detest these people, he did not feel so superior as to pity them, it was rather he felt a sad sorrowful respect."

After all, what Mailer saw in their faces was:

> the muted tragedy of the Wasp—they were not on earth to enjoy or even perhaps to love so very much, they were here to serve, and serve they had in public functions and public charities (while recipients of their charity might vomit in rage and laugh in scorn), served on opera committees, and served in long hours of duty at the piano, served as the sentinel in concert halls, and the pews on the aisle in church, at the desk in schools, had served for culture, served for finance, served for salvation, served for America—and so much of America did not wish them to serve any longer, and so many of them doubted themselves, doubted that the force of their faith could illumine their path in these new modern horror-head times.

In this yearning, "in San Francisco in '64 they had been able to be insane for a little while, but now they were subdued, now they were modest, now they were looking for a leader to bring America back to them, their lost America, Jesusland."[19]

More than an increasingly subdued party, though, Mailer also recognized a startling change within himself. He suddenly found sympathy for these people, and sympathy for—could he really say it?—Nixon. Mailer was always open to the possibility of finding a new hero, and Nixon now looked to Mailer like . . . a president. Mailer was forty-five at the time, maybe not mellowing just yet, but more mature, less enchanted by the pure energy of youth—which still had its appeals, but which, he was seeing, could also careen off into paths for personal fulfillment, the "apocalyptic orgasm" that Buckley had tried to pin on him a few years earlier. In transformative times like these, a grizzled ego might not be such a bad thing in a leader.

But still, it was *Nixon*.

As Mailer left Miami, he watched the final proceedings from a television set and it dawned on him "for the first time he had not been able to come away with an intimation of what was in a politician's heart, indeed, did not know if he was ready to like Nixon, or detested him for his resolutely non-poetic binary system, his computer's brain, did not know if the candidate were real as a man, or whole as a machine, lonely in his sad eminence or megalomaniacal, humble enough to feel the real wounds of the country or sufficiently narcissist to dream the tyrant's dream." In the end, Mailer "had no idea at all if God was in the land or the Devil played the tune."[20] Was Nixon the future? And if so, what did that possibly mean?

When he got home to Brooklyn, Mailer saw a column in the newspaper from an obviously tired Buckley. The column proposed that convention speeches be shorter and that rules be made to allow anyone to be nominated for president, but that their candidacy must be voted on during the first day of the convention and "that the one with the fewest votes at the end of the first ballot would be publicly executed."[21]

Where was Buckley's satirical joviality? Mailer may have thought back to Buckley's ponderous, "But I don't know, I don't know" line from a few weeks earlier.

Thumbing through his mail, Mailer also found a letter from his friend. "I shudder at the thought of what you will be writing about that august convention," Buckley wrote.[22]

But before Mailer put pen to paper in response, he had to head to Chicago. Who knew what would happen at the Democratic National Convention? Buckley was packing his bags, too.

If Miami represented the last stand of the American WASP as it incorporated its angry, more ideologically pure offspring in order to restore a sense of order to the country, it was Chicago, where the Democrats were battling it out, that would prove to be more dynamic, and more violent. There, the blood of 1968 would spill freely in the streets, the subterranean blues coming well above-ground, as the radicals and the liberals fought for control of the party and, perhaps, the future of the country.

The young radicals who organized the march to the Pentagon in 1967, the hippies and the Yippies, had sought to parade outside the Chicago convention center in 1968. They wanted spectacle, and the spectacle they most sought was having the President of the Free World accept his party's nomination under armed guard. They wanted the world to see that Americans did not unilaterally support America, and that they would make Johnson pay for his sins.

But then Johnson had stepped down. The young radicals decided they would still rally in opposition to the war, but it seemed as though things might fracture apart depending on who got the nomination. The protest might lack focus. No matter. They'd still gather.

As the convention approached, this concern became more ominous. The RSVPs were mounting, coming from a wide variety of groups with little in common. Even though only somewhere near ten thousand people would come to Chicago to protest, they were an unruly bunch, hard to control.

Meanwhile, Chicago's mayor, Richard Daley—wide-nosed and perpetually five-o'clock shadowed, the laughable epitome of Chicago's historic meatpacking stench ("Daley looked in fact like a vastly robust old peasant woman with a dirty gray silk wig," Mailer wrote, not inaccurately)[23]—had refused to allow the protestors to march anywhere. This had the unfortunate consequence of penning them in a public park across the street from the main hotels, barricaded in by chain-link fencing. Their curfew to be off the streets and out of the park was at eleven o'clock each night. And so, until eleven every evening, from the penned-in grassway down the street from the convention itself, directly across from the hotel where the delegates were staying, the rowdy protestors shouted and sang.

Mailer was one of them, but only sort of. Many saw him as a leader of the movement, but he knew this was now not his movement to lead, if it ever had been. The subtle awareness that had come upon him in 1967—that the birthing pangs of a new order were about to create something he wasn't quite comfortable with—was becoming increasingly clear. He hated the Vietnam War just as much as these protestors, but he was coming to recognize that their demands for "liberation" were just too much for him. It was too mindless. Yes, demanding "freedom" was fair and proper, but to free oneself from the commonweal didn't make any sense. As he put it, the principles of these new lefties, the unwashed hippie and Yippie masses, were "simple—everybody, obviously must be allowed to do (no way around the next three words) his own thing, provided he hurt no one doing it—they were yet to learn that society is built on many people hurting many people, it is just who does the hurting which is forever in dispute."[24]

Mailer feared that, even as the technocratic liberalism of postwar America seemed to be fading, it might make a dramatic comeback if the only alternatives on offer were mindless liberation for the sake of individual fulfillment or Nixonian conservatism (which was impossible to define but didn't smell good nonetheless; it might just be unshaven liberalism all over again. Or worse: it might be the baton, the true totalitarianism of the right).

Worryingly, no one in Chicago looked like they were ready with a careful answer. "Just as he had known for one instant at the Republican Gala in Miami Beach that Nelson Rockefeller had no chance of getting the nomination," wrote Mailer, referring to himself again in the third person, "so he knew now on this cool gray Sunday afternoon in August, chill in the air like the chill of the pale and the bird of fear beginning to nest in the throat, that trouble was coming, serious trouble."[25] And then he wondered: "Were these odd unkempt children the sort of troops with whom one wished to enter battle?"[26]

He wasn't sure. In writing about the convention later, Mailer talked about "politics as property," by which he meant people would give you their support, but only if you traded for it. No one ever gave away a vote or a contract or a piece of property for free. The only people unaffected by this iron-clad rule of politics were complete ideologues, because they thought their cause was more valuable than property; you couldn't barter with them, and thus they were dangerous.

Aware of this, Mailer looked at all the "liberation" being demanded by the protestors, the constant demand to "do your own thing," and he wondered if their sensibilities were too fixed, too hard-nosed, without any property to barter. Again, he just didn't know how things would play out, but it didn't look good.[27]

Violence between the protestors and police began even before the convention started. The Thursday before Monday's opening speeches, a seventeen-year-old Sioux Indian named Dean Johnson was killed in a skirmish with police. The police said he pulled a gun, so they shot him. Protestors planned an ad hoc march in his honor. The police watched the march closely, lending an ominous air to the procession.

On Friday, as the Yippies nominated their own candidate for president, Pigasus the Pig ("Vote Pig in '68" their placards said), more than six thousand National Guardsman showed up expecting bigger riots. At Fort Hood, Texas, sixty soldiers were being readied for Chicago, but then had protested their assignment and refused to go. Given the choice of Vietnam or Chicago, they'd choose Vietnam. Forty-three of them, all black, were arrested and put in the stockade.[28]

By Sunday, the protestors numbered several thousand, so numerous now that they fanned out across the city, staging protests wherever they could. The police followed them everywhere and arrested them if they became insubordinate. The mob was still orderly enough to honor its eleven o'clock curfew, although some of the more animated kept protesting as they made their way home, leading to greater violence in spots across Chicago. When the police went to disperse the crowd in the Lincoln Park neighborhood, for example, the protestors threw bottles and smashed car windows all the way home.[29]

That Monday was when all hell broke loose for the first time. "[T]he city was washed with the air of battle," as Mailer recalled.[30] Mayor Daley opened the convention that day saying, "As long as I'm mayor of this city, there's going to be law and order in this city." He had been under pressure to give up the convention to another locale, perhaps a place like Miami. But Daley threatened that some facets of support might disappear from the victorious Democratic candidate should the convention be taken from Chicago. He didn't care about national wrath; he wasn't a national politician. As Mailer understood, "he could get 73% of the vote in any constituency made up of people whose ancestors were at home with rude instruments in Polish forests, Ukrainian marshes, Irish bogs—they knew how to defend the home: so did he."[31] Now Daley had to keep his word about preserving law and order. He put his police on extended twelve-hour patrols. He had plainclothes cops follow the protest leaders. Tom Hayden, one of the most conspicuous of the radicals, said they were at "the fairly claustrophobic distance of about ten feet wherever we went."[32]

As Mailer observed things that Monday, he recognized that there was no organization or even any real motive for the protests other than to vent collective anger. At one point he saw several young protestors building a barricade out of picnic benches in the middle of Lincoln Park, where they knew cops would try to remove them at eleven o'clock. To Mailer, this was ridiculous: "the police cars would merely drive around it, or tear-gas trucks would push through it." And to what end? To protest being kicked out of the park? Mailer "could not make the essential connection between that and Vietnam. If the war were on already, if this piece of ground were essential to the support of the other pieces of ground . . . but this ridiculous barricade, this symbolic contest with real bloody heads—he simply did not know what he thought."[33]

Mailer surveyed the terrain again and decided this wasn't his battle. These were not his people; they were too empty of ideas, too woozy, too theatrical. This was the politics of emotion from the left about to confront the politics of emotion from the right. He wanted no part of it. He left.

An hour later, when the curfew came, sure enough a police car rammed through the barricade, scattering the scurrying protestors like rats exposed to light. Some jumped on the car and smashed its windshield. Fifty officers charged forward, and then the tear gas began. Army jeeps showed up. The jeeps were lined with barbed wire, which reminded everyone of the Soviet jeeps they had seen on the news coverage of the failed Czech revolution just a week earlier. Even reporters got clubbed that night; the police had planned ahead, though, and removed their nameplates, lest they get caught on camera. Parallels between Soviet totalitarianism and Chicago's law and order were almost too easy to make. Editors of major newspapers greeted one another at the Henrotin Hospital north of downtown, there to claim their own.

———

The next afternoon, on Tuesday, a few dozen Quakers led a march from their meeting hall north of downtown to the convention center, demanding peace in Chicago and in Vietnam. Soon, a thousand others joined them. When the police stopped the protestors at Thirty-ninth and Halsted, about a half-mile north of the convention, the Quakers set up a picket line at that exact spot and peacefully marched in circles. If they couldn't go further, they'd stay right there. And they did. For almost twenty-four hours. The Quakers!

While police contained the pacifists, another interfaith group, four hundred strong, began marching to Lincoln Park to protest the eleven o'clock curfew, this time carrying a twelve-foot wooden cross. By nightfall, the lower half of the cross was shrouded in an amorphous cloud of tear gas.

Ironically (or perhaps not), the cross was the scene of the fiercest of the battles that day. As clergy spoke out against the war, the police encircled them and closed in. The curfew had come. Someone helpfully announced over the loudspeaker, "If it's gas, remember, breathe through your mouth, don't run, don't pant, and for Christsake don't rub your eyes." Then the gas came. Panic ensued. Kids threw whatever they could find, shielding their eyes as they blindly hurled stuff at the cops. Some started pulling up the pavement in the street, a desperate tactic, as if to say the reason these young people did not want to go to Vietnam was not because they were afraid to fight, but because they would only sacrifice themselves for a proper cause. Like this one. Their hands bled as they dug into the street.

"From where I lay, groveling in the grass," said Steve Lerner, a reporter for the *Village Voice*:

> I could see ministers retreating with the cross, carrying it like a fallen comrade. Another volley shook me to my feet. Gas was everywhere. People were running, screaming, tearing

through the trees. Something hit the tree next to me, I was
on the ground again, someone was pulling me to my feet, two
boys were lifting a big branch off a girl who lay squirming hys-
terically. I couldn't see. Someone grabbed onto me and asked
me to lead them out of the park. We walked along, hands
outstretched, bumping into people and trees, tears streaming
from our eyes and mucus smeared across our faces. I flashed
First World War doughboys caught in no-man's-land during a
mustard gas attack. I felt sure I was going to die.

Eventually, Lerner found an underground station on the El:
"Diving down into the subway, I found a large group of refugees
who had escaped the same way. The tunnel looked like a busy
bomb shelter; upstairs the shooting continued."[34]

Like a faulty firework, protests landed all over the city as the
protestors fled Lincoln Park, sparking fires here and there, spreading the police and National Guard thin. To alleviate things, the
National Guard allowed the protestors to camp for the night at
Grant Park. Better to keep them there than to send them out into
parts unknown. Meanwhile, the hospitals continued to fill.

Wednesday would be the worst of the violence, the "Massacre
of Michigan Avenue" it would later be called, and it would be televised. Just before the nominating vote in the convention hall, some
ten thousand to fifteen thousand people gathered in Grant Park
for the only officially sanctioned antiwar protest of the convention
week. Mailer was there, joined by Dick Gregory, David Dellinger,
Allen Ginsberg, and other luminaries to speak out against the war
and hope against hope that the Democratic Party would take a
stance for peace.

As the speeches wore on, voices increasingly desperate, news
broke over a radio that the Democratic Party had rejected a peace
plank in its platform.

That was it. As word spread, the threat of violence manifested
itself fully. People threw things and shrieked and attacked anyone

sniffing of authority. One protestor, "a shirtless longhair," recalled
Tom Hayden, climbed up the band shell where the speeches were
being given and removed the American flag. In its place went a
bloody shirt.[35]

Police, heretofore watching from the sidelines, began to move
in. But the protestors had organized. They had selected marshals,
who lined up to allow the protest on stage to continue. The police
didn't heed the young marshals, though. One protestor was beaten
unconscious with a single blow. Others were attacked with billy
clubs. Thousands fled from the park, screaming.

The screamers quickly discovered that National Guardsmen had
blocked several of the park's exits, and the only outlet led straight
onto Michigan Avenue. Thousands of protestors soon flooded
Chicago's Magnificent Mile, an unruly, scared mob of somewhere
close to ten thousand.

By coincidence, the ten thousand smashed into another group
of protestors. This one was marching toward the Conrad Hilton
Hotel, which served as the headquarters for Hubert Humphrey,
the sitting vice president and presumptive Democratic nominee.
To the protestors, Humphrey's foreign policy was essentially President Johnson's, and so they planned to march to the Hilton to let
him hear their protests.

The movements came together, but still there was no violence.
The lid was kept on the smoldering fire, ready to erupt at any
moment.

And then the oddest thing happened. At that exact moment
when the chaos seemed to reach its peak, when the thousands of
protestors crashed into one another wondering where to go next,
the Reverend Ralph Abernathy, Martin Luther King, Jr.'s right-
hand man who had taken up his fallen friend's cudgel in advocating for the poor and downtrodden, was traveling down Michigan
Avenue on a dopey old mule. His "mule train"—three mules toting
Reconstruction-era wagons—was a symbol of poverty, and Abernathy, being a man who garnered respect, had received a permit to

march to the convention with his mules. The same mule train had been used at Martin Luther King, Jr.'s funeral three months prior, and the police didn't want to mess with that symbol. In the midst of utter chaos, then, there was this slow-moving mule train plodding down the middle of Michigan Avenue, Eeyores of the night.

Everyone paused to watch. It was like a breather in the middle of a fight, a collective inhale and exhale before the dukes went up again. Some protestors had the idea to follow them—yes, that was a good idea. After all, the mules were headed toward the convention hall and the police were allowing them to proceed. Soon, thousands began to follow the mules. "It was a magic moment," said David Lewis Stein, one of the protestors, "the ghost of Martin Luther King rising up to lead us."[36]

What the protestors didn't know was that they had stepped into a trap. As the mules and the thousands behind them approached the convention hall, they came to a four-way intersection at Balbo and Michigan Avenues, a few long blocks north of the convention center but right in front of the Hilton. In anticipation of their arrival, Chicago police had cordoned off three sides of the intersection, leaving the line of protestors to snake toward them from the fourth. As the marchers crossed into the intersection, the police allowed the mules to pass through but then closed ranks. For nearly thirty minutes, there was a quiet standstill. The line of protestors kept pushing forward under the inertial weight of the march, the police not allowing them relief. The intersection bulged.

Then, with horrific suddenness, the police commissioner ordered the streets cleared. Had he spent thirty minutes consulting with Mayor Daley? Consulting the president? Had he made this decision on his own? Nobody knew. And why there, right below the delegates' hotel, where everyone was aware the whole thing would be televised? Was it a deliberate attempt to show the world that the protestors could push authority only so far without suffering repercussions?

Regardless, the beatings began. According to the official report, the melee lasted seventeen minutes.[37] Mailer watched the whole thing from the nineteenth floor of the Hilton, no longer a man of action. He had removed himself from the scene at some point during the march from the band shell to the Hilton, eventually taking the elevator up to his room. Looking down at the battle, he winced at the horror, but also detected a cool beauty in the thing, a result of his torn commitments and the artfulness of silent destruction. Mailer too wondered if the forces of the land had wanted the whole thing to be televised, as if to say, "Look at the costs associated with your protest. If you push, we'll push back, and we probably have more backing us up than you do." Still, the police looked undisciplined and vicious, like they had held up their resolve for days, and were now exhausted and needed to release the tension.

The exhale was brutal. Billy clubs were swung; cans of tear gas sputtered around. More police jeeps with barbed wire showed up carrying policemen wearing gas masks. As they disembarked from their jeeps, they armed themselves. They had been asked to clear the streets, and that's exactly what they'd do—but first they'd shed a little blood. "The police were angry," said one witness. "Their anger was neither disinterested nor instrumental. It was deep, expressive and personal. 'Get out of here you cock suckers,' seemed to be their most common cry."[38]

Perhaps the most dramatic moment came when, as the *New York Times* put it:

> For no reason that could be immediately determined, the blue-helmeted policemen charged the barriers, crushing the spectators against the windows of the Haymarket Inn, a restaurant in the hotel. Finally the window gave way, sending screaming middle-aged women and children backward through the broken shards of glass. The police then ran into the restaurant and beat some of the victims who had fallen

through the windows and arrested them. At the same time, other policemen outside on the broad, tree-lined avenue were clubbing the young demonstrators repeatedly under television lights and in full view of delegates' wives looking out the hotel's windows. Afterward, newsmen saw 30 shoes, women's purses and torn pieces of clothing lying with shattered glass on the sidewalk and street outside the hotel and for two blocks in each direction.[39]

And it was all televised. Alongside the dozens of journalists, network cameras had been covering the protest. When the march approached the Hilton, the cameras there to cover the dignitaries at the hotel simply turned their lenses toward the street. The battle was shown live.

Inside the convention hall, the venerable Senator Abe Ribicoff from Connecticut, a salt-and-peppered icon who had served Kennedy well but had never been noted for speaking out, surprised everyone by showing a bit of backbone, lambasting, on national television, "the turmoil and violence that is competing with this great convention for the attention of the American people." He was typically an unremarkable speaker, and he went on to nominate the peace candidate, George McGovern, for president. But as he ended his speech, he said something that had been only hinted at in his earlier rebuke. If McGovern were elected president, said Ribicoff, "We wouldn't have these Gestapo tactics in the streets of Chicago." He looked right at Mayor Daley as he said it.

Everyone stopped. Had he really likened the Chicago police to the Gestapo? There were men in the room who had suffered at those Nazi hands. You don't play around with a metaphor like that, especially from the podium of a national convention.

Daley, who had sat passively through the first line about turmoil and violence in the streets, couldn't let the second one go. He stood up, pointed his thick finger in Ribicoff's direction, and screamed something at him. The comment was unmiked, but it didn't take a practiced lip reader to understand what he said: "Fuck you, you Jew son of a bitch, you lousy motherfucker, go home."[40]

So much for decorum. Ribicoff stared him down, now suddenly standing tall. "How hard it is to accept the truth," he taunted Daley from on stage.

Hubert H. Humphrey, the unloved vice president who vowed to maintain the war in Vietnam until it was won with honor, took the party's nomination on the first ballot, overcoming the "Dump the Hump" chants from outside. Ten days later, Mayor Daley defended the actions of his police but made a slip of the tongue: "The policeman isn't there to *create* disorder; the policeman is there to *preserve* disorder." But the official report afterward was clear in its assessment, calling it unequivocally a "police riot."

In a television studio high above the floor of the convention, Buckley sat watching the screen display the violence outside. He was highly irritable that day, just like the nation, and he hadn't slept well the night before. His hotel room at the Hilton overlooked Grant Park, normally a highly prized view of the greenscape across Michigan Avenue and then to the glistening lake beyond. The evening before, however, the park had been nothing but a sea of protest, kids yelling and screaming until three o'clock in the morning. The curfew had been lifted at the park, of course, and now they sounded to Buckley and Pat like a pack of angry wounded animals, ready to pounce on whatever came close. The air was uncertain and scary. The smell of tear gas had drifted into the hotel's air-conditioning system.

Buckley winced at the thought of what he was expected to do next. Once again he'd confront Gore Vidal, and this time he'd have to make some effort to defend the police and their mayor. Law and order were important, necessary, to civil society, but it was hard to suggest the police were defending "freedom" when "freedom" looked as it had the night before. Buckley hated Mayor Daley, too, and thought his actions on the streets were close to authoritarianism. Later, in a private letter to Nancy Reagan, he referred to the police actions as the result of Daley's "fascist dicta-torship." That too was a metaphor one didn't deploy lightly. In fact, Buckley didn't intend it as a metaphor at all.[41]

But there was no way he was going to say that on live television, nor would he let Vidal say it either. The protestors knew what was coming when they did what they did, had provoked it even, and so were just as indefensible as the cops. If he had to choose the lesser of two evils, he'd choose Daley's law and order. Although when it looked like that, enthusiasm was hard to muster.

When the cameras started rolling, Buckley said the protestors had provoked the response they got. They had raised the flag of the Vietcong and taunted the police until they got their made-for-TV moment. It was like what Martin Luther King, Jr., had done with all his televised confrontation, but without any moral high ground to defend. The protestors brought it on themselves.

Vidal disagreed, saying Daley was little more than a monster "who believes in order without law," adding that the demonstrators were "absolutely well behaved" at the Grant Park band shell, a fact later confirmed by both the *New York Times* and the city's internal report.[42]

Buckley threw his head back with exasperation.

As the back and forth continued, the moderator saw temper-atures rising between the two and tried to head things off. He attempted to get Vidal to grant Buckley's point that raising an enemy flag was a provocative act, and wouldn't "raising a Nazi flag in World War II . . . have had similar consequences?"

Vidal waffled around a bit, eventually arguing, "I assume it is the point of American democracy that you can express any point of view you want. . . ."

But Buckley cut him off: "And some people *were* pro-Nazi, and some people were pro-Nazi. . . ."

"Shut up a minute," said Vidal, a bit too tartly.

"No I won't," said Buckley. "And some people were pro-Nazi, and the answer is that they were well treated by people who ostracized the . . . And I am for ostracizing people who egg on other people to shoot American Marines and American soldiers. I know you don't care because you don't have any sense of identification. . . ."

He was defending American nationalism and shouting down Vidal's over-the-top criticism of the country that had supported him. If you shouted it down too long, Buckley was saying, there were bound to be consequences.

Vidal retorted: "As far as I am concerned, the only sort of pro- or crypto-Nazi that I can think of is *yourself.* Failing that, I would only say we can't have the right of assembly if they're. . . ."

At this point, the moderator saw Buckley lose his cool completely. Buckley had hated the Nazis during World War II. Now he was being called one.

"Let's—let's not call names . . . ," the moderator said meekly, trying to fend off what he knew was coming.

But it was too late.

"Now listen, you queer," snarled Buckley, the coil unsprung, "stop calling me a crypto-Nazi or I'll sock you in the goddam face. . . ."

"Oh, Bill," Vidal interrupted, loving every minute of it, "you're so extraordinary. . . ."

". . . and you'll stay plastered," continued Buckley. "Let the author of *Myra Breckenridge* go back to his pornography and stop making allusions of Nazism to somebody who was in the last war and fought Nazis. . . ."

"You were *not* in the infantry," said Vidal, rightly pointing out that Buckley had graduated Officer Candidate School just as the war ended and never went abroad.

The moderator flailed around, trying to get the conversation back on track, but both men, and Buckley especially, had lost their tempers. The moderator spoke for most of the rest of the time, with Buckley and Vidal only offering closing remarks.

Afterward, as Buckley and Vidal were taking out their earpieces,

Vidal whispered to Buckley, "I guess we gave them their money's worth tonight." Buckley didn't respond. He was distraught at what had happened. He turned his back and stormed away, more angry at himself than Vidal.[43]

That evening put on display the costs of celebrity intellectual life, of what happens when intellectual life is trimmed down to little more than entertainment. Who wins? No one but the networks. Why hadn't ABC chosen someone else, Buckley must have wondered, someone eager to probe the depths of an issue or of the nature of man, someone like Norman Mailer?

When *Esquire* asked Vidal and Buckley to write a piece about the incident, the name-calling continued. Buckley eventually sued *Esquire* for printing Vidal's lies about him (Vidal countersued). Buckley's friends urged him not to litigate. "A celebrity is simply one who accepts pay for having no privacy," wrote Hugh Kenner, perhaps America's greatest literary critic and Buckley's close friend. "ABC is . . . putting on a show. . . . What you have in fact done is accept a role as a Celebrity. You will be playing William F. Buckley, Old Antagonist of Gore Vidal. And you will be conceding the right to have your privacy violated, which means in the first instance being taxed with past statements you never made and leads right up to such imputations—bisexuality, anti-Semitism, etc.—as make up the texture of Gore Vidal's *Esquire* piece."[44]

Too true, thought Buckley. But there was something more to it than that: Buckley had become frayed by the times. As all hell broke loose outside and inside the convention hall, it was hard not to think of it as a giant metaphor for the nation. The revolution he had sought for so long was not supposed to look like this, not at all. Mayor Daley was not his George Washington.

Buckley fell into bed that night exhausted and hollowed out.

Later that night, Mailer walked among the wreckage. He was aghast. He hated everyone. He had done so much to destabilize the Liberal Establishment, to unglue the premises of postwar American life, to challenge The Rules, to push back against the overly rational bird's-eye view of things, to resist corporate capitalism. But now he was confronted by what he had helped wrought. On one side it was the totalitarian forces of an authoritarian state, and Richard Daley was their leader. On the other side was a collection of miscreants and drug addicts who didn't possess enough smarts to figure out how to lead, or if they could, or what they stood for other than a whole lot of "do your own thing." With the streets now speckled with blood, Mailer walked right down the middle of Michigan Avenue. "The disease was beneath the skin," he wrote of the event, "the century was malignant with an illness so intricate that the Yippies, the Muslims, and the rednecks of George Wallace were all in attack upon it. They might eat each other first, but that was merely another facet of the plague—cannibalism was still the best cure for cancer."[45]

And then it hit him: for the first time in his life, he was afraid of the future. Mailer discovered within himself a "reluctance to lose even the America he had had, that insane warmongering technology land with its smog, its superhighways, its experts and its profound dishonesty. Yet," he continued, "it had allowed him to write. . . . He had lived well enough to have six children, a house on the water, a good apartment, good meals, good booze, he had even come to enjoy wine."

Then he wrote one of his best lines: "A revolutionary with a taste in wine has come already half the distance from Marx to Burke."[46] Was he, the great revolutionary, in mid-transition? Like a sex-crazed young man now confronted with the pregnancy that he helped bring about, did he now want to go back to a time when things were simpler?

Looking at the carnage on Michigan Avenue, the real question for Mailer was "where his loyalties belonged—to the revolution or to the stability of the country"?[47] He just didn't know. So he did what he always did at times like this—he went to a bar and got a drink.

When he gave a speech later that night with four bourbons under his belt, he had the speakers turned first to the National Guardsmen watching over things, and talked to them about the time he spent in the Army, sympathizing with their inner struggle. Then, in a symbolic gesture only he himself understood, he had the speakers turned 180 degrees to the protestors and spoke of his sympathies for them and their revolution.

Knowing nothing of his inner turmoil, the protestors responded by telling him to "Write good baby, write good." With those lines, he knew he'd have to cast his lot with the protestors. They'd let him lead. They'd put him on stage. Who could say no to that? Certainly not Norman Mailer. But still, as he put it in his own inimical way, "Put your fingers in V for victory and give a wink. We yet may win, the others are so stupid. Heaven help us when we do."[48]

It was a half-hearted endorsement to say the least, one filled with more than a bit of dread.

Over the next few days, Buckley tried to make sense of it all. In a series of columns, he showed himself to be just as torn as Mailer was about the future, although with a slight inclination toward the forces of order, an inclination that grew more pronounced as his distance from the convention grew. The days of the convention, he wrote, were "horrible," expressing a "fatigue that came naturally to all who had participated actively or passively" in an event where the "mood of the minority was, as we all know, not merely mutinous, but mutinous in that especially determined way that characterizes the morally arrogant."[49] How could the youth be so arrogant? How could they be so sure of their cause? Their call for liberation was social suicide. And it was on the march!

Still, Buckley knew the police bore some responsibility for the rupture. Even those willing to defend them, he wrote in a column titled, "On Rioting," "*were* horrified at what they saw, because what they saw included the redundant blow of the nightstick, at the head or shoulder or rump of a victim already incapacitated; included, on one notorious occasion, policemen calling for the vacating of a street at a speed at which, literally, unpracticed sprinters could not comply."

The police were, nevertheless, defenders of order. They were there to preserve a basic function of American democracy. Political conventions were part of that. He lingered, though, over the central question at hand: "Do we really desire to enforce police regulations adamantly, or do too many people suspect that such regulations, promulgated under pressure, are arbitrary and constricting, and therefore lacking in sufficient moral authority to justify automatic acceptance?"

Well, he just didn't know. What did it mean when the preservation of order required a bloodletting? Were those in Chicago who were throwing "themselves into police lines . . . saying to us things which we ought to hear"? As was typical for Buckley, he punted on this, the most valuable question: "The initiative, at this point, is with the intellectuals," he said, "who should tell us-folk how to square off to these problems."[50] He asked all the right questions but then left the search for answers to someone else.

He did make one attempt to understand the dynamics of 1968 in terms he was comfortable with—the set of assumptions from the past. A few weeks after the riots, he wondered out loud if he could safely impugn the rioters as communists. This would return him to more comfortable Cold War grounding. His conclusion was that of a man trying desperately to make sense of things when the old analogies no longer held up. No, they weren't communists, he decided, but their actions did serve communist ends: "the ideological compatibility of the two is the existentialist reality," he said, a bit too easily.[51] But still, his America was drifting away, and he knew it. The ground had shifted too much, the language of understanding was different.

The morning after the convention, Mailer pondered the mess. On his way out of town, he made one final pass through Grant Park, the encampment of the distraught. The place was mostly empty now, save for an odd assortment of injured troops from the previous night, when the police had actually stormed the McCarthy headquarters, thinking Clean Gene's volunteers were hurtling projectiles at them from their hotel rooms. As Mailer walked the line, he saw "mountaineers, varlets, knaves, Hindu saints, musketeers, tank men, and wanly beautiful Yippie girls." A collared priest recited a Catholic Mass over the diversity of bloodied heads, the combination of the counterculture and the antiwar movement presided over by a symbol of authority nearly two thousand years old. As Mailer pondered the odd assortment, he wrote, "The sight, after all the sights, seemed perfectly conventional."

He finally turned to enter his hotel across the street, the same hotel where Buckley and Pat had tried to sleep the previous night. As Mailer turned, he ran headlong into Senator McCarthy's daughter—a young brunette, politically involved, the daughter of the peace candidate who had just been defeated and whose troops had just been battered, someone who sympathized with the soldiers now being tended in the field.

"What should we do about this mess?" she asked, her youthful intrepidness betraying more than an ounce of hope.

Mailer recoiled at the question. Did he really want to keep fighting? In the end, he said what he had to say, the truth. "I'm going to catch a plane and see my family," he said, raising his head just in time to see the flash of disapproval come across her face as she became aware that one of the Generals was removing himself from battle.

But Mailer didn't tell her what he was really thinking. When he wrote it all down a few weeks later, he wrote the wizened words of a wounded warrior: "Dear Miss, we will be fighting for forty years."[52]

PART IV

THE NEW ORDER
(1969–76)

12

One Last Try

n January 1969, with the dark clouds of the convention still hovering over the nation, Richard Nixon took the oath of office as the thirty-seventh president of the United States. "We find ourselves rich in goods, but ragged in spirit," he said in his inaugural address. "We cannot learn from one another until we stop shouting at one another." But the chances of that seemed slim.[1]

A month later, Buckley sent Mailer an invitation to get away from it all.

"Dear Norman," he wrote.

> I'd like you to share with me a high point of my year. In May
> . . . I sail my schooner from Miami to New York (non-stop).
> The trip last year took six and a half days . . . the weather was
> fine, though we could have used a little more wind. The drill
> is four hours on-duty, eight hours off; so that there is plenty
> of time to read, sun, etc. We stop in mid-ocean a couple of
> times a day for a quick swim. The crew of four looks after
> essentials. The cabins are air-conditioned, and won't remind
> you of Guadalcanal. The company, need I say, is choice. You,
> Murray Kempton, Garry Wills, and a couple of other old
> friends.

"Besides," Buckley concluded, "I'm reminded . . . that contact with you is necessary for my social respectability."[2]

It was a snarky response to a recent *New York* magazine article about Buckley that suggested the only reason people tolerated him was because people on the left cared for him. Mailer was prominently mentioned among Buckley's admirers.[3]

Mailer was ecstatic. He was ready, he said, to send "a letter full of enthusiasm and shout yes." But then a magazine got in touch with him about writing an assignment "that's extraordinarily tempting," an assignment covering the lunar landing of 1969. He told Buckley he'd have to mull it over for a week. "If you want to fill out your list by then I understand all to [*sic*] well, if sadly. But if you can keep the space open for a time I'll let you know so soon."[4]

The magazine assignment—advance interviews with the astronauts —got delayed, so Mailer signed on for the sail.

In April, Buckley sent a memo to his shipmates: Mailer, Wills, Evan Galbraith, radio entrepreneur Peter Starr, and engineer Reggie Stoops (Murray Kempton couldn't go). "The plan is to set sail from Miami at noon," he wrote. "Miscellaneous information: Please don't bring suitcases—only duffle bags and briefcases. There is a typewriter on board. Come to think of it, there is everything on board." Guests only had to bring topsiders. "I'll bring acrylic paints and canvases," he added, leaving aside the fact that seeing Buckley's seascapes had once prompted painter Marc Chagall to say, "poor paint."[5] "If you wish to present an apple to the skipper," Buckley continued, "wine please. If you don't you will get wine anyway. . . . Isn't it glorious!"[6]

By that time, though, something else had come up for Mailer. After deliberating and taking two weeks to decide, Mailer finally scribbled his regrets to Buckley: "It looks as tho I'll be running for mayor. I must, I fear, decline your splendid invitation—unless of course you'd consider coming out for me."[7] Buckley of course would do no such thing, not in 1969 nor at any other time. But he would watch Mailer the candidate perform the same dance he himself had done four years earlier, and it would be no less fun, even if it meant his friend couldn't join him on the sail.

Mailer had always wanted to be mayor. He had of course admitted to wanting to be president many times, but that was fanciful, a rhetorical flourish with just a slight kernel of truth. The nation was huge, and politics was dirty. He never wanted to do the dirty work necessary to enter national politics.

But New York City was different. It was not amorphous. It was gritty and dirty and glorious and home, and what happened there simply happened faster and more dramatically than anywhere else. Mailer thought he could articulate the hopes and dreams of the precocious city, understand and articulate the rage of the late 1960s, and direct it toward a fulfilling future. It was an attempt to save the country from itself.

This was not Mailer's first time running for mayor. There had been the 1961 plan to run on the existential ticket. Thinking he could bring together the city's artists and its poor, Mailer had planned to announce his candidacy at a party. Instead, he had gotten too drunk, stabbed his wife, and was sent to Bellevue. So much for the campaign of 1961.

Then, in 1965, as Buckley was making speeches, shaking hands, and putting forward ideas for the future, Mailer, perhaps a bit longingly, began to construct a huge model city of the future— out of Legos. As he wrote to his friend Don Carpenter, "I've been working with plastic, 10,000 pieces of plastic, on an idea I have for a new kind of city. I think my ideas about plastic are right: handle 10,000 pieces of plastic and you feel flat and dead. What a cheerisome [sic] note this is."[8]

The Lego Group, of Danish origin, began in 1932 as a wooden toy manufacturer. It only began making Lego pieces out of plastic in 1947, and then only exclusively out of plastic in 1960, when its warehouse of wood supplies burned to the ground. The founder, Ole Kirk Christiansen, won his own company-wide competition to name the plastic brick he'd just invented, the name coming from the Danish *leg godt*, or "play well." Despite a host of immediate competitors, the Lego bricks were wildly successful, giving kids (and their parents) the freedom to create and destroy with infinitesimal variety in a relatively controlled environment.

Once the company went plastic, one of Mailer's sons got some Legos as a birthday present, and a light bulb went on in Mailer's head. He hated the sprawl of the modern city, and he had long sought an alternative. In 1964, in both the *New York Times Magazine* and even the lofty *Architectural Forum*, Mailer had expounded on the theme. "If we are to avoid a megalopolis five hundred miles long, a city without shape or exit, a nightmare of ranch houses, highways, suburbs and industrial sludge," he wrote in an article called "Cities Higher Than Mountains," "then there is only one solution: the cities must climb, they must not spread, they must build up, not by increments, but by leaps, up and up, up to the heavens."[9] His 1965 Lego-made "City of the Future" would serve as a model.

Before long Mailer had two workers helping him, and he ordered crates and crates of red, blue, white, and black Legos from a factory in New Jersey. He moved all the furniture to one side of his oversized Brooklyn living room and, for two months, the three men built a huge Lego city on a four-by-eight-foot piece of plywood with several five-foot aluminum legs supporting the various high-rises. It ended up being more than seven feet tall, eight feet wide, and four feet deep, a huge oval city with various high-rises connected to one another by cables. Mailer would scribble down ideas, pop into the living room, discuss things with the workers, then disappear to write. At night, he'd come down and adjust things.

"I can't stand this shit in my living room," Beverly said.

Mailer didn't care; he kept on building, a maniac constructing his own kingdom while watching his friend Buckley run for mayor of a real city.

"It was very much opposed to Le Corbusier," Mailer later said, adding weight to his tinker with kid's toys. "I kept thinking of Mont Saint-Michel."

"Each Lego brick represents an apartment," he'd explain. "There'd be something like twelve thousand apartments. The philosophers would live at the top. The call girls would live in the white bricks, and the corporate executives would live in the black." Zip lines would connect the towers, and "[o]nce it was cabled up," he said, "those who were adventurous could slide down. It would be great fun to start the day off."[10]

After a few months, a friend from the Museum of Modern Art saw the creation, took pictures, and asked Mailer if he would allow him to display it at MoMA. Mailer loved the idea and promised to deliver it right away, but he quickly discovered that the city was too big to get out of his house. The doors were too narrow. He sought cranes to carry it upward off his balcony. That didn't work. He thought to have several of the front windows removed from his apartment. It still wouldn't fit. In the end, they'd have to take Mailer's "City of the Future" apart, but with that, Mailer refused. They'd already glued several sections together, and he knew they'd forget exactly how they built the thing.

In the end, Mailer said, "Fuck it, that's it. It stays." He paid the workers to build a small fence around it, and Mailer's Lego city remained in his living room for the next forty years.[11] Beverly claimed to eventually come to love it, but conceded, "It was a bitch to dust."[12]

In typical Mailer fashion, frustrated hopes had transitioned into yet another creative outlet. But, of course, Legos were not New York City. His "campaign" of 1965 was a bust. That was Buckley's irascible moment anyway.

By 1969 Mailer was in his professional prime. He was a National Book Award winner, the holder of a Pulitzer Prize, and probably the most famous writer in America. But he also saw the right and left falling apart, succumbing to their worst incarnations—

authoritarianism on the one hand, and "do your own thing"-ism on the other—and he sought, ironically enough, to create a new middle, the basis for a new establishment that would curtail the worst of either flank. What he wanted to do in 1969 was develop more fully what he called his Left-Conservatism in an attempt to find some last-gasp peace in the late 1960s.

The city had its troubles—and then some. In 1965, when John Lindsay defeated Abe Beame and Buckley to replace Robert Wagner as mayor, the middle class was already leaving in droves, deficits were skyrocketing, the educational system was under duress, crime rates showed danger, the budget was out of whack, and there was a water shortage. By 1969, things had gotten worse. The city was still bleeding the kinds of jobs that made up the middle class. Everything was cheaper outside New York City, and even corporate headquarters began moving to the suburbs. The crime rate had continued to climb. As one of Lindsay's competitors put it, under the Wagner administration, "People were afraid to leave their homes at night. Now, after four years of Lindsay, the people are afraid to leave their homes in the daytime."[13]

Meanwhile, the day Lindsay entered office in 1965, transit workers went on strike to protest a lack of raises and lack of concern for improving the infrastructure. The strike wasn't Lindsay's fault, but he handled it so poorly that it stuck with him for the rest of his career. As a publicity stunt, Lindsay simply walked from place to place, smilingly saying he thought New York was still a "fun city." "Fun city" was the kind of thing a wealthy person from the Upper East Side like Lindsay would say, not the kind of thing uttered by workers in the outer boroughs. The phrase attached itself to Lindsay derisively, and more than one journalist told harrowing tales of the city's decline while Lindsay whistled in the clouds about a "fun city." As Buckley put it in a column titled "Revolution in Fun City," "Three terms of Wagner (who went down to ignominious defeat) produced a city which every year was worse off than the year before. Four years of Lindsay . . . matured almost every problem Mr. Wagner had coaxed along into adolescence during his long tenure."[14]

Things only got worse. In 1968, Lindsay attempted to answer the needs of his constituents and grant more local control to the sprawling New York School District by breaking it into several smaller parts. The plan backfired. It was perceived as union busting. The mostly Jewish-run teachers' union fought against local control and for preserving seniority within the union, while neighborhood residents, mostly African American and Puerto Rican, demanded even more control than Lindsay's plan granted.

The issue came to a head in Ocean Hill, an insular all-black neighborhood in Brooklyn. There, "neighborhood control" had grown increasingly radical, its goal "to teach our black youth how to survive in the hostile society that we do not yet control" and to defeat the "Anglo Saxon based curriculum" which had led to the "enslavement" of black children, according to one activist. The area's new Ocean Hill–Brownsville Governing Board fired a bunch of unionized teachers in order to take control.[15]

Repercussions came quickly. A huge teachers' strike commenced a few weeks later. The issue of whether or not the teachers could be dismissed by a local board lasted through the summer of 1968, and led to a huge city-wide teachers strike on the first day of school in August 1968. When the strike ended inconclusively two days later, the schools in Ocean Hill were blocked off by parents who wanted to keep the unionized teachers out. It was a mess.

There was a second strike, and then a third. Kids missed more than a month of classes. The episode finally ended in late 1968 through a complicated settlement made without the help of either the parents' organization or the union, leaving Lindsay's chief aide on schools to conclude, "We didn't gain squat by this. This was not a win-win, it was a lose-lose-lose-lose."[16]

More importantly, the issue became synonymous with the decline of one of the key coalitions making up the postwar left, African Americans and Jews. The racial and ethnic dynamics of the Ocean Hill–Brownsville debacle put on display some of the limits of postwar liberalism. Dueling constituencies, who had been willing to sacrifice in the name of the common good, pulled back from that effort to allow their own group to thrive. It wasn't that they were being greedy; it was that the top-down approach of postwar liberalism had too long ignored the plight of certain neighborhoods. Lindsay, like most politicians, had a difficult time navigating the growing demands. When he at first sided with the neighborhoods over the unions, many Jewish advocates began calling him anti-Semitic. When he eventually caved to some of the demands made by the unions, Lindsay alienated African Americans. John Lindsay, the supposed savior of postwar liberalism, was reeling from tensions within his own camp.

As he proceeded to face his doom, one image haunted Lindsay above all else. In February 1968, a sanitation workers' strike made the city look like a bona fide post-apocalyptic movie set. As the strike went on for nine full days, mounds of garbage piled up throughout the city, ten thousand tons a day, eventually totaling almost one hundred thousand tons of trash, its stench everywhere. Sometimes the winds were strong enough to knock over the growing piles, launching garbage swirling in the streets. At one point, some of the garbage caught fire, sending black smoke high into the urban air. With cops speeding around dealing with crime, the place stinking like a dump, and smoke billowing above, it was hard to deny that 1968 New York City represented a liberal dystopia.

Politicians didn't seem up to the task of handling the problem as they bickered rather than clean up the place. Lindsay had first ludicrously asked the governor, Nelson Rockefeller, to send in the National Guard to pick up the garbage. Rockefeller refused. "I would just like to say that having military men come in [not only] to collect garbage but to break a strike in this city would have the most serious repercussions, be inflammatory, there could be fighting on the streets, and I think we've got trouble enough in this city," the governor said.[17]

In the end, after nine days of stink, Rockefeller threatened to have the state health commissioner declare a public emergency, which would have allowed the state to take control of the sanitation department. He promised to give the workers what they wanted, and he would send the bill to the city. Eventually the two sides submitted to arbitration, with the arbitrator splitting the differences.[18] Lindsay may have stood up to the demands of the unions, but the city still stank.

Lindsay did have one triumphant moment as mayor: on April 4, 1968, the night Martin Luther King, Jr., was shot and violence escalated throughout the country, Lindsay drove straight to Harlem, got out of his car, and walked into the angry mass of people who were about to riot. At six-foot-six, he raised his hands and shared their sorrow. He talked and talked and talked about their pain, and listened to what they had to say, validating their anger. There was no riot in Harlem that day. Lindsay had been a soothing force.

It was one of only a handful of good moments, and those who looked more closely saw that it simply masked the violence and anger among New York's black community that seeped out slowly in 1968, not all at once, so that the property damages in 1968 were pretty bad, at the level of a riot even. But the images presented to the public—of a city saved by John Lindsay—were different. When he ran for reelection in 1969, one of Lindsay's ubiquitous television commercials told residents that if they wanted to see the good that Lindsay had done for New York City, they should drive through the Holland Tunnel to Newark, a city devastated by riots. The television commercial conveniently skipped over the fact that Lindsay had paid overtime to have the city's garbage collectors go to Harlem early each morning to preserve the sense of order.

With memories of burning trash piles, economic decline, and the coalitions that used to be dependable now faltering, Lindsay and the liberalism he represented looked vulnerable. Buckley was unrelenting. "What is happening in New York City, no question about it," he wrote, "is the return of bread cast thoughtlessly on the waters over a period of time, and Lindsay has as enthusiastically as anybody sided with the fanatic interpreters of the Bill of Rights, so much so as to help to immobilize those who believe that above all it is the responsibility of government to maintain law and order and protect its citizens."[19] The city seemed to be reeling out of control, and not only Lindsay but all of postwar liberalism was to blame. Bread had been thrown to all the ducks that swam over; it was inevitable the bread would eventually run out and the ducks would fight over the scraps. Buckley had been predicting this for decades.

As if God wanted to punish Lindsay more, in February 1969, shortly after Buckley wrote these lines, more than fifteen inches of snow fell on New York City. Eventually forty-two people died and 288 were injured as a result of the storm. Lindsay, following the predictions of the National Weather Service (which called for rain), hadn't planned for snow, and the snow removal process went excruciatingly slow. Once the snow removers finally made it to work, they discovered that many of their machines were inoperable due to poor maintenance, and that the director who was supposed to organize things was upstate and unavailable until, ironically enough, roads had been cleared enough for him to come home. For three days the city was impassable. United Nations Undersecretary General Ralph Bunche said in a letter to the mayor, "As far as getting to the United Nations is concerned, I may as well be in the Alps." He lived in Queens.[20]

After four days the plows had cleaned up several sections of the city, but everyone realized that Manhattan had been the first borough cleared. The white working classes in the outer boroughs seethed.

A day late and a dollar short, Lindsay made a trip to Queens, trying to re-create the magic that had prevented race riots in Harlem the previous year. Instead, his limousine got stuck in the snow. A truck with four-wheel drive took him part of the way, but then it got stuck, too. As he walked through the borough on foot, residents heckled him. "You should be ashamed of yourself!" and "Go back to Manhattan!" they yelled from their second- and third-floor windows.

Finally, one woman approached Lindsay and said he was "a wonderful man," to which Lindsay replied, "And you're a wonderful woman, not like the fat Jewish broads up there," pointing to the hecklers up above. The comment likely would have cost Lindsay his political career, but the Associated Press, the *New York Times*, and WNEW radio all declined to run the story. As one of the writers for the *Times* recalled, they didn't want to kick a man when he was down.[21] More than likely, though, the reporters all supported Lindsay and his liberalism; it's hard to imagine them showing such restraint with someone like Nixon or Goldwater.

And so in 1969 the city was a mess. Perhaps unsurprisingly then, the New York City mayoral campaign of 1969 was a bit of a mess, too. As Buckley saw things, "What's happening in New York is that the people-at-large simply don't want to re-elect John Lindsay," specifying, "The fact is that the majority, the overwhelming majority of New Yorkers, believe that Lindsay has failed them, Lindsay and his politics have failed them."[22] One observer on the left put it more bluntly: "there was a jaunty feeling of 'fuck-youism' running throughout the town."[23] Mailer, never short of chutzpah, thought he could channel all the "fuck-youism" into creative directions by running for mayor.

It was a ridiculous assumption, really. Mailer for Mayor? The front cover of *New York* magazine said it all when it displayed a picture of Mailer and asked: "SERIOUSLY?"[24] But in the face of mounting anxieties, a crumbling political middle, and the worst of either extreme coming to the fore, Mailer thought he could invent a new kind of center and push the city, and the country, into more promising directions. Most of the alternatives—Mario Procaccino, John Marchi, and former mayor Robert Wagner—were white ethnics who promised little more than law and order. There was no original thinking or creativity. Mailer thought this might be his moment, a time when his revolutionary ambitions finally matched the mood of the people.

He wasn't alone in making this assumption. In February, barely after the snow had melted, Jack Newfield, a left-wing reporter for the *Village Voice*, and Noel Parmentel, a conservative writer for *National Review*, who knew of Mailer's long-standing ambition to be mayor, urged him to run. Mailer jokingly called the coming together of the two men "the Hitler–Stalin pact," but it was hard to deny that the anti-liberal critiques that Buckley and Mailer had each chronicled in their journals from 1955 were coming together in 1969 to advocate for the mayoral candidacy of Norman Mailer.[25]

For his part, Mailer hoped "a few sparks from the fires on the right and left will fly up and form this coalition."[26] Later in the campaign he said, "The left and the right have almost no meaning in municipal politics. People whose national politics are right-wing—and find my ideas on, say, Vietnam atrocious—may nonetheless believe I hate air pollution and neighborhoods ruined by ugly buildings as much as they do and might be the one man running to do something about it."[27]

Mailer's political insight was that there was a huge hole in the governing of the city—and in liberalism generally. He saw Lindsay, a limousine liberal who ran most of his well-funded campaigns out of the coffers of Upper East Side bankers, offering generous programs to the lower classes, especially African Americans and Puerto Ricans, while also taking care of his own. The gap, then, was that the elite seemed to be doing everything it could to help the city's poorest while ignoring the working classes that constituted the four outer boroughs of New York—the broad middle. These working-class whites were the people who had voted for Buckley in 1965; they were the "girls who want to work at Bell Telephone," as Mailer had put it back then. And they were still feeling angry and ignored. As Mailer saw it, their anger could go in one of two directions: a tortoise-like reversion to law and order, or into more promising solutions for the future. He hoped to provide a path to the latter.

An antiwar Jew with a Harvard degree and a Pulitzer, Mailer was not the ideal voice to represent the white working class. So he brought into his campaign as an advisor Pete Hamill, a drinking buddy and the writer who had chastised Capote's Black and White Ball for ignoring the plight of the Vietnamese. By the late 1960s, Hamill had become one of the most articulate writers on the subject of the white working classes, which was no surprise considering they were his people. Mailer wanted to learn from Hamill.

In April 1969, just as Mailer was gearing up his campaign, Hamill wrote an article for *New York* magazine entitled "The Revolt of the White Lower Middle Class." In his piece he recalled chatting with his literary friends, who saw the working class as:

> murderous rabble: fat, well-fed, bigoted, ignorant, an army of beer-soaked Irishmen, violence-loving Italians, hate-filled Poles. Lithuanians and Hungarians (they are never referred to as Americans). They are the people who assault peace marchers, who start groups like the Society for the Prevention of Negroes Getting Everything (S.P.O.N.G.E.), the people who hate John Lindsay and vote for George Wallace, presumably because they believe that Wallace will eventually march every black man in America to the gas chambers, sending Lindsay and the rest of the Liberal Establishment along with them.

But Hamill explained the anger:

> The working-class white man spends much of his time complaining almost desperately about the way he has become a victim. Taxes and the rising cost of living keep him broke, and he sees nothing in return for the taxes he pays. The Department of Sanitation comes to his street at three in the morning,

and a day late, and slams garbage cans around like an invading regiment. His streets were the last to be cleaned in the big snowstorm, and they are now sliced up with trenches that could only be called potholes by the myopic. His neighborhood is a dumping ground for abandoned automobiles, which rust and rot for as long as six weeks before someone from the city finally takes them away. He works very hard, frequently on a dangerous job, and then discovers that he still can't pay his way; his wife takes a Thursday night job in a department store and he gets a weekend job, pumping gas or pushing a hack. For him, life in New York is not much of a life.[28]

In short, not only had postwar liberalism ignored the white working classes, but the liberals had worried more about the plight of the poor than their own. The white working class, which thought it was doing what it was supposed to be doing to succeed, felt disrespected. Rather than vent about the system (how did one do that, anyway?), they often took out their anger on those they saw as getting a free ride, most especially African Americans. No wonder Buckley's bootstraps argument was catching on.

Mailer understood the feeling. While covering Nixon in 1968, he himself candidly admitted he "was getting tired of Negroes and their rights." The realization came to him as he was waiting at a press conference for Rev. Ralph Abernathy, who was at that point forty-five minutes late.[29] Mailer felt guilty about these thoughts, but also was "heartily sick of listening to the tyranny of soul music, so bored with Negroes triumphantly late for appointments, . . . so weary of being sounded in the subway by Black eyes, so despairing of the smell of booze and pot and used-up hope in blood-shot eyes of Negroes bombed at noon, so envious finally of that liberty to abdicate from the long year-end decade-drowning yokes of work and responsibility."[30] Mailer objectively understood the anger of the white working classes, but he knew their violence and racism wasn't the answer. He sought something better.

In March 1969 he agreed to run for mayor. Oddly, the haphazard coalition that had recruited him, Parmentel, Newfield, and the famous feminist writer Gloria Steinem, had also asked Jimmy Breslin to run. Breslin was a hard-nosed working-class newspaper columnist and saloon-goer with a reputation for being both smart and salt of the earth. To their great surprise, both men said yes. Stuck sorting out the mess, they were saved by the bell. Just as the campaign was gearing up, it was announced that Mailer had won the Pulitzer Prize for *Armies*, so putting him atop the ticket made more sense. Breslin gruffly agreed to run for City Council president instead. They asked Steinem to run for comptroller, but she declined, afraid her presence would make it look like "a campy literary exercise."[31] The two men went it alone.

Mailer announced his candidacy at the Overseas Press Club, the same venue Buckley had used four years earlier. In a speech entitled "Why They Run," he answered the titular question in typical Mailerese: "It has to do, above all else, with what has been squeezed out of us by outside, abstract forces, chiefly by that gross technology which straddles us, insatiably sapping our spirit. . . . To deal with the enormous complexities of this all-embracing alienation . . . Jimmy Breslin, who is running for City Council President, and Norman Mailer, mayoralty candidate, propose to return political power to the people of New York City."[32]

The two central planks on their platform promised just as much: "turning New York City into a 51st state and shifting the powers of this state to neighborhoods." After all, "Only with local control by men and women at the neighborhood level will we ever be able to achieve safe streets and schools . . . and rebuild our slums room by room. Mailer–Breslin hold that New York should be for New Yorkers . . . geared for neighborhood control, not run by remote control."[33]

The boundaries of the smaller counties within the newly created fifty-first state would be decided by the people, they promised. From there, the people would choose what they wanted the city-state to look like. A neighborhood of old people, for instance, "might wish to purchase massive police protection, while, on the other hand, a poor neighborhood would obviously be more concerned with money spent on education and housing. Who among us is so arrogant to say we know the needs of neighborhoods better than those who populate its streets?"[34]

The campaign figured that revenues would go up in the Fifty-first State Plan because the city-state would no longer have to send money to Albany and could use all its revenues locally. It could also apply for federal funds independently. Real estate taxes could be lowered to encourage the renovation of substandard housing. Neighborhoods could implement their own welfare programs, such as one (they proposed) that hired the needy to work in locally run daycare centers so mothers could pursue professions. If a neighborhood wished, police could be required to live in their locality, and they could have prisons there, too, transforming "our jails from mere inhumane detention centers to environments conducive to genuine social rehabilitation." To alleviate juvenile delinquency, the city-now-state could fund neighborhood recreation programs in each locality, then host a statewide competition (stickball tournaments, for instance, would be held in the caverns of Wall Street on weekends).[35]

In addition to his numerous calls for increased local control, Mailer, like Buckley, sought to end the area's pollution. Mailer's method? Similar to Buckley's: a monorail around the island of Manhattan that spidered into each borough and was met by cable cars that swooped riders through the metropolis. It was so popular that civil engineers began to draw schematics. It was dubbed "Mailer Rail."

Along similar lines, Mailer proposed to prohibit "all traffic but trucks, taxis and buses" on the island of Manhattan. In addition, there would be a "once-a-month so-called 'Sweet Sunday,' where there would be no traffic in the city at all, no trains or buses moving in or leaving and no planes."

"Nothing would fly but the birds," the platform read.[36]

At one point, Mailer even thought to outlaw all power on Sweet Sunday, save for generators in hospitals. But then he thought better of it: "On the first hot day the populace would impeach me."[37] He scrapped that plan.

There were hundreds of ideas emanating from the campaign. Loan out the city's demolition fund to people who wanted to rehabilitate buildings through Neighborhood Housing Banks. Break up the school districts into neighborhood-controlled districts. Make Coney Island "Las Vegas East." Offer free bicycles in all parks, to be returned on the honor system. Put a zoo in every neighborhood. For motor enthusiasts, a U.S. Grand Prix in Central Park.

In sum, Mailer's main effort was to increase local control in order to allow each group to seek its own vision of fulfillment. His platform, he said, offered "a new beginning," ranging from "Free Huey Newton to end fluoridation," from "compulsory free love in those neighborhoods which vote for it, [to] compulsory church attendance on Sunday for those neighborhoods who vote for that . . . What we are running on," Mailer said, "is one basic, simple notion—which is that till people see where their ideas lead, they know nothing; and that, my fine friends, is why I am running. I want to see where my own ideas lead."[38] His hope was that by allowing more local control, he could end the right–left split then tearing the nation apart, the right–left split that had emerged out of a feeling of helplessness brought on by years of the Liberal Establishment's bureaucratic control. "The cry of Power to the Neighborhoods," he said, "addresses itself from the left across the divide to conservatism. Speaking from the left, it says that a city cannot survive unless the poor are recognized, until their problems are underlined as not directly of their own making." And from the right, Mailer's plan "recognizes that man must have the opportunity to work out his own destiny, or he will never know the dimensions of himself, he will be alienated from any sense of

whether he is acting for good or evil." The plan "even recognizes
the deepest of conservative principles—that a man has a right to
live his life in such a way that he may not know if he is dying in a
state of grace. Our lives, directed by abstract outside forces, have
lost that possibility most of all."[39]

Did it sound crazy? Of course. Was it even possible to secede?
They were checking. How would the neighborhoods organize?
That was up to them. But if intellectuals were supposed to provide
ideas, here they were, attempting to give people a stake in society
again, to allow differing dreams to flourish. Mailer was pleased
when the *New York Times* wrote, "His political program is a blend of
radicalism, conservatism, invention, and, perhaps, prophesy [*sic*]."
Mailer was even more pleased that the *Times* quoted him as saying,
"It is impossible to change this city for the better without creating a
new political basis. Lindsay is the proof of this because he worked
manfully in the old tradition, tried to wed a new tradition to it,
and failed. Despite his best efforts, the city is in unhappier shape
than ever."[40]

As the primary approached, Mailer hit the stump. He had famous
friends working for him. Not only were his New York writer-friends
supportive of the venture, but folks like Andy Warhol, who screened
his, *I, a Man* film with proceeds going to Mailer's campaign. The
Doors showed their documentary *Feast of Friends* at the same rally,
and Jim Morrison read poetry at a fundraiser on the Sunset Strip
in Hollywood, proceeds going to Mailer for Mayor. "Run, Run
Fast," Morrison wrote to Mailer.[41]

Mailer had some great moments on the campaign. He and
Breslin, one an unpredictable non-practicing Jew from Brooklyn,
the other an unpredictable Irish Catholic familiar with the bars
of Queens and the Bronx, made a great one-two punch. Breslin
could talk to cops, Mailer to brownstoners. In a line he'd use again
and again, Breslin would talk about his high school, John Adams
High in Queens, where he went "for five years." The school was

located right on the quarter pole at Aqueduct Racetrack, and, as Breslin put it, "The first English sentence I ever learned was 'It is now post time.'" When the district remodeled the school, they had to move the quarter pole, which "was the cultural high point in the school's history." The working-class audiences ate it up. Of his graduating class, Breslin said, "We produced sixteen New York City policemen, seventeen New York City firemen, and thirty-two of the most prominent felons in this city." After the laughter died: "And seventy-five body and fender men who were open to any proposition." More laughter.[42]

During one stop at New York University, Breslin showed up woefully hung over from the night before. He looked at Mailer, saw deeply bloodshot eyes, and realized Mailer was suffering from the same affliction. Then he noticed Mailer was wearing dark pants, an ugly plaid sports coat, and a white dress shirt unbuttoned at the neck. Breslin laughed: "This is the way it should be—both of us hung over, you dressed like a detective in those fuckin' Seventeenth Precinct clothes. Just the way it should be."[43]

At his best, Breslin could be magical. When he went to the police academy, he wore a dark suit with a dull sheen, the wool not sedate enough to be Wall Street, not shiny enough for Mafioso: "A plainclothesman out on the make," concluded the campaign manager. "A nice touch."[44]

Then Breslin proceeded to tell the police it wasn't their fault, this mess the city was in. "The police," he said:

> get blamed for all the mistakes of all the people who are supposed to be more important and smarter than us. You're asked to go out and take care of, patch up holes made in forty years of history by Congressmen from New York who sat still while federal housing bills were being passed that didn't help us. . . . You're being asked to pay for a Board of Education which sat at 110 Livingston Street and kept everybody in the city illiterate in the areas you worry about most. And you're

being asked to pay for the mistakes of white politicians who walked around and never even knew one Black person and made the decisions which affected their lives and caused an awful lot of the rancidness that's now in everyone's mouth over this situation.

"Now *they* created the problems," Breslin continued. But "now they turn to you, the policemen of the city of New York, and say: 'You go out and handle them.' In my estimation, it's a disgrace. As usual it comes down to us—give it to the fellow on the bottom. Let him handle the problem."[45]

By seceding from the state and returning the city to local control, cops could better understand the various situations they found themselves in, because local cops would know their beat. "We think," Breslin said, "the only way that this can be handled is to send everybody to his own room, and we'll talk in the morning. . . . Let's ventilate, let's separate, let's have people in control of their own education. Make this city a state, and later on somewhere along the line we can start to mingle. I think the people are much better at controlling their own destiny."

It was in some ways a speech clouded with racial overtones, but it was mostly a class speech. It was a way to discuss the merits of their esoteric ideas—fifty-first statehood, neighborhood control— in a non-esoteric way. As the campaign manager put it, their platform attacked "the soft underbelly of liberalism," the plight of the middle class and the perspective of the bird's-eye view.[46]

Mailer had his moments, too, although rarely at white working-class venues. Instead, he excelled with students. On one occasion, Queens College was in a state of turmoil, with a thousand students on a sunbaked mall still fresh from protesting a ghetto enrollment program and calling for open admissions. Mailer looked at the students and saw all the flesh and the steam and the sensualized anger of a nineteen-year-old who is mad, the girls in short shorts "whose brown thighs were covered with the veil of blond algae," the boys with their bare chests. Breslin approached the podium to speak first, as per the norm, when the students started chanting, "What about Nixon? What about Daley?" The students laughed and jostled. Breslin looked at the crowd, waiting for them to die down, but he couldn't think of a way to connect. Racetrack jokes wouldn't work here. Mailer was chomping at the bit to speak, and eventually couldn't resist. Before Breslin opened his mouth, Mailer pushed him aside with a bold right arm, grabbed the podium, and screamed into the microphone, "Fuuuuuuuck!!!!!"

He won them over in an instant. He gave an impromptu speech and, "As he spoke and they responded," reported the campaign manager, "you felt like a voyeur as he wallowed in their collective heat."[47] Mailer knew what animated this crowd: the lusty physicality of sex and action.

His best moment on the campaign was probably when he saw a vision of his promised land, his own Elysian Field. He went to a block party in the Park Slope section of Brooklyn and saw everything he thought the city could be. Brownstones with stoops, not skyscrapers with elevators. White folk, black folk, Puerto Rican, all chasing their kids around as they rode bikes on the cordoned-off street. Hot dogs and beer, small talk, intimacy. Some neighbors had organized a pageant. Neighbors from another block brought over foods they'd learned to cook in another country. Proceeds from a raffle went to buy flowers and plants to help maintain the neighborhood. It was beautiful. "It's exactly what I have been talking about," Mailer said, as he gripped his wife's hand a bit tighter and looked over his own brood of children and his mother, whom he had brought along. "I'm running against urban renewal!"[48] So much for cities higher than mountains: he wanted local control.

When he was asked to speak at the Time-Life Building, the symbolic belly of the beast of postwar liberalism, a place where one might have expected him to falter, Mailer excelled. "[W]e run on the notion," he said to the gathered reporters, "that politics is philosophy and that one cannot begin to solve the problems of a city without engaging in philosophical arguments with oneself and with one's neighbor." Perhaps ironic in light of the fact that Buckley had critiqued Mailer for having no "ground wire" in 1962, now Mailer was advocating neighborhood power in order to "find an objective ground where we can begin to locate whether some pet idea of ours or some profound idea of ours is partially true or partially untrue."

For example, were right-wingers correct when they felt "that Black people are lazy, spoiled, ungrateful, and incapable of managing their own society"? "Black people feel, I would guess," said Mailer, "on the one hand they have extraordinary possibilities and that they are great people. On the other hand, they have to feel that they can't possibly know, because they never had an opportunity to express that desire. So, if nothing else, Black communities working with their own power in their own neighborhoods could show to other neighborhoods one of two things, which is either that Black people were right about their potentiality for the future, or that they were wrong."

At the same time, "we would have the marvelous, if somewhat comic, alternatives of considering all those magical LSD communities where you would have children living on LSD for five years. At the end of that time, they would either be creating castles, or they might be two-thirds dead of liver disease."

"'The notion we're running on," he concluded, "is that until we begin to know a little more about each other—not through the old-fashioned New Deal governmental methods of tolerance—but through the quality of human experience in societies . . . we know nothing at all."[49]

Creative ideas plus a love for the city plus humor: Mailer was serious. When he gave a talk at Brooklyn College, one student interrupted to ask what Mailer would have done about the recent snowstorm. Mailer looked at the kid and said he would have "pissed all over it."[50] When he visited a synagogue, his mannerisms were so forceful that his yarmulke fell off his head. Silence greeted the room, and Mailer, instead of bending over to pick it up, looked heavenward and said, "I hope the Lord has not spoken."[51]

But of course the Lord had spoken, and much of the inevitable outcome was Mailer's fault. The press was ready to view his campaign as nothing but a publicity stunt, and Mailer gave them plenty of material to work with.

In one heartbreaking instance, he was planning to give a speech in Greenwich Village when young hippy protestors arrived and prevented any civil discourse. They stood on their seats and played volleyball with a balloon. When one protestor brought a Vietcong flag to the stage, Mailer left. Strikingly, more than a hundred people followed Mailer out of the room, and someone suggested he go to Union Square to give his speech there. As he headed in that direction, the crowd behind him swelled. He was a bona fide Pied Piper about to make New York legend. A full moon even lit the sky.

Then he messed it all up. When he finally got to the park, he walked right past it. Where was he going? It turned out someone had handed him a card with an address, and Mailer went there instead. The card led him to a fashionable bar that eagerly welcomed Mailer, putting him at a prominent table near the window— but then demanded a cover charge from all his followers. Mailer somehow missed it all, as though he had never even thought to speak to the hordes who followed him. He ordered a drink and chatted with friends, while his supporters held their hands to the windows to get a better look, before heading home in disgust. He missed the moment.[52]

The most remarkable mistake though (if not the most damning) took place at a rally at the Village Gate, a famous jazz club where John Coltrane, Nina Simone, and Aretha Franklin had all performed. The campaign had just acquired enough signatures to appear on the ballot, and the event was to honor the volunteers who had made it happen and raise a few bucks from people who wanted to see the ticket. Everyone, including Mailer, got too drunk. When it came time for him to speak, he approached the audience with hostility. He told them it was his "evening and you know it." He shouted them down when they started to chant his name. When he went off on a dangerous tangent (on, say, "the Jews"), they tried to bring him back to safe ground. But he greeted those suggestions with an angry "fuck you." At the end, he finished "with a small story, which you can shove down your throats." It turned out to be a self-indulgent story about how none of their efforts was worth a damn anyway: "We're all expendable," he said. The crowd left angry and confused.

The next morning, when Beverly and his campaign manager told him what he had done, Mailer actually cried in his pillow. The press and the city hadn't been taking him seriously, and now he had justified them. "I felt contrite," he said later. "You know, it was a real fuck-up."[53]

He struggled to make up for it, showing up at campaign head-quarters early, shaking everyone's hands. But it went only so far. In a book of position papers published immediately after the campaign (actually, the nine-thousand-dollar advance for the book helped finance the campaign), Mailer wrote an apologetic fore-word: "I wish to dedicate this collection to the hard-working staff and the enthusiastic volunteers of the Mailer–Breslin Campaign. To the extent we were successful," he continued, head dutifully bowed, "much of the credit can be given to the long hours they put in, to the extent we failed the candidate can appropriate his full and thorough share."[54]

In the end, the campaign slogans varied from "No More Bullshit" to "Vote the Rascals In" to "I Would Sleep Better If Norman Mailer Were Mayor." Mailer and Breslin had performed the intellectu-als' task of coming up with new ideas about how to confront the future. Unfortunately, as was all too common, Mailer was better at describing ailments than at proposing solutions, and many of his ideas were just too far-fetched to reach an electorate more eager to vent its frustrations through rage than creativity.

In both the Democratic and Republican primaries, white ethnic law-and-order candidates ended up winning. In the crowded Democratic primary, Mailer finished fourth, receiving 41,136 votes.

"I was so naïve," Mailer recalled, "I thought I was going to win! For me, it was a religious venture. I thought God had chosen me because I had been a bad man, and I was going to pay for my sins by winning and never having an easy moment ever again."[55]

He watched election returns come in from his campaign headquarters at Columbus Circle. Breslin, it turned out, got more votes than Mailer, probably in part because he could play to the white working class better than his running mate. In the aftermath, Breslin addressed the press to apologize for having engaged in an activity that had closed the bars for the day (the required closure of bars on election days has since been rescinded).[56]

Meanwhile, the toughest law-and-order conservative in the Democratic primary, Mario Procaccino, won the nomination, capturing 255,529 votes. Former mayor Wagner was second with 224,464 votes, while Herman Badillo, a Puerto Rican and the only other progressive aside from Mailer, finished third with 217,165 votes.

Among the Republicans, Buckley's favorite candidate, a boring state senator named John Marchi, delivered the shock of the election by upsetting Mayor Lindsay. Buckley had called Marchi "one of the world's sweetest, most reasonable men, [and] by everyone's reckoning one of the two or three most conscientious public servants in Albany."[57] But even Buckley had a hard time getting excited about the possibility of a Marchi mayoralty. He was just a dull guy. Nevertheless, the electorate wanted a tough conservative, and they found Marchi more promising than four more years of Lindsay.

A political dance began. Lindsay, a mayor rejected by his own party, found a home in the Liberal Party of New York, which made him concede to many of their demands before allowing him to run under their banner. He agreed, becoming as liberal as they required.

In November, the two law-and-order candidates (Procaccino and Marchi) split 57 percent of the vote, which allowed Lindsay to slide through and hold onto his mayoralty even though he won just 42.4 percent of voters. Lindsay may have won the election, but he certainly hadn't won the city.

After the Democratic primary, James Wechsler, a prominent editorialist and a supporter of Herman Badillo's progressive candidacy, wrote, "On the morning after, one man who must have felt peculiarly foolish and frustrated was Norman Mailer. Surely nearly all of the 41,136 votes Mailer polled would have gone to Herman Badillo if he had pulled out; they would have been sufficient to carry the night for the Bronx insurgent."[58] If Badillo had gone up against Marchi, Lindsay would have lost the endorsement of the Liberal Party (which would have supported Badillo), and Badillo probably would have become mayor. Even Mailer himself said that if he had known how well Badillo would do in the primary, he "might have hesitated about running."[59]

Wechsler noted, "in a perverse way, John Lindsay is once again indebted to a member of the writing fraternity who allowed dreams of glory to befuddle his sense. In the 1965 mayoralty race Bill Buckley's candidacy—bitterly aimed at Lindsay—backfired when he drew more votes away from Democrat Abe Beame than from Lindsay. In the current circumstance Mailer's motives were quite different, but the final posture was equally grotesque; by remaining in the race, he prevented the Badillo miracle and opened the door to Procaccino."[60]

Two elections in a row, then, Buckley and Mailer's opposition to mainstream liberalism had helped ensure liberalism's electoral victory.

That is not to say liberalism won the day. In New York at least, people voted their fears, not their hopes. Both major party candidates were from the white working classes; both were law-and-order men; and many progressive New Yorkers couldn't support either one. As then-Congresswoman Shirley Chisholm said, "It was impossible for me to support Procaccino. His background, his statements, and his speeches gave black voters every reason to suspect that he was hostile to them. He seemed cut from the same cloth as the Republican nominee, a reactionary in the strict sense of the word." She, like many other progressives, backed Lindsay's campaign, but did so unenthusiastically, the lesser of three evils.[61]

At the end of the day, it looked as though Mailer had been right: the city was losing its sense of itself and was living in fear. Rather than opt for new solutions, it simply sought more regimented control. As Mailer put it, his campaign "had been a scheme with all the profound naiveté of assuming that people voted as an expression of their desire when he had yet to learn the electorate obtained satisfaction by venting their hate."[62] Even if the liberal mayor remained in office for four more years, it was clear the right and the left were attempting to force a realignment. It was unclear, however, how Mailer would fit into the new formation.

Buckley was curiously silent throughout the campaign. He commented on the mayoral election in early 1969 and near Election Day, but he took the early fall off, when the Mailer campaign was in full swing.

Buckley did write one column on Mailer in 1969, but he never published it. Late in that year, Buckley's writing syndicate sent him to Vietnam to do a series of columns "from the front." The first column came back so quickly they scrapped the essay Buckley had written in advance. Atop that first Vietnam piece, the syndicate's version to its subscribers reads: "Editor: Kill Norman Mailer Column."[63] The column has since vanished.

For his part, Buckley was pondering his place in the emerging new order, too. Publicly, he dismissed the idea of running for office ever again after his 1965 mayoral run, saying he would only do it if "voting was by invitation only."[64] But that's what would-be politicians always say. In truth, Buckley loved the experience of the campaign, telling his brother, "Nothing is quite the same again. . . . There's a certain exhilaration in making one's points well, in feeling the response of a crowd in reaction to one's own rhetorical arguments."[65] His run for mayor in 1965 had given him the bug.

After his loss in 1965, Buckley privately decided to challenge Robert F. Kennedy for his New York Senate seat in 1970. He assumed LBJ would be reelected in 1968 and that Kennedy would be operating on Johnson's left, gearing up for a White House bid in 1972. By challenging Kennedy in 1970, Buckley could stir the pot once again and do so with as much fanfare as possible: America's two great Irish-Catholic families, squaring off face to face. But then RFK was killed, and Buckley scrapped the plan. He didn't want to be a politician for the sake of governing. He wanted to give his ideas the broadest venue possible. He simply thought a Kennedy versus Buckley battle would be good for the country and for his movement. That all died with RFK.

Still, several Conservative Party strategists wanted him to run anyway. The man who had been chosen to replace Bobby Kennedy after his assassination in 1968 was a Republican named Charles Goodell, and Goodell had moved to the left as soon as he was sworn in. He had moved so far to the left, in fact, that he was bound to split the vote with whomever the Democrats nominated, opening the door for a true conservative. Buckley could win in 1970.

Knowing they'd need to sweeten the deal, Conservative Party leaders invited Buckley to lunch. They surprised him by bringing along Clifton White, the mastermind behind the Goldwater campaign, the guy who had sewn up the nomination in all the small states before Goldwater had even decided to run. White was the resident genius of conservative political numbers.

Over lunch, White explained how Buckley, as a senator from New York, could go on to make a legitimate challenge for the White House in 1972. Buckley could be president! Nixon had done nothing but move to the left since his election, White argued, and the American people didn't really like him anyway. They only elected him in 1968 because the Democrats were such a mess. If a true conservative, one who talked law and order and preached conservative principles, entered the race, that person could be assured of winning almost two hundred electoral votes. That wasn't enough to win—you needed 272—but it was a good start. And once the campaign began in earnest, who knew what might happen? Maybe the president would get caught trying to break into the headquarters of the Democratic National Committee, or something crazy like that.

Buckley had little interest in small-town politics at this point. He was too big a celebrity and didn't want to risk his successes for the sake of nuts-and-bolts governing. When he was asked in 1970 if he wanted to be a member of the House of Representatives, he laughed at the idea, saying: "Not unless I can have all the seats simultaneously."[66]

But being president was different. Buckley thought over the proposition. Yet after a few weeks, he decided against it. He just didn't want to risk his media empire to run what might be a quixotic campaign. Or worse still, to win the Senate seat in 1970, then lose the presidency in 1972 and be stuck in the Senate for four more years. "If somebody had said that I could be President," he later recalled, "I would have said yes, which is different from saying, 'I can give you a twenty percent chance of being President, if you desert your career and try to climb this particular ladder.' The answer is no, and I said no."[67]

Instead, he allowed himself to be wooed by Nixon. At one memorable meeting before the 1968 election, Nixon served South African brandy as a way of showing ideological sympathy. Then Nixon sung from the conservative songbook for three hours, eventually winning Buckley's support. When he was eventually nominated, Nixon asked Buckley to recommend a vice president. (Buckley named John Gardner, a progressive who had served as LBJ's secretary of health, education, and welfare. Nixon was exasperated, but he grinned and bore it.) And once he was elected, Nixon appointed Buckley to the United States Information Agency, the highest appointment a working journalist can have. The Agency could make no policy and was accountable to no one. Buckley was bored there, but he served at the pleasure of the president. Then, in 1973, Nixon appointed Buckley as a delegate to the United Nations. Buckley hated that work, too.

More intimately, Nixon started having occasional thirty-minute meetings with Buckley, with only Henry Kissinger or H. R. Haldeman in attendance. Buckley was moved, saying in a 1970 *Playboy* interview, "I have discovered a new sensual treat, which, appropriately, the readers of *Playboy* should be the first to know about. It is to have the President of the United States take notes while you are speaking to him, even though you run the risk that he is scribbling, 'Get this bore out of here.' "[68]

Nixon was playing him, though. As Kissinger recalled, "He liked him, but Buckley would make him uneasy, and he thought he was not really relevant to the decisions that he had to make."[69] But the play worked. *National Review* supported almost everything Nixon did. Most amazingly, Buckley even came to defend Nixon's Family Assistance Plan, probably the most radical economic redistribution plan ever pushed by an American president. Its offer of guaranteed income to the poorest Americans through cash handouts struck against every nerve in the libertarian body. But Buckley was a good soldier. He entertained a personal visit from Nixon's envoy, Daniel Patrick Moynihan (Buckley later sent Moynihan the recipe for the apple soup they had eaten for dinner), and then he massaged the plan in his columns: it was "daring and attractive," Buckley wrote; its appeal was "its directness. It accosts, for the first time, the sprawling mass that has grown up around a few humanitarian postulates, grown utterly out of hand, as witnessed in New York City."[70]

What had become of the great conservative? A generous interpretation is that Buckley was strategically integrating himself and his movement into the Republican Party, finally merging his vision of conservatism with the dictates of governing. He was ready to accept partial success in exchange for a place at the table. A less generous interpretation might be that he was sick of fighting for a cause that seemed no longer his to control.

13

Jokers

In very late 1969, Mailer wrote a short letter to his friend Allen Ginsberg. The letter was nothing special, a quick note about the progress of his latest book, which Mailer described as being "like a string one follows through the caves." In a postscript, though, which was almost as long as the letter itself, Mailer revealed something to his friend: "P.S." he wrote, "People keep asking me to do pieces on what I think the 70's will be like. Do you know I don't have the remotest idea. We were sure of what would happen in the 60's and we weren't far from wrong. The 70's are just a fearful blank to me. I hope it's age rather than presentaments [*sic*]."[1]

It was a candid admission, especially coming from Mailer, who throughout the 1950s had been predicting much of the rupture that came during the 60s, and more often than not had been right. In 1956 he had detected "the hints, the clues, the whispers of a new time coming," even saying: "There is a universal rebellion in the air," consisting of "the sexual revolution one senses everywhere . . . and the growing power of the Negro."[2] In 1959, he "had the feeling of an underground revolution on its way," a "moral and sexual revolution which is yet to come upon us."[3] That same year, he even remarkably predicted "the green plant marijuana . . . will become for the sixties what the saloon was for the twenties."[4] Most especially, though, he predicted the challenges coming to the Liberal Establishment and the loss of belief in the triptych of ideas that made up American postwar liberalism. As he had said of one of his films, "loss was everywhere."

But when it came to the 1970s, "a blank like the windowless walls of the computer city came over his vision," he wrote of himself. "It was not despair he felt, or fear—it was anesthesia. He had no intimations of what was to come. . . . He was adrift."[5] As he further explained, "the world . . . had changed in ways he did not recognize, had never anticipated, and could possibly not comprehend now. The change was mightier than he had counted on."[6] Mailer didn't have a clue what was coming next.

Buckley too had been a relatively reliable reader of the crystal ball. He had correctly sensed that the mid-1950s was the right time to braid together a new kind of conservatism, one shorn of its harshest edges, ideologically balanced between anti-government libertarianism and respect-for-The-Rules traditionalism. He had excommunicated the more egregious outliers, harsh libertarians like Ayn Rand, anti-Semites like the readers of *The American Mercury*, and Cold War conspiracy theorists like Robert Welch and his John Birch Society. Cleaning out the gunk had done wonders for the movement.

He even recognized the glue that was needed to keep the coalition from splintering, at first alternating between staunch Cold Warriorism and perpetually rebuking the Liberal Establishment, then picking up on the anxieties provoked by the civil rights movement. Buckley had even recognized that Goldwater had no chance to win in 1964 because there hadn't been enough groundwork laid.

But by the early 1970s, factions were forming within the right that he could no longer contain. In 1969, Buckley even had to break up fistfights during his annual jaunt to the Young Americans for Freedom convention. The libertarians and the traditionalists were in open war with each other, and when Buckley stood up to reconcile the two sides, he was shouted down. When he finally did get a hold of the microphone, his magic was gone. The traditionalists, who dressed like him, talked like him, and hated their libertarian peers for embracing the radicalism of the counterculture, saw that being a Buckleyite might be their ticket to later success in the Republican Party. Most of the time, they were right. But their traditionalism didn't seem heartfelt; it seemed opportunistic. The libertarians, meanwhile, kept arguing that tradition and The Rules needed to be swept aside to make way for a new order. When Buckley finally spoke, his words—that freedom only comes to those who respect tradition—were not taken seriously by anyone. An opposition movement began outside. More fights broke out the next day. One YAFer even stood in the middle of the convention and, in the name of libertarianism, burned his draft card. Buckley had lost his touch.

Meanwhile, the language of the Cold War, language on which Buckley had always fallen back to bring together the various conservative strands, had lost its strength. When he harped on the Cold War, his words sounded dated. In the wake of Vietnam, fewer and fewer Americans were able to accept the United States as purely good while other nations were purely bad. The revelations of 1968 and 1969 complicated the narrative. But Buckley didn't change course—he just began to sound old.

By the early 1970s, many Americans clearly had new moral imperatives, and they no longer mirrored Buckley's. When *Time* did a piece on the twenty-fifth anniversary of *National Review* in 1980, it named six other conservative publications "enjoying a new legitimacy." Buckley had created the space for these other conservative journals of opinion, but as the crowd swelled, he lost his centrality.

What was happening was that the rebellion against postwar American liberalism that Mailer and Buckley had helped usher in during the 1950s and early 1960s was now in the process of redefining the set of premises by which Americans lived. New understandings of the story of the nation, of the capabilities for human rationality, of The Rules, were all taking hold. The foundations of culture were changing. And yet, neither man was fully equipped to handle all the changes; they were perhaps too old, or had peaked too soon, or had become inflexible, or had perfectly embodied a time and place they could now never escape. Nothing brought this home to them more than a series of events from 1969 to 1972 that failed to animate their imaginations and, worse, painted them into calcified positions, remnants of yesteryear, forever men of the 1950s and 1960s.

For Buckley, the first real signs of his declining force occurred in 1970, and came from within his own family. Dan Mahoney and Kieran O'Doherty looked for alternatives after they had failed to convince Buckley to run for Senate in 1970, and found the next best thing in James Buckley, Bill's older brother.

Jim was widely thought of as a sweet guy, not as articulate as Bill, although his politics were much the same. Jim had spent his post-Yale years in the family's oil business. He was not a firebrand. His passion was bird-watching. But like Bill, he felt he should pay his dues to the cause he supported. He had run for Senate in 1968 and finished third, winning a respectable 1,139,402 votes. In 1970, after much persuasion, he agreed to run again.

Jim's 1970 run was aided considerably by the liabilities of the sitting senator, Charles Goodell, who was deemed more left-wing than any of his fellow Republicans and most Democrats, too. Goodell was so left-wing, in fact, that even Nixon quietly decided to help Jim Buckley defeat the sitting Republican. In one White House meeting, Nixon told Bill, "Tell [Jim] when he is being heckled at one of his speeches to go right up to spitting distance of the protester. The television cameras will catch that face-to-face encounter and that means votes for the law and order candidate."

Haldeman, Nixon's chief of staff, also gave advice: "Bill, get a couple of guys from Young Americans for Freedom. Tell them to dress up like Woodstock protesters and have them throw an egg or some ketchup at your brother. That will make it into the evening television news."

As Haldeman spoke, the president leaned over to Buckley, "a Madame Tussaud smile on his face," recalled Buckley, and said: "I didn't hear that, Bill."[7]

With all these factors working for him, Jim gained momentum, crested at the right moment, and won with 38.7 percent of the vote—Goodell and Democrat Richard Ottinger split the left-wing vote.

Many saw Jim's election as a harbinger of a new political realignment—the incorporation into the Republican Party of a slightly tamed Buckleyite conservatism—although the Buckley in question was Jim, not Bill. As Jim gave his victory speech, he said, with what came across as uncharacteristic immodesty, "I am the voice of the new politics." He was of course making a point about the rise of conservatism in America, finally capable of challenging, and beating, the Liberal Establishment. But the statement came across as undignified.

Standing offstage, Bill winced. He knew the press would pick up the line, and he wasn't wrong. A few days later, he sent his senator-elect brother a framed copy of the *New York Post*, which ran a banner headline reading: "Buckley: 'I Am The New Politics.'"

But for Bill there was something else in it, too. He quietly seethed that other voices, even (perhaps especially) his brother's, were now speaking for the movement he, by his own reckoning, had "midwifed" into existence. While he didn't want to be a politician, he distinctly felt this was *his* Senate seat, that *he* had earned it, not Jim.

When Bill heard Jim utter the "new politics" line, he turned to his sister and said, with a touch more bite than he would have liked, *"La nouvelle politique, c'est goddam well moi!"* ["The new politics is goddam well me!"][8]

Buckley's sister laughed, unsure how playful the comment was meant to be.

As usual, Buckley sought to write his way to clarity. Immediately after the election, he began to imagine a book that would articulate his role in the conservative movement, and justify his actions—to himself, if to no one else. What emerged a year later (as always, the book was written in February and March in Switzerland) was *Cruising Speed: A Documentary*. The thing was, it wasn't a political book. Not really. Instead, Buckley told the world with semi-candid detail about a week in the life of William F. Buckley, Jr. In the diary, Buckley plays with his dog, who jumps in the limousine to go wherever Buckley has to go. Buckley meets dignitaries, concert pianists, journalists, students, historians. He wines and dines them all. The catalog of events (as *Firing Line* host or syndicated columnist or *National Review* editor or public speaker) allowed Buckley to demonstrate how busy he was, how in demand he was, how important he was. It's good to be Bill Buckley, he was saying; it's a hectic life, but fun. He laughed at some of the silly things he did, showed deep emotion at the misfortune of others, and only incidentally talked politics.

It wasn't until the final two stories that Buckley revealed his hand. One of the tropes he used throughout the book was to describe his method of responding to letters, which he usually dictated into a tape recorder from the back of his limousine as he raced from place to place. The technique had the benefit of allowing readers to see how popular he was (all those letters!) and how generous he was (he responds to nearly all of them), and how brilliant he was (reading between the lines of a correspondent's argument, pointing out the weaknesses in the line of thought, etc.). A lot of letters impressed him, especially the ones from the younger generation (see, he's hip!).

In the book, the final letter to which Buckley responds was from a college student named "Herbert." Herbert professes to admire Buckley's skill, but critiques him for trying to drape his conservative philosophy onto a pluralistic nation. Didn't Buckley recognize that the traditions he was so eager to uphold came from a privileged minority of wealthy white folks, that this particular group no longer deserved to impose its traditions on others, and that in fact the federal government was necessary to ensure they couldn't use their wealth and power to do so?

Buckley scoffs at the important challenge too blithely, referring to it as "the enduring effort to harness America to the epistemological skepticism of Mill." But he pauses to consider Herbert's plea for him to be more flexible. "You are a symbol," Herbert had said, "and, so the legend goes, symbols never change. Conservatism in America, in my opinion, owes everything to your efforts alone." But if Buckley wanted to retain his place atop the American conservative hierarchy, Herbert suggested, he'd have to become something more than a static symbol. He'd have to change.[9]

Buckley had never thought of himself in this way before. He knew people had started imitating him in ways less favorable than those YAFers from just a few years earlier. Pen in mouth, clipboard in lap, vocabulary expansive, voice drawn and elaborate: people took turns doing their best impersonations. When Buckley appeared on the comedic variety show *Laugh-In* in 1970, Lily Tomlin spoofed him, declaring herself the real "William Fuhbuckleyyyy." Buckley took it well. When asked if the reason he sat down during *Firing Line* was because he couldn't think on his feet, Buckley waited a moment, then said, "It is hard . . . to stand up . . . under the weight . . . of all that I know." When asked if his two favorite comedians were Flip Wilson and Democratic Senator and noted Vietnam dove William Fulbright, Buckley replied: "I don't think Flip Wilson is so funny." When asked, "Did you see the film *Myra Breckenridge* and why not?" Buckley answered: "Because it folded before the New York public transportation system could get me there."

Being a "celebrity playing the role of William F. Buckley," as Hugh Kenner had put it, was one thing. But being a symbol of something seemed altogether different. It seemed so unbendable. Was he now unable to be an effective voice?

"One wishes for the powers of John Henry Newman," Buckley writes back to Herbert, referring to the great Catholic Cardinal and teacher of students. "But assuming that one possessed them, are the certitudes worthy? The certitudes of a middle-aged mid-twentieth century American conservative?"[10]

He seemed to pause. He didn't have an answer. He had become a symbol . . . but of what? Of a bygone era?

If the letter from Herbert provoked questions about Buckley's role in the 1970s, the book's final story attempted to answer them. In the book's last pages, Buckley is taken aback when his friend John Kenneth Galbraith says point-blank: "Give it up. The whole thing. *National Review*, journalism, television, radio, lecturing. Come to the academy, and write *books*. It is only *books* that count. I did it. I left *Fortune*, and went to Harvard. The break must be absolute. You will need the *trauma*. Then—only then," said Galbraith, "you will discover the means to give a theoretical depth to your ideological positions." Otherwise, you will soon be forgotten, forever a salesman for a product approaching its expiration date.[11]

Buckley pushed back. Being a professor was not his thing; writing thoughtful books was not his talent; that wasn't where his strengths lay. "[T]he theoretical depth is already there," he said, referring to the work of other thinkers, "and if I have not myself dug deeper the foundations of American conservatism, at least I have advertised their profundity."

He just couldn't stop being a salesman. There was too much that was appealing in that life. Plus, doing something else was hard. "What," he pondered, thinking about his life, "does it take to *satisfy*, to satisfy *truly*, *wholly*?" His answer: "A sense of social usefulness." Right then and there he vowed to maintain his role as salesman, to be satisfied with it, "imperfectly which is not to say insufficiently," at, of course, "cruising speed," which became the book's title.[12]

It was a startling admission—a middle-aged man too tired to change, one who felt he had done enough. He would remain the same because that was where he was comfortable. *Cruising Speed* was a perfect example of the fact that people were more interested in Buckley the celebrity than in Buckley the conservative. In Buckley's mind, that was how he could best sell the conservative movement. The book was serialized in *The New Yorker* before it was released in hardcover. It became a bestseller.

What Buckley only partially realized was that the sands were rapidly shifting beneath him. The new set of premises coming into existence had changed the important features of American conservatism. While Buckley was pondering his role as symbol and celebrity, others on the right were refashioning the movement—and they were doing so without the help of Bill Buckley. They even had the nerve to call themselves "the New Right."

A political strategist named Kevin Phillips most articulately described (and advocated on behalf of) the New Right. He was fifteen years younger than Buckley and saw the potential to tap more forthrightly into the stewing anger of white working classes, forsaking Buckley's aristocratic excesses. Phillips put it this way in 1975: "[T]oday's New Right tends to be overtly populist where the Old Right is generally elitist. Many in the older Buckley-oriented 'Conservative Movement' regard ideological conservatism as a surviving high-church religion unhappily now practiced only by the elite handful who have kept uncontaminated by mass culture and politics. . . . Today's 'New Right,'" Phillips continued, ". . . is designedly anti-elitist—preferring mobilization of Levittown, Georgia, and South Boston to false pretenses of political gentility."[13] The New Right was to be a populist movement. It wouldn't have the ideological problems Buckley had had when he weighed the conundrum of elite versus mass rule in his one and only effort to write a Big Book.

Not only was there a new style, there was also new substance. As opposed to the Cold War and free-market economics, the New Right, Phillips said, "puts its principal emphasis on domestic social issues—on public anger over busing, welfare spending, environmental extremism, soft criminology, media bias and power, warped education, twisted textbooks, racial quotas, various guidelines and an ever-expanding bureaucracy."[14] Phillips expanded on this new kind of angry conservatism in numerous books and columns throughout the 1970s, coming off as the innovative coach eager to help Republicans move beyond Buckley's brand of elite conservatism in order to get elected by the populace.

Phillips was not alone in sensing the transition. George Will, Rowland Evans, and Robert Novak all emerged in the early 1970s as prominent conservative columnists. Compared to Buckley, they seemed livelier, and to have a better grasp on the direction of the country. Will was perhaps as erudite as Buckley, if less colorful, but he appeared to be more in tune with the goings-on in Washington. Evans and Novak were not as literary as Buckley, but they were closer to the action and related better to readers. They were also unabashed supporters of the New Right, and thus better able to capture the spirit of rebellion that Buckley himself had once personified. By the mid-1970s, as Buckley approached fifty, if a newspaper wanted to have just one conservative columnist, they were increasingly choosing Will, Evans, or Novak. In 1975, when the hugely popular *Newsweek* sought a conservative voice, it skipped Buckley in favor of George Will.

Faced with this competition, all of Buckley's outlets began to suffer. *National Review* went into a decline, not so much in readership as in its ability to shape debate. Most of the old editors were retiring or dying and being replaced by younger ones who had grown up with *National Review* but didn't understand its philosophical foundations. They liked Buckley's style, not necessarily the more considered aspects of his substance, and thus the magazine became predictable and mean-spirited. Even *Firing Line* grew dull in the 1970s. It was still one of a handful of thoughtful shows on television, but guests became repetitive, debates were predictable, and the whole endeavor lacked fire. As Pat Buchanan said, "Now it is an exploration in issues rather than an engagement." Others simply called it a "snooze."[15]

Many thought Buckley was asleep at the tiller, and it would be hard to say they were wrong. The times had changed, but his ideas and temperament hadn't. The energy, the vibrancy, seemed gone.

At almost the exact same time, Mailer began to lose his way, too. As with Buckley, it was a host of internal opponents who demonstrated just how out of touch he'd become. For Mailer, though, it wasn't a group of young men showing him the door; it was women.

Without really understanding why, Mailer had become a prime target of the women's liberation movement in the spring and summer of 1970. He discovered this when an editor from *Time* asked if he could send a reporter to interview Mailer for a cover story on the subject of women's liberation. Mailer was surprised to get the call. Why him?

"Well, you may as well face it," the editor said. "They seem to think you're their major ideological opposition."[16] Mailer was shocked. The editor went on to explain the popularity of Kate Millett, a young graduate student whose book of literary criticism, *Sexual Politics*, had become one of the bibles of the women's liberation movement. The book was brash and combative, trampling over the accepted norms within the postwar literary canon. But its argument was simple: all those writers you were taught to love and respect? They all hated women.

Millett didn't hesitate to name names. She targeted three at length: D. H. Lawrence, whose sex scenes were groundbreaking if subtle by the standards of the 1970s; Henry Miller, whose more vivid sex scenes had led his books to be banned; and Norman Mailer, whose writings mostly came after the censorship battles had been fought, but who, one could make the case, most epitomized the inherent gender discriminations within postwar American life.

Millett was no prude, and it wasn't the graphic sex scenes that bothered her. In fact, she seemed to glory in them, comfortably quoting bad words and lurid details. What bothered Millett was the power relations that the sex scenes exemplified, what she called "sexual politics." Her central argument was that, despite the brilliance of these men (and she respected Mailer's writings on politics and foreign policy), they had a view of women that consigned them to being secondary citizens, useful only for domestic chores and sexual conquest.

Millett had special ire for Mailer. Her attack on him spanned more than twenty-five pages, and she recited entire passages from *An American Dream.* Her favorite scene to lambast, of course, was the sex scene between Mailer's doppelgänger Rojack and the German maid Rita, whom Rojack finds masturbating immediately after he has murdered his wife. Rojack, Millett pointed out, "takes" the maid, doesn't say a word the entire time they engage, and exerts his dominance through physical power and then buggering her into submission. In sum, the maid has no control. The worst part, as Millett saw it, was that the maid purported to love it all. "Mailer's *An American Dream,*" Millet wrote, "is an exercise in how to kill your wife and be happy ever after. The reader is given to understand that by murdering one woman and buggering another, Rojack became a 'man.'"

Millett understood what Mailer was trying to do in his critique of American culture. But she sensed Mailer was too embedded in his own era's assumptions to recognize the ramifications of some of his positions. His anti-technology stance, for instance, placed an onus on women who, more often than not, bore the brunt of having a baby in the absence of birth control. "I think Mailer's journalism is super," she said later. "I loved *Armies of the Night* and there's a good deal in *Why Are We in Vietnam?* that is superb. He has great insight into the whole American psyche." Nevertheless, she said, "There's still an allegiance [to masculine domination]. It's as if one wrote about white supremacists and criticized them, yet at the same time hankered after their view."[17]

What's more, Mailer had risen to the top ranks of outlaw estab-

lishmentarians, a rebel in some respects but also still wedded to
some of the stale aspects of a fading culture. Millett didn't want his
sensibilities about women passed on. "I felt," she said, "he was the
leading spokesman of that particular point of view for his generation and his voice was the most prevalent. You got it, for example,
through his influence upon *The Village Voice* and the young men
who wrote for that paper. He had many, many imitators. In the sixties one heard Mailer's point of view a great deal. It was the reign-
ing attitude, the current, fashionable literary male chauvinism,
and Mailer was its famous progenitor. At that point, there wasn't
any counter voice because the women's movement was just emerging. So Mailer's view had enormous power and was extremely
oppressive to women with literary interests or ambitions."[18]

Mailer was stunned by the onslaught. *He* hated women? Sure,
his track record wasn't exactly stellar on the marital front, and he
had stabbed one of his wives, and he led a meandering love life
with mistresses and girlfriends and one-night stands. But hating
women? That didn't sound right to Mailer.

After he hung up with the editor from *Time*, past episodes began
to come back to him. When Gloria Steinem first asked Mailer to
run for mayor in 1969, he said no, twice. "Well," she had responded,
"at least I won't have to explain you to my friends at Women's Lib."
Mailer asked her what they could possibly have against him. She
laughed: "Try reading your books someday."

Mailer was surprised. He very well may have been quoted as
saying, "Women at their worst are low, sloppy beasts." But she
should know that he would have gone on to say, had he not been
interrupted, "that women at their best are goddesses."

"That," replied Steinem, "is exactly what's wrong with your attitude." There was nothing between the pedestal and the prostitute.
He didn't see women as normal human beings.[19]

Perhaps New York Congresswoman Bella Abzug put it best when
she said she agreed with Mailer on many things, but said to the
then-candidate, "We think your views on women are full of shit."[20]

While he was trying to understand the attack, he appeared on a television show hosted by Orson Welles in the summer of 1970. When the subject of women came up, Mailer's words became immediate proof that Millett was right: "Women should be kept in cages," he said, remarkably and inexplicably. When Welles pressed Mailer, he responded cryptically: "Orson, we respect lions in the zoo but we want them kept in cages, don't we?"[21]

It was an incredible line for someone already under attack for hating women. A small firestorm erupted, and when *Time* came out that fall, it was, to Mailer's shock, Millett's face on the cover, not his.

Like Buckley, Mailer sought to write his way to clarity. What dawned on him as he wrote about women's liberation, though, was that there were limitations to the kinds of freedom he could support. As he thought it through, Mailer's great fear was not that women would displace men atop the economic or cultural hierarchy. That kind of liberation was fine. Instead, he feared that women would eventually work to make men biologically meaningless and thus take the dirty, earthy aspects of humanity away. To him, Millett appeared "as Robespierre was beyond Rousseau," because she sought to end "the tyranny of the vagina" for women, which was, she argued, "nothing but a flunky to the men."[22] For Mailer, this was one liberation too much. It made no sense to be liberated from nature. Men were men and women were women, and there were certain aspects of that fact that couldn't be denied. The idea of pure biological equality "gave him a species of aesthetic nausea," he wrote.[23] He would, he said, "agree with everything they asked but to quit the womb."[24]

These were not the words of someone staunchly against women's liberation. But he could only go so far. "Women's Liberation," he wrote, "if it accomplished nothing else, had pushed him back into an obsession he wished to quit—which was whether the revolution was the most beautiful or diabolical idea of man—a hateful question: because thoughts about the revolution were never too far from thoughts about the size of his waist and the potential Humphreys of his ass."[25] The man who in 1959 promised to settle for nothing less than a revolution of the soul was now beginning to rethink his stance.

While Mailer's position on women's liberation was hardly trite or ill conceived, Mailer was shocked when he realized that hardly anyone cared. As was typical of nearly all his latest work, Mailer's article on women's liberation—which once again took up every page in *Harper's*—was turned into a book, which he called *The Prisoner of Sex*. It was unclear how many people bothered to read it, but what was clear was that those who did saw in Mailer not what he wrote but what they expected to see: a big, galumphing white man no longer current with the times, more interested in the Humphreys of his ass than revolutions of the soul. They ignored his arguments and portrayed him as little more than an image of himself. He too had become a symbol.

Mailer saw what was happening and didn't fight it. Instead, he milked it. In early 1971, he invited a handful of prominent feminists to a Theater of Ideas forum at the Town Hall Theater at New York University, and he promoted the whole thing. He hoped to sell a few copies of his book.

Hundreds of students, activists, and women's liberationists gathered into a crowded auditorium to hear Mailer emcee a panel on women's liberation that included literary critic Diana Trilling; radical lesbian poet Jill Johnston; president of the New York chapter of the National Organization for Women (NOW) Jacqueline Ceballos; and, the star of the evening, Australian feminist Germaine Greer, whose new book, *The Female Eunuch*, had catapulted her to the top of the women's liberation movement. (Millett declined to appear.) Mailer's friend D. A. Pennebaker, who filmed *Maidstone*, recorded the whole event.[26]

Mailer showed up straight out of central casting, in a full dark three-piece suit, an increasingly rotund belly, and a flirty, old-school sensibility about women. He referred to the women on stage as "ladies." He was booed more than once, and he loved it.

When Ceballos gave her remarks, she said she was grateful to have the opportunity to finally address the Establishment, by which she meant Mailer. The audience laughed at what they knew to be true. Ceballos wondered out loud if she should correct herself— was Mailer now the Establishment? He had been so radical on so many fronts for so long. But then she thought better of it, saying Mailer is "sort of the liberal side of the Establishment, but still he represents the Establishment."[27]

And it was true. By 1971, so much of what Mailer had sought— overhauling The Rules, critiquing corporate capitalism, questioning the expansive use of technology, taking seriously the irrational side of humankind—had come to pass. Mailer had been one of the best chroniclers of the transformation. What's more, the Establishment had rewarded him for doing it, bestowing upon him some of their most prestigious prizes and awards. Now, as the revolutions he had helped spawn continued without him, he had become part of the Establishment trying to preserve at least a small portion of the old order. It was a stunning recognition for Ceballos, Mailer, and the audience. In her comments at the Town Hall debate, she skipped over *Prisoner of Sex*, and lambasted Mailer for representing an Establishment that thinks a woman "gets an orgasm when she gets the shiny floor!"

Trilling, Mailer's old friend, was the most balanced of the panelists, rejecting Mailer's dependence on biology but also rejecting the feminists' rejection of *his* rejection. "I would gladly take even Mailer's poeticized biology in preference to the no biology at all of my spirited sisters," she said. "I think there is not only more life in it, but better life. *But*, and this is a big but, I am also not inclined to join in any attack upon even the extreme female liberationist, much as I might reject their views, if this attack has its source in the wish to protect the sexual culture in which we now live. Mailer accepts our sexual culture pretty much as given or at least that part of it which has to do with the relative status of the sexes. I do not."

Then Greer, a tall, stunning woman, walked up to the podium. She accentuated her appearance with a long fox stole and a flirtatious vibe, suggestively taunting Mailer for not being smart enough to see through the Western world's domination of women, especially in its art. "[T]he art on which we nourish ourselves is sucking our vitality and breaking our hearts," Greer said, thinking purely of Norman Mailer's fiction.

When Mailer opened the panel to questions, he tried to keep the discussion from becoming overly theatrical. "If you wish me to act a clown," he said, "I will take out my modest little Jewish dick and put it on the table. You can all spit at it and laugh at it, and then I'll walk away and you'll find it was just a dildo I left there. I hadn't shown you the real one. But if we're going to have a decent discussion . . . let's have it on the highest level we can."

Betty Friedan asked the first question, about why Mailer essentialized women based on their biology. He hadn't essentialized women, other than to point out the biological traits that made them women, but of course that wasn't the role Mailer was playing in the audience's imagination. He was Mailer the Powerful.

Susan Sontag asked why Mailer referred to Diana Trilling as "our foremost lady literary critic" in his introductory remarks. Didn't he understand that this was patronizing? "It seems like gallantry to you," Sontag said, "but it doesn't feel right to us."

It was a fair question, but it missed the fact that Mailer had intended it as a joke. Sontag didn't get it. "I will never use the word 'lady' again in public," Mailer finally acquiesced.

Then Cynthia Ozick stood up to ask the best question of the night. The novelist was tiny, but she wore huge glasses. She slowly eked out her question: "This question," she said, "I have been fantasizing for many, many years, since *Advertisements for Myself,* only I always thought it would take place at the Y [laughs]. Now, . . . This is my moment to live out a fantasy. Mr. Mailer, in *Advertisements for*

Myself, you said, 'A good novelist can do without everything but the remnant of his balls.' For years and years I have been wondering, Mr. Mailer, when you dip your balls in ink, what color ink is it?"

Everyone laughed. After some stammering, Mailer finally smiled and said: "[I]f I don't find an answer in a hurry, I think we're gonna have to agree the color is yellow. I will, I will, I will cede the round to you. I don't pretend that I've never written an idiotic or stupid sentence in my life and that's one of them."

While the audience didn't dwell on his response, it was in fact a demonstration that Mailer understood the cause of women's liberation better than they were willing to let on. When he had, more than a decade before, urged his fellow writers to write with more courage, he had used "balls" as a metaphor. Now he understood the metaphor's limitations.

Elizabeth Hardwick and Anatole Broyard asked other questions Broyard's was simple enough but raised hackles in the crowd as he slowly let it out: "I really don't know what women are asking for. Now . . . suppose I wanted to give it to them." Greer cut him off and said to Broyard: "Listen. You may as well relax, because whatever it is they're asking for, honey, it's not for you."

Only Johnston veered toward the theatrical. She read an off-color poem that was acceptable on its merits, then she had two women jump onstage to start making out with her. The trio fell to the floor, the audience hooting and laughing, but Mailer got mad. "You can get as much prick and cunt as you want around the corner on Forty-second Street for two dollars and fifty cents. We don't need it here," he said. He wanted to talk about women's liberation. Several audience members booed Mailer, but the theatrics underscored the showy aspect of the entire evening. "You had all those powerful egos at work, elucidating absolutely nothing, and everybody had his or her own style," said the cartoonist Jules Feiffer, who was also there. "That evening was show business, just as most of those evenings were. But that doesn't mean they weren't worthwhile. . . . You're getting a lot of intelligent people saying interesting, amusing, and even sometimes perceptive things, complex people working off each other, playing off each other, even though a lot of what they're saying is pure bullshit based on the moment."[28]

Later, Diana Trilling had an equally perceptive take. "[T]hough its calendar date was 1971," she said, "the sixties had come to a close with that evening." By which, she meant "the fierce improvisation of the evening and its particular kind of sexual license." The old order had come and gone, and the new order, with the decline of The Rules and the emphasis of individualistic role-playing, had come into vogue.[29]

In an essay that appeared a few months later in *Esquire* entitled "My Mailer Problem," Greer tried to figure out what had happened to Mailer, how this thinker of radical thoughts had so completely moved beyond the realm of radicalism. How could he no longer *get it?* How could he succumb to the world of image?

She concluded that Mailer was simply too old, his art and ideas one generation removed from the present. His war metaphors, she said, were stoked by phallic imagery that came out of World War II, and in the era of Vietnam they were no longer appropriate. As with those war metaphors, she said, "For Mailer, Women's Liberation had become simply another battle of the books in a war in which he had been campaigning all his life."[30] For women, though, this was no game. It was "a fight for life, no holds barred," and "As long as Mailer sees his spirit as a triumvirate of phallus, ego, and talent, he cannot discern the fantasy nature of his conquests," he could not understand what it was they wanted to be liberated from; he was unable to see that it was him.[31]

"Concepts of aristocracy are breaking down all over," Greer concluded, "and Mailer's chagrin swells when he considers that he was maybe just about to make it" when the times changed on him. Now he couldn't even celebrate his intellectual offspring because of their differences. Instead, he rejected the new radicals as an "ill-mannered, drug-leached, informer-infested, indiscriminate ripping up of all the roots, yes, spoiled young middle-class heroes with fleas in their beard and ruses doubtless in the groin."[32] Unlike Mailer and his generation, the younger radicals "don't care whether Eldridge Cleaver writes better than Mailer or not, they just want to know what both are into, whether they will serve a purpose. Suddenly, wryly, but foreseeably, Mailer abandons the Jewish troublemakers, [Abbie] Hoffman, [Jerry] Rubin and friends (and me) and takes up with" the Establishment.[33]

The cover of *Esquire* that week featured a gigantic image of a greying Mailer, wearing a gorilla suit and carrying in his hands a helpless Germaine Greer, who uses both her hands to cover her vagina. Mailer was the unevolved King Kong taking powerful but unartful swipes at the people he thought he loved but was in fact crushing.

After the Town Hall debate, Mailer rented a house in Vermont to relax. He did a little writing, but not much. Instead he kept to himself, quietly out of the limelight. He wrote to a friend in September, saying, "My summer passed quietly. I had all seven children with me on a farm in Vermont, about 200 miles north of New York. . . . It was a summer in which I did, for once, almost no writing and just lay fallow like an old field. Now I feel the stirrings of literary work. It would be nice if the time has come to begin a long book."[34]

He wasn't quite ready, though. He would write several quick books for money over the next few years—on fights, on celebrities— but not a major work for almost a decade. It would take him that long to recalibrate.

In 1971, a toy company called Politicards produced a deck of cards featuring cartoonish images of the era's central political figures. Nixon was the king of spades, smiling, wearing a crown, a staff, a red robe, and nothing else. His queen was his wife, Pat, as angular and harsh as her reputation. The jack was Spiro Agnew, the vice president.

Among the politicians and personalities humorously imagined in the deck, there were two jokers: William F. Buckley, Jr., and Norman Mailer. Buckley resembled the perfect courtier, with a high, white medieval collar and a silly jester's hat, as he wistfully looked off to the right, his face's famous angles on full display. Mailer too wore the jester's costume, but his image was straight-on and full-bodied, legs open, arms crossed, looking imperious and challenging, greying curls popping from the silly hat.[35]

The cards were a spoof, and it's likely both Buckley and Mailer laughed if they saw them. But they were also a further piece of evidence of what they had become in the public mind by the 1970s. They were calcified images stuck in the just-recent past. The two men had crafted these images so well, in fact, that they proved almost unshakable.

For both Buckley and Mailer, there would be more books, but they would be different than those that came before, and neither could claim to be writing about the entirety of the nation. Those days, for both men, and perhaps for the nation at large, were gone. A new order prevented such wistful imaginings.

14

Moving On

I n 1976, the producers of the sprightly morning show *Good Morning America* called Buckley to ask if he wanted to debate Norman Mailer about the upcoming Carter versus Ford election. Buckley raised a hopeful eyebrow. Could people be ready to listen again? Would the energy from the 1962 debate, just fourteen years past but seemingly a million years gone, return? Was America eager to engage the ideas of Buckley and Mailer, aging icons of the right and left, once again? He asked the producer how long they would have on air.

"Six minutes."

"No," said Buckley, his smile fading fast.

"What!"

"No."

"Why?"

"Because in six minutes you can't count on getting anything said," replied a deflated Buckley. After a quick conference of executives on the other end of the line, *Good Morning America* agreed to give Buckley and Mailer eleven minutes. Would that work? Buckley said yes, but he wasn't exactly basking in the minor victory.

On November 2, 1976, the two men met at the studio, did the program, argued a bit, and affected hardly anyone's vote that either man could recall. Now comfortably over fifty, they looked like aging lions. The papers didn't cover it, neither man spoke much of it afterward, and the "debate" was forgotten about almost as soon as the cameras stopped rolling.[1]

Despite the lack of energy, they both recognized that appearing together on *Good Morning America* was the first time they'd argued in a while. Indeed, just a few months earlier, Buckley had written Mailer to ask for a blurb for the back of his new book, and he began his letter saying, "It's been ages since we have screamed at each other."[2] They'd socialized a bit and seen one another at fashion shows and the like. "As early as 1973, '74," recalled Dotson Rader, one of Mailer's old writer friends, "one had begun to see Norman in places one wouldn't expect to see him—say . . . at a fashion-show opening or at the Buckleys', in a wide variety of circles where he was by nature an outsider."

But of course he was no longer an outsider in such company. When Rader threw Mailer a birthday party in the mid-1970s, Mailer gave him a list of one hundred and fifty people to invite. Rader didn't recognize half the names. They were "socialite types," Radar realized, "like Peter Glenville and Jan Cushing," both wealthy Upper East Siders.

One person who didn't come to Mailer's party despite an invitation was Truman Capote, who saw that snowstorms were predicted and didn't want to get stuck in a house with Mailer. "Oh-h-h, Dotson," said Capote, according to an account by Radar, "there's going to be a blithard; we're going to be thnowed in at the houth and I know what's going to happen. I'll be trapped in the little bedroom upstairs, and in the middle of the night Norman's going to come in my room and rape me. I just can't chance it. Give my regret."[3]

Mailer's reputation hadn't stopped preceding him.

Buckley too had become less involved in the political fray. The book Buckley asked Mailer to blurb was, as Buckley put it, "a non-ideological book" called *Airborne*, a tale of Buckley's thirty-day voyage across the Atlantic Ocean from Miami to Marbella, a journey he undertook with his son and a handful of crew in his sixty-foot schooner, *Cyrano*. It was a reflective diary, somewhat like *Cruising Speed* on the high seas. But unlike *Cruising Speed*, which had used Buckley's anecdotes to reflect on his place within the conservative movement, *Airborne* had nothing to say about politics at all. The anecdotes were the book. Instead of selling ideas, he was selling his celebrity. "Would you have a look?" Buckley asked Mailer.

Mailer was too busy writing his own non-ideological book. He scribbled back, "The following quote is yours without reading any more than your letter. 'I do not know a writer in the CIA whose work I enjoy more.' If this can't carry the day, let me know, and I'll lift my tired eyes to *Airborne*. Cheers, Norman."[4]

Buckley was unimpressed.

"I quite understand," Buckley wrote back tersely. "But would you please return the galleys as they are scarce. I enclose a suitable envelope."[5]

Mailer wasn't going to let Buckley be impetuous. "Dear Bill," he wrote. "You really can't have it both ways. Cheers, Norman."[6] Mailer returned the book unread.

After that back and forth, the next time they saw each other was on *Good Morning America*. After the taping, they decided to catch up over breakfast at Buckley's New York City apartment.[7] As they forked their food, it must have been clear to both of them what had happened over the course of the fourteen years since their first debate, that each tenet of the postwar liberal triptych had taken severe hits, some of which they were happy about, some of which they weren't, but which, taken all together, had altered the central set assumptions of most Americans.

The weakest of the three tenets had always been the perceived requirement to obey The Rules, and so when challenges came, it

presented a lackluster defense and crumbled easily. By the early
1970s, scarcely anyone was surprised to see not just miniskirts but
pants on a woman, or bearded men not just without neckties but
even without collars on their shirts. Casual attire was carrying the
day in a society in which tradition was not to be respected but questioned. At the same time, it had become increasingly common and
hardly even provocative to hear coarse language in public or bad
words in a movie. Pornography was legal to view and even participate in if you were older than eighteen. In 1969, the U.S. Supreme
Court had declared that the First and Fourteenth Amendments
protected the possession of obscene images, and in 1970, a presidentially appointed Committee on Obscenity and Pornography
shockingly found "insufficient evidence that exposure to explicit
sexual materials played a significant role in the causation of delin-
quent or criminal behavior." In 1973, the U.S. Supreme Court loosened its definition of "obscene material" even more. The courts
were following the culture.

There were dramatic changes in sexual behavior and family life,
too, including the acceptance of more premarital sex, more cohab-
itation without marriage, more fatherless children, and more
divorce. Long hair became acceptable for men; women and girls
were encouraged to wear their hair more naturally. Contraceptives
were legal and widespread by the end of the decade.

In short, The Rules had proven themselves unworthy and—
worse—masking hidden hierarchies. Now they were being
flaunted, and no one could explain why they shouldn't be. When
parents tried to explain to the youth why they should respect The
Rules, they ended up sounding like Archie Bunker.

In a way, the entire culture seemed to have picked up on Mailer's insights from the previous decade. His rejection of The Rules
had long been one of his central complaints. Buckley had said of
Mailer in 1965, "As a citizen, he is wild, defying not only those
starched conventions that are there primarily to stick out your
tongue at, but the other conventions, the real McCoys: those that

are there to increase the small chance we have, whether as children or as adults, for a little domestic tranquility." But in just a few short years Mailer had moved to the conservative side of the culture; he had become one of the defenders of at least some of The Rules. As Mailer understood things, we should be bound by some rules in order to create a middle ground for society. But when everyone did his or her own thing, there was little to keep society together.

The decline of the rules-based society helped initiate another kind of society, one that both Buckley and Mailer recognized as centered on rights. People from all walks of life were borrowing the language of the civil rights movement and proclaiming rights for themselves. Americans had a right to wear their hair however they wanted; or dress in whatever fashion they wished; or protest in the streets, whether against the war in Vietnam or against income taxes. They were proclaiming their independence from the past, from the strictures of tradition, from the Liberal Establishment. The "Black is Beautiful" campaign from the late 1960s, for instance, which encouraged black men and women to grow their hair into Afros and embrace the dynamism of an African past, was in part a rejection of postwar cultural norms about how they should proceed if they wanted to get ahead. The "Gay is Good" campaign from 1968 made a similar argument in its title alone. Most parents of baby boomers had little difficulty providing example after example of the shocking demands made by their rights-loving children.

By 1976, the rights-based society had spread into areas most Americans hadn't even thought of. In 1968 the Architectural Barriers Act forced federal contractors to consider the rights of disabled people when building new structures. Equal rights were expanded to the disabled in 1973. In 1969, Native Americans took over Alcatraz to demand their right to repossess lands taken from them illegally. "Asian Americans have assumed white identities," proclaimed poet Amy Uyematsu in a breakthrough 1969 article, "The

Emergence of Yellow Power." "Now they are beginning to realize that this nation is a 'White democracy' and the yellow people have a mistaken identity."[8]

What's more, rights were being granted not only to people but to things. In 1965, the courts protected a marital couple's "right to privacy" (thus legalizing access to contraception).[9] In 1973, the courts protected a woman's "right to choose" whether or not she would have an abortion.[10] Many Americans, including Mailer and Buckley, thought this was an awful lot of rights-giving, and in fact that it risked destabilizing the entire social order. But it was true that all the demands stemmed from a simple complaint: the liberal consensus of the postwar era had not done enough to give all sectors of American society any semblance of genuine power. There were wrongs that needed correcting. If the Liberal Establishment wouldn't correct things, those left behind would do it on their own. And to do so, they would use the best American words they could find: rights in the name of freedom.

One thing both Buckley and Mailer noticed, though, was that the transition from a rules-based to a rights-based society all but eliminated the need for a ruling class. When The Rules were in fashion, someone had to adjudicate and enforce. When The Rules were gone, a ruling elite became less vital. No one wanted to follow their rules anyway. The elite might be wealthier or more powerful than the rest, but they were not necessarily more moral.

Both Buckley and Mailer were torn about the transition from rules to rights. They hadn't much liked the Liberal Establishment during their formative years, so inroads were welcome. On the other hand, the new rights-based model seemed devoid of any center. There was little concern for the larger community, and how could a nation bind together if all anyone wanted to do was go their own way?

Once The Rules began to be challenged, the other panels of the postwar triptych did not look quite the same. Perhaps surprisingly, rational thought came under assault, too. Alternative faiths like Zen Buddhism, Eastern meditation rituals, Native American spirituality, and even more esoteric "faiths" like est (a dogmatic seminar-like training session designed to free people from the constraints they felt in life), seemed to pop up everywhere. Their appearance signified more than just a rejection of traditional establishment faiths like Protestantism, Catholicism, or Judaism (although rejecting them was part of it). Instead, the movement was seen as a yearning to find truths that had seemed unattainable via avenues that prioritized the rational. These were richer ways to truth than the rational bird's-eye view of the liberals, a declaration that everyone came to truths differently and couldn't be atomized by faceless bureaucrats.

It was no surprise that the hippies and Yippies held séances and exorcisms at their rallies, and that the older generation, men like Mailer, didn't quite feel comfortable with it. Ken Kesey and his Merry Pranksters may have been on the far end of the spectrum in 1964 when they drove to the San Francisco Republican National Convention while full of acid, but by the end of the decade there were "trip-ins" across the country. Mind-altering drugs were designed to open up arenas beyond the rational, to open one up to the man behind the curtain. If six turned out to be nine, sang Jimi Hendrix, he wouldn't mind, because he had his own world to live in, and he wasn't going to copy anyone else's.

If drugs weren't everyone's cup of tea, the attack on rationalism echoed an older complaint—one that struck at the heart of the liberal endeavor. This complaint hung on the question of whether or not rational thought could be employed to improve the entire lot of American society or just that of a privileged few. What all the rights-demanders were claiming, not incorrectly, was that the progressive, rational endeavors of the Liberal Establishment still left many people behind. It was also clear that those left behind were the ones *always* left behind: racial minorities, the poor, women. This suggested some kind of conspiracy, or at the very least, some prioritizing. Robert Moses's hope that rational bureaucrats were going to usher in the millennium hadn't been fulfilled, and it didn't look like it was ever going to be, either. But for middle-class white achievers able to take advantage of the GI Bill, union seniority systems, or race-based segregation laws, well, all things looked fairly plausible.

This suspicion prompted still another question: if rational thought couldn't be trusted as impartial, shouldn't the very notion of progress be questioned as well? A more proper way of putting the question might be: progress for whom? Deep-seated mistrust about large bureaucracies crept into the tenor of the nation. It was a most American suspicion, but by the early 1970s it once again became a widespread sentiment; bureaucracies were seen as little more than self-serving monoliths out to garner profits and power. Meanwhile, all those exhibits about the "America of the future" that had dominated popular culture in the 1950s and 60s, with their futuristic techno-progress societies where guardians of science ushered in a spectacular future, were replaced by apocalyptic versions where various factions have succumbed to civil war. Philip K. Dick's *Do Androids Dream of Electric Sheep?* (1968) set the tone for a flurry of imaginative dystopian stories throughout the 1970s and early 1980s. (Dick's novel was turned into the dystopian film *Blade Runner* in 1982.) As the 1960s turned into the 1970s, belief in progress faded.

The federal government didn't help. The Tet Offensive of 1968 was followed in short order by the revelation of the My Lai massacre in 1969, in which American troops slaughtered up to five hundred unarmed Vietnamese women and children; the National Guard's murder of four students at Kent State University in 1970 as they were protesting the expansion of the Vietnam War; the release of the Pentagon Papers in 1971, showing the government had known for years it was lying about progress in Vietnam; and eventually the Watergate revelations of 1972, 1973, and 1974, which led to the Nixon's resignation as president. The following year, in

1975, the last American troops ignominiously left Vietnam, and shortly thereafter Vietnam came under communist leadership. Confidence in the federal government, as with most things considered "establishment," waned on all fronts.

What replaced it wasn't a complete rejection of rational thought, though. Instead, what emerged was a greater awareness that rational thought and progress were limited, not only in their capacity to succeed, but also in their reach. Rather than have one concept of "the good" or even "the nation," factions formed to promote progress for their own faction. Throughout the 1970s, there was a white ethnic revival, a movement by people who previously had thought of themselves simply as Americans but were now opting to prioritize their ethnic heritage. St. Patrick's Day parades expanded, as did those celebrating Columbus Day. The number of people claiming to be Native American rose exponentially, too.[11] The idea of a unified America has always been something of a fiction, but one that has had its share of adherents over time. Now, the pie seemed to be breaking apart. Those doing the splitting were doing it gleefully, and those resisting could harness few successful arguments on their own behalf. One historian has called it the age of fracture.[12]

As The Rules faltered and the power of rational thought and progress were shown to possess limits, the third arm of the postwar triptych suffered as well. This shouldn't be surprising considering how reliant corporate capitalism was on both federal regulators and the sense that paying taxes contributed to a viable commonweal. As the "do your own thing" attitude of the late 1960s and 1970s emerged, it led to rising demands for lowered income and real-estate taxes and for decreased governmental regulation. These demands hearkened back to those made by business leaders throughout the twentieth century. But in the 1970s, these complaints changed form and took on populist appeal. If the nation was proving to be a fiction, what was the point of contributing to the greater good?

The assault on corporate capitalism took its most obvious form in the world of politics. Since the early 1970s, the lobby to reduce taxes had been growing in Washington. Think tanks like the American Enterprise Institute began making the case for supply-side economics, which argued that rather than having the federal government be responsible for economic redistribution, it was more reliably done by increasing the freedom and wealth of individuals and corporations, who could then expand the economy on their own. The National Tax Limitation Committee, meanwhile, sought constitutional limitations on federal spending in an effort to starve the beast that was now the predominant image of the federal government.[13] In 1978, Californians declared a "taxpayer revolt" and overwhelmingly passed Proposition 13, which put limits on the rate that real-estate taxes could rise in any given year.

That same year, Congress abolished price regulations on the airline industry. Fares went down and profits rose during the first year, which led to an immediate (and ill-conceived) domino effect. Between 1979 and 1982, trucking, long-distance bus transport, railroads, telecommunications, oil, and the savings and loan industries all experienced governmental deregulation. The results were mixed and led to numerous abuses, as well as lower costs. But the transformation reflected the sentiment of the times, that large establishments were not to be trusted compared to individual entrepreneurs. The corporate capitalism of the postwar era, with its friendly relations between business and the state, was undergoing significant changes in the 1970s. It was now conceivable to think of an instance where what was good for General Motors was perhaps not so good for the nation.[14]

Certainly these changes were aided by complex transformations within the structure of global capitalism. Beginning in the early 1970s, the American economy began to shrink rather than grow. Foreign competition, increased dependence on foreign energy sources, including oil, and the decline of American manufacturing all took their toll on the American people. It was only in the context of this larger transformation that some of the libertarian dreams came true, but that it happened is undeniable.

Mailer mostly liked the rejection of The Rules and the turn against the rational, and Buckley thought it was about time the government began to lower taxes and reduce regulations on business. But these transformations came so quickly and in tandem that it looked damningly unclear how the future would unfold.

The irony was that most everything was done in the name of a word well loved by both Mailer and Buckley: freedom. People demanded their rights in the name of freedom. Business demanded lower taxes in order to preserve freedom. What was the meaning of "do your own thing" besides a call for more freedom? Businesses reverted to more laissez-faire kinds of operations. People increasingly sought the good life on their own terms. Freedom, in both its right and left meanings, was the true victor of the tremors of the late 1960s and early 1970s. For men raised to argue against and urge the transformation of the community, there was little left to argue with.

Perhaps this helps explain why, despite the narrative made fashionable in popular magazines, the American people were not in fact any less happy in the 1970s than in the 1960s. Throughout the 1970s pollsters found Americans to be a generally contented lot. In one 1976 survey, Americans reported to be happy in their marriages, to like their children, to like their jobs (no matter what kind), and generally to feel they were getting ahead in life. A duplication of the famous 1927 survey of Middletown done in 1977 showed that when it came to personal satisfaction, Americans' feelings had hardly changed at all throughout the course of the twentieth century.[15]

Instead of a story of decline or interminable revolution, then, what Buckley and Mailer came to be aware of was a break in the set of norms that governed American society. The triptych needed refashioning. Rights for the individual had replaced The Rules of

the community. Free-market capitalism replaced its corporate sib-
ling. And sources of truth moved from the rationalization of a traditional bureaucratic elite that could speak to the entirety of the
nation to the prioritization of local, more individualistic voices.

In the end, there was less preoccupation with the life of the
nation. Efforts at patriotism looked phony, or dangerously jingo-
istic. Men and women who once thought they might speak on
behalf of America, as Mailer and Buckley and many others had
in the 1950s and 1960s, now seemed to recognize that the idea
of a nation was something of a fiction, an imagined community.
For those like Buckley and Mailer, who had spent the 1960s craft-
ing platforms for the country and plotting an escape from the
doldrums of the Liberal Establishment, the awareness that the
country was a mythical being for whom no one could rightfully
speak was a dispiriting shock. The idea, of course, was always a
fiction: how could Mailer, Buckley, Vidal, Schlesinger, any of them
speak about the "life" of the nation? That they thought they could
was a function of the time and place in which they grew up and
matured. Once the times changed, that fiction was unmasked.

Both Mailer and Buckley recognized these changes, and tried to
assimilate them into their own worldviews. But for men raised with
an older set of assumptions, it was hard work. It would take time
to recalibrate.

After breakfast at Buckley's apartment, Buckley escorted Mailer
downstairs to help him flag a taxi. As they looked down the street,
they saw a station wagon careening toward them. They watched
it closely. It wasn't altering course and was heading right at them.
At the last minute, they jumped out of the way, ready to holler at
the reckless driver. When the vehicle screeched to a halt, the back-
seat window rolled down, and Daniel Patrick Moynihan was sitting
there smiling as he was being driven around town.

Moynihan would on that very day be elected to the U.S. Senate, defeating Bill's brother Jim. As a happy Moynihan opened his window, he yelled, "Damn. I could have got you both with one swipe!"

Without missing a beat, Buckley, thinking of the debate on *Good Morning America*, said, "Norman has already been killed once this morning."[16]

Epilogue

They wouldn't be killed that day, or any other for the next thirty-plus years, but they would be forced to shift courses and come to grips with the fact they were no longer central to the life of the nation. They continued to write journalistic pieces, cover political conventions, and be newsworthy personalities. But in the 1970s, 1980s, and 1990s, both removed themselves from the pitch of battle, patron saints already.

For his part, Buckley made a surprise turn to fiction in the 1970s. "After Watergate," recalled his friend and editor Sophie Wilkins, "he felt a lot of despair with right-wing politics and with the kind of fellows he had to support for the President. Writing with his imagination he was free to have everything according to his heart's desire."[1]

At a 1975 meeting, Sam Vaughan, president of Doubleday Publishing, presented Buckley with a table full of ideas for a new book, trying to entice him to write for them. Buckley, Vaughan recalled, brushed the ideas "on the floor as you would clean crumbs from the table." Vaughan then asked Buckley, "What would you like to write that you are not now writing?"

Buckley's reply startled him: "[A] novel," Buckley said.[2]

Vaughan thought about the prospect and immediately saw the

upside, knowing Buckley's skill at writing quickly and imaginatively. Vaughan rushed over a contract the very next day.

Vaughan thought he would get a highly literate, idea-laden novel with a complex plot. But Buckley had other things in mind. When he sent the first draft to Doubleday four months later, it was a pulpy spy novel filled with sex, intrigue, and celebrity. Buckley loved the page-turning quality of the spy-novel genre, but he had grown tired of morally ambiguous books like John le Carré's spy novels or movies like *Three Days of the Condor*, in which both the Soviets and the Americans received scorn for their duplicity and untrustworthiness. Buckley's book had little ambiguity in it. Yes, Buckley said in his fiction, the Americans might lie and cheat, but they were doing so in the name of freedom. Because of that, they were not operating on the same moral plane as those who acted duplicitously to create human misery, like the Soviets.

The hero of Buckley's novel was Blackford Oakes, an American James Bond who was more or less an improved version of Buckley himself. Like Buckley, Oakes is a Yale graduate, tall, with straw-colored hair and blue eyes. Like Buckley, Oakes served in World War II. But Oakes is also a talented fighter, mathematician, engineer, bomb-constructor, art historian, and wooer of women. In the novel, *Saving the Queen*, the CIA sends Oakes to discover how the Soviets keep getting America's secrets about the H-bomb, which have only been shared with the Queen of England and the British prime minister. Oakes discovers it's the Queen's cousin doing the deed. Her cousin hates Stalin but believes in the Leninist future, and has been turned by a Soviet handler in London.

The message of the book, about the lack of moral equivalence between East and West, gets somewhat overshadowed by the thrilling narrative, the James Bond–like antics, and the sex scenes, which might be called Maileresque. When Oakes deflowers the young Queen Caroline, the scene is downright saucy: "She arched back her neck and pointed her firm breasts up at the ceiling, and he was on her, kissing her softly, saying nothing. Her thighs began to heave, and she said in a whisper, 'Now.' He entered her smoothly. . . ."[3] The queen is one of three women Oakes beds in the book. It became a bestseller.

When a reporter asked John Kenneth Galbraith if he could explain the book's success, Galbraith replied, "Bill Buckley has a genuine talent for fiction, as his discriminating readers have always known." And of Buckley's decision to write novels, Galbraith said it was "a quantum step in self-recognition."[4] When actor David Niven said he was too busy filming a movie to blurb the back of the book, but that Buckley was welcome to write a blurb under his name, Buckley jokingly responded: "Probably the best novel ever written about fucking the Queen. David Niven." Niven, British-born, was caught off guard by the irreverence but then laughed heartily with Buckley at what was, thankfully, a joke.[5]

The book's success prompted Buckley to keep at it. Throughout the later 1970s and early 1980s, five more Blackford Oakes novels appeared. Buckley had become a novelist.

It was odd, Buckley writing fiction. Not that he was bad at it, but the once-upon-a-time enfant terrible of American political life was rattling his saber in the most subtle of forms. Unfortunately, while the form of the novel sometimes leads to great insights, more often than not Buckley used it to create a more comfortable world for himself, one that lacked the complexity of real life. "I do resist introspection," he wrote in 1983, "though I cannot claim to have 'guarded' against it because even to say that would suppose that the temptation to do so was there, which it isn't." Instead, he remained busy. "The search for virtue is probably best drowned out by *commotion*, and this my life is full of," he said. "It is easier to stay up late working for hours than to take one tenth the time to inquire into the question whether the work is worth performing."[6]

This refusal to contemplate the new order and place himself within it sometimes led to disastrous results, especially in 1983, when he wrote a kind of sequel to 1971's *Cruising Speed*. The 1983 novel, called *Overdrive*, was far worse, far more self-indulgent, and showed exactly how out of touch Buckley had become. "[W]hen part of this book first appeared in the *New Yorker*," wrote Grace Lichtenstein in the *Washington Post*, "I thought it was a joke, a Buckley parody of how some leftist might view Buckley's preoccupation with material possessions and his aristocratic lifestyle. Alas, it is not an intentional parody."[7]

The book casually mentioned the thirty-foot-long swimming pool Buckley had installed in his basement; his efforts to customize his limousine (by adding two feet to accommodate his long legs); the wines he drank during lunch, how the president (now Ronald Reagan) was an old friend and a charter subscriber of *National Review* (Reagan was mentioned no less than eight times in the book, each time more casually than the last); and finally how Buckley was so in demand that he was bouncing around more than ever before, from Tampa to Toledo to New York, from Huey Newton to Merv Griffin to Jeane Kirkpatrick.

Buckley's old friend, John Leonard, was biting in his criticism. "I thought *Overdrive* was a piece of self-indulgence," he said bluntly. Buckley "simply doesn't understand to this day that when you talk about getting your limousine customized that people are going to take offense; he doesn't understand it, he resents it. One of the questions you have to ask yourself is how much irony there is in the man. The style is ironic, but I sometimes wonder whether he really gets the irony."[8]

Without the irony, the book was little more than an example of how far removed Buckley had become. He had run out of ideas, was repeating himself, and was living off his celebrity. Buckley, said novelist John Gregory Dunne, "seems distracted and disjointed, as he approaches his fifty-eighth birthday. The show has been on the road too long. There have been too many plane trips, too many nights spent in Executive West hotels. Mr. Buckley has spread himself so thin that he has begun to repeat himself, repeatedly." Of

Overdrive, Dunne said, Buckley "is so sublimely unselfconscious, so 'blasphemously happy' with his own life that he wants to share with his reader what amounts to a 50,000-word advertisement for himself."

Buckley's advertisement, unlike Mailer's, left out all the insights. As Dunne realized:

> Among those of his huge cast of characters who are known personally to me, there is incidence of alcoholism, drug addiction, pederasty, pedophilia, adultery, cuckoldry, and various other manifestations of life's stigmata, not a hint of which darkens Mr. Buckley's journal. The result is a truly alarming vision of a life without shadows. In the world according to Buckley, Gatsby would marry Daisy, Tom Buchanan would find eternal happiness with Jordan Baker, Myrtle Wilson would open a chic and successful boutique, and Nick Carraway would become the Republican-Conservative governor of New York, with William F. Buckley, Jr., as his mentor/adviser/*éminence blanche.*[9]

In an era filled with irony and suspicion and dark motives, Buckley was out of place.

Mailer took a different approach to locating himself within the new order. Throughout the 1970s he made a few ventures at keeping himself in the news, with essays on celebrities that seemed to recall his early writings of the 1960s but lacked the same penetrating gaze into the heart of the nation. He was asked to write the foreword to a picture book on Marilyn Monroe, but got so caught up in the subject he ended up writing a short biography instead. Unfortunately, his insights about a celebrity who no longer animated the imaginations of the new generation weren't that insightful.[10] Meanwhile, a book on Muhammad Ali's 1974 fight against George Foreman, the famous Rumble in the Jungle, lacked the verve and depth of his earlier writings on boxing, and his attempts to draw large conclusions about America fell flat. In fact, he hardly attempted them anymore.[11] These books were short, thirty-thousand-word essays printed in big fonts with wide margins.

Mailer finally located his muse once again in the later 1970s, compelled, like much of the rest of the nation, by the 1976 double murder of two Salt Lake City men. What interested Mailer, though, was the personality of the murderer. Gary Gilmore was handsome, often articulate, and, most of all, unafraid to die. When he was given his sentence, Gilmore immediately responded by saying to the judge, "You sentenced me to die. Unless it's a joke or something, I want to go ahead and do it."

Of course, it took longer than that, and while Gilmore waited for the punishment for his crime, details emerged that made him seem even more fascinating. He had a lover who wanted to die with him, and who had even tried to commit suicide with him. He wrote poetry. The interviews he gave were thoughtful and thought provoking. He captivated the nation. Gilmore appeared on the cover of *Newsweek* in November 1976 under the headline, "Death Wish."

In studying the case, Mailer discovered a story about a country he didn't really know anymore. The story wasn't really about the country at all, in fact, but about the desolation of the West, the culture of Mormonism, and the violence that lay latent in each of us, a tiny swath of a larger whole. Mailer compiled all the materials available and ended up with more than three hundred interview sessions totaling more than fifteen thousand pages. This was more material than he had ever had to work with before, and it provoked him to think about storytelling differently. Throughout the 1960s, he had relied almost entirely on his own memory and intelligence to craft a story. The material was what he observed, and the story was told through his lens. In Gilmore's story, Mailer could not be the central player. He chose to write it in a standard third-person narrative, where the narrator is outside the story looking in. He hadn't used the style since *The Naked and the Dead*, three decades earlier.

In addition to the choice of narrator, Mailer also created an icy, morally ambivalent tone. The story of the murders is told through cold description. When the families of the victims find out what happened, we've already learned about their lives and struggles, about the most recent fights they've had with their partners, and then we watch them break down upon hearing of the murders. When Gilmore is finally executed, there is a long section on the history of the firing squad and on the remnants of Gilmore's heart. Mailer would eventually call the book *The Executioner's Song*, but its style was simple and clear. "The deity," reviewer Ted Morgan said, "orchestrates the voices, but does not join the song." Gone are "the existential musing, the outrageous ideas, the over-characterizing."[12] As Buckley observed, "This is not a book about Mailer, and not a book, were you to pick it up not knowing the identity of the author, [that] would lead you to guess his identity. You would, however, know instantly that you were in the hands of a master."[13] Many people think it's his best book.

Executioner's Song was Mailer in transition. More than just the ambivalent tone, what was different was the narrower terrain. The book is stuck in working-class, often poor Utah, a place with a unique culture and a unique history. It wasn't a book about America, but about a small part of it. Mailer still imagined himself as something of a Dostoevsky, but gone were the pretensions that he, or anyone, could be an American Tolstoy. He said as much in a letter to his aunt and uncle; his goal was to understand the deep psychology of the murderer, "which has never been touched by anyone, except for that author sitting next to God himself, old Dostoyevsky."[14] As he wrote a friend, "The worst is that all the people who like my other books will probably not like this one. It's not searching, but panoramic and descriptive, almost pedestrian."[15]

The book spent twenty-five weeks on the *New York Times* best-seller list, topping out at number three. It won Mailer his second Pulitzer Prize and was a finalist for both the American Book Award and the National Book Critics Circle Award. It was reviewed positively in nearly every venue. But it was not, as Alfred Kazin had described Mailer's work a decade earlier, a mirror to the nation. To do that, it seemed, was now impossible.

Ultimately, *The Executioner's Song* brought Mailer back to being a novelist again. The books he wrote after *Executioner's Song* were almost all novels: *Ancient Evenings, Harlot's Ghost, Oswald's Tale, The Gospel According to the Son.* This would be his métier for the next twenty-five years.

Buckley loved *Executioner's Song.* The narrative was compelling, the writing spare. Mailer had trimmed his ego from the work, allowing the artistic genius to come out. The two men discussed the book on *Firing Line* in 1979. The show was quiet and contemplative. There were no arguments about their dueling visions of America. They were there to chat about Mailer's book. Buckley even invited Jeff Greenfield to serve as an examiner in order to help stir the pot, a common practice in *Firing Line*'s mellowing years. But it didn't help. One reflective moment in the interview came when Mailer opened up about the kind of portrait he was painting in the novel. "One of the things I discovered while writing the book is I began to think that there is such a thing as the American character," he said. "I think in America we are all enormously concerned with being virtuous. It doesn't matter what we do. We can be anything from a drug pusher to a clergyman. We measure ourselves by our virtue. . . . We are obsessed with it."

It hearkened back to Mailer's "virtuous heart" analogy he had scribbled down after his first debate with Buckley. It was, perhaps, one of Mailer's lasting insights about the country—trying to preserve its virtuous heart in the midst of challenges posed by the increasing speed of modern life. But if back then Mailer had hoped to save the nation from itself, *Executioner's Song* was more ambivalent, less engaged, and less transformative. Now, it seemed, Mailer just wanted to tell a good story.

As Mailer put it toward the end of the show, "I've been in the habit for years of feeling that I could dominate any question pretty quickly—it's been my vanity," he said. "[But] I thought it might be very nice for once just to write a book which doesn't have an answer, but poses delicate questions with a great deal of evidence and a great deal of material and lets people argue over it. I feel there are any number of areas in this book where there are people who have better answers to give than I have." And so, "I felt that maybe the time had come—at least for me in my own work—to do a book where I don't explain it to the reader, and in part I *can't* explain all of it to the reader. I can merely make the reader tremendously familiar with material they usually don't encounter." He would, he said, keep his "opinions to the side."[16]

For Buckley and Mailer, the end would come not by assassination or the station wagon, but with old age. Mailer would succumb to acute renal failure in November 2007 and Buckley would die of a heart attack a few months later, in February 2008.

A predictable flood of tributes followed. All the major newspapers, all the magazines had been affected by these intellectual heavyweights who had interpreted, debated, and differed on almost every important topic in the latter half of the past century. Looking back, it was clear Buckley had shaped the politics of the previous fifty years, if not as much as he would have liked, and that Mailer had affected its culture and its tone, if not as much as he would have liked. Fittingly, their public funerals were held just five days and one subway stop apart in April 2008.

"If I'm still famous, do it at Saint Patrick's," Buckley had said to his son a few years earlier. "If not, just do it in Stamford at Saint Mary's."[17]

He was, of course, still famous, and on that April day in New York City, St. Patrick's Cathedral was filled to capacity with 2,200 souls. Henry Kissinger spoke, as did Buckley's only son, novelist Christopher Buckley. George McGovern and Tom Wolfe sat in the pews. President George W. Bush had called the Buckley family hours after Buckley's death; he was unable to attend the service but sent the vice president. Everyone acknowledged Buckley's role in the conservative moment. One biographer (of many) had called him the "Patron Saint of the Conservatives." President Reagan had bestowed upon him the Medal of Freedom. Buckley, they agreed, had altered the way American politics looked and sounded in the late twentieth century. Some loved what he had done, others didn't, but his impact was undeniable.

Five days later, some of the very same luminaries headed to Carnegie Hall to give Norman Mailer his sweet goodbye. Joan Didion, Don DeLillo, Gay Talese, and other literary giants were in attendance, as well as two thousand others. In addition to all of Mailer's early successes and his work from the 1960s, they mentioned his presidency of PEN the writers' society, in the early 1990s, which allowed him to take a stance defending Salman Rushdie. They mentioned the Iraq War of 2003, which had seemed to inspire the protestor inside Mailer once again. His screeds against George W. Bush resembled those previously reserved for Lyndon B. Johnson. Mailer, they agreed, had altered the way Americans thought about their country, the way they looked at their leaders, and the perceptions they had when they thought of themselves. More than just a literary giant, Mailer had shaped the cultural and political outlook of a generation of Americans. Some loved it, some didn't, but the impact was undeniable.[18]

John Buffalo Mailer, Mailer's youngest son, read a family treasure, a humorous obituary Mailer wrote for himself in 1979, almost three decades before his actual passing:

> Norman Mailer passed away yesterday after celebrating his fifteenth divorce and sixteenth wedding. "I just don't feel the old vim," complained the writer recently. He was renowned in publishing circles for his blend of fictional journalism and factual fiction, termed by literary critic William Buckley: Contemporaneous Ratiocinative Aesthetical Prolegomena.

Buckley was consequentially sued by Mailer for malicious construction of invidious acronyms. "Norman does take himself seriously," was Mr. Buckley's reply. "Of course he is the last of those who do."[19]

Of course, funny as the line was, Buckley didn't think Mailer was CRAP at all.

Another assessment came from Reid Buckley, Bill's youngest brother. In 2008, Reid wrote a colorful, doting book about his family. Toward the end, he identified the heights of the Buckley family's "fame and influence," seeing it near its peak in 1965, when Bill ran for mayor, hitting new heights with Bill's *Time* magazine cover from 1967, and then in 1970, with Jim Buckley's election to the New York Senate. From there it went downward "with diminishing panache," through the 1970s and the Reagan administration. Despite Jim's election to Senate, during those exciting years from 1965 to 1970 everything "centered around Bill," Reid wrote, "his books, his magazine, his column, his articles, his debates, his television program, his charm."

In fact, Reid wrote, "The only figure of those times who came close to him in fame and notoriety was Norman Mailer." Both operated in "the center of New York, Washington, and also national television." Both were icons of an era.[20]

Reid was of course partial, but that doesn't mean he was wrong. While there were other talismans of the era, none rises so imperiously over the right wing as Bill Buckley. Not only did he organize a ragtag bunch of conservatives into a formidable national movement, but by the 1970s he also spent a large amount of energy serving as a mentor to a younger generation. It should be no surprise, then, that the style of modern American conservatism is defined by some of the traits Buckley first brought to the table—adversarial, confident, sometimes witty—even if the terms on which the American right has centered never came to look exactly as Buckley might have hoped.

Making a case for Norman Mailer's position on the left is more difficult, in part because the left was populated by many significant figures during the 1960s, none of whom braided together the causes as successfully as Buckley did for the right. But also because Mailer's strengths were different than Buckley's; he was rarely capable of sacrificing his philosophical temperament in order to tolerate the egos of others. Perhaps his ego was too large. Either way, he mostly wanted to talk about the nature of man.

What is undeniable is the respect they had for each other.

In 1970, when Buckley did a long interview for *Playboy*, he was asked, "To whom do you personally feel inferior?"

Buckley waffled around a bit, saying "millions of people—or hundreds of thousands of people."

Digging for some dirt, *Playboy* pressed the issue.

"Norman Mailer?" it asked.

Buckley answered quickly, "[He's] much more talented than I am."

He then modified his answer a bit: "Now, there are certain things in which I am Mailer's manifest superior. Politically, he's an idiot. And he's botched his life and the lives of a lot more people than I've botched, I hope."

"On the other hand," Buckley said of his old friend, "he's a genius and I'm not."[21]

Mailer's appraisal of Buckley would in some ways be typically Mailerian—long and more difficult to decipher, but worth the effort.

In 1975, Mailer was asked to auction off an evening with William F. Buckley, Jr. He went into full hyperbole, making fun of what was so easy to make fun of in Buckley: his ridiculous vocabulary. Mailer stood up at the auction and said:

> Here to auction off an hour with that intellectual inchling, that pride of conservatism erumpant (if not always ideologically erugate) I am happy to say that the successful bidder

will receive a full hour of conversation and attention from
Sharon, Connecticut's own buckeen, William F. Buckley, right
in his New York home among his lares and penates.

. . . At any rate, we must breathe deep, avoid the ganch and
the garlion, and prepare to bid up our wallets for the right to
be received by that scollardical exponent of holophrasis, that
natural practitioner of misosophy and misocainia, that sedu-
lous seeksorrow of the CIA, now rendered semi-ustilate I fear
by the likes of Spiro Agnew, but nonetheless phenomenally
well worth bidding up if you have a taste for tongue-tallying
with America's own sempiternal columnist, that upper Yahoo
from Yale, Mr. William F. Buckley and his gang of trillibubs.

After the auction, Mailer sent Buckley a clean copy of the speech:
"Dear Bill: Yours to frame or flip away."[22]

Buckley responded: "Dear Norman: Thanks a million for the
text of the introduction, which I shall attempt to decipher as soon
as I find myself next to a substantial dictionary. I have not yet met
the highest bidder, but I shall attempt to sound as you would have
me sound! Let's meet soon. As ever, Bill."[23]

Acknowledgments

It's certainly better to have written a book than to be writing one, partly so you can thank those who helped you along the way

For me, special mentions go to: David Hollinger, John D'Emilio, and Deirdre McCloskey, who supported the project from its inception; the early readers, who include David Sehat, Andrew Hartman, Maura Jane Farrelly, Jim Sack, my mother-in-law Susan Rivers, my mother Jill Schultz, and the late, great Peter Bacon Hales; and Bob Goldberg, who not only read an early draft but supported me for a year at the Tanner Humanities Center at the University of Utah.

Acknowledgements are also due to those who opened doors for this project, including Christopher Buckley, William Massa at the Sterling Memorial Library at Yale University, Lawrence Schiller and the Norman Mailer Estate, the Harry Ransom Center, which not only houses the Norman Mailer Papers but which also made me a Research Fellow, and Peter Manso.

My agent, Andrew Stuart, helped turn the kernel of an idea into a proposal, and my editor, Matt Weiland, helped turn that proposal into the book that is now in your hands. Sam MacLaughlin at Norton made everything go smoother, even, very occasionally, tolerating an irritable author in the throes of navigating permissions and the like. The production, publicity, marketing, and sales teams at Norton have also done yeoman's work; I can only shout so loudly. To all of them, this book is better because of you. Thanks.

Finally, I must express gratitude to the large web that is my family, who always enthusiastically supported me in this project. This is especially true for Terra and the kids, Thaddeus, Eleanor, and Quincy. Humor when I needed it, many welcome distractions along the way, and tangible love: I'm grateful everyday. Thanks, too, to Ava the dog.

Notes

Epigraph

1   Norman Mailer, "Buckley notes," folder 4, box 17, Mailer Papers.

Introduction

1   Christopher Buckley, *Losing Mum and Pup: A Memoir* (New York: Twelve, 2009), p. 185.
2   For the reports on Buckley's urine color, ibid., pp. 96-101. On his habit of urinating out of his limousine, see p. 163.
3   On Buckley contemplating suicide, see Buckley, *Losing Mum and Pup*, pp. 157–58 and 210.
4   Ibid., p. 36.
5   On his devotion to her, and on its connection to his thoughts of suicide, see ibid., p. 150.
6   Norman Mailer to William F. Buckley, Jr., n.d. (probably March 1966), box 570, folder 10, Mailer Papers.
7   Norman Mailer, "Ten Thousand Words a Minute," reprinted in Norman Mailer, *The Presidential Papers*, (New York: G. P. Putnam's Sons, 1963), p. 265.
8   William F. Buckley, Jr., "Norman Mailer, R.I.P.," *National Review* (December 3, 2007): 14.
9   Ibid.
10 Ibid.

Chapter 1. The Nature of Man

1 Gore Vidal, "The Norman Mailer Syndrome," *The Nation*, January 2, 1960, reprinted in Gore Vidal, *United States: Essays, 1952–1992* (New York: Broadway, 2001), pp. 31-40.

2 Lewis Nichols, "In And Out of Books," *New York Times*, October 7, 1962, p. BR5.

3 "America," in Allen Ginsberg, *Howl and Other Poems* (San Francisco, CA: City Lights, 1956), p. 31. For more on this, see generally Elaine Tyler May, *Homeward Bound: American Families in the Cold War Era* (New York: Basic Books, 1988).

4 The *Life* series was made into a book: John K. Jessup, ed., *The National Purpose* (New York: Holt, Rinehart and Winston, 1960), p. 83 for Rossiter and p. 28 for Stevenson.

5 A good recapitulation of these intellectual yearnings can be found in Howard Brick, *Age of Contradiction: American Thought and Culture in the 1960s* (New York: Twayne Publishers, 1998).

6 Nichols, "In And Out of Books," p. BR5.

7 Barry Goldwater, *The Conscience of a Conservative* (New York: Macfadden Books, 1960), p. 3.

8 John Golden to William F. Buckley, Jr., August, 21, 1962, box 562, folder 5, Mailer Papers.

9 Mailer recounts this story in a collection of oral histories, *Mailer: His Life and Times*, ed. Peter Manso (New York: Washington Square Press, 1985), p. 127.

10 The quotation is from Adele Mailer, *The Last Party: Scenes from Life with Norman Mailer* (New York: Barricade Books, 1997), p. 349.

11 For Mailer's thoughts on the design of *Advertisements*, see J. Michael Lennon, *Norman Mailer: A Double Life* (New York: Simon & Schuster, 2013), pp. 242–52. On New Journalism see, for instance, Marc Weingarten, *The Gang That Wouldn't Write Straight: Wolfe, Thompson, Didion, and the New Journalism Revolution* (New York: Crown, 2005).

12 Norman Mailer, *Advertisements for Myself* (New York: G. P. Putnam's Sons, 1959; quote from Cambridge, MA: Harvard University Press, 1992), p. 19. Later observers would be stunned to see how presciently Mailer had predicted the uprisings that came to be known as "the Sixties." From pot to protests, *Advertisements* had predicted it all.

13 Ibid., p. 17.

14 Reagan recounted this story at the thirtieth anniversary dinner for *National Review*. For his role as a charter subscriber, see Rick Perlstein, *Before the Storm: Barry Goldwater and the Unmaking of the American Consensus* (New York: Hill and Wang, 2001), p. 122.

15 For a selection of comments on the importance of *National Review* to the movement, see Rebecca E. Klatch, *A Generation Divided: The New Left, the*

New Right, and the 1960s (Berkeley, CA: University of California Press, 1999), pp. 66–70.

16   Harold Conrad quoted in Manso, ed., *Mailer*, p. 355.

17   Posters are in folder 10, box 559, Mailer Papers.

18   Harold Conrad, quoted in Manso, ed., *Mailer*, p. 355.

19   Stan Isaacs, "Will Sonny-Floyd Match Left-Right?" *Newsday*, September 24, 1962, p. 19C.

20   Norman Mailer, *The Presidential Papers* (New York: G. P. Putnam's Sons, 1963), p. 257.

21   Harold Conrad, *Dear Muffo: 35 Years in the Fast Lane* (New York: Stein and Day, 1982), p. 150.

22   Roger Donoghue quoted in Manso, ed., *Mailer*, p. 362.

23   Hugh Hefner to Norman Mailer, October 2, 1962, box 562, folder 5, Mailer Papers.

24   Norman Mailer to Eiichi Yamanishi, September 12, 1962, box 553, folder 5, Mailer Papers.

25   Mailer, *Presidential Papers*, p. 174.

26   William F. Buckley, Jr., to Irving Kupcinet, September 7, 1962, box 562, folder 5, Mailer Papers.

27   "Instructing Norman Mailer on the True Meaning of the American Right Wing," in William F. Buckley, Jr., *Rumbles Left and Right: A Book about Troublesome People and Ideas* (New York: G. P. Putnam's Sons, 1963), pp. 71–84.

28   Norman Mailer, *The Deer Park* (New York: G. P. Putnam's Sons, 1955; quote from New York: First Vintage Edition, 1997), p. 131.

29   "Instructing Norman Mailer on the True Meaning of the American Right Wing," in *Rumbles Left and Right*, pp. 71–84.

30   Isaacs, "Will Sonny-Floyd Match Left-Right?"

31   "Mater si, Magistra no," *National Review* (August 26, 1961): 114. The line originated with Garry Wills when he used it in a phone call with Buckley, who then deployed it in *National Review*. See Garry Wills, *Why I Am a Catholic* (New York: Houghton Mifflin Harcourt, 2003), p. 48.

32   Buckley, "Instructing Norman Mailer," in *Rumbles Left and Right*, pp. 82–83.

33   In the last phrase, Buckley was quoting an essay on Mailer by "his friend, my enemy, Gore Vidal," as Buckley put it. Ibid., p. 81.

34   Ibid., p. 83.

35   Ibid., p. 84.

36   Mailer, "The Debate with William Buckley—The Real Meaning of the Right Wing in America," in *Presidential Papers*, p. 165.

37   Mailer, "The Debate With William Buckley," in *Presidential Papers*, p. 170.

38   On Mailer's "libertarian socialism," see "The Homosexual Villain" in Mailer, *Advertisements For Myself*, p. 225.

39   Mailer, "The Debate With William Buckley," in *Presidential Papers*, p. 173.

40   Ibid., p. 171.

41 Ibid., pp. 173–74.

42 William F. Buckley, Jr., and Norman Mailer, "The Role of the Right Wing: A Debate," *Playboy*, February 1963, pp. 115–16.

43 Ibid., p. 116.

44 On Mailer's Manichaeism, see Norman Mailer with Michael Lennon, *On God: An Uncommon Conversation* (New York: Random House, 2008), pp. 15–38.

45 Buckley and Mailer, "The Role of the Right Wing," p. 116.

46 In Hilary Mills, *Mailer: A Biography* (New York: Empire Books, 1982; quote from New York: McGraw-Hill, 1984), p. 292.

47 Gay Talese, "Mailer Debates William Buckley; Chicago Political Bout a Draw," *New York Times*, September 24, 1962, p. 31.

48 Norman Mailer to Eiichi Yamanishi, October 17, 1962, box 553, folder 5, Mailer Papers.

49 Isaacs, "Will Sonny-Floyd Match Left-Right?"

50 Roger Donoghue in Manso, ed., *Mailer*, p. 362.

51 Talese recounted the story many times; see for instance: Leon Neyfakh, "The Id (and Imp) of American Literature," *New York Observer*, November 14, 2007.

52 Mailer, *Presidential Papers*, p. 174.

53 William F. Buckley, Jr., "Naked & Half Alive," September 23, 1962. All of Buckley's columns, and most of his other work as well, can be read and downloaded from the website of Hillsdale College, Hillsdale, Michigan. See https://cumulus.hillsdale.edu/Buckley/ (accessed September 13, 2013).

54 William F. Buckley, Jr., "Listen, Mills," *National Review* (December 17, 1960): 369.

55 Buckley, "Naked & Half Alive."

56 Norman Mailer to Dick Koffler, March 8, 1963, box 566, folder 1, Mailer Papers.

Chapter 2. Placid Seas

1 Norman Mailer to A. C. Spectorsky, September 28, 1962, box 562, folder 5, Mailer Papers.

2 Norman Mailer to Aaron Berlin, November 28, 1962, box 560, folder 18, Mailer Papers.

3 See Liz Smith, "My 'Ancient Evenings' With Norman Mailer," *Chicago Tribune*, September 7, 2012, and Steven Marcus, "Norman Mailer: The Art of Fiction No. 32," *Paris Review* (Winter–Spring 1964), available at http://www.theparisreview.org/interviews/4503/the-art-of-fiction-no-32-norman-mailer (accessed October 27, 2014).

4 Midge Decter quoted in *Mailer: His Life and Times*, ed. Peter Manso (New York: Washington Square Press, 1985), p. 345.

5 There is some dispute about whether Buckley's first and second languages really were Spanish and French, or if it was simply a story he liked to tell.

There is also some dispute about the seminar-like atmosphere of the family dinner table.

6 For Pat's "library," see Christopher Buckley, *Losing Mum and Pup: A Memoir* (New York: Twelve, 2009), pp. 57–58.

7 "Sixty-Nine Questions and Answers," from *Expose* 1952, and found in Norman Mailer, *Advertisements for Myself* (New York: G. P. Putnam's Sons, 1959; quote from Cambridge, MA: Harvard University Press, 1992), p. 272. For the story of Spinoza, see the recollection of Marjorie "Osie" Radin, Mailer's cousin, in Manso, ed., *Mailer*, p. 25 and Mary V. Dearborn, *Mailer: A Biography* (New York: Houghton Mifflin Company, 1999), p. 17.

8 For this story, see Dearborn, *Mailer*, p. 13.

9 Recounted in John B. Judis, *William F. Buckley, Jr.: Patron Saint of the Conservatives* (New York: Simon and Schuster, 1988), p. 59.

10 Recounted by Galbraith in Judis, *Buckley*, p. 79.

11 John Golden to William F. Buckley, August 21, 1962, box 559, folder 10, Mailer Papers.

12 Norman Mailer to Aaron Berlin, November 28, 1962, box 560, folder 18, Mailer Papers.

13 In addition to the meeting at Buckley's house, the potential debates are described in a series of letters between the two men. See, for instance, Norman Mailer to William F. Buckley, April 29, 1963, box 26, Mailer folder, Buckley Papers; William F. Buckley to Norman Mailer, June 18, 1963, box 26, Mailer folder, Buckley Papers; Norman Mailer to William F. Buckley, July 3, 1963, box 26, Mailer folder, Buckley Papers; William F. Buckley to Norman Mailer, August 20, 1963, box 26, Mailer folder, Buckley Papers; and, when they finally decided to "let it go for awhile," Norman Mailer to William F. Buckley, September 12, 1963, box 26, Mailer folder, Buckley Papers.

14 Brent Bozell was the most famous convert to conservatism via Buckley's demonstration of good living. See Judis, *Buckley*, pp. 56–57.

15 Homer, *The Odyssey*, Book IX, ll. 82–104.

16 William F. Buckley, Jr., *Up From Liberalism* (New York: McDowellm Obolensky Inc., 1959; quote from New York: Stein and Day, 1984), pp. 117–18.

17 Mailer, *Advertisements for Myself*, p. 17.

18 President Eisenhower, "Remarks at a Safety Conference," February 17, 1954, http://www.fhwa.dot.gov/interstate/audiotext.htm#s06 (accessed May 27, 2014).

19 Robert Moses, *Working for the People: Promise and Performance in Public Service* (New York: Harper & Brothers, 1956), p. 62.

20 Moses, *Working for the People*, p. 2.

21 Found in Charles R. Morris, *A Time of Passion: America 1960–1980* (New York: Penguin, 1986), p. 3.

22 John Maynard Keynes, *The General Theory of Employment, Interest and Money* (New York: Harcourt, Brace & World, 1936), p. 378.

23 Daniel Bell, *The End of Ideology: On the Exhaustion of Political Ideas in the Fifties*, (1960; Cambridge, MA: Harvard University Press, 2000), pp. 403–4.

24 Historians will note my homage to the great work of Henry F. May, who uses the triptych image to describe the intellectual premises of Victorian America in his *The End of American Innocence: A Study of the First Years of our Own Time, 1912–1917* (New York: Knopf, 1959).

25 Robert A. Caro, *The Power Broker: Robert Moses and the Fall of New York* (New York: Vintage, 1975).

26 Norman Mailer, "Letter to the Editor," *Playboy*, April 1963, p. 8.

27 William F. Buckley, Jr., "Norman Mailer, R.I.P.," *National Review*, (November 14, 2007): 14.

28 Hoke Norris, "Mailer Brings Existentialism to City," *Chicago Sun-Times*, May 12, 1963, p. 58.

Chapter 3. American Golem

1 William F. Buckley to Norman Mailer, October 31, 1962, box 21, Mailer folder, Part 1, Buckley Papers.

2 Pat Buckley to Norman Mailer, n.d. (probably February 1963), box 564, folder 14, Mailer Papers.

3 Ibid.

4 William F. Buckley to Norman Mailer, n.d. (probably February 1963), box 564, folder 14, Mailer Papers.

5 Pat Buckley to Norman Mailer, n.d. (probably February 1963), box 564, folder 14, Mailer Papers.

6 Norman Mailer to William F. Buckley, Jr., April 3, 1963, box 564, folder 14, Mailer Papers.

7 William F. Buckley, Jr., to Norman Mailer, October 31, 1962, box 21, Mailer folder, Part 1, Buckley Papers.

8 William F. Buckley, Jr., to Norman Mailer, April 26, 1963, box 26, Mailer folder, Buckley Papers.

9 Norman Mailer to William F. Buckley, Jr., December 16, 1964, box 31, Mailer folder, Buckley Papers.

10 All quotes from William F. Buckley, Jr., "To My Admirers at Chapel Hill," January 3, 1963, box 52, folder 13, Mailer Papers.

11 It appears in both William F. Buckley, Jr., *Rumbles Left and Right: A Book about Troublesome People and Ideas* (New York: G. P. Putnam's Sons, 1963), pp. 71–84 and William F. Buckley, Jr., *Let Us Talk of Many Things: The Collected Speeches* (New York: Forum, 2000; quote from New York: Basic Books, 2008), pp. 48–57.

12 Hoke Norris, "Mailer Brings Existentialism To City," *Chicago Sun-Times*, May 12, 1963, p. 58.

13 Hugh Hefner to Norman Mailer, January 21, 1963, box 567, Playboy (1963) folder, Mailer Papers.

14 Norman Mailer to William F. Buckley, July 3, 1963, box 26, Mailer folder, Buckley Papers.

15   Buckleys to Norman Mailer, April 31, 1963, box 26, Mailer folder, Buckley Papers.

16   Richard Kluger, "To dig, get off the middleground," *Book Week*, November 10, 1963, p. 4.

17   Norman Mailer to William F. Buckley, July 3, 1963, box 26, Mailer folder, Buckley Papers.

18   William F. Buckley, Jr., to Norman Mailer, June 18, 1963, box 26, Mailer folder, Buckley Papers.

19   Norman Mailer to William F. Buckley, July 3, 1963, Mailer folder, box 26, Buckley Papers.

20   For *Open End*, see Steven Battaglio, *David Susskind: A Televised Life* (New York: St. Martin's Press, 2010), pp. 42, 46–47, 57, 57–71, and 91; on the UN Plaza apartment complex, see Charlotte Curtis, "Notables Living in U.N. Plaza 'Compound' Finally Get Acquainted," *New York Times*, May 18, 1967, p. 51.

21   Battaglio, *David Susskind*, p. 120.

22   Ibid., p. 118.

23   William F. Buckley, Jr., "On the Right" column, April 15, 1962 and Aug. 13, 1963, and found in John B. Judis, *William F. Buckley, Jr.: Patron Saint of the Conservatives* (New York: Simon and Schuster, 1988), p. 206.

24   Norman Mailer to Eichii Yamanishi, December 15, 1963, Mailer Papers, and found in J. Michael Lennon, *Norman Mailer: A Double Life* (New York: Simon & Schuster, 2013), p. 335.

25   Norman Mailer to Mickey Knox, December 17, 1963, Mailer Papers, and found in Lennon, *Mailer*, pp. 334–35.

26   William F. Buckley to Norman Mailer, December 17, 1963, box 26, "Mailer" folder, Buckley Papers.

27   Paul Gardner, "Mailer and Buckley Talk on 'Open End,'" *New York Times*, February 3, 1964, p. 51.

28   William F. Buckley to Miss Anna Steele, February 12, 1964, box 52, folder 13, Mailer Papers.

29   Norman Mailer to William F. Buckley, February 20, 1964, box 52, folder 13, Mailer Papers.

30   Paul Gardner, "Mailer and Buckley Talk on 'Open End,'" *New York Times*, February 3, 1964, p. 51.

31   Norman Mailer to Eiichi Yamanishi, April 17, 1964, box 553, folder 6, Mailer Papers.

32   Norman Mailer, "Freedom or Virtue? Take a Vote Gentleman, Why Freedom, etc.," n.d. (probably December 1963), box 52, folder 13, Mailer Papers.

33   All Mailer quotes on these three pages from Norman Mailer, "So the Kid went . . . ," n.d., box 52, folder 13, Mailer Papers.

Chapter 4. The Fires

1   Norman Mailer, "In the Red Light: A History of the Republican Convention in 1964," *Esquire* (November 1964), and reprinted in Norman Mailer, *Cannibals and Christians* (New York: Dial Press, 1966), p. 13.

2   For the success of White and Manion, see Rick Perlstein, *Before the Storm: Barry Goldwater and the Unmaking of the American Consensus* (New York: Hill and Wang, 2001), pp. 6–16 and 172–94.

3   Norman Mailer, *Miami and the Siege of Chicago* (New York: D. I. Fine, 1968; quote from New York: *New York Review of Books*, 2008), p. 68.

4   Norman Mailer, "In the Red Light," reprinted in *Cannibals and Christians*, p. 17.

5   Perlstein, *Before the Storm*, p. 374.

6   Ibid.

7   Norman Mailer, "In the Red Light," reprinted in *Cannibals and Christians*, p. 19.

8   Ibid., p. 23.

9   Ibid., p. 24.

10   Ibid., p. 28.

11   Perlstein, *Before the Storm*, p. 108.

12   Ibid., and Alan MacKay, quoted in Rebecca E. Klatch, *A Generation Divided: The New Left, the New Right, and the 1960s* (Berkeley, CA: University of California Press, 1999), p. 20.

13   Perlstein, *Before the Storm*, p. 473.

14   John B. Judis, *William F. Buckley, Jr.: Patron Saint of the Conservatives* (New York: Simon and Schuster, 1988), p. 221.

15   William F. Buckley, Jr., "The Young Americans for Freedom," *National Review* (September 24, 1960): 172.

16   Lee Edwards quoted in Judis, *Buckley*, p. 189.

17   Ibid., p. 184.

18   Perlman, *Before the Storm*, p. 108.

19   Judis, *Buckley*, p. 191.

20   William F. Buckley, Jr., to Clinton Davidson, December 1, 1954, box 2, "Davidson" folder, Buckley Papers.

21   Perlstein, *Before the Storm*, p. 472.

22   Judis, *Buckley*, pp. 222–23.

23   Ibid., p. 221.

24   William F. Buckley, Jr., "The Impending Defeat of Barry Goldwater," September 11, 1964, reprinted in Buckley, *Let Us Talk of Many Things: The Collected Speeches* (New York: Forum, 2000; quote from New York: Basic Books, 2008), pp. 75–76.

25   Ibid., p. 76.

26   Ibid., p. 77.

27   Ibid., p. 78.

28 Barry Goldwater, "Acceptance Speech," Republican National Convention, July 16, 1964. The speech is available to view in full at http://www.c-span .org/video/?4018-1/goldwater-1964 acceptance-speech (accessed October 21, 2014).

29 For more on this, see Judis, *Buckley*, p. 202.

30 William F. Buckley, Jr., "The Aimlessness of American Education," *Newsday*, March 5, 1960, p. 6. Buckley originally used the locality of Garden City to make his comparison, which would have made sense to the local Long Island readers of *Newsday*, but he changed it to Boston in reprints when the line became famous. See Buckley, "A Reply to Robert Hutchins: The Aimlessness of American Education," in *Rumbles Left and Right: A Book about Troublesome People and Ideas* (New York: G. P. Putnam's Sons, 1963), p. 134.

31 William F. Buckley, Jr., to Norman Mailer, n.d. (probably February 1963), box 564, folder 14, Mailer Papers.

32 Perlstein, *Before the Storm*, p. 371.

33 Betty Friedan, *The Feminine Mystique* (New York: W. W. Norton & Company, 1963), pp. 15–16.

34 Klatch, *Generation Divided*, p. 20.

35 The Port Huron Statement is easily available but see *"Takin' It to the Streets": A Sixties Reader*, Alexander Bloom and Wini Breines, eds. (New York: Oxford University Press, 2003), pp. 50–61.

36 Klatch, *Generation Divided*, p. 138.

37 Diana Trilling to Norman Mailer, June 27, 1963, box 566, folder 1, Mailer Papers.

38 Norman Mailer, "Superman Comes to the Supermarket," *Esquire* (November 1960) and reprinted in Mailer, *The Presidential Papers* (New York: G. P. Putnam's Sons, 1963), pp. 46–47 and 58.

39 Hamill quoted in *Mailer: His Life and Times*, ed. Peter Manso (New York: Washington Square Press, 1985), p. 357.

40 Ibid.

41 Carol Polsgrove, *It Wasn't Pretty, Folks, but Didn't We Have Fun?: Esquire in the Sixties* (New York: W. W. Norton & Co., 1995), p. 67.

42 Mailer, *Presidential Papers*, p. 5.

43 Ibid., p. 11.

44 Ibid., pp. 12–13, 269–71.

45 Ibid., pp. 2–5.

46 Richard Kluger, "To dig, get off the middleground," *Book Week*, November 10, 1963, p. 4.

47 John Kenneth Galbraith, "The Kennedys Didn't Reply," *New York Times Book Review*, November 17, 1963, p. 6.

48 Garry Wills, "The Art of Not Writing Novels," *National Review* (January 14, 1964): 31.

49 Mailer, "In the Red Light," reprinted in *Cannibals and Christians*, p. 34.

50 Ibid., p. 43.

51 Ibid., p. 45.

52 See *Historical Tables: Budget of the U.S. Government, Fiscal Year 2012*, produced by the Office of Management and Budget and found at: http://www
.whitehouse.gov/sites/default/files/omb/budget/fy2012/assets/hist.pdf
(accessed July 24, 2014).

53 Doris Kearns Goodwin, *Lyndon Johnson and the American Dream* (New York:
St. Martin's Press, 1991), pp. 54 and 220, and found in David Wyatt, *When America Turned: Reckoning with 1968* (Amherst: University of Massachusetts
Press, 2014), p. 103.

54 William F. Buckley, Jr., to Norman Mailer, November 18, 1964, box 542,
folder 3, Mailer Papers.

55 Norman Mailer to William F. Buckley, Jr., November 24, 1964, box 542,
folder 3, Mailer Papers.

56 George H. Gallup, *The Gallup Poll: Public Opinion, 1935–1971*, Vol. 3 (New
York: Random House, 1972), p. 1764. For the transition from other problems to race, see also pp. 1723–24, 1769, 1770, 1786, 1788, and 1802.

Chapter 5. American Dreams

1 For a good exploration of the complex relationship between Mailer and
Baldwin, see W. J. Wetherby, *Squaring Off: Mailer vs. Buckley* (New York:
Mason/Charter, 1977). For the quotation, see pp. 31–32.

2 For Mailer approaching the *New York Times Book Review* asking to review
Baldwin's *Giovanni's Room*, see Norman Mailer to James Baldwin, August
16, 1956, box 531, folder 10, Mailer Papers.

3 Wetherby, *Squaring Off*, p. 31.

4 "Nation: The Root of the Negro Problem," *Time*, May 17, 1963, available at
http://content.time.com/time/subscriber/article/0,33009,830326,00.html
(accessed November 5, 2014).

5 Norman Mailer, "The White Negro," *Dissent* (1957) and republished in
Norman Mailer, *Advertisements for Myself* (New York: G. P. Putnam's Sons,
1959; quote from Cambridge, MA: Harvard University Press, 1992), p. 341.

6 James Baldwin, "A Black Boy Looks at a White Boy," *Esquire* (May 1961),
and reprinted in James Baldwin, *The Price of the Ticket: Collected Nonfiction,
1948–1985* (New York: St. Martin's Press, 1985), pp. 289–303, quotation
from pp. 289–90.

7 Baldwin, *Price of the Ticket*, p. 292.

8 Norman Mailer to Francis "Fig" Gwaltney, November 9, 1963, box 566,
folder 4, Mailer Papers.

9 Mailer revealed the price in a letter: Norman Mailer to Adeline "Lub"
Lubell-Naiman, November 5, 1963, box 567, folder 17, Mailer Papers.

10 Norman Mailer to Francis "Fig" Gwaltney, November 9, 1963, box 566,
folder 4, Mailer Papers.

11 Norman Mailer, *An American Dream* (New York: Dial Press, 1965; quote
from New York: Vintage, 1999), pp. 31–32.

12 Norman Mailer to Adeline "Lub" Lubell-Naiman, November 5, 1963, box 567, folder 17, Mailer Papers.

13 Norman Mailer to Don Carpenter, June 1, 1964, box 542, folder 5, Mailer Papers.

14 Norman Mailer to Francis "Fig" Gwaltney, December 20, 1963, box 566, folder 4, Mailer Papers.

15 Mailer, *An American Dream*, p. 134.

16 For Cybill Shepherd playing Cherry, see Norman Mailer to Peter Bogdanovich, August 8, 1975, box 636, folder 4, Mailer Papers.

17 Mailer, *An American Dream*, p. 45.

18 Mary V. Dearborn, *Mailer: A Biography* (New York: Houghton Mifflin Company, 1999), p. 205.

19 Norman Mailer to Mickey Knox, February 17, 1964, found in J. Michael Lennon, *Norman Mailer: A Double Life* (New York: Simon & Schuster, 2013), p. 339.

20 Norman Mailer to Eiichi Yamanishi, April 17, 1964, box 553, folder 6, Mailer Papers.

21 Jason Epstein to Norman Mailer, March 9, 1965, box 569, folder 3, Mailer Papers.

22 Norman Mailer to Jason Epstein, March 25, 1965, box 569, folder 3, Mailer Papers.

23 Jason Epstein to Norman Mailer, April 1, 1965, box 569, folder 3, Mailer Papers.

24 Norman Mailer to Eiichi Yamanishi, June 3, 1965, box 553, folder 7, Mailer Papers.

25 Norman Mailer to Susie Mailer, April 1965, box 569, folder 2, Mailer Papers.

26 Eliot Fremont-Smith, "Mailer's Fantasy About Mailer," *New York Times*, March 17, 1965, p. 43.

27 Joan Didion, "A Social Eye," *National Review*, April 20, 1965, pp. 329–30.

28 Norman Mailer to William F. Buckley, Jr., April 20, 1965, box 36, Mailer folder, Buckley Papers.

29 Patricia Buckley to Norman Mailer, n.d. (probably 1965), box 542, folder 3, Mailer Papers.

30 William F. Buckley, "From the Right: *Life* Goes to Norman Mailer," "On the Right," for release September 25 or 26, 1965.

31 "Never the Champion, Always the Challenger: A First-Rank Writer's Reckless Quest for—What?" *Life*, September 24, 1965, p. 100.

32 For Buckley's copy, see box 36, Mailer folder, Buckley Papers.

33 Buckley, "*Life* Goes to Norman Mailer."

34 Buckley's collection of reviews on *An American Dream* can be found in box 36, Mailer folder, Buckley Papers.

35 Buckley, "*Life* Goes to Norman Mailer."

36 Mailer Papers includes the rough version of the column that was sent to newspapers across the country for syndication.

37 Norman Mailer to "Bill-elect," October 18, 1965, box 542, folder 3, Mailer Papers.

38 William F. Buckley, Jr., to Norman Mailer, n.d. (probably late October 1965), box 542, folder 3, Mailer Papers.

39 Wetherby, *Squaring Off*, p. 137.

40 Mailer, *An American Dream*, pp. 180, 185.

41 Norman Podhoretz, "My Negro Problem—and Ours," *Commentary* (February 1963): 93–101, quotation at 97.

42 Andrew O'Hagan, "Norman Mailer: The Art of Fiction, No. 193," *The Paris Review* (Summer 2007), http://www.theparisreview.org/interviews/5775/ the-art-of-fiction-no-193-norman-mailer (accessed May 28, 2014).

43 Norman Mailer to Eiichi Yamanishi, June 3, 1965, box 553, folder 7, Mailer Papers.

44 Ibid.

Chapter 6. The Most Hated Man in America

1 The debate is easily found on the Internet, but a slightly condensed transcription appeared in "The American Dream and the American Negro," *New York Times Sunday Magazine*, March 7, 1965, pp. 32–33, 87–89.

2 William F. Buckley, Jr., *Up From Liberalism* (New York: McDowellm Obolensky Inc., 1959; quote from New York: Stein and Day, 1984), p. 157.

3 William F. Buckley, Jr., "Segregation and Democracy," *National Review* (January 25, 1956): 5.

4 William F. Buckley, Jr., "The South Girds Its Loins," *National Review* (February 29, 1956).

5 William F. Buckley, Jr., "Why The South Must Prevail," *National Review* (August 24, 1957): 149.

6 Ibid.

7 Buckley, *Up From Liberalism*, p. 155.

8 Ibid., p. 157.

9 William F. Buckley, Jr., "Desegregation: Will It Work?" *Saturday Review*, November 11, 1961, pp. 21–22.

10 William F. Buckley, Jr., to Edward T. Kraft, December 1, 1964, box 31, KPFA-Kraft folder, Buckley Papers.

11 For an excellent discussion of the bootstraps argument and its role in the American conservative resurgence of the 1970s, see Matthew Frye Jacobson, *Roots Too: White Ethnic Revival in Post-Civil Rights America* (New York and Cambridge, MA: Harvard University Press, 2008). For the structural inhibitions created to limit the possibilities for African Americans, see Thomas J. Sugrue, *Sweet Land of Liberty: The Forgotten Struggle for Civil Rights in the North* (New York: Random House, 2009).

12 *Public Papers of the Presidents of the United States: Lyndon B. Johnson, 1965*, Vol. 2, entry 301 (Washington, D.C.: Government Printing Office, 1966), pp. 635–40.

13 As recounted in Carl T. Bogus, *Buckley: William F. Buckley, Jr. and the Rise of American Conservatism* (New York: Bloomsbury, 2011), p. 161.

14 Ibid.

15 See note 1.

16 Garry Wills, "Buckley, Buckley, Bow Wow Wow," *Esquire*, January 1968, found in Bogus, *Buckley*, pp. 172–73.

17 On Selma, see Taylor Branch, *At Canaan's Edge: America in the King Years, 1965–68* (New York: Simon and Schuster, 2007), pp. 5–193; and see Townsend Davis, *Weary Feet, Rested Souls: A Guided History of the Civil Rights Movement* (New York: W. W. Norton & Company, 1998), pp. 88–120.

18 *Public Papers of the Presidents of the United States: Lyndon B. Johnson, 1965*, Vol. 1, entry 107 (Washington, D. C.: Government Printing Office, 1966), pp. 281–87.

19 These recollections are from David Wyatt, *When America Turned: Reckoning with 1968* (Amherst: University of Massachusetts Press, 2014), p. 105.

20 Buckley reprinted the speech in William F. Buckley, Jr., *The Unmaking of a Mayor* (New York: Bantam Books, 1966).

21 William F. Buckley, "Remarks to the New York Police Department Holy Name Society," April 4, 1965, reprinted in Buckley, *The Unmaking of a Mayor*, pp. 355–59, quotation at 359.

22 For a recapitulation, see Buckley, *The Unmaking of a Mayor*, pp. 10–11.

23 Sam Tanenhaus, "The Buckley Effect," *New York Times Magazine*, October 2, 2005.

24 Norman Mailer to William F. Buckley, Jr., April 20, 1965, box 36, Mailer folder, Buckley Papers.

25 Ibid.

26 William F. Buckley, Jr., to Norman Mailer, n.d., box 542, "Correspondence WFB and Patsy, 1962–66" folder, Mailer Papers.

27 When Buckley recounted this story the following year, he put a gentler gloss on it. He told *Harper's* Larry King that he had done it as a joke because he knew Mailer would "immediately go to the index to evaluate his own role, and that 'Hi!' will just kill him!" See Larry King, "God, man, and William F. Buckley," *Harper's*, March 1967.

28 James Carney, "10 Questions for William F. Buckley," *Time*, April 12, 2004.

29 Kevin Phillips, *The Emerging Republican Majority* (New Rochelle, NY: Arlington House, 1970), p. 37.

Chapter 7. Catching All the Falling Bodies

1 James T. Patterson, *The Eve of Destruction: How 1965 Transformed America* (New York: Basic Books, 2012), pp. xi–xii.

2 "New York, Greatest City in the World—and Everything Is Wrong with It," *New York Herald Tribune*, January 25, 1965, and found in Vincent J. Cannato, *The Ungovernable City: John Lindsay and His Struggle to Save New York* (New York: Basic Books, 2001), pp. 22–23.

3 Found in Cannato, *The Ungovernable City*, p. 30.
4 Sam Tanenhaus, "The Buckley Effect," *New York Times Magazine*, October 2, 2005.
5 William F. Buckley, Jr., *The Unmaking of a Mayor* (New York: Bantam Books, 1966), p. 105.
6 Tanenhaus, "The Buckley Effect."
7 William F. Buckley, Jr., "Mayor, Anyone?" "On the Right" column for May 22 or 23, 1965.
8 Buckley, *The Unmaking of a Mayor*, p. 102.
9 Ibid., p. 97.
10 Tanenhaus, "The Buckley Effect."
11 For Buckley's thoughts on Lindsay, see Buckley, *The Unmaking of a Mayor*, pp. 42–47 and 67–96; and for his hopes that the Conservative Party could alter the shape of the Republican Party, see Buckley, *The Unmaking of a Mayor*, pp. 67–96.
12 "Statement by Wm. F. Buckley Jr., Announcing His Candidacy For Mayor of New York, June 24, 1965," reprinted in *National Review* (July 13, 1965): 586–89.
13 Buckley, *The Unmaking of a Mayor*, p. 345.
14 Norman Mailer, "Norman Mailer on Lindsay & the City," *Village Voice*, October 28, 1965.
15 Buckley, *The Unmaking of a Mayor*, pp. 367–68.
16 William F. Buckley to Norman Mailer, May 26, 1966, box 542, folder 3, Mailer Papers.
17 Tanenhaus, "The Buckley Effect."
18 All press quotations come from the extended index of Buckley, *The Unmaking of a Mayor*, pp. 366–71.
19 Tanenhaus, "The Buckley Effect."
20 Cannato, *The Ungovernable City*, p. 53.
21 Found in Buckley, *The Unmaking of a Mayor*, pp. 336–37, and Tanenhaus, "The Buckley Effect."
22 Tanenhaus, "The Buckley Effect"
23 "Statement by Wm. F. Buckley Jr., Announcing His Candidacy For Mayor of New York, June 24, 1965," reprinted in *National Review* (July 13, 1965): 588.
24 Norman Mailer to "Bill-elect," October 18, 1965, box 542, folder 3, Mailer Papers.
25 William F. Buckley, Jr., to Norman Mailer, June 30, 1965, box 36, Mailer folder, Buckley Papers.
26 Norman Mailer to William F. Buckley, Jr., July 14, 1965, box 36, Mailer folder, Buckley Papers.
27 William F. Buckley, Jr., to Norman Mailer, n.d., box 542, WFB and Patsy correspondence, 1962–66 folder, Mailer Papers.
28 Norman Mailer to William F. Buckley, Jr., October 18, 1965, box 36, Mailer folder, Buckley Papers.
29 Buckley, *The Unmaking of a Mayor*, p. 340.

30 It should be pointed out that Buckley's voice of conservatism brought several white working-class voters to the Republican Party, and these voters ended up voting for Lindsay—and staying Republicans. See Cannato, *The Ungovernable City*, p. 71.

31 Buckley, *The Unmaking of a Mayor*, p. 344.

32 Ibid., p. 350.

33 Norman Mailer, "In the Red Light: A History of the Republican Convention in 1964," *Esquire* (November 1964) and reprinted in Norman Mailer, *Cannibals and Christians* (New York: Dial Press, 1966), p. 44.

34 Norman Mailer, "Lindsay and the City," reprinted in Mailer, *Cannibals and Christians*, p. 63.

35 Ibid.

36 Ibid., p. 64.

37 Norman Mailer to William F. Buckley, Jr., November 24, 1964, box 31, Mailer folder, Buckley Papers.

38 Norman Mailer to William F. Buckley, Jr., November 24, 1964, box 542, folder 3, Mailer Papers.

39 Norman Mailer to "Bill-elect," October 18, 1965, box 542, folder 3, Mailer Papers.

40 Norman Mailer to William F. Buckley, Jr., June 8, 1965, box 36, Mailer folder, Buckley Papers.

Chapter 8. Fly in the Ointment

1 Plimpton recalls the scene in his oral biography of Capote. George Plimpton, *Truman Capote: In Which Various Friends, Enemies, Acquaintances, and Detractors Recall His Turbulent Career* (New York: Doubleday, 1997), p. 250.

2 The comment was made by R. Couri Hay and found in Plimpton, *Truman Capote*, p. 251.

3 James T Patterson, *The Eve of Destruction: How 1965 Transformed America* (New York: Basic Books, 2012), p. 13. For more examples, see Howard Brick, *Age of Contradiction: American Thought and Culture in the 1960s* (New York: Twayne Publishers, 1998), pp. 152–53, Todd Gitlin, *The Sixties: Years of Hope, Days of Rage* (New York: Bantam, 1987), pp. 178–79, or David Farber, *The Age of Great Dreams: America in the 1960s* (New York: Hill and Wang, 1994), pp. 153–56.

4 There are plenty of good descriptions of the Vietnam War. See, for example, Michael Belknap, *The Vietnam War on Trial: The Mai Lai Massacre and Court-Martial of Lieutenant Calley* (Lawrence: University of Kansas Press, 1999), chapter 1, and Farber, *The Age of Great Dreams*, pp. 117–37.

5 Dwight D. Eisenhower, *Mandate for Change, 1953–1956: The White House Years* (New York: Doubleday, 1963), p. 372.

6 Jerry Rubin quoted in *Mailer: His Life and Times*, ed. Peter Manso (New York: Washington Square Press, 1985), pp. 406–7, and Hilary Mills, *Mailer: A Biography* (New York: Empire Books, 1982; quote from New York: McGraw-Hill, 1984), p. 290.

7   Norman Mailer, "A Speech at Berkeley on Vietnam Day," reprinted in Norman Mailer, *Cannibals and Christians* (New York: Dial Press, 1966), p. 70.

8   Ibid., p. 75.

9   Ibid., pp. 79–80.

10 Ibid., pp. 81–82.

11 Paul Krassner, quoted in Manso, ed., *Mailer*, p. 407.

12 Rubin quoted in Manso, ed., *Mailer*, pp. 406–7, and Mills, *Mailer*, p. 291.

13 Abbie Hoffman quoted in Mills, *Mailer*, p. 291.

14 Don Carpenter, quoted in Mailer, *Manso*, ed., p. 408.

15 Mailer, *Cannibals and Christians*, p. viii.

16 Norman Mailer to Eiichi Yamanishi, June 3, 1965, box 553, folder 7, Mailer Papers.

17 William F. Buckley, Jr., "In the End, We Will Bury Him," address to a rally protesting the visit to the United States by Nikita Khrushchev, Carnegie Hall, New York, September 17, 1960, reprinted in William F. Buckley, Jr., *Let Us Talk of Many Things: The Collected Speeches* (New York: Forum, 2000; quote from New York: Basic Books, 2008), pp. 33–38.

18 William F. Buckley, Jr., *National Review*, January 12, 1965, found in John B. Judis, *William F. Buckley, Jr.: Patron Saint of the Conservatives* (New York: Simon and Schuster, 1988), p. 268.

19 A good discussion of Buckley's position on rollback and Cuba can be found in Carl T. Bogus, *Buckley: William F. Buckley, Jr. and the Rise of American Conservatism* (New York: Bloomsbury, 2011), pp. 246–55.

20 Ibid.

21 Donald Lambro to Norman Mailer, August 13, 1966, box 569, folder 22, Mailer Papers.

22 Norman Mailer to Donald Lambro, September 24, 1966, box 569, folder 22, Mailer Papers.

23 William F. Buckley, Jr., to Norman Mailer, February 16, 1966, box 569, folder 22, Mailer Papers.

24 Norman Mailer to William F. Buckley, Jr., n.d. (probably March 1966), box 570, folder 10, Mailer Papers.

25 Mailer's quotation found in Plimpton, *Truman Capote*, p. 134.

26 Norman Mailer, *Advertisements for Myself* (New York: G. P. Putnam's Sons, 1959; quote from Cambridge, MA: Harvard University Press, 1992), p. 465.

27 For Capote's efforts at selling his book, see Deborah Davis, *Party of the Century: The Fabulous Story of Truman Capote and His Black and White Ball* (New York: John Wiley & Sons Inc., 2006), pp. 96–100, quotations at pp. 98 and 96.

28 Ibid., p. 113.

29 Ibid., p. 121.

30 Katharine Graham quoted in Plimpton, *Truman Capote*, p. 248.

31 As quoted in ibid., p. 276.

32 Leo Lerman quoted in ibid., p. 249.

33 Quotation found in *Too Brief a Treat: The Letters of Truman Capote*, ed. Gerald Clarke (New York: Vintage Books, 2004), p. 274.

34 Charlotte Curtis, "Capote's Black and White Ball: 'The Most Exquisite of Spectator Sports,'" *New York Times*, November 29, 1966, p. 53.

35 As quoted in Plimpton, *Truman Capote*, p. 264.

36 Davis, *Party of the Century*, p. 233.

37 Ibid., pp. 232–33.

38 Ibid., p. 230.

39 As quoted in Plimpton, *Truman Capote*, p. 215.

40 As quoted in ibid., pp. 214–15.

41 As quoted in ibid., p. 238.

42 Lumet and Mailer quoted in ibid., p. 258.

43 As quoted in Mary V. Dearborn, *Mailer: A Biography* (New York: Houghton Mifflin Company, 1999), p. 223.

44 Buckley and Galbraith quoted in Plimpton, *Truman Capote*, p. 261.

45 Mailer quoted in ibid., pp. 276–77.

46 From W. J. Wetherby, *Squaring Off: Mailer vs. Buckley* (New York: Mason/ Charter, 1977), p. 123.

47 Mailer quoted in Plimpton, *Truman Capote*, pp. 268–69.

48 Ibid., p. 269.

49 Ibid.

50 Davis, *Party of the Century*, p. 233.

51 William F. Buckley, Jr., "The Politics of The Capote Ball," *Esquire* (December 1967): 160.

52 Pete Hamill is quoted in ibid.

53 Ibid., 159.

54 Ibid., 159–60.

55 Ibid., 116.

56 Found in Davis, *Party of the Century*, p. 246.

57 Mailer, "In the Red Light: A History of the Republican Convention in 1964," *Esquire* (Nov. 1964), and reproduced in Mailer, *Cannibals and Christians*, p. 26.

58 Paul Potter, "The Incredible War," April 17, 1965, and reprinted in *"Takin' It to the Streets": A Sixties Reader*, Alexander Bloom and Wini Breines, eds. (New York: Oxford University Press, 2003), pp. 174–78.

59 Farber, *The Age of Great Dreams*, p. 167.

Chapter 9. A Searing Love of Country

1 Norman Mailer, *The Armies of the Night: History as a Novel, the Novel as History* (New York: Signet, 1968), pp. 19–20.

2 Dotson Rader, who was there, tells the story in *Mailer: His Life and Times*, ed. Peter Manso (New York: Washington Square Press, 1985), pp. 454–55.

3 Mailer, *Armies*, p. 20.

4 Ibid., p. 43.

5 Ibid., pp. 91–92.

6 Ibid., p. 124.

7 Ibid., p. 129.

8 On the fate of MacDonald and Lowell, see Mailer, *Armies*, pp. 293–95. For the poem, see Robert Lowell, "The March," first printed in *New York Review of Books*, November 23, 1967, and available online at http://www.nybooks.com/articles/archives/1967/nov/23/the-march/ (accessed November 5, 2014).

9 As quoted in Mailer, *Armies*, p. 303.

10 Ibid., p. 306.

11 Ibid., pp. 307–8.

12 Ibid., p. 157.

13 Robert McNamara quoted in Maurice Isserman and Michael Kazin, *America Divided: The Civil War of the 1960s*, 3rd ed. (New York: Oxford University Press, 2008), p. 194.

14 Norman Mailer, "Armies of the Night," *Firing Line*, May 28, 1968, Firing Line Collection, program 102, Hoover Institution Archives, copyright Stanford University.

15 J. Michael Lennon, *Norman Mailer: A Double Life* (New York: Simon & Schuster, 2013), p. 390.

16 Ibid., p. 391.

17 Hilary Mills, *Mailer: A Biography* (New York: Empire Books, 1982; quote from New York: McGraw-Hill, 1984), p. 322.

18 Ibid.

19 Ibid.

20 Robert Lowell to Norman Mailer, March 13, 1968, box 580, folder 3, Mailer Papers.

21 Found in Mills, *Mailer*, p. 323.

22 Robert Lowell to Norman Mailer, March 13, 1968, box 580, folder 3, Mailer Papers.

23 Mailer, *Armies*, p. 136.

24 Ibid., p. 77.

25 Ibid., p. 204.

26 Ibid., p. 160.

27 Alfred Kazin, "The Trouble He's Seen," *New York Times Book Review*, May 5, 1968, p. BR26.

28 Richard Gilman, *The New Republic*, excerpted and reprinted in Manso, *Mailer*, pp. 466–67.

29 Eliot Fremont-Smith, "Mailer on the March," *New York Times*, April 26, 1968, p. 41.

30 Mailer, *Armies*, p. 33, italics mine.

31 Robert Lowell to Norman Mailer, March 13, 1968, box 580, folder 3, Mailer Papers.

32 Dwight Macdonald to Norman Mailer, April 19, 1968, box 580, folder 4, Mailer Papers.

33 Jerry Rubin quoted in Manso, *Mailer*, p. 461.

34 William, F. Buckley, Jr., "Legal Demonstrations?" "On the Right" column for March 12, 1968.

35 Freeman quoted in John B. Judis, *William F. Buckley, Jr.: Patron Saint of the Conservatives* (New York: Simon and Schuster, 1988), p. 267.

36 Norman Thomas, "Vietnam: Pull Out? Stay In? Escalate?" *Firing Line*, April 8, 1966.

37 The famous remark appeared in "The Sniper," *Time*, November 3, 1967.

38 Judis, *Buckley*, p. 267.

39 "The Sniper," *Time*.

40 *Time* cover, November 3, 1967.

41 "The Sniper," *Time*, November 3, 1967.

42 Norman Mailer, *Why Are We in Vietnam?* (New York: Henry Holt and Co., 1967), pp. 203 and 208.

43 Ibid., p. 7.

44 Norman Mailer to Eiichi Yamanishi, August 30, 1967, box 577, folder 2, Mailer Papers.

45 The reviews are reprinted in Manso, *Mailer*, p. 454.

46 William F. Buckley, Jr., "Let the Rich Alone," December 30, 1967, reprinted in William F. Buckley, Jr., *The Jeweler's Eye: A Book of Irresistible Political Reflections* (New York: Putnam, 1968), p. 276.

47 Norman Mailer, "Armies of the Night," *Firing Line*, May 28, 1968, Firing Line Collection, program 102, Hoover Institution Archives, copyright Stanford University.

48 Mailer, *Armies*, p. 131.

49 Mel Lyman, "Buckley & Mailer," *New York Avatar*, August 18, 1968, p. 18.

50 "Accepting the National Book Award," in Norman Mailer, *Existential Errands* (New York: Little, Brown, 1972), p. 254.

51 Ibid., p. 255.

52 Mailer, *Armies*, p. 320.

Chapter 10. The Assassination of Politics

1 Mailer to Eiichi Yamanishi, June 15, 1968, box 584, folder 5, Mailer Papers.

2 Quoted in A. J. Langguth, *Our Vietnam: The War 1954–1975* (New York, Simon & Schuster, 2000), p. 467.

3 For a reading of his iconic newscast, and for Cronkite's reflections on it, see "Final Words: Cronkite's Vietnam Commentary," *NPR News*, July 18, 2009, http://www.npr.org/templates/story/story.php?storyId=106775685 (accessed June 1, 2014).

4 Walter Cronkite, *A Reporter's Life* (New York: Alfred A. Knopf, 1996), p. 258.

5 Quoted in Todd Gitlin, *The Sixties: Years of Hope, Days of Rage* (New York: Bantam, 1987), p. 299.

6 Quoted in David Wyatt, *When America Turned: Reckoning with 1968* (Amherst: University of Massachusetts Press, 2014), p. 38.

7　William F. Buckley, Jr., "Kennedy Has A Secret," "On the Right" column for April 16, 1968.

8　"President Lyndon B. Johnson's Address to the Nation Announcing Steps to Limit the War in Vietnam and Reporting His Decision Not to Seek Reelection," online archives of the Lyndon B. Johnson Presidential Library, http://www.lbjlib.utexas.edu/johnson/archives.hom/speeches.hom/680331.asp (accessed October 25, 2014).

9　William F. Buckley, Jr., "The Withdrawal of Johnson," "On the Right" column for April 4, 1968.

10　Wyatt, *When America Turned*, p. 91.

11　Quoted in Taylor Branch, *At Canaan's Edge: America in the King Years, 1965–68* (New York: Simon and Schuster, 2007), p. 734.

12　Quoted in Wyatt, *When America Turned*, p. 155.

13　Westmoreland quoted in ibid., p. 115.

14　Harry Edwards quoted in "The Sixties: 1968" (season 1, episode 8), CNN, August 1, 2014.

15　William Sloane Coffin, *Once to Every Man: A Memoir* (New York: Atheneum, 1977), p. 302.

16　Quoted in Bruce J. Schulman, *The Seventies: The Great Shift in American Culture, Society, and Politics* (New York: Da Capo Press, 2002), p. 9.

17　Ibid.

18　Joan Didion, *Slouching Towards Bethlehem* (New York: Farrar, Straus & Giroux, 1968), p. 123.

19　Pete Hamill, "Two Minutes to Midnight: The Very Last Hurrah," *Village Voice*, June 13, 1968.

20　Norman Mailer, "RFK," read to Tom Harris of the Associated Press, June 6, 1968, box 581, folder 10, Mailer Papers.

21　John F. Kennedy, "Address on the First Anniversary of the Alliance for Progress," March 13, 1962, available online in Gerhard Peters and John T. Woolley, *The American Presidency Project*. http://www.presidency.ucsb.edu/ws/?pid=9100 (accessed October 25, 2014).

22　Norman Mailer, "Some Dirt in the Talk," *Esquire* (December 1967), reprinted in Norman Mailer, *Existential Errands* (New York: Little, Brown, 1972), p. 103.

23　Ibid., pp. 121–22 and 110.

24　Hilary Mills, *Mailer: A Biography* (New York: Empire Books, 1982; quote from New York: McGraw-Hill, 1984), pp. 327–28.

25　Ibid.

26　William F. Buckley, Jr., to Norman Mailer, July 16, 1968, box 52, Mailer folder, Buckley Papers.

27　John B. Judis, *William F. Buckley, Jr.: Patron Saint of the Conservatives* (New York: Simon and Schuster, 1988), p. 269.

28　William F. Buckley, Jr., "The Politics of Assassination," *Esquire* (October 1968): 163 and 230.

29 William F. Buckley, Jr., to Norman Mailer, July 16, 1968, box 52, Mailer folder, Buckley Papers.

30 William F. Buckley, Jr., "Did You Kill Martin Luther King?" April 19, 1968, and reprinted in William F. Buckley, Jr., *Let Us Talk of Many Things: The Collected Speeches* (New York: Forum, 2000; quote from New York: Basic Books, 2008), pp. 117–23.

31 Norman Mailer to William F. Buckley, Jr., July 30, 1968, box 52, Mailer folder, Buckley Papers.

32 "Loss" is found in Mailer, "A Course in Film-Making," *Existential Errands*, p. 151; the cutting process is described in Norman Mailer to Eiichi Yamanishi, December 12, 1968, box 584, folder 5, Mailer Papers.

33 The cameraman's reflection is recorded in Mills, *Mailer*, p. 330.

34 Mailer, "A Course in Film-Making," *Existential Errands*, p. 167.

35 William F. Buckley, Jr., to Norman Mailer, August 1, 1968, box 52, Mailer folder, Buckley Papers.

36 Norman Mailer to William F. Buckley, Jr., July 30, 1968, box 52, Mailer folder, Buckley Papers.

Chapter 11 Halfway to Burke

1 Robert Sherrill, "Miami Beach, the All-Too-American City," *New York Times*, August 4, 1968, p. 7.

2 Norman Mailer, *Miami and the Siege of Chicago* (New York: D. I. Fine, 1968; quote from New York: *New York Review of Books*, 2008, p. 12.

3 Ibid., p. 14.

4 Headley quoted in Sherrill, "Miami Beach, the All-Too-American City," 54.

5 The debate is easily found on the internet, including at http://www.youtube .com/watch?v=jy68qXMcGn8 (accessed December 5, 2013).

6 John B. Judis, *William F. Buckley, Jr.: Patron Saint of the Conservatives* (New York: Simon and Schuster, 1988), p. 291.

7 Ibid., p. 290.

8 Mailer, *Miami and the Siege of Chicago*, p. 68.

9 Richard Nixon, "If Mob Rule Takes Hold in the U.S.," 1966, reprinted in *"Takin' It to the Streets": A Sixties Reader*, Alexander Bloom and Wini Breines, eds. (New York: Oxford University Press, 2003), pp. 294–97.

10 Quoted in David Wyatt, *When America Turned: Reckoning with 1968* (Amherst: University of Massachusetts Press, 2014), p. 122.

11 Joe McGinniss, "Rapt Young Right-Wingers Hear 'Rambling' Buckley," *Philadelphia Inquirer*, August 7, 1968, p. 3.

12 Tom Wicker, "Reagan Avows Candidacy," *New York Times*, August 6, 1968, p. 1.

13 William F. Buckley, Jr., "Condescending at Miami," "On the Right" column for August 6, 1968.

14 Bill Barry, "A Trip Into Idea Land With William Buckley," *Miami News*, April 18, 1967, p. 6A.

15 Mailer, *Miami and the Siege of Chicago*, p. 42.
16 Ibid., p. 44
17 Ibid., p. 48.
18 Ibid., p. 35.
19 Ibid., pp. 35–36.
20 Ibid., pp. 81–82.
21 William F. Buckley, Jr., "Reform the Conventions," "On the Right" column for August 17 or 18, 1968.
22 William F. Buckley, Jr., to Norman Mailer, August 1, 1968, box 52, Mailer folder, Buckley Papers.
23 Mailer, *Miami and the Siege of Chicago*, p. 114.
24 Ibid., p. 140.
25 Ibid., p. 144.
26 Ibid.
27 Ibid., pp. 105–9 and 132.
28 "Protest Riot Duty," *Chicago Tribune*, August 25, 1968, p. 8.
29 Wyatt, *When America Turned*, p. 238.
30 Mailer, *Miami and the Siege of Chicago*, p. 146.
31 Ibid., p. 104.
32 Tom Hayden, *Reunion: A Memoir* (New York: Random House, 1988), p. 301.
33 Mailer, *Miami and the Siege of Chicago*, p. 148.
34 Quoted in ibid., pp. 151–53.
35 Hayden, *Reunion*, p. 315.
36 David Lewis Stein, *Living the Revolution: The Yippies in Chicago* (Indianapolis: Bobbs-Merrill, 1969), p. 117, and quoted in Wyatt, *When America Turned*, p. 241.
37 *Rights in Conflict: Convention Week in Chicago, August 25–29, 1968*, Report Submitted by Daniel Walker, director of the Chicago Study Team, to the National Commission on the Causes and Prevention of Violence (New York: E. P. Dutton, 1968).
38 Quoted in *Rights of Conflict* and found in Wyatt, *When America Turned*, p. 241.
39 J. Anthony Lukas, "Humphrey Nominated on the First Ballot after his Plank on Vietnam is Approved; Police Battle Demonstrators in Streets; Hundreds Injured," *New York Times*, August 29, 1968.
40 Todd Gitlin, *The Sixties: Years of Hope, Days of Rage* (New York: Bantam, 1987), p. 334.
41 Buckley's letter to Nancy Reagan from October 1969 is quoted in Judis, *Buckley*, p. 291.
42 J. Anthony Lukas, "Humphrey Nominated on the First Ballot . . ."
43 The debate is widely available on the Internet and the context is described well in Judis, *Buckley*, pp. 288–95.
44 Found in Judis, *Buckley*, p. 294.
45 Mailer, *Miami and the Siege of Chicago*, p. 182.
46 Ibid., pp. 186–87.

47 Ibid., p. 188.

48 Ibid., p. 223.

49 William F. Buckley, Jr., "Toujours Humphrey," "On the Right" column for September 3, 1968.

50 William F. Buckley, Jr., "On Rioting," "On the Right" column for September 5, 1968.

51 Buckley, "Are the Rioters Communists?" "On the Right" column for September 21 or 22, 1968.

52 Mailer, *Miami and the Siege of Chicago*, pp. 222–23.

Chapter 12. One Last Try

1 Richard Nixon: "Inaugural Address," January 20, 1969, available online in Gerhard Peters and John T. Woolley, *The American Presidency Project.* http://www.presidency.ucsb.edu/ws/?pid=1941 (accessed October 25, 2014).

2 William F. Buckley, Jr., to Norman Mailer, n.d. (probably February 1969) sent from Switzerland, box 586, folder 4, Mailer Papers.

3 Jack Newfield, "Hatred Amid the Junk," *New York* (November 18, 1968): 57.

4 Norman Mailer to William F. Buckley, Jr., March 7, 1969, box 586, folder 4, Mailer Papers.

5 James K. Galbraith, "On Bill Buckley," *New Republic*, February 28, 2008, and available online at http://www.newrepublic.com/blog/the-plank/james-k-galbraith-bill-buckley (accessed November 5, 2014).

6 Memo to Galbraith, Mailer, Starr, Stoops, Wills, from Bill Buckley, April 8, 1969, box 586, folder 3, Mailer Papers.

7 Norman Mailer to William F. Buckley, Jr., April 14, 1969; penciled note written by Mailer atop Memo to Galbraith, Mailer, Starr, Stoops, Wills, from Bill Buckley, April 8, 1969, box 586, folder 3, Mailer Papers.

8 Norman Mailer to Don Carpenter, January 27, 1965, box 542, folder 5, Mailer Papers.

9 Norman Mailer, "Cities Higher Than Mountains," *New York Times Magazine*, January 31, 1965, and reprinted in Mailer, *Cannibals and Christians*, p. 235.

10 Anthony Lane, "The Joy of Bricks," *The New Yorker*, April 27, 1998, pp. 102–3.

11 *Mailer: His Life and Times*, ed. Peter Manso (New York: Washington Square Press, 1985), pp. 418–19.

12 Mary V. Dearborn, *Mailer: A Biography* (New York: Houghton Mifflin Company, 1999), p. 218.

13 As quoted in Mary V. Dearborn, *Mailer: A Biography* (New York: Houghton Mifflin Company, 1999), p. 401.

14 William F. Buckley, Jr., "Revolution in Fun City," "On the Right" column for June 21 or 22, 1969.

15 As quoted in Vincent J. Cannato, *The Ungovernable City: John Lindsay and His Struggle to Save New York* (New York: Basic Books, 2001), p. 306.

16 Ibid., p. 337.

17 Damon Stetson, "Garbage Strike is Ended on Rockefeller's Terms," *New York Times*, February 11, 1968, pp. 1 and 76.

18 Ibid.

19 William F. Buckley, Jr., "Mayor Lindsay and the Jewish Community," "On the Right" column for January 1969.

20 Quoted in Cannato, *The Ungovernable City*, p. 396.

21 Ibid., pp. 396–97.

22 William F. Buckley, Jr., "Confusion Abounding in New York," "On the Right" column for October 16, 1969.

23 Joe Flaherty, *Managing Mailer* (New York: Coward-McCann, 1970), p. 31.

24 *New York*, May 5, 1969, cover.

25 As quoted in Flaherty, *Managing Mailer*, p. 15.

26 Ibid., p. 20.

27 Bernard Weinraub, "Mailer Aims to be Everyman's Mayor," *New York Times*, April 17, 1969.

28 Pete Hamill, "The Revolt of the White Lower Middle Class," *New York*, April 14, 1969.

29 Norman Mailer, *Miami and the Siege of Chicago* (New York: D. I. Fine, 1968; quote from New York: *New York Review of Books*, 2008), p. 51.

30 Ibid., p. 53.

31 As quoted in Flaherty, *Managing Mailer*, p. 21.

32 Norman Mailer, "Why They Run," box 83, folder 5, Mailer Papers.

33 Ibid.

34 Ibid.

35 Ibid.

36 Ibid.

37 Flaherty, *Managing Mailer*, p. 52.

38 Norman Mailer, "At the Village Gate," found in Peter Manso, ed., *Running Against the Machine: The Mailer-Breslin Campaign* (New York: Doubleday and Company, 1969), p. 64.

39 Mailer, "Why They Run."

40 Bernard Weinraub, "Mailer Says that Alienation is Major Problem in City," *New York Times*, May 12, 1969, p. 26.

41 The Doors to Norman Mailer, n.d. 1969, folder 3, box 589, Mailer Papers.

42 Flaherty, *Managing Mailer*, pp. 48–49.

43 Ibid., p. 59.

44 Ibid., p. 96.

45 Ibid., pp. 98–99.

46 Ibid., p. 97.

47 Ibid., p. 73.

48 Ibid., p. 154.

49 The speech is reprinted in Manso, ed., *Running Against the Machine*, pp. 78–79.

50 Breslin recalled the incident in Sam Roberts, "Mailer's Nonfiction Legacy: His 1969 Race for Mayor," *New York Times*, November 19, 2007.

51 Flaherty, *Managing Mailer*, p. 158.

52 Ibid., pp. 139–40.

53 Michael Gross, "Norman Mailer: The Writer as Candidate," *New York*, April 6, 1998.

54 Manso, ed., *Running Against the Machine*, p. v.

55 Gross, "Norman Mailer: The Writer as Candidate."

56 Ibid.

57 William F. Buckley, Jr., "Who's For Mayor?" "On the Right" column for March 1 or 2, 1969.

58 James A. Wechsler, "Victory in Defeat," *New York Post*, June 19, 1969, and reprinted in Manso, ed., *Running Against the Machine*, p. 135.

59 Cannato, *The Ungovernable City*, p. 411.

60 Wechsler, "Victory in Defeat," p. 136.

61 Chisolm quoted in Cannato, *The Ungovernable City*, p. 415.

62 Norman Mailer, *The Prisoner of Sex* (New York: Primus Press, 1985, orig. pub. 1971), pp. 228–29.

63 William F. Buckley, Jr., "Hue-A Full Day," "On the Right" column for December 9, 1969.

64 John B. Judis, *William F. Buckley, Jr.: Patron Saint of the Conservatives* (New York: Simon and Schuster, 1988), p. 310.

65 Ibid., p. 311.

66 "William F. Buckley, Jr.: Interview," *Playboy*, May 1970, and reprinted in William F. Buckley, Jr., *Inveighing We Will Go* (New York: Putnam, 1972), p. 62.

67 Judis, *Buckley*, p. 312.

68 "William F. Buckley, Jr.: Interview," *Playboy*, reprinted in Buckley, *Inveighing We Will Go*, p. 33.

69 Judis, *Buckley*, p. 299.

70 Ibid., pp. 300 and 304.

Chapter 13. Jokers

1 Norman Mailer to Allen Ginsberg, December 9, 1969, box 586, folder 6, Mailer Papers.

2 Norman Mailer, *Advertisements for Myself* (New York: G. P. Putnam's Sons, 1959; quote from Cambridge, MA: Harvard University Press, 1992), p. 325.

3 Ibid., p. 278.

4 Ibid., p. 388.

5 Norman Mailer, *Of a Fire on the Moon* (Boston, MA: Little, Brown, and Co., 1970), p. 141.

6 Ibid., p. 55.

7 Buckley told this story in an op-ed in the *New York Times*: William F. Buckley, Jr., "The Watergate Moment," *New York Times*, August 8, 1994.

8   Buckley relates the story, with charity for himself, in William F. Buckley, Jr., *Cruising Speed: A Documentary* (New York: Bantam Books, 1972), pp. 120–21. The story is corrected and placed in context in John B. Judis, *William F. Buckley, Jr.: Patron Saint of the Conservatives* (New York: Simon and Schuster, 1988), pp. 314–16.

9   Buckley, *Cruising Speed*, p. 249.

10   Ibid.

11   Ibid., pp. 249–50.

12   Ibid., p. 250.

13   Kevin Philips quotation from July 7, 1975, found in Judis, *Buckley*, pp. 377–78.

14   Ibid.

15   Judis, *Buckley*, p. 440.

16   Norman Mailer, *The Prisoner of Sex* (New York: Primus Press, 1985, orig. pub. 1971), p. 16.

17   Hilary Mills, *Mailer: A Biography* (New York: Empire Books, 1982; quote from New York: McGraw-Hill, 1984), p. 360.

18   Ibid., p. 359.

19   Mailer, *The Prisoner of Sex*, p. 19.

20   Ibid., p. 21.

21   Ibid., pp. 28–29.

22   Ibid., p. 55.

23   Ibid., p. 134.

24   Ibid., pp. 232–34.

25   Ibid., p. 56.

26   *Town Bloody Hall*, dir. Donn Alan Pennebaker (Pennebaker Hegedus Films, 1979). The event took place on April 30, 1971.

27   This quote from Ceballos and all following quotes from the panel are from *Town Bloody Hall*.

28   Mailer's and Jules Feiffer's quotations are from *Mailer: His Life and Times*, ed. Peter Manso (New York: Washington Square Press, 1985), pp. 522–24.

29   Trilling quoted in ibid., p. 523.

30   Germaine Greer, "My Mailer Problem," *Esquire* (September 1971): 90.

31   Ibid., 92.

32   Quoted in ibid., 93.

33   Ibid.

34   Norman Mailer to Eiichi Yamanishi, September 21, 1971, box 613, folder 5, Mailer Papers.

35   The cards are in the author's possession.

Chapter 14. Moving On

1   William F. Buckley, Jr., "A Journal—Overdrive I," *The New Yorker*, January 31, 1983, p. 64.

2 William F. Buckley, Jr., to Norman Mailer, July 6, 1976, box 653, folder 1, Mailer Papers.

3 Capote quoted by Dotson Rader, in *Mailer: His Life and Times*, ed. Peter Manso (New York: Washington Square Press, 1985), pp. 576–77.

4 Norman Mailer to William F. Buckley, Jr., July 15, 1976, box 653, folder 1, Mailer Papers.

5 William F. Buckley, Jr., to Norman Mailer, July 22, 1976, box 653, folder 1, Mailer Papers.

6 Norman Mailer to William F. Buckley, Jr., handwritten on letter from William F. Buckley to Norman Mailer, July 22, 1976, box 653, folder 1, Mailer Papers.

7 Buckley, "A Journal—Overdrive I."

8 Amy Uyematsu, "The Emergence of Yellow Power," *GIDRA* (October 1969): 9–13.

9 *Griswold v. Connecticut* 381 U.S. 479 (1965).

10 *Roe v. Wade* 410 U.S. 113 (1973) and *Doe v. Bolton* 410 U.S. 179 (1973).

11 For a dynamic look at the white ethnic revival, see Matthew Frye Jacobson, *Roots, Too: White Ethnic Revival in Post-Civil Rights America* (Cambridge, MA: Harvard University Press, 2008).

12 Daniel T. Rodgers, *Age of Fracture* (Cambridge, MA: Belknap Press of Harvard University Press, 2011).

13 Ibid., pp. 70–71.

14 Ibid., pp. 62–63.

15 Charles R. Morris, *A Time of Passion: America 1960–1980* (New York: Penguin, 1986), p. 228.

16 Buckley, "A Journal—Overdrive I."

Epilogue

1 Quoted in John B. Judis, *William F. Buckley, Jr.: Patron Saint of the Conservatives* (New York: Simon and Schuster, 1988), p. 372.

2 Ibid.

3 William F. Buckley, Jr., *Saving the Queen* (New York: Doubleday, 1976; quote from Nashville, TN: Cumberland House Publishing, 2005), pp. 217–18.

4 Galbraith quoted in Judis, *Buckley*, p. 385.

5 Niven story in ibid.

6 William F. Buckley, Jr., *Overdrive: A Personal Odyssey* (New York: Doubleday, 1983), pp. 77–78.

7 Found in Judis, *Buckley*, p. 436.

8 Leonard interview found in ibid., p. 437.

9 John Gregory Dunne, "Happy Days Are Here Again," *New York Review of Books*, October 13, 1983.

10 For instance, ". . . as Jackie Kennedy married Aristotle Onassis and Teddy Kennedy went off the bridge at Chappaquiddick, so the decade that began

with Hemingway as the monarch of American arts ended with Andy Warhol as its regent, and the ghost of Marilyn's death gave a lavender edge to that dramatic American design of the Sixties which seemed in retrospect to have done nothing so much as to bring Richard Nixon to the threshold of imperial power." Norman Mailer, *Marilyn: A Biography* (New York: Grosset & Dunlap, 1973), p. 15.

11 Norman Mailer, *The Fight* (Boston, MA: Little, Brown & Co., 1975), p. 239.

12 Found in J. Michael Lennon, *Norman Mailer: A Double Life* (New York: Simon & Schuster, 2013), p. 516.

13 William F. Buckley, Jr., "Crime and Punishment: Gary Gilmore," *Firing Line*, October 11, 1979, Firing Line Collection, program S390, Hoover Institution Archives, copyright Stanford University.

14 Quoted in Lennon, *Mailer*, p. 520.

15 Norman Mailer to Mary Breasted, July 17, 1978, box 667, folder 3, Mailer Papers.

16 Buckley, "Crime and Punishment: Gary Gilmore," *Firing Line*.

17 Christopher Buckley, *Losing Mum and Pup: A Memoir* (New York: Twelve, 2009), p. 226.

18 The two funerals are treated together in Sam Tanenhaus, "One Final Round: Requiem for Two Heavyweights," *New York Times*, April 13, 2008.

19 Norman Mailer, "Novelist Shelved," *Boston*, September 1979.

20 Reid Buckley, *An American Family: The Buckleys* (New York: Threshold Editions, 2008), p. 382.

21 Reprinted in William F. Buckley, Jr., *Inveighing We Will Go* (New York: Putnam, 1972), pp. 59–60.

22 Norman Mailer to William F. Buckley, Jr., May 19, 1975, box 610, folder 3, Mailer Papers.

23 William F. Buckley, Jr., to Norman Mailer, July 9, 1975, box 610, folder 3 Mailer Papers.

Credits

Text Credits

Image Credits

Buckley and wife Pat at the ball: AP Images.

James Baldwin sitting smoking a cigarette: © Bettmann/Corbis.

Portrait of Truman Capote: © Bettmann/Corbis.

Portrait of Gore Vidal: © Bettmann/Corbis.

Gloria Steinem: © Bettmann/Corbis.

Buckley at his desk: © Condé Nast Archive / Corbis.

Mailer's Lego city: © Fred W. McDarrah / Premium Archive / Getty Images.

March on the Pentagon: © Fred W. McDarrah / Premium Archive / Getty Images.

William F. Buckley and Richard Nixon: © Bettmann/Corbis.

Esquire, September 1971: courtesy Hearst Media and George Lois.

Buckley and Mailer on *Firing Line*: *Firing Line* Collection, Program 102, Hoover Institution Archives, copyright © Stanford University.

Index